Today's Economic Issues

Recent Titles in the Across the Aisle Series

Today's Economic Issues

Democrats and Republicans

NANCY S. LIND, ERIK T. RANKIN,
and
GARDENIA HARRIS

Foreword by
JOSEPH R. BLANEY

Across the Aisle

 ABC-CLIO™

An Imprint of ABC-CLIO, LLC
Santa Barbara, California • Denver, Colorado

Library of Congress Cataloging-in-Publication Data

Names: Lind, Nancy S., 1958- author. | Rankin, Erik, author. | Harris, Gardenia, 1961- author.

Title: Today's economic issues : Democrats and Republicans / Nancy S. Lind, Erik T. Rankin, and Gardenia Harris ; foreword by Joseph R. Blaney.

Description: Santa Barbara, California : ABC-CLIO, 2016. | Series: Across the aisle | Includes bibliographical references and index.

Identifiers: LCCN 2016025878 (print) | LCCN 2016029465 (ebook) | ISBN 9781440839368 (print : alk. paper) | ISBN 9781440839375 (ebook)

Subjects: LCSH: United States—Economic policy—2009- | United States—Social policy—1993- | Economic security—United States. | Public welfare—Economic aspects—United States. | Democratic Party (U.S.) | Republican Party (U.S. : 1854-)

Classification: LCC HC106.84 .L56 2016 (print) | LCC HC106.84 (ebook) | DDC 330.973—dc23

LC record available at https://lccn.loc.gov/2016025878

ISBN: 978-1-4408-3936-8
EISBN: 978-1-4408-3937-5

20 19 18 17 16   1 2 3 4 5

This book is also available as an eBook.

ABC-CLIO
An Imprint of ABC-CLIO, LLC

ABC-CLIO, LLC
130 Cremona Drive, P.O. Box 1911
Santa Barbara, California 93116-1911
www.abc-clio.com

This book is printed on acid-free paper ∞
Manufactured in the United States of America

Contents

Foreword

Differences between Democrats and Republicans: In Their Own Words

When discussing the fundamental differences between Democrats and Republicans on economic issues (or any issues for that matter) it is helpful to understand that politics is primarily a comparative process. As William L. Benoit, Joseph R. Blaney, and P. M. Pier advanced with the Functional Theory of Political Communication, in participatory democracy, candidates engage the electorate by trying to appear preferable (Benoit, Blaney, and Pier 1998). This is done by pointing to one's strengths (acclaiming), detracting from the opponent's strengths (attacking), and responding to attacks with potential to damage one's candidacy (defending). Understanding that all political discourse can be categorized into this tri-partite schema is essential to understanding politics (Benoit, Blaney, and Pier 1998). However, the Functional Theory offers further levels of categories for consideration. For instance, political messages can be further categorized as dealing either with *policy* or *character*. Policy considerations (the subject of the remainder of this book as it concerns economics writ large) can include past deeds, future plans, or general goals. Character considerations can include ideals (ideology), leadership qualities, and personal qualities (Benoit, Blaney, and Pier 1998). The framework of Benoit and his colleagues has been applied in dozens of studies addressing television and radio advertisements, press releases, nomination acceptance speeches, convention keynote speeches, primary and general election debates, talk radio appearances, direct mail and social media campaigns. In short, it is the gold standard for understanding the nature and function of political communication. Couple this with the notion that political "reality" is defined by communication. Berger and Luckmann (1966) made a very strong argument for the idea that our social realities (i.e., the way we view the world and assumptions we make about everything from gender roles to division of labor and wealth) are completely a matter of construct between persons as they exchange symbols and create shared social environments. As political audiences' understanding of politics is similarly socially constructed through the messages they consume, the key differences between Democrats and Republicans can be illuminated by political function analyses of the last 20 years. In *Communication in Political Campaigns*, Benoit (2007) found that party affiliation influences messages produced by political candidates. In particular he shed light on the potential effects of affiliation on the functions (acclaiming, attacking, or defending) and topics (policy or character). Specifically, he found that when looking at discourse in general (not differentiating advertisements, speeches, etc.), Democrats were slightly more likely to attack and Republicans were slightly more likely to acclaim. Both parties used only 2 percent of their discourse to defend themselves. He also found that Democrats discussed policy more, and character less, than Republicans (Benoit 2007). However, in terms of relevance to this book, the question of "issue ownership" may be the key to understanding the nature of differences between parties/candidates and what they would ask us to believe about the political and economic state of affairs.

Petrocik's Theory of Issue Ownership holds that over time voters believe that one party is better suited to address particular issues. For instance, the public holds the belief that Democrats are better able to advocate for health care, education, social security, and the environment, while Republicans better represent the country's interests with respect to taxes, national defense, and terrorism prevention. To the extent that the voting public holds these prejudices about parties and issues one can claim that a party "owns" an issue or issues (Petrocik 1996). Given this, the modest differences in function and topic that Benoit found could be attributable to the fact that some issues are more important in a given year, leaving a party's ownership of an issue (and ability to acclaim its record, as opposed to attacking an opponent's record) a central focus of a campaign. For instance, as national security was very important in the 2004 election, one might not be surprised that the Republican Party and candidates acclaimed themselves for the policies they implemented. Likewise, as the national economy was sinking during the 2008 campaign, it is not surprising that the Democrats attacked Republican policies as the culprit. In short, the functional discourse of a party will necessarily adapt to the political environment as it presents opportunities and challenges to the parties based on their "ownership" of issues.

Why begin a book about the differences between Democrats and Republicans with an understanding of how election campaigns socially construct economic issues? Because the parties and candidates themselves beg for us to understand economics from frames that suit their desired policies. Only when parties are given power via consent of the electorate can their policies be pursued and implemented.

Is the attention in this book given to differences between Democrats and Republicans on economic issues merited? The political communication research supports an unequivocal "yes" to this question. The vast majority of political communication (i.e., speeches, advertisements, talk radio appearances, etc.) ultimately addresses economic issues. Benoit, Blaney, and Pier (1998) found that political discourse could be categorized as addressing issues the following amounts of time: the economy (22 percent), education (20 percent), Medicare and health (15 percent), taxes (9 percent), and crime and drugs (6 percent) with 28 percent of all discourse addressing other sundry topics (e.g., national defense, social issues, etc.). However, their understanding of "economy" was too narrow. The chapters in this volume point to a much broader understanding of economic issues, one that would collapse education, Medicare/health, and taxes under the economic umbrella accounting for *fully 66 percent* of all political discourse (when collapsing the data the same way as the seminal study of the 1996 election, which subsequent election cycles have mirrored in many ways). Given this preponderance of campaign messages addressing economic issues, it is safe to say that Bill Clinton's presidential campaign adviser James Carville was striking a chord with his admonition that "It's the Economy, Stupid" (Galoozis 2015).

This expanded understanding of "economy" merits discussion here as this volume details the issues in minutiae. Several chapters in this book address differences between Democrats and Republicans as understood by the classic "jobs and the economy" category. Just to name a few, Osaore Aideyan's chapter on free trade, Grace Allbaugh's chapter on inflation, and Vanette Schwartz's chapters on infrastructure investment and job creation might all be typical of topics directly rated to the economy. They all address the heart of economic activity with their focus on the exchange of goods and services and assignment of capital investment for public works. Likewise Michael R. Potter's chapter on stimulus spending, Lucas Lockhart's essay on financial industry regulation and George Waters's chapter on progressive taxation address economic issues head-on as they define the central role of government in regulating/intervening in questions of how tax liability should be assigned to best ensure shared prosperity and which industries ought to receive governmental investment to provoke growth. These chapters may be rather obvious in terms of ideological differences between the parties, with Democrats tending to favor intervention as a matter of fairness and Republicans tending to oppose intervention as a barrier to market efficiencies. However, the editors of this volume rightly understand how so many seemingly unrelated issues have direct (not even indirect) impacts on the economy. For instance, Rabe-Hemp, Navarro, and Comens address the issue of differences between the parties on corruption. While this might seemingly be a matter of criminality, think for a moment about the consequences of corruption. Will the taxpayer who perceives his/her hard-earned dollars are being systematically skimmed for dubious purposes, benefiting only people with inside clout, be anxious to fund important initiatives for education and infrastructure? One might argue that the polity would be less interested in making such important investments if corruption is perceived as widespread. This illustrates how corruption, aside from the misallocation of resources in an economy, can reduce confidence in government's ability to address economic problems.

Similarly, Karen Flint Stipp's chapter on scientific and medical research might appear only tangential to economic issues, but think again. According to the World Bank, between 2010 and 2014, health care expenditures accounted for 17 percent of the United States' gross domestic product (GDP) (Health Expenditure 2015). Aside from the tiny country of Tuvalu (19.7 percent) this is by far the greatest amount spent on health care by any country in the world (Health Expenditure 2015). Though scientific and medical research expenditures may be a small portion by comparison, the ability to identify public health problems and proffer scientifically tested solutions eventually impacts the larger figure. For instance, a relatively small National Institute of Health grant that could result in an effective treatment for obesity could offer multiple economic returns/impacts. If obesity were effectively reduced even minimally the health care industry (and insured citizens) would spend fewer resources on treatment of diabetes, osteoarthritis, and other obesity-related conditions. This scenario demonstrates the relevance of such research (a very modest portion of the national budget) to health care (a very large portion of the nation's GDP).

Elizabeth Wheat's chapter on energy policy is also illustrative of a large, yet indirect economic issue. Specifically, in May of 2014 U.S. consumers were paying an average of $3.70 for a gallon of gasoline. In May of 2015 the same product cost $2.60, or over a dollar less per gallon (GasBuddy.com 2015). The roughly $20 per tank of gas difference between the two time periods has potential for great fluctuation in the amount of expendable income in people's pockets. This in turn can affect consumer spending on retail, housing, entertainment, and so on. This makes Wheat's other chapter, addressing green energy subsidies, relevant as well to the extent that less reliance on fossil fuels can theoretically result in lower demand and prices.

An example of an "indirect" economics topic that should be of great interest to the electorate is the issue of student loans and debt. College affordability impacts the extent to which individuals can enroll in higher education. Moreover, as students and parents seek a return on investment (ROI) for their college expenditures, institutions may be tempted to align their curricula with professional/vocational offerings setting an agenda not only for courses of study, but industries to be valued over other industries. Availability of college financial aid and the pressures put on students to choose direct paths to jobs has the potential to affect the American workforce in its earliest stages, for better or worse. As such, understanding differences between the political parties on this issue is important for voters to discern their choices in elections.

Mark Olson's chapter on social security and Chad Kahl's offering on pensions have similar relevancies insofar as they both involve the economic viability of the elderly. However, an ongoing theme gets buried in the political talk of economic challenges for seniors (prescription drug prices, cost of living inflation, etc.) and what to do about those challenges. That theme is the idea that some retirees do not need or are not worthy of social security benefits. Scholars refer to the ongoing collections of stories that contribute to a society's unwitting assumptions about social order as message systems, and the cumulative effect of those ongoing stories as "Cultivation Theory," developed by the late George Gerbner (1998). As stories of persons who are, or are not, deserving of these benefits unfold the primary function of social security can get lost: namely, workers who pay into social security in their youth will collect the benefits in their old age as a simple matter of economic justice. Talk of "means tests" for seniors who by some standards are economically privileged, if left unchallenged, will reduce the program's reputation to another welfare entitlement. Olson addresses the magnitude of the pay-in, borrow from, and potential trouble with long-term payout.

The chapters mentioned above are not meant to detract from the inherent value of all of the chapters in this book. They are mentioned in particular as they provide excellent examples for the need for this entire project. In summary, the work of the political theorists, economists, social workers, and other social scientists in this volume is most justified. Widely accepted content analytics of political campaigns show that two-thirds of all candidate messages in major campaigns address economic issues broadly understood. Politicians address these issues because of their salience for the voting public. It is the reader's obligation in these pages to discern the differences between Democrats and Republicans to be better prepared as citizens and consumers of information in a self-governing society.

Joseph R. Blaney

Further Reading

Benoit, William. 2007. *Communication in Political Campaigns*. New York: Peter Lang.

Benoit, William, Joseph Blaney, and P. M. Pier. 1998. *Campaign '96: A Functional Analysis of Acclaiming, Attacking, and Defending*. Westport, CT: Praeger.

Berger, Peter L., and Thomas Luckmann. 1966. *The Social Construction of Reality: A Treatise in the Sociology of Knowledge*. Garden City, NY: Anchor Books.

Galoozis, Caleb. 2015. "It's the Economy, Stupid." *Institute of Politics at Harvard University*. Accessed September 30. http://www.iop.harvard.edu/it's-economy-stupid-2.

GasBuddy.com. 2015. "Eighteen Month Average Retail Price Chart." Accessed September 30. http://www.gasbuddy.com/Charts.

Gerbner, George. 1998. "Cultivation Analysis: An Overview." *Mass Communication and Society* 3/4: 175–194.

Petrocik, J. R. 1996. "Issue Ownership in Presidential Elections with a 1980 Case Study." *Journal of Political Science* 40: 825–850.

World Bank. 2015. "Health Expenditure, Total (% of GDP)." Accessed November 14. http://data.worldbank.org/indicator/SH.XPD.TOTL.ZS.

Introduction

Both the Democratic and Republican parties claim that they have the best interests of the nation and its people at heart, and they are equally adamant that they have the best policy solutions to address America's problems and challenges. This volume in ABC-CLIO's *Across the Aisle* series examines the proposals and positions of the two parties—from profound disagreements to areas of common ground—in the realm of economic policy.

Today's Economic Issues: Democrats and Republicans sorts through the rhetorical clutter and partisan distortions that typify so many disputes between Republicans and Democrats in the 21st century in order to provide an accurate, balanced, and evenhanded overview of the parties' respective policy positions and attitudes on the most important and divisive social issues in the United States. Coverage also details instances in which the rhetorical positions staked out by Democrats and Republicans are inconsistent with their voting records and policy priorities.

Finally, in addition to explaining the differences between the two parties on today's hot-button economic issues, this volume also documents significant differences of opinion *within* the parties where present. After all, neither Republicans nor Democrats march in complete lockstep on a wide range of issues, from green energy subsidies to social security to the estate tax. Nor do the policy positions of Republican and Democratic politicians always reflect the views of Republican and Democratic voters.

Throughout this volume, the text features actual quotes from conservative and liberal party leaders, think tanks, and media figures, public opinion poll results, and other valuable, authoritative information to enhance its coverage. This information serves as the foundation for the volume's summaries of the philosophies and records of the two parties in such diverse realms as deficit spending, the national debt, financial industry regulation, income tax reform, income inequality, stimulus spending, and entitlement programs.

Entry Features

Each essay in *Today's Economic Issues: Democrats and Republicans* begins with an "At a Glance" summary of the prevailing sentiments and policies of the two parties on the issue being discussed. This section also includes reader-friendly "bullet points" listing the most important views of each party.

Each essay then provides an "Overview" of historical trends, events, and attitudes displayed by both Republicans and Democrats regarding the issue in question. This section explores party attitudes toward key pieces of legislation, details their political alliances, and tracks evolutions in party thought over time.

From there each essay moves into a deeper exploration of the history and attitudes of the two parties on the issue in question. Every essay features two special sections—one devoted to the Democratic record on the issue, the other concerned with the Republican record. As with the "At a Glance" and "Overview" sections, these sections are carefully crafted to provide an accurate and impartial overview of the parties' respective positions.

Every essay in this collection is further supplemented with sidebars featuring illuminating excerpts from speeches, court decisions, and editorials from liberal and conservative presidents, senators, pundits, and justices on the issue being studied. Each essay then concludes with a helpful Further Reading section to direct users to other information sources. The collection is also enhanced with a helpful glossary of economic policy terms, programs, and organizations mentioned in the book.

Bankruptcy

At a Glance

Most support for bankruptcy reform lies within the Republican Party. Republicans pushed for and ultimately passed legislation that aimed to prevent consumer abuse, encourage repayment of debts, cut down on fraud, and still provide assistance for those who need it. Advocates contend that the bankruptcy system in the United States is too easily abused by those who do not truly require assistance.

Most opposition to the reform comes from the Democratic Party with a few key Democrats voting for reform. The opposition contends that the bankruptcy system should be preserved, especially for those who face unforeseen problems like unemployment or illness.

Many Democrats . . .

- Believe bankruptcy reform would accommodate the credit card industry, which invested over $100 million lobbying since 1999
- Assert bankruptcy reform would harm those that needed it most as a result of unemployment or medical expenses
- Contend bankruptcy reform proposals would create unnecessary fees and administrative obstacles with its required credit counseling

Many Republicans . . .

- Support steering individual bankruptcy cases toward Chapter 13 (reorganization of debt) instead of Chapter 7 (straight liquidation) and forcing repayment of some debt
- Advocate mandatory credit counseling and completion of financial management courses for people declaring bankruptcy to help prevent future financial issues
- Would like to make credit more accessible
- Complain that fraud and abuse are problems with current bankruptcy law

Overview

The history of U.S. bankruptcy law can be traced back to the time of Henry VIII, allowing creditors to seize debtors' assets and imprison them until debts were paid. As credit use increased, imprisonment became less realistic, and seizing all of a debtor's assets was deemed inappropriate for every case. This set the stage for the evolution of bankruptcy law, and in the 20th century the relief of a discharge of debt became available. The bankruptcy system was not originally intended to provide a fresh start to a debtor.

The U.S. Congress has the power to enact national bankruptcy legislation as stated in Article I, Section 8, Clause 4, or the Bankruptcy Clause of the U.S. Constitution: "To establish a uniform rule of naturalization, and uniform laws on the subject of bankruptcy throughout the United States." The framers of the Constitution believed interstate commerce would require a national bankruptcy law to establish a remedy for debts to be collected out of state. There were also issues with land speculation as people purchased acreage as investment but were then unable to pay their obligations and were being jailed leaving debts unpaid (Frimet 1991).

The great panic of 1837, which was caused by relaxed credit practices, land speculation, state government debt, crop failures, and bank instability, led to a severe depression. The resulting the Bankruptcy Act of 1841 allowed debtors to file bankruptcy and receive a discharge after assets had been distributed to the creditors with several stipulations. The Bankruptcy Act of 1898 eliminated the need for a percentage of creditors to agree to a discharge and for a minimum payment toward the debt, in order to provide a fresh start to the debtor. Creditors were to be treated equitably and be paid a pro rata share of the debtor's assets. The Bankruptcy and Supremacy Clauses of the Constitution give the federal bankruptcy court jurisdiction over both creditors and debtors forcing cooperation.

A bankruptcy estate is created after a bankruptcy petition is filed. The debtor's property is then controlled by the bankruptcy court. An automatic stay prevents creditors from acting outside of the court; they are notified of the bankruptcy, and they must file a claim. If a claim is not filed, they receive nothing but the debt is still discharged. Creditors will not necessarily get the same percentage of their claims. They will be given equal consideration under the law and paid what is available from the estate according to state and federal law. No bankruptcy law includes state and federal statutes, and it creates the rules between creditors and debtors.

Debtors were further protected by the Bankruptcy Reform Act of 1978, which allowed debtors to avoid non–purchase money liens on property such as furniture and appliances. This act created the bankruptcy code, Title 11 of the U.S. code, which is the substantive law of bankruptcy. Congress gave the Supreme Court authority to enact procedures, and the Advisory Committee on Bankruptcy Rules meets twice a year to review rules and propose changes. This group consists of law professors, lawyers, and federal judges appointed by the chief justice. Proposed amendments are published for public comment. The Advisory Committee reviews comments, and if the amendment is approved, it is submitted to the Standing Committee, the Judicial Conference, and then the Supreme Court. The Supreme Court submits the rule changes to Congress on May 1, and Congress has three months to reject it. If the rule is not rejected, it goes into effect December 1.

The Bankruptcy Reform Act of 1994 allowed bankruptcy processes to move more quickly and created the National Bankruptcy Review Commission, which makes recommended revisions to the bankruptcy code (Nelson 2000). Republicans, however, believed major reforms were needed and pushed for more change. The House and Senate were able to pass the Bankruptcy Reform Act of 2000, which President Clinton killed using a pocket veto. The Bankruptcy Reform Act was reintroduced each year in Congress, backed by Republicans and opposed by most Democrats. After the 2004 elections, Republican majorities in the Senate and House passed a bill signed into law by President Bush in 2005.

This still-debated revision, the Bankruptcy Abuse Prevention and Consumer Protection Act of 2005 (BAPCPA), is the last major revision of bankruptcy law. This law added provisions to limit acts of bad faith including the following:

- A means test forcing debtors into Chapter 13, which means paying more debt back
- Mandatory credit counseling prior to filing for bankruptcy and before receiving a discharge
- A lender can get a lien for the full amount of a car bought within 910 days of filing for bankruptcy instead of its depreciated value
- The homestead exemption is limited to $146,450 if purchased 1,215 days before filing
- An automatic stay of 30 days for a second filing unless a debtor has had more than two filings
- No discharge if within four years of a previous filing with a discharge
- No discharging debts greater than $500 to one creditor within 90 days of filing or cash advances received within 70 days of filing
- An attorney must review and sign off on the bankruptcy petition
- Student loans cannot be discharged

BAPCPA passed the Senate by a vote of 74 to 25 and the House by a vote of 302 to 126. All Republicans in both houses voted for the bill. Democrats were divided with slightly stronger support in the Senate where the bill originated. Nineteen Senate Democrats voted for and 25 voted against the bill. Democratic support came from southern states, with senators from more liberal states in the west and northeast voting in opposition. One exception is Delaware, where Democratic Senators Biden and Carper both voted for the bill. Only 73 House Democrats voted for the bill with 123 voting against it. Again most of the votes against the bill came from western and northwestern states with all Democratic representatives from Michigan, Illinois, and Massachusetts voting against the bill.

Democrats on Bankruptcy Reform

Throughout the 1990s and culminating with the BAPCPA of 2005, Democrats widely opposed bankruptcy reforms that they contended benefited businesses and complicated the bankruptcy process for consumers. In the late 1990s, then professor Elizabeth Warren, now a senator, wrote against the act and pointed out that almost half the people who filed for bankruptcy were dealing with medical debt, and two-thirds were unemployed (Kuhlman 2005).

Opponents of the 2005 bill argued that the over $100 million spent by the credit card industry to lobby for it since 1999 proved that it would work in their favor. Democrats argued that the need for the bill had been overstated, echoing Senator Warren's earlier argument that most bankruptcy filings were due to unemployment or medical expenses (Himmelstein et al. 2005). The means test triggered by the debtor's income ignored causes of bankruptcy including illness, job loss, and even predatory lending. It also required debtors to accumulate more debt on attorney and court costs (Sabatini 2005). The required credit counseling was deemed questionable in terms of value by the Government Accountability Office (GAO), which noted that the education was too late to be useful but was creating both administrative obstacles and an additional fee (Jones 2007).

There were a few key Democrats that supported the bankruptcy reform, most of them citing the need to end abuses of the system. During the Senate debate, Senator Carper of Delaware noted, "Concerns have been raised, justifiably, over the last decade or more that some people who have the ability to repay don't; they simply run up their debts and walk away from those obligations" (Carper 2005). Minority Leader Harry Reid echoed this sentiment by stating the bill "embodies a principle I agree with: Those who have the means to repay their debts should be required to do so" (Reid 2005). There were many who opposed the bill despite agreeing with these sentiments. Senator John Kerry acknowledged these concerns but raised his own concerns about the bill as written. "I strongly believe that reform of our bankruptcy law is necessary: Too often, bankruptcy is used as an economic tool. . . . However, I am unable to support the Bankruptcy Reform Act before us today because I believe it is unfair and unbalanced. . . . Inexcusably, this bill helps creditors without helping consumers" (Kerry 2005). Senator Kerry encouraged Republicans and fellow Democrats who supported the bill to accept some of the offered amendments in order to alleviate some of the concerns about its fairness.

Democrats attempted to protect consumers from what they saw as the most damaging of the act's changes with amendments. These were rejected by Republicans and a few Democrats: Senator Nelson from Nebraska, Senator Johnson from South Dakota, Senator Carper from Delaware, and Vice President Biden, who was then the senator from Delaware. For example, Senator Schumer attempted to limit the exemption for asset protection trusts, which would close a loophole protecting money stashed in "protected trusts" (and therefore untouchable by bankruptcy

Senator Hillary Clinton Criticizes BAPCPA

On March 11, 2005 then Senator Hillary Clinton spoke regarding the Bankruptcy Abuse Prevention and Consumer Protection Act (BAPCPA), which Republican President George W. Bush signed into law:

> Mr. President, while I strongly believe that Congress should act to fix the problems in our bankruptcy system, I also believe that this bill is misguided and deeply flawed.
>
> This bankruptcy bill fundamentally fails to accord with the traditional purposes of bankruptcy, which recognize that we are all better off when hard-working people who have suffered financial catastrophe get a "fresh start" and a second chance to become productive and contributing members of society. With the passage of this legislation, which makes obtaining this fresh start more expensive and more difficult, we are ensuring that many responsible Americans will continue to be buried under mountains of debt, and unable to take back control and responsibility for their lives.
>
> Our Nation's bankruptcy law developed out of a recognition that the world can be a competitive, often unforgiving place. Bankruptcy reform should therefore be directed toward creating a civil society in which valuing individual responsibility is not incompatible with admitting the enduring truth that sometimes bad things happen to responsible, hardworking people. Sometimes, conscientious Americans need help and support against forces that are too big for them to stand against alone. It should be about making sure that both large corporations and individual citizens are held to the same standards of responsibility and accountability.
>
> . . . Almost without exception, the majority has voted across the board against these and other amendments, apparently under strict orders from the Republican leadership to oppose any and all amendments, regardless of whether the amendments were designed to help our troops, to remove loopholes for millionaires, to help families facing medical and financial crisis.
>
> . . . This legislation, especially after refusal, after refusal, after refusal to support amendments to improve it, is unfair and unjust.

Source

Clinton, Hillary. 2005. "Bankruptcy Abuse Prevention and Consumer Protection Act 2005." *Project Vote Smart*. March 11. Accessed May 17, 2015. https://votesmart.org/public-statement/83566/bankruptcy-abuse-prevention-and-consumer-protection-act-of-2005#.VWTMZ89Vikp.

laws). This was rejected by all Senate Republicans, as well as Democratic Senators Nelson, Johnson, and Carper.

Other rejected amendments included the following:

- Protecting retirement savings for employees when a business files for bankruptcy
- Discouraging predatory lending practices

- Protecting consumers affected by identity theft
- Protecting caregivers experiencing economic distress
- Protecting debtors whose financial problems were caused by serious medical problems
- Protecting the elderly from losing their homes
- Protecting service members and veterans

Although the 2005 changes aimed to stem personal bankruptcy filings, personal bankruptcy filings rose dramatically in the aftermath of the 2008 economic crisis. Democrats have focused lately on curing the cause of bankruptcy. By passing the Affordable Care Act and working to improve unemployment numbers, the hope is to eliminate some of the need to file for bankruptcy. Most recently 13 Democrats in the Senate introduced the Fairness for Struggling Students Act of 2015, which would treat private bank issued student loans the same as other unsecured debt in bankruptcy proceedings. This would reverse a portion of the 2005 bill. Senator Dick Durbin, one of the sponsors, stated, "Too many Americans are carrying around mortgage sized student loan debt that forces them to put off major life decisions like buying a home or starting a family. We can no longer sit by while this student debt bomb keeps ticking" (Durbin 2015). The senator's website also points out that prior to passage of the BAPCPA in 2005, only government issued or guaranteed student loans were protected from bankruptcy.

Republicans on Bankruptcy Reform

The BAPCPA was a Republican-led initiative, which they claimed had bipartisan support. All of the bankruptcy reform bills submitted to Congress, including the BAPCPA and the 2000 version that passed both houses before being pocket vetoed, were sponsored and strongly supported by Republican Senator Grassley of Iowa. The law for bankruptcy has changed very little since 2005, although there have been some attempts to clarify the law.

One of the main reasons the Republicans pushed for bankruptcy reform was a dramatic increase in bankruptcy filings, from just over 300,000 in 1980 to nearly 1.4 million in 1999. After the passage of the 2005 version, Senator Grassley noted on his website that "the number of bankruptcies has been growing at record levels in recent years, including a 57 percent increase in Iowa since 2000" (Grassley 2005). The concerns were echoed during the Senate floor debate in 2005 by Senator Hatch, who stated that "bankruptcy claims have skyrocketed since the last major bankruptcy reform bill in 1978" (Hatch 2005). Senator Frist also mentioned that in 2004 there were over 1.6 million bankruptcies. He further stated, "The total number of bankruptcies more than doubled during the 1980s and then doubled again from 1990 to 2003. . . . Personal bankruptcies outnumber business bankruptcies by a multiple of more than 45 to 1" (Frist 2005).

President George W. Bush Touts BAPCPA

On April 20, 2005, President George W. Bush spoke before signing the Bankruptcy Abuse Prevention, Consumer Protection Act (BAPCPA) (2005).

Today we take an important action . . . to continue strengthening our nation's economy. The bipartisan bill I'm about to sign makes common-sense reforms to our bankruptcy laws. By restoring integrity to the bankruptcy process, this law will make our financial system stronger and better. By making the system fairer for creditors and debtors, we will ensure that more Americans can get access to affordable credit.

. . . Our bankruptcy laws are an important part of the safety net of America. They give those who cannot pay their debts a fresh start. Yet bankruptcy should always be a last resort in our legal system. If someone does not pay his or her debts, the rest of society ends up paying them. In recent years, too many people have abused the bankruptcy laws. They've walked away from debts even when they had the ability to repay them. This has made credit less affordable and less accessible, especially for low-income workers who already face financial obstacles.

. . . Under the new law, Americans who have the ability to pay will be required to pay back at least a portion of their debts. Those who fall behind their state's median income will not be required to pay back their debts. This practical reform will help ensure that debtors make a good-faith effort to repay as much as they can afford. This new law will help make credit more affordable, because when bankruptcy is less common, credit can be extended to more people at better rates. . . .

America is a nation of personal responsibility where people are expected to meet their obligations. We're also a nation of fairness and compassion where those who need it most are afforded a fresh start. The act of Congress I sign today will protect those who legitimately need help, stop those who try to commit fraud, and bring greater stability and fairness to our financial system. I'm honored to join the members of Congress to sign the Bankruptcy Abuse Prevention and Consumer Protection Act.

Source

Bush, George W. 2005. "President Signs Bankruptcy Abuse Prevention, Consumer Protection Act." (statement made at the president's signing of the BAPCPA, Washington, DC, April 20). Accessed May 21, 2015. http://georgewbush-whitehouse.archives.gov/news /releases/2005/04/ print/20050420-5.html.

The main reason given by strong supporters of the reform bill was a belief that those who could repay their debts should, therefore BAPCPA was meant to force more individuals to choose Chapter 13 bankruptcies (Gargotta 2006). There was a strong belief that there were some individuals who abused the current system and that even if it was only a small percentage of all filers who were stopped, it would make a difference. Senator Grassley noted that a majority of bankruptcies are filed under Chapter 7 with only about one-third of individuals choosing Chapter 13. Chapter 13 bankruptcy requires the debtor to repay at least some of their debt, and one of the major pushes for reform was ensuring that those who could pay did. According to Senator Grassley, "The bankruptcy bill preserves a fresh start for people who are overwhelmed by medical debts, loss of a job, or sudden unforeseen emergencies" (Grassley 2005). However, he goes on to say that those who can repay their debts should. There was a strong consensus that the fundamental principle behind this bill was to ensure that people who could repay their debt did.

The Republican supporters also touched on many of the issues brought up by those in opposition to the bill during the debate on the Senate floor in order to further bipartisan support. Senate Majority Leader Frist spoke on the Senate floor about the special circumstances that were protected by the bill. Acknowledging that the number one reason for filing bankruptcy was medical expenses, he points out that the legislation allows filers to deduct all of their medical costs as part of the means test. He also points out that private school tuition is an allowable deduction in order to protect educational opportunities. Finally, he emphasizes that child support and alimony payments get paid first, before creditors get paid. He finished by saying, "The legislation before us is thoughtful. It is well considered. It is family centered. It closes unfair loopholes so that the system and the people it is designed to help can get that fresh start and get back on track" (Frist 2005).

Although most Republicans in Congress are happy with the new law, there have been attempts to clarify interpretations of the law. Most recently, Senator Grassley introduced a bill entitled Family Farmer Bankruptcy Clarification Act of 2015, which is meant to overturn the 2012 Supreme Court decision in *Hall v. United States*. He believes the decision is contrary to the 2005 act. Grassley claims the Supreme Court overrode the intent of Congress. The bill is cosponsored by Democratic Senator Al Franken of Minnesota. According to Senator Grassley, "The Supreme Court screwed everything up by ruling that the law may have been changed in the bankruptcy code, but it was not changed in the tax code" (Boden 2015).

Amanda Swartzendruber and
Renee Prunty

Further Reading

Associated Press. 2000. "Clinton Vetoes Bankruptcy Bill." *Lubbock Online,* December 19. Accessed April 14, 2015. http://lubbockonline.com/stories/121900/upd_075-5725.shtml#.VTvLiCFViko.

Boden, Sarah. 2015. "Grassley Wants Bankruptcy Protections for Farmers." *Iowa Public Radio,* January 20. Accessed May 26, 2015. http://iowapublicradio.org/post/grassley-wants-bankruptcy-protections-farmers.

Carper, Thomas. 2005. "On Bankruptcy Reform." *Statements and Speeches, Tom Carper, U.S. Senator for Delaware.* Accessed April 21, 2016. http://www.carper.senate.gov/public/index.cfm/otherstatements?ID=b7cf98a6-9b85-48c2-bf88-3905415b4745.

Dickler, Jessica. 2008. "Personal Bankruptcies on the Rise." *CNN.com.* October 24. Accessed April 12, 2015. http://money.cnn.com/2008/10/24/pf/bankruptcy_filings/.

Durbin, Dick. 2015. "As Rising Student Load Debt Nears $1.2 Trillion, Durbin Introduces Legislation to Address Crisis." *Dick Durbin, United States Senator for Illinois.* March 12. Accessed May 19, 2015. http://www.durbin.senate.gov/newsroom/press-releases/as -rising-student-loan-debt-nears-12-trillion-durbin-introduces-legislation-to-address -crisis-.

Durbin, Dick, et al. 2015. "Fairness for Struggling Students Act of 2015." *Scribd.com,* March. Accessed May 22, 2015. http://www.scribd.com/doc/258543672/Fairness-for -Struggling-Students-Act-of-2015.

Frimet, R. 1991. "The Birth of Bankruptcy in the United States." *Commercial Law Journal* 96: 160–188.

Frist, William. 2005. "Bankruptcy Reform." Remarks in the U.S. Senate. *Congressional Record Volume 151, Number 21,* March 1, S1813–S1814. Accessed April 21, 2015. https:// www.gpo.gov/fdsys/pkg/CREC-2005-03-01/html/CREC-2005-03-01-pt1-PgS1813 -7.htm.

Gargotta, Craig A. 2006. "Selected New Consumer Provisions to the Bankruptcy Abuse Prevention and Consumer Protection Act of 2005." *United States Attorneys' Bulletin* 54 (4): 9–11.

Grassley, Chuck. 2005. "Word On: Bankruptcy Reform." *Chuck Grassley, United States Senator for Iowa.* April 22. Accessed May 21, 2015. http://www.grassley.senate.gov/news /news-releases/word-bankruptcy-reform.

Hatch, Orrin. 2005. "Bankruptcy Reform." Remarks in the U.S. Senate. March 10. Accessed April 21, 2016. http://weberlaw.com/BAPCPA/s.256/sec-mat/Senate-Debate-Transcripts /senate-debate-05.03.10.pdf.

Himmelstein, David U., Elizabeth Warren, Deborah Thorne, and Steffie Woolhandler. 2005. "MarketWatch: Illness and Injury as Contributors to Bankruptcy." *Health Affairs.* February 2. Accessed March 8, 2015. http://content.healthaffairs.org/content /suppl/2005/01/28/hlthaff.w5.63.DC1.

"House Vote #108 IN 2005." 2005. *Govtrack.us.* Accessed May 22, 2015. https://www .govtrack.us/congress/votes/109-2005/h108.

Jones, Yvonne D. 2007. "Bankruptcy Reform: Value of Credit Counseling Requirement Is Not Clear (GAO-07-203)." April 24. LCCN 2007414394.OCLC 156274430. Washington, DC: Government Accountability Office.

Kerry, John. 2005. "Bankruptcy Reform." Remarks in the U.S. Senate. March 10. Accessed April 21, 2015. http://weberlaw.com/BAPCPA/s.256/sec-mat/Senate-Debate-Transcripts /senate-debate-05.03.10.pdf.

Kuhlman, A. 2005. "Bankruptcy Changes Will Hurt Society." *American Banker 170* (53): 11.

Nelson, J. 2000. "Consumers Bankruptcies and the Bankruptcy Reform Act: A Time-Series Intervention Analysis." *Journal of Financial Services Research* 17: 181.

Reid, Harry. 2005. "Bankruptcy Reform." Remarks in the U.S. Senate. March 1. Accessed April 21, 2016. http://capitolwords.org/date/2005/03/01/S1814-2_bankruptcy-reform/.

"S.194—Family Farmer Bankruptcy Clarification Act of 2015." 2015. *Congress.gov.* Accessed May 22. https://www.congress.gov/bill/114th-congress/senate-bill/194.

Sabatini, Patricia. 2005. "New Law's 'Means' Test Just Mean, Bankruptcy Experts Say." *Pittsburgh Post Gazette,* April 26. Accessed April 25, 2015. http://old.post-gazette.com /pg/05116/494270.stm.

Sahadi, Jeanne. 2015. "The New Bankruptcy Law and You." *CNNMoney.com.* October 17. Accessed April 25, 2015. http://money.cnn.com/2005/10/17/pf/debt/bankruptcy_law /index.htm.

"Senate Passes Grassley Overhaul of Bankruptcy System; Bill on Way to White House." 2000. *Chuck Grassley, United States Senator for Iowa.* December 6. Accessed May 21, 2015. http://www.grassley.senate.gov/news/news-releases/senate-passes-grassley-overhaul -bankruptcy-system-bill-way-white-house.

"Senate Vote #44 IN 2005—Bankruptcy Abuse Prevention and Consumer Protection Act of 2005." 2005. *Govtrack.us.* Accessed May 22, 2015. https://www.govtrack.us/congress /votes/109-2005/s44.

U.S. Congress. 2005. *Congressional Record—Daily Edition,* 109th Cong., 1st sess., March 1 to April 14. Vol. 151, no. 21 to 54.

U.S. Senate. Committee on the Judiciary. 2005. *Bankruptcy Reform: Hearing before the Committee on the Judiciary.* 109th Cong., 1st sess., February 10. Accessed January 4, 2015. http://www.gpo.gov/fdsys/pkg/CHRG-109shrg42675/html/CHRG-109shrg42675. htm.

U.S. Senate. 2005. *U.S. Senate Roll Call Votes 109th Congress—1st Session.* Accessed May 13, 2015. http://www.senate.gov/legislative/LIS/roll_call_lists/vote_menu_109_1.htm.

Corporate Taxation

At a Glance

Both parties favor the taxation of corporate income and reform of the current corporate tax code. However, they disagree over issues such as tax rates, the distribution of tax preferences and expenditures, and the degree to which the corporate tax code can spur economic growth. Democrats typically prefer higher and more progressive effective corporate tax rates than Republicans. Democrats are also more likely to view corporate taxation in terms of economic fairness between higher and lower income groups. Republicans favor lower effective rates and less progressivity. They also argue that all Americans, regardless of income, ultimately pay the costs of corporate taxation.

Historically, both parties are responsive to industry lobbying for special tax credits, deductions, and exemptions, but individual congress members differ in terms of which economic sectors they believe are most deserving of special treatment. Similarly, both parties support deductions and credits for business investment, research and development (R&D), and the declining value of firms' physical assets (i.e., depreciation), but have serious disagreements over the size and timing of these deductions and credits. Republicans are more likely to believe that low and minimally progressive rates as well as aggressive deductions for business investment will directly translate into higher economic growth and international competitiveness. Although sharing a desire to keep U.S. corporations competitive, Democrats see a more complicated relationship between effective corporate tax rates and investment incentives on the one hand, and economic growth and competitiveness on the other.

Many Republicans . . .

- Believe corporate tax rates should be low by international standards and minimally progressive
- Assert that the costs of corporate taxes are ultimately paid by employees, consumers, and shareholders
- Contend that the primary goal of corporate tax policy should be to boost business confidence and incentivize investment

Many Democrats . . .

- Say that corporate tax rates should be progressive and comparable to the average rate for developed countries
- Believe that corporations have sufficient revenue to pay most of their taxes without shifting the costs onto others
- Feel that in addition to incentivizing investment and promoting growth, the corporate tax system must generate significant revenue and respect many Americans' desire for economic equity

---

Overview

When Republicans rose to political dominance following the Civil War, they rolled back President Abraham Lincoln's (1861–1865) emergency taxes on corporate shareholders and instituted a fiscal system based upon tariffs and consumption taxes (Brownlee 2004, 34–38). As the twentieth century approached, this regressive fiscal regime came under political pressure due to the efforts of agrarian populists, southern and western Democrats, and progressive Republicans. Their continued agitation regarding economic and political inequality led to the ratification of the Sixteenth Amendment and the passage of the first non-excise corporate income tax in 1913. However, it was not until World War I that President Woodrow Wilson (1913–1921) and congressional Democrats were able to raise rates into the double digits. Although these Democratic gains were partially rolled back during the Republican-dominated 1920s, President Franklin Delano Roosevelt (1933–1945) utilized the congressional leadership of southern Democrats and the economic emergency associated with the Great Depression to gradually raise rates and add progressivity during the 1930s. By the height of the World War II hostilities, the top two corporate income brackets were taxed at 53 percent and 40 percent (Taylor 2003, 287–289). Corporate tax revenues as a percentage of GDP followed a similar pattern as rates. From 1909 until the onset of the WWII, corporate taxes amounted to just fewer than 2 percent of GDP. Following Roosevelt's significant wartime tax hikes, corporate tax revenues reached nearly 7 percent of GDP (Slemrod and Bakija 2008, 23).

The political battle lines surrounding corporate taxation remained remarkably similar from the end of the nineteenth century until the end of the Great Depression. The struggle was often ideological, viewed as zero-sum, and cross-cut both parties. Pro-tax rhetoric emphasized class divisions between the "virtuous" masses on the one hand and the undeserving and politically corrupt rich on the other. Class cleavage was reinforced by a sectional conflict with the agricultural south and west facing off against the more industrialized north and east. Southern Democrats and western Republicans had the strongest preferences in favor of corporate taxation. Northeastern Republicans were uniform in their opposition and viewed progressive corporate taxation as the manifestation of backward-looking agrarian populism and dangerous working-class agitation (Brownlee 2004, 42–47)

The politics surrounding corporate taxation in the post-WWII era differed significantly. The decades following WWII witnessed gradual corporate tax declines and a shift to a less ideological and more technocratic interest group based politics. In a pattern that continues today, post-war corporate tax politics were based upon a loose bipartisan consensus that viewed the corporate tax code as a policy tool to boost economic growth rather than explicitly redistribute wealth. Industry lobbies jockey to pressure congressional committees and executive branch officials for special treatment and incentives. They are often successful (Martin 1991, 1–49).

Rate hikes during the Korean War, in combination with a booming economy, increased corporate tax revenues to their post-war peak of roughly 6 percent of GDP or nearly a third of federal government tax revenues. With the Korean War cease-fire, corporate tax revenues and rates began a decades-long decline. Tax rates declined at a slower pace than tax revenues and occurred across both Republican and Democratic administrations. By the beginning of the 1980s, corporate tax revenues dropped below 2 percent of GDP for the first time since the Great Depression. They remain at similar levels today (Keightley and Sherlock 2011). Top rates declined slowly and reached 34 percent at the end of the 1980s. Although revenues will increase temporarily during periods of brisk economic growth, the current 35 percent top rate generates only around 10 percent of federal revenues (Gravelle and Hungerford 2011, 3).

There are many reasons behind this decline in the importance of corporate taxes for federal revenue. Declines in rates play only a small part. More important were long-run declines in taxable corporate profits, the increased use of foreign tax shelters, the exclusion of an increasing number of businesses from the corporate code, and statutory changes to the corporate tax base such as depreciation allowances and credits for business investment and research and development.

Besides controversies over rates and foreign tax shelters, the distribution of special tax incentives to industry generates some of the most heated debates. Both Republicans and Democrats have a long historical track record of funneling tax credits, deductions, exemptions, exclusions, and allowances to their favored economic sectors. These tax expenditures take on a variety forms with the largest being deferrals for active income generated by controlled foreign corporations; deferrals of gains on like-kind exchanges; exclusions of interest on public purpose state and local government bonds; credits for investment in physical capital and R&D; and deductions for the accelerated depreciation of assets (Keightley and Sherlock 2011). The politics surrounding these expenditures is complex since each change to the tax code generates winners and losers across industries.

Currently, industries with the lowest effective tax rates due to credits, allowances, or deductions tend to be those that are more likely to make large investments in depreciable assets or expenditures on R&D. Tax-favored industries include biotechnology, communications equipment, mining structures, renewable energy, and petroleum and natural gas production. In contrast, industries disadvantaged by the current tax code in terms of effective tax rates include retail, food services, utilities, and industrial and commercial construction. In terms of the most taxes paid, manufacturing ranked first in 2008. Manufacturers paid about 32 percent of total federal corporate taxes despite the fact that manufacturing firms account for only 6 percent of all corporate businesses (Keightley and Sherlock 2011). Divisions between industries often prevent business from speaking with one voice regarding the specifics of corporate tax provisions. Rather than pure partisanship, it is often the presence or absence of different industries within congressional districts and regions that best explains many politicians' corporate tax preferences.

Although the two parties share the goal of promoting growth, they continue to disagree over the specifics of tax rates, levels of progressivity, and which industries do and do not deserve special treatment. Both parties are divided over the acceptable level of deficits and the degree to which changes in corporate taxation must be offset with changes in spending.

Republicans on Corporate Tax Policy

The tax legislation signed by President Ronald Reagan (1981–1989) reflects divisions within the Republican Party that remain today. As a result, they deserve special attention and serve as a useful frame of reference for contemporary controversies. Policy factions within the Republican Party include supply-side tax-cutters who believe the incentive effects of cutting taxes will in and of themselves boost growth; monetarists focused on controlling inflation; and more traditional conservatives who shared the supply-siders' desire to cut taxes but often insist that tax cuts be paid for by reductions in spending rather than government borrowing.

Reagan and other top Treasury officials entered office as enthusiastic supply-siders who believed that only a robust system of investment incentives and steep cuts to top individual tax rates could restore America's economic prowess. As a result, Reagan and his congressional Republican allies passed the Economic Recovery Tax Act of 1981 (ERTA), the largest tax cut in American history. The ERTA cut tax rates for corporate income; introduced the Accelerated Cost Recovery System that significantly increased the rate at which depreciating property could reduce corporate tax burdens; created a safe harbor provision that gave lessors the same tax benefits as normal owners; increased tax credits for investment and R&D; liberalized rules for the writing off of operating losses; reduced windfall profits taxes on oil companies; and excluded even more companies from the corporate tax code altogether (Martin 1991, 107–108). Many of these provisions were a result of political haggling rather than a pure technocratic application of supply-side thinking. Monetarist, traditional deficit-averse Republicans, conservative Democrats, and financial trade associations all expressed fears that the 1981 tax cuts would create massive deficits that could crowd out private investment and ultimately lead to inflation. In order to overcome this bipartisan resistance, supply-siders struck a deal with industry. If industry groups lobbied recalcitrant Republicans to support the supply-side tax cuts, they would get their desired loopholes and incentives within the tax code. The deal stuck and ERTA was passed in August of 1981.

A mere year later, sluggish business investment, double-digit unemployment, and the largest budget deficits in history emboldened critics and weakened the position of supply-siders within the administration. President Reagan, loathe to repeal the individual tax cuts that were his signature first-term achievement, viewed closing loopholes within the corporate tax code as the most attractive option to raise revenue (Brownlee 2004, 151–154). Negotiations between traditional deficit-averse Senate Republicans and the House Democratic majority produced the Tax Equity and Fiscal Responsibility Act of 1982. The legislation repealed scheduled increases in accelerated depreciation deductions, tightened safe harbor leasing rules, reduced the generosity of the investment tax credit, and instituted a 10 percent withholding on corporate dividends and interest payments to bondholders. The legislation infuriated ardent supply-siders in the House, but their minority status undermined their ability to meaningfully shape the legislation (Martin 1991, 135–136).

The Tax Reform Act of 1986 followed the pattern set by the 1982 legislation in that it closed rather than opened corporate tax loopholes. The bill also signaled the abandonment of one of the core tenets of supply-side thinking: generous investment incentives as an essential pillar of pro-growth economic policy. More traditional congressional Republicans joined a chorus of neo-classical economists in arguing that investment credits and accelerated depreciation had failed to boost the absolute levels of investment and contributed to inefficient distortions in capital allocation (Martin 1991, 159–169). The implications of the 1986 reform for corporations were transformative. Although corporate rates were reduced from 48 to 34 percent, the effective corporate tax burden for many firms would increase as some of their most treasured tax preferences were eliminated. Reforms included the elimination of the investment tax credit, greater limitations on the deduction and carryovers of losses, and an updated system of accelerated depreciation that was more neutral across industries and assets. Supply-siders and industry interests may have opposed the elimination of investment incentives, but they were ultimately persuaded by the promise of across-the-board rate reductions. With the exception of tax preferences for the oil industry, the 1986 reform of the tax code was largely a success. While corporate tax expenditures increased from 6 to 8 percent of GDP between 1980 and 1985, this trend reversed after the reform. In the first four years after passage, tax expenditures to business declined by two-thirds to less than 6 percent of GDP.

The reforms to the corporate tax code remained largely intact during the administrations of George H. W. Bush (1989–1993), and Bill Clinton (1993–2001). George H. W. Bush was a clear fiscal traditionalist among Republicans. Despite his strong preferences for rate cuts and tax preferences for the oil industry, he agreed to a modest tax hike in the name of balanced budgets and did not oversee a major expansion of corporate tax expenditures during his presidency. George H. W. Bush's electoral loss in 1992 and the ascension of Newt Gingrich to the House Speakership in 1994 marked a reassertion of a supply-side tax-cutting philosophy within the Republican Party. However, it was not until the George W. Bush presidency (2001–2009) that corporate tax preferences and expenditures would see significant expansion.

A Conservative Congressman Speaks Out in Support of Bonus Depreciation

In 2014 Congressman Dave Camp, Michigan Republican and Chairman of the House Ways and Means Committee, made the following floor statement in support of the permanent extensions of bonus depreciation:

> Our current Tax Code is a wet blanket on this economy. It puts our businesses, their workers, and their products at a severe disadvantage. . . .
>
> Adding insult to injury, the United States is the only country that allows important pieces of its Tax Code to expire. The result: businesses and their workers are left constantly guessing whether certain policies will be around next year, hurting their ability to plan for the future. The National Association of Manufacturers told congress that the "expiration of bonus depreciation at the end of 2013 has had a chilling effect on the economy.". . .
>
> A survey of NAM members found that nearly a third of business owners would not make any investments this year without bonus depreciation and section 79 expensing . . .
>
> The legislation we have before us today would provide a permanent 50 percent bonus depreciation deduction and make the deduction available to more farmers and business owners across the country . . .
>
> . . . The effects of making bonus depreciation permanent are real. Analysis done by the Tax Foundation found that permanent bonus depreciation would grow the economy by 1 percent, which would add $182 billion to the economy; would increase capital stock by over 3 percent; would increase wages by about 1 percent, or $500 for an individual making $50,000 a year; and would create 212,000 jobs. . .
>
> . . . Making 50 percent bonus depreciation permanent is supported by associations representing a variety of industries: farmers, telecommunications, manufacturers, energy, construction, retailers, and technology. Over 100 groups have voiced their support for bonus depreciation stating that it "will provide an immediate incentive for businesses to make additional capital investments, thereby boosting the U.S. economy and job creation."

Source

Camp, Dave. 2014. Statement. *Congressional Record*. H 6112, July 11. Accessed April 18, 2015. http://thomas.loc.gov/cgi-bin/query/B?r113:@FIELD(FLD003+d)+@FIELD(DDATE +20140711.

Republican-sponsored tax legislation in 2002, 2003, and 2004 clearly expressed supply-side beliefs in the growth benefits of tax cuts and diminished concern over deficits. Provisions included the creation and then expansion of expensing for certain capital asset purchases, extended exceptions for active financing income, increased carrybacks of net operating losses to five years, and a new deduction for income from U.S. production activities (Tempalski 2006, 14). These changes, paired with large reductions in individual rates and capital gains taxes, were all passed without equivalent reductions in government spending. Despite their criticisms of the Obama Administration's deficits, Republicans' adherence to supply-side thinking was most recently demonstrated through their attempts to make bonus depreciation allowances permanent without offsetting them through increased revenues or spending cuts (Tiberi 2014).

Democrats on Corporate Tax Policy

The 1980 election was viewed by many Democrats as a rejection of overly generous spending programs and Keynesian policies of macroeconomic stabilization. When Reagan proposed his massive tax cut in 1981, the Democratic chair of the House Ways and Means committee, Dan Rostenkowski, rallied the liberal wing of the party by depicting the individual cuts in Reagan's plan as inequitable. He also mobilized fiscally conservative southern Democrats by suggesting that Reagan's cuts would create large deficits. Rostenkowski then attempted to outflank Senate Republicans by offering business interests generous tax expenditures and preferences. In an effort to defeat this nascent legislative coalition, Reagan and his Senate allies moved to outbid Rostenkowski by offering even more generous preferences to the oil industry and other key economic sectors. The strategy was successful. Business interests and southern Democrats from oil producing districts abandoned Rostenkowski's legislative alternative and aided Senate Republicans and President Reagan in passing the largest tax cut in American history (Martin 1991, 120–131).

Despite the weak economy and complaints from liberal constituents regarding the 1981 legislation, Democratic leaders avoided conflict within the party in 1982. Although liberals wanted to raise taxes in order to fund social programs and conservative southern Democrats wanted to raise taxes in order to reduce deficits, intraparty divisions over tax preferences for the oil industry crippled the Democratic leadership. Fearing another defeat, the Democrats let Senate Republicans craft the tax hikes of 1982.

Democrats took a more active role when tax reform emerged onto the agenda in 1986. Reform appealed to both liberals and conservatives within the party. Liberal Democrats feared that Reagan was attempting to undermine their Party's reputation as the agent of reform and viewed the current tax system as unfair and full of giveaways to wealthy corporations. Conservative Democratic support was once again driven by concerns over deficits (Brownlee 2004, 167–169). Although congressional leaders were not completely successful in protecting the legislation from particularistic demands, the final result was a landmark departure from the status quo that purged the tax code of a wide variety of special industry provisions.

The nomination and election of President Bill Clinton marked the ascension of more centrist and deficit-averse forces within the Democratic Party. Clinton did not oversee major changes to corporate tax policy beyond a very modest increase in the top corporate tax rate from 34 percent to 35 percent and the simplification of equipment depreciation rules.

In contrast, the Obama administration (2009–2017) significantly expanded special tax breaks for business within the American Recovery and Reinvestment Act of 2009 (ARRA). Corporate provisions included a temporary (bonus) increase in allowable expensing of depreciable business assets and tax credits for investments in advanced energy facilities (Recovery.gov 2009). President Obama also joins congressional Democrats and Republicans in their desire to reform corporate taxation by repealing some corporate tax preferences and expenditures and

---

A Liberal Democrat Criticizes Bonus Depreciation

In 2014 Sander Levin, a Michigan Democrat and Ranking Member of the House Ways and Means Committee, made the following remarks objecting to the permanent extension of bonus depreciation:

> Essentially, what it does is to make permanent what has always been considered temporary. Bonus depreciation, which has been temporarily enacted during the previous two recessions to help assist the economy during the short term—that is what it has been—allows companies to write off investments more quickly than normal, providing them an incentive to make capital investments now rather than later.
>
> And that incentive actually disappears when the provision is made permanent. That is why CRS has said its temporary nature "is critical to its effectiveness." Secondly, it is unpaid for. Talk about consistency, talk about a budget bill that talks about the importance of deficit reduction, and here you have the Republicans proposing a bill that would add $287 billion in debt. . . .
>
> When all is said and done, House Republicans will have added more than $1 trillion to the deficit by permanently extending a select group of corporate tax cuts.
>
> But let me just say I must confess I am amazed at the inconsistency of this position. It was 5 months ago in the chairman's and the Republican Ways and Means draft that they proposed to eliminate this provision entirely. Bonus depreciation was gone. And now they come forth and they say, Let's make it permanent. That gives inconsistency a bad name. It is appalling. It is really also dangerous.

Source

Levin, Sander. 2014. Statement. *Congressional Record.* H 6113, July 11. Accessed April 18, 2015. http://thomas.loc.gov/cgibin/query/D?r113:6:./temp/~r113PhxdWS.

lowering rates (Pozen 2015). Whether this consensus can withstand continued partisan and intra-party disagreements over effective rates, progressivity, and what will surely be aggressive anti-reform industry lobbying is an open question.

Lucas Lockhart

Further Reading

Brownlee, W. Elliot. 2004. *Federal Taxation in America: A Short History*. Cambridge, UK: Cambridge University Press.

Gravelle, Jane G., and Thomas L. Hungerford. 2011. *Corporate Tax Reform: Issues for Congress*. CRS Report No. RL34229. Washington, DC: Congressional Research Service. Accessed on April 3, 2015 http://taxprof.typepad.com/files/crs-rl34229.pdf.

Keightley, Mark P., and Molly F. Sherlock. 2011. *The Corporate Income Tax System: Overview and Options for Reform*. CRS Report No. R42726.Washington, DC: Congressional Research Service. Accessed April 2, 2015. https://www.fas.org/sgp/crs/misc/R42726 .pdf.

Martin, Cathie J. 1991. *Shifting the Burden: The Struggle Over Growth and Corporate Taxation*. Chicago: University of Chicago Press.

Pozen, Robert. 2015. "U.S. Corporate Tax Reform: Why Obama's Good Ideas Don't Add Up." The Brookings Institution. February 5. Accessed April 4, 2015. http://www .brookings.edu/research/opinions/2015/02/05-us-corporate-tax-reform-obamas -good-ideas-dont-add-up-pozen.

Recovery.gov. 2009. Accessed on April 15, 2015. http://www.recovery.gov/arra/Transparency /fundingoverview/Pages/fundingbreakdown.aspx#TaxBenefits.

Slemrod, Joel, and Jon Bakija. 2008. *Taxing Ourselves: A Citizens Guide to the Debate over Taxes*. Cambridge, MA: MIT Press.

Taylor, Jack. 2003. "Corporation Income Tax Brackets and Rates, 1909–2002." *Statistics of Income (SOI) Bulletin* 23(2): 284–290. Accessed April 5, 2015. http://www.irs.gov/pub /irs-soi/02corate.pdf.

Tempalski, Jerry. 2006. *Revenue Effects of Major Tax Bills*. U.S. Department of the Treasury OTA Working Papers 81, 1–20.

Tiberi, Patrick. 2014. "H.R. 4718—To amend the Internal Revenue Code of 1986 to modify and make permanent bonus depreciation." May 22. Accessed April 2, 2016. https:// www.congress.gov/bill/113th-congress/house-bill/4718.

Corruption

At a Glance

Some political observers contend that corruption in the United States' political system has more to do with how Republicans and Democrats define corruption rather than any differences in actual behavior. In addition to recognizing widely acknowledged forms of corruption like outright political bribery, Republicans define corruption based on the wastefulness of government growth and spending, and vehemently oppose any regulation of the competitive political process. For this reason, they oppose campaign finance reform, arguing that people should be encouraged to financially participate in the political process. In the same manner, Republicans tend to oppose earmarking arguing that it contributes to wasteful spending and excessive legislative dealmaking that is not in the public interest.

Democrats tend to believe corruption is rooted in the individual behavior of people entrusted with political power that usurp that power for their own ends, rather than for the people they were tasked with representing. They believe this happens because the political system in the United States is biased toward unrestrained capitalism and greed. Wealthy individuals and corporations buy political favoritism through campaign contributions. For this reason, Democrats tend to support campaign finance reform and the use of earmarking as a way of ensuring that projects for the people get funded, even if the projects are not in the best interests of the wealthy.

Many Democrats . . .

- See corruption as primarily an issue of lawmakers lining the pockets of business elites and political supporters at the expense of poor and middle-class Americans.
- View political corruption as motivated by greed for money and influence
- Believe corruption is inevitable in an environment where unlimited campaign contributions by the wealthiest corporations and individuals can buy political influence
- See Republicans as unduly influenced by their key constituencies

Many Republicans . . .

- See ineffective social service programs and "big" government as rife with political corruption
- Believe corruption has been promoted historically through the funding of "pet projects" via the earmarking process
- See Democrats as unduly influenced by their key constituencies

---

Overview

America's two-party political system presumes deep-seated ideological differences in how the Republican and Democratic parties define political corruption, but close analysis suggests that most of the political party differences in corruption have little to do with the behaviors of corruption and much more to do with how the groups understand and define political corruption. This is exacerbated by the fact that there is no universal, agreed upon definition of corruption. The most commonly cited definition is by Transparency International, an organization that scores countries on how corrupt their public sectors are in their Corruption Perceptions Index. Transparency International defines corruption as "the misuse of entrusted power for private gain" (2015). In reality, corruption embodies several situations, which speak to the heart of political influence, namely the issues of bribery and campaign finance, where public officials use their political position to gain resources or more power for their private gain. How these acts are defined varies according to party platform.

From its earliest days, the Republican Party has framed itself as a party dedicated to fiscal responsibility, balanced budgets, and the elimination of waste from federal spending (Davis 2006). They define corruption as the wastefulness of social programs and the expansion of government. For example, Thomas Frank, author of the *Wrecking Crew* argued:

> [t]he welfare state isn't a 'safety net' or an improved, scientific form of civilization, according to this view; it's a systematically organized rip-off in which all the liberal elements—from the media to the trial lawyers—have a designated role to play. (Frank 2008, 241)

For Republicans, political corruption has less to do with individual rule infraction and more to do with the systematic decay of political culture. For this reason, Republicans are more likely than Democrats to define acts that lead to government spending, such as earmarks, or legislative provisions that guarantee federal expenditures to particular recipients as corruption (Frisch and Kelly 2010)

Democrats, by comparison, define corruption in terms of breaking the rules. Corruption occurs when those entrusted with political power do not act in the

---

Democratic House Speaker Nancy Pelosi Decries GOP "Culture of Corruption"

When Democrats took control of the House in 2006 and the White House in 2008 from the GOP, some observers asserted that their success was due in part to their accusations that the Republican majority had allowed a "culture of corruption" to flourish in Washington. In January 2006, for example, Congresswoman Nancy Pelosi (D-CA) asserted that if voters returned Congress to control of the Democrats, her party would "drain the swamp of Washington":

> For a long time now, an ethical cloud has hung over the Capitol. For years, Democrats have called for an end to the Republican culture of corruption.
>
> . . . Republicans are resisting true reform because they generally benefit from the enabling culture of corruption to continue. Republicans have allowed this poison tree of corruption to bear the fruit of bad policy for the American people.
>
> . . . The intention of our Founding Fathers was for Congress to be a marketplace of ideas. The Republicans have turned Congress into an auction house—for sale to the highest bidder. You have to pay to play. It is just not right.
>
> . . . Democrats are leading the effort to turn the most closed, corrupt Congress in history into the most open and honest Congress in history.
>
> . . . Ours must be a government 'of the people, by the people, and for the people.' That means all of the American people. Republicans have made it a government of, by, and for a few of the people. America can do better. We can and we will. With this agenda, Democrats will create the most open and honest government in history, and put power back where it belongs—in the hands of all the people. Together, America can do better.

Source

Pelosi, Nancy. 2006. "We Will Create the Most Open and Honest Government in History." Speech Delivered January 18 at the Thomas Jefferson building at the Library of Congress. Accessed November 16, 2015. https://pelosi.house.gov/news/press-releases/pelosi-we -will-create-the-most-open-and-honest-government-in-history.

---

interest of those who the state was founded to protect and instead usurp that power for their own ends. In this way, Democrats see corruption in terms of the weakening of ethical constraints on individual conduct in public office resulting in the abuse of political power. For example, Democrats accuse the Republican Party of using its political base to line the pockets of business elites. As Paul Krugman of the *New York Times* argued, Democrats believe they are fighting "crony capitalists," "corporate insiders," and "malefactors of great wealth" (Krugman 2003). For this reason, Democrats tend to oppose unlimited spending on campaigns, arguing that it establishes a political system that favors the rich and leads to quid pro quo, a Latin phrase meaning simply, "something for something," relationships.

It is clear that corruption occurs in both political camps; however, since the Watergate scandal, the Democratic Party has sought—and been successful to some

---

A Conservative Commentator Condemns the Democrats' "Culture of Corruption"

After Democrats reclaimed control of both Congress and the White House in 2008, conservative critics claimed that President Obama, House Speaker Nancy Pelosi, and other members of their party let a culture of corruption take root. In 2014 Michelle Malkin, author of *Culture of Corruption: Obama and His Team of Tax Cheats, Crooks and Cronies* (2010), detailed a series of scandals and investigations plaguing Democratic local and state officials around the country, then mocked Pelosi for her claims that Democrats were above such behavior:

> Has Nancy Pelosi seen a newspaper lately? . . . I'd love to see her face in the wake of the veritable epidemic of Democratic corruption now sweeping the country. . . . Nancy Pelosi famously promised to "drain the moral swamp" and end the "culture of corruption." She cast herself her minions as America's political cleanup crew. But once again, the culture of corruption boomerang has swung back around to smack Democrats in their smug mugs.

Source

Malkin, Michelle. 2014. "A Whole Lotta Democrat Corruption Going On." March 28. *Michellemalkin.com*. Accessed November 23, 2015. http://michellemalkin.com/2014/03/28/a-whole-lotta-democrat-corruption-going-on/.

---

degree—in positioning itself as the party of reform in terms of reducing money's impact on politics and policy. Stronger attempts to control corruption began in response to the Watergate scandal, which culminated in Republican Richard Nixon's resignation from the presidency in August of 1974. Jimmy Carter's subsequent comments, when he accepted the Democratic nomination for president, defined the Democrats as the party of reform: "We can have an American government that has turned away from scandal and corruption and official cynicism and is once again as decent and competent as our people" (Carter 1976). In 2006, the Democratic Party was still defining the Republican Party as a one awash in a "culture of corruption." Governor Howard Dean, a Democrat from Vermont, commented on allegations of insider trading by Senator Bill Frist, a Republican from Tennessee to the then-emerging Abramoff scandal, asserting: "Republicans have made their culture of corruption the norm" (NBC 2006).

The reality is that political activity in the United States may not be driven as much by political principle or ideological conviction but rather by pragmatism and reciprocity. Once an allegation is made, many individuals accused of corruption fire back at their accusers, creating so-called "corruption wars." The public's increased awareness of corruption is a direct result of public partisan allegations of corruption. For example, recently, the Republicans have turned the Democrats' language against them and sought to paint the Obama Administration as one stained by a "culture of corruption," citing Democratic congressman Anthony Weiner's sex scandal, the conviction of Representative Jesse Jackson, Jr. for using campaign funds for personal use, and the fallout over the large-scale government surveillance and intelligence gathering scandals (Batley 2013). While there are no reliable data about which political party is more corrupt in the United States, it is clear that the American public sees its government as corrupt. A 2013 public opinion poll showed that 72 percent of respondents believed that corruption has increased since 2007 and 76 percent of respondents felt that political parties were corrupt or extremely corrupt (Transparency International 2015). The costs of corruption and the resulting scandal wars thus not only include the loss of billions of dollars in taxpayers' money, but also a reduction in the legitimacy of government.

Republicans on Corruption

The Republican Party views actions that destabilize the separate powers of large entities as corruption (Kleinig and Heffernan 2004). To illustrate, Republicans generally oppose regulations that interfere with the competitive political process, including campaign finance reform and earmarking. In the 2012 Republican Platform, the GOP stated that they believe that there should be no limitations on the amount an individual should be able to contribute to a campaign (Republican National Convention 2012). This position is naturally beneficial to the GOP, as the Republican Party has historically been able to secure more high-end individual contributions than the Democratic Party (Lowenstein 1989). Republican Governor of New Jersey Chris Christie defined the perceptions of campaign corruption, not in terms of what is spent, but in terms of transparency: "I think what is corrupting in this potentially is we don't know where the money is coming from" (Gold 2015). His statement has prompted a solution to this perception that is currently being batted around within the Republican Party: reveal campaign contributions to the public. This solution has not been popular with contributors, however. "I don't think my contribution should be disclosed," said one such individual. "I don't think my group should be hassled" (Gold 2015). There is some research that suggests that spending limits benefit the Democrats and handicap the Republicans, due to the Republican Party being smaller, but with deeper pockets. To be competitive, Republican candidates must win over a larger number of independent voters, which requires a well-funded and highly visible campaign. And campaign finance reforms, depending on their specifics, could make this outcome much more difficult.

On April 2, 2014, the United States Supreme Court struck down the aggregate limits on the amount an individual can contribute to federal candidates, parties, and political action committees over a two-year period. This decision essentially removed the overall cap on individual contributions but left the base limits on federal candidates' campaigns, PACs, or party committees. Currently, individuals who wish to contribute to a campaign are allowed to contribute up to $2,600 per election to a federal candidate. This decision was widely interpreted as a major victory for the Republican stance on campaign financing.

While the Republican Party rejected limits on campaign spending, it has supported limitations on earmarks, citing that earmarks encourage wasteful spending and unethical behavior (Davis 2014). What are earmarks? The Office of Management and Budget defined earmarks as:

> Funds provided by the Congress for projects, programs, or grants where the purported congressional direction circumvents otherwise applicable merit-based or competitive allocation processes, or specifies the location or recipient, or otherwise curtails the ability of the executive branch to manage its statutory and constitutional responsibilities pertaining to the funds allocation process. (Office of Management and Budget 2015)

In 2010, the House of Representatives enacted a ban on earmarks when the Republicans took control of the House. This ban, which was widely supported by the GOP base of "small government" adherents, was renewed in 2014 (Pappas 2014).

Democrats on Corruption

Democrats are concerned not only with cases of outright bribery, but with forms of political corruption that are perceived to interfere with the ability of the government to fairly distribute resources and carry out policies for the benefit of the public. From this perspective, a corrupted democracy is one that disempowers the public through the uneven administration of rights, inefficiencies, and misdirected public funds (Warren 2015). Two issues of concern to the Democratic Party are earmarking and campaign finance.

Traditionally, earmarking assists in the funding of pet projects within the districts of lawmakers. Democrats have demonstrated mixed support for earmarking. In his 2011 State of the Union address, President Obama stated that he would veto any bill that was designated for earmarking purposes (Wong 2011). This was primarily done as a deficit-reduction measure, as well as potentially preventing earmarks from being used for improper financial benefits toward specific donors or constituents. However, many Democrats oppose the earmarking ban, arguing that the power of Congress' purse is necessary to guarantee that the needs of the people are met. Harry Reid, the Democrat Senate Majority Leader of Nevada and Democratic Senator Dick Durbin of Illinois argued that earmarking should be brought back (Ricci 2014). Specifically, Reid called for greater transparency than what was previously given to re-introduce earmarking (McAuliff 2014).

The call to make earmarking a more transparent process is an acknowledgment that earmarking conducted behind closed doors has greater potential for corruption. For example, institutions ranging from specific organizations to entire industries that have received earmarks from political members may in due time express their gratitude financially with campaign contributions and the like (Lessig 2011). Where some may call this exerting political influence, others may call it corruption. Historically, quid pro quo ("something for something") has been used as a dividing line between criminal corruption, and what Kevin D. Williamson calls the "moral ickiness" of the democratic process (Williamson 2015).

The U.S. Supreme Court's decision in 2010 *Citizens United* clarified this historical definition of corruption: if it is not punishable by a bribery statute, it is not corruption (Lessig 2015). In 2010, Democrats called for a reversal of the *Citizens United* decision arguing that it has contributed to corruption. Democrats tend to believe that removing restrictions on campaign funding unfairly favors the rich (Rosen 2014). Instead, they argue for campaign finance reform, as well as legislation, to close loopholes and require greater disclosure of campaign spending. The 2014 *McCutcheon* decision that struck down the aggregate limits on the amount an individual could contribute to federal candidates, parties, and political action committees over a two-year period, was a clear defeat for the Democratic stance on campaign financing. Since that time, in an alleged attempt to level the playing field, some Democrats have embraced the *Citizens United* and *McCutcheon* decisions (Sirota 2015). For example, Hillary Clinton has accepted millions of dollars from major corporations to finance her presidential campaign, compared to Bernie Sanders who has not pursued funding through a Super PAC, instead choosing to receive most of his campaign funds from small, individual donations (Lichtblau 2015).

Cara E. Rabe-Hemp,
John C. Navarro, and
Cayla Comens

Further Reading

Batley, Melanie. 2013. "Democrats Have 'Culture of Corruption' They Once Blamed GOP For," *Newsmax*, July 25. Accessed November 1, 2015. http://www.newsmax.com /Politics/dms-culture-corruption-gop/2013/07/25/id/517037/.

Davis, Lanny. 2006. *Sandal: How Gotcha Politics Is Destroying America*. New York: Palgrave Macmillan.

Carter, James E. 1976. "1976 Democratic Convention Acceptance Speech". July 15. Accessed October 30, 2015. http://www.americanrhetoric.com/speeches/jimmycart er1976dnc.htm.

Davis, Susan. 2014. "Read Boehner's Lips: No New Earmarks." *USA Today*, May 12. Accessed October 21, 2015. http://onpolitics.usatoday.com/2014/05/12 /read-boehners-lips-no-new-earmarks/.

Federal Election Commission. *McCutcheon, et al. v. FEC*. Accessed May 23, 2015. http:// www.fec.gov/law/litigation/McCutcheon.shtml.

Frank, Thomas. 2008. *Wrecking Crew*. New York: Metropolitan Books.

Frisch, Scott A., and Sean Q. Kelly. 2010. *Cheese Factories on the Moon: Why Earmarks Are Good for American Democracy,* Boulder, CO: Paradigm Publishers.

Gold, Matea. 2015. "Big Money in Politics Emerges as a Rising Issue in 2016 Campaign." *Washington Post*, April 19. Accessed June 10, 2015. http://www.washingtonpost.com /politics/big-money-in-politics-emerges-as-a-rising-issue-in-2016-campaign/2015/04/19 /c695cbb8-e51c-11e4-905f-cc896d379a32_story.html?hpid=z1.

Kleinig, John, and William C. Heffernan. 2004. "The Corruptibility of Corruption." In *Private and Public Corruption*, edited by William C. Heffernan and John Kleinig, 3–22. Lanham, MD: Rowman & Littlefield Publishers, Inc.

Krugman, Paul. 2003. "The Acid Test." *New York Times*, May 2, 1.

Lessig, Lawrence. 2011. *Republic, Lost: How Money Corrupts Congress—and a Plan to Stop It.* New York: Twelve.

Lessig, Lawrence. 2015. "Democrats Embrace the Logic of 'Citizens United.'" *Washington Post*, May 8. Accessed May 5, 2015. http://www.washingtonpost.com/opinions/the-clintons-citizens-united-and-21st-century-corruption/2015/05/08/7f11a0d6-f57b-11e4-b2f3-af5479e6bbdd_story.html.

Lichtblau, Eric. 2015. "Bernie Sanders's Success in Attracting Small Donors Tests Importance of 'Super PACs.'" *New York Times*, August 15, 1.

Lowenstein, Daniel H. 1989. "On Campaign Finance Reform: The Root of All Evil Is Deeply Rooted." *Hofstra Law Review 18* (2): 301–367.

McAuliff, Michael. 2014. "Harry Reid Defends Earmarks, Says Obama Is 'Wrong'." *Huffington Post*, June 6. Accessed May 1, 2015. http://www.huffingtonpost.com/2014/05/06/harry-reid-earmarks_n_5275591.html.

NBC. 2006. "Howard Dean: Culture of Corruption." *Hardball with Chris Matthews*, May 1. Accessed October 1, 2015. http://www.nbcnews.com/id/12580289/ns/msnbc-hardball_with_chris_matthews/t/howard-dean-culture-corruption/.

Office of Management and Budget. 2015. "Earmarks." Accessed May 23. https://earmarks.omb.gov/earmarks-public/.

Pappas, Alex. 2014. "Behind Closed Doors, Republicans Push to End Earmark Ban." *The Daily Caller*. Last modified November 14. Accessed May 15, 2015. http://dailycaller.com/2014/11/14/behind-closed-doors-republicans-pushing-to-end-earmark-ban/.

Republican National Committee. 2012. "We Believe in America: 2012 Republican Platform." Republican National Convention, 12. Accessed May 22, 2015. http://www.presidency.ucsb.edu/papers_pdf/101961.pdf.

Ricci, Mike. 2014. "No Ifs, No Buts, No Earmarks." *Office of the Speaker of the House*. May 13. Accessed September 7, 2015. http://www.speaker.gov/general/no-ifs-no-buts-no-earmarks.

Rosen, Jeffrey. 2014. "Clarence Thomas does not Share the Founding Fathers' View of Corruption." *New Republic*, October 11. Accessed May 27, 2015. http://www.newrepublic.com/article/115152/mccutcheon-case-corruption-and-supreme-court.

Sirota, David. 2015. "Democrats Embrace Citizens United in Defense of Clinton." *Buzz Flash.com*, May 6. Accessed May 15, 2015. http://www.truth-out.org/buzzflash/commentary/democrats-embrace-citizens-united-in-defense-of-clinton/19300-democrats-embrace-citizens-united-in-defense-of-clinton.

Transparency International. 2015. "Country Overview: United States." Accessed May 26. http://www.transparency.org/country#USA_Overview.

Warren, Mark E. 2015. "The Meaning of Corruption in Democracies." In *Routledge Handbook of Political Corruption*, edited by Paul M. Heywood, 42–55. New York: Routledge.

Williamson, Kevin D. 2015. "Defining 'Corruption' Corruptly," *National Review*, May 9. Accessed May 25. http://www.nationalreview.com/corner/418158/defining-corruption-corruptly-kevin-d-williamson.

Wong, Scott. 2011. "Senate Dems Give in on Earmark Ban." *Politico*, February 1. Accessed May 27, 2015. http://www.politico.com/news/stories/0211/48623.html.

Debt Ceiling

At a Glance

Both Republicans and Democrats understand the potential dangers of an aggressively rising debt ceiling. Their ideological differences come from the preferred methods of decreasing American deficits and limiting the rise of the debt ceiling.

Democrats see budget deficits and the accumulation of the national debt as a problem to be managed through an increase in taxes and careful monitoring of the costs of much-needed services. Many Democrats believe that increasing budgets reflect an increased demand for government assistance and support. The best way to mitigate the rising costs without adding more debt is to increase revenue, some of which needs to come through higher taxes on the wealthiest Americans or corporations.

Recently, Republicans have become more aggressive in emphasizing their belief that a reduction in the national debt is essential. Many have stated that the consistently growing debt ceiling is a danger to the economic stability of the country. To keep from adding to that debt, they propose cutting national spending and government services. Their refusal to consider raising taxes on the wealthy, however, has sparked debate about whether they truly see the national debt as a crisis.

Many Democrats . . .

- Say that some debt may be necessary to provide government-funded services
- Believe strongly in maintaining a large budget regarding social services, and are more willing to cut spending for other expenses, like national defense.

Many Republicans . . .

- Express concern that maintaining a large national debt is hazardous for the American economy
- Feel that excessive government spending is responsible for national debt and needs to be curtailed

- Believe Congress should approve considerable spending cuts to unnecessary or wasteful social services programs

---

Overview

As the needs and resources of the country change, so do the cost of services for which the government must pay. When the money coming in through the various revenue streams the United States government generates is greater than the amount being spent on services, it is referred to as a budget surplus. However, the revenue is often exceeded by annual spending, creating a budget deficit. To pay for services that cannot be accounted for with internal revenue streams, the U.S. government can borrow money from international organizations or foreign governments. Deficits held over multiple years create national debt. Most of this debt comes from loans with international organizations, other nations, or large international banks. When the government is able to develop a surplus, they can use those excess funds to pay off some of the accrued debt. The limit placed on such debt is called the debt ceiling, and is the total amount of money the government is allowed to borrow to pay off its extra expenses from deficits. Each year the budget runs a deficit, additional debt is accrued, and eventually the amount borrowed begins to reach that maximum. The government then needs to vote to raise the limit of how much they can borrow; otherwise it would be forced to cut billions of dollars in expenses (public services) to balance the budget.

If Congress does not vote to raise the debt limit, the government cannot borrow the necessary funds to support the various government departments and organizations under its purview, and those departments will not be able to function. This forces a shutdown of all the underfunded departments. Simultaneously, the government will have promised to pay more money than it has, pushing the government to default on its loans. A federal default would have a negative impact on the United States economy and the world at large. The dollar is a global currency. A default on American loans would imply that the worth of that dollar has decreased significantly, severely disrupting the financial well-being of the American economy as well as the banks and other governments that own American debt. This would then impact financial markets worldwide. A default on loans could potentially create a crash in the global stock market, throwing the world's economy into an economic depression (Frank 2004, 69–71).

Budget deficits have been common since the nation's inception, but a formal debt limit was not created until 1917, with the passage of the Second Liberty Bond Act. The decision to raise the debt ceiling or cut spending is where controversies arise. It is typically a two-step process. First, Congress must create a budget to see how much is to be spent. If that spending exceeds revenue, they vote to raise the debt limit. This process was briefly altered when, in 1979, to eliminate the inefficiencies of this two-step process, Congress passed the Gephardt Rule, named for

Congressman Richard Gephardt. This rule stated that each time the new budget was passed with a deficit; the debt ceiling was automatically raised to accommodate that debt. This rule was kept in place until 1995, when the Republican-controlled House repealed it. In 2015, Congress is using the two-step process.

Historically, raising the debt ceiling was a fairly non-partisan exercise, so these consequences were of no great concern. However, beginning in the 1990s, many in the Republican Party became concerned with increased government spending. This trend continued to grow, and peaked when a sharply conservative wing of the Republican Party, the Tea Party, gained popularity in 2009. The Tea Party platform is based on the libertarian ideology of a small government with as little interaction with and cost to citizens as possible (Maltsev and Skaskiw 2013, 1–2). The Tea Party gained momentum in Congress when it won a significant number of congressional seats in the 2010 midterm elections.

The increase in conservative congressional votes led to more political discord about how to approach a budget, particularly as the United States once again neared the debt limit. When it became necessary to raise the debt ceiling in 2011, a number of Republicans drew the conclusion that it was not in the public's best interest to raise the debt ceiling without the promise of significant spending cuts. House Speaker Boehner, a Republican from Ohio, declared that to raise the debt ceiling without these cuts would be fiscally irresponsible, and called on Republicans to refuse to vote for an increase in the debt limit until their requirements of reduced government spending and a smaller budget were met. This debate took Congress very near the deadline for voting to actually raise the debt ceiling. The United States came dangerously close to defaulting on its loans. Ultimately, Democrats felt forced to concede billions of dollars in spending cuts for domestic programs and services over 10 years as a concession for Republicans to agree to raise the debt limit (Hulse and Cooper 2011). Due to how perilously close Congress came to defaulting, the Standard & Poor Financial Services Company lowered the United States' credit rating from a AAA grade to a AA+ grade for the first time in modern history, stating that the international community had lost some confidence in America's ability to pay its national debt (U.S. Congress, Joint Economic Committee 2013, 59–60).

This close call had other significant negative consequences. The Republican victory emboldened them to demand more cuts when Congress was again forced to vote to raise the debt ceiling in 2013. However, this time Democrats stood firm in their decision not to agree to anything less than a debt ceiling bill free of attached partisan spending cuts. This debate took the country so close to a default that some government agencies were forced to shut down, to avoid going over the spending limit until Congress could reach an agreement. They were finally able to come to a consensus and vote to raise the limit with only hours left before the country would default. Democrats came out victorious, with an almost completely clean bill (Cohen, Botelho, and Yan 2013).

The United States neared its debt limit of $18.1 trillion in October 2015, and was forced to begin another high-stakes fight over whether or not to raise it. Again,

Partisan Divisions over Raising the Debt Ceiling

On February 11, 2014, Senator Ted Cruz, a Republican and vocal member of the Tea Party movement issued a statement about the irresponsibility of raising the debt ceiling without also cutting national spending. His stance, which he has repeated on many occasions, echoed what many other conservative Republicans have said about adding to the national debt. Among other things, Senator Cruz stated:

> If you ask anybody outside of Washington whether we should keep increasing the debt ceiling without fixing the underlying problem of out-of-control spending, the answer is 'of course not.' This answer cuts across party lines and ideology—outside the Beltway, Republicans, Democrats, Independents, and Libertarians all agree that living within your means is basic common sense. And yet Washington is not listening to the American people. Under President Obama, our national debt has increased from $10 trillion to $17 trillion, and now the President is asking for yet another blank check to keep increasing our debt without doing anything to reform Washington's spending problem. This is wrong, and it's irresponsible. Our parents didn't do this to us, and we shouldn't do it to our kids and grandkids. Historically, the debt ceiling has proven the most effective leverage for reining in spending; 28 times, Congress has attached meaningful conditions to debt ceiling increases. We should do so again to address the real problem.

Democrats, on the other hand, have harshly criticized GOP reluctance to raise the debt ceiling since President Obama took office. On March 6, 2105, House Minority leader Nancy Pelosi suggested that Republicans routinely use the threat of a debt default to try to force Democrats to concede to their budgetary demands. She further implied that Republicans are not taking the issue of raising the debt limit seriously, and that they are compromising the stability of the country. As she stated:

> There is no reason that the Republican Congress should not act immediately to take the prospect of a catastrophic default off of the table. Failure to act would have savage impacts on American families: tumbling retirement savings and soaring interest rates for student loans, mortgages, credit cards, and car payments. Republicans' unending manufactured crises present a very real danger to the security of American families. As critical deadlines loom that threaten millions of seniors' access to their doctors, jeopardize critical infrastructure projects at the dawn of the summer construction season, and other challenges, the American people cannot afford a Republican Congress more interested in hostage-taking than legislating. Republicans are only stoking the fires of uncertainty—needlessly threatening to derail our historic 12-month stretch of 200,000 plus monthly job creation. House Republicans need to stop creating crises and work with House Democrats to advance the needs of America's families.

Sources

Cruz, Ted. 2015. "Cruz: I Intend to Object to Any Effort to Raise the Debt Ceiling with a Simple Majority Vote." Accessed October 5. http://www.cruz.senate.gov/?p=press_release&id=920.

Pelosi, Nancy. 2015. "Pelosi Statement on Treasury Secretary Letter to Congress on Debt Limit." Accessed October 6. http://www.democraticleader.gov/newsroom/pelosi-statement-treasury-secretary-letter-congress-debt-limit/.

Republicans demanded billions of dollars in cuts to services like Medicare and Social Security, with Democrats refusing to negotiate under those strict and unfair terms. With just a few days to spare, Republican leadership and President Obama came to a compromise to pass a bill that would raise the debt ceiling again. This bill also increases spending limits, while cutting the budgets of some social programs, giving into some of the demands from both sides (Herszenhorn 2015). Even with this compromise, Republican leadership stated that they would have trouble securing conservative votes to pass the bill.

Democrats on the Debt Ceiling

While Democrats understand the importance of the debt ceiling debate, they do not make it a vocal priority unless there is an imminent vote on the matter. For example, there is no mention of it in their official party platform. Historically, Democrats tend to focus on the services government can provide for its constituents first, and then decide how to pay for those new services. As more government-funded programs and projects are implemented, larger budgets are also required to pay for those new services. They believe that the government should be responsible for paying for services to address certain needs, like health care, public transportation, and financial assistance for the poor or disabled. In return, there are taxes on consumptive goods and income to make sure everyone receives the basic level of care and to offset increased expenses (U.S. Congress, Joint Economic Committee 2013). This leads Democrats to weigh funding these necessary programs against creating a budget that can be paid for without accruing more debt. A majority of Democrats typically vote in favor of ensuring American programs are being funded, and accept the potential accrual of debt. This is not to say that Democrats blindly increase spending in every situation; they are much more willing to cut spending which does not positively and directly impact America's welfare. When Republicans criticize them for spending thoughtlessly, and creating a bloated budget, Democrats often cite defense spending, which they are more than willing to cut to keep national costs low.

In discussions of spending, Democrats also emphasize that not all government services add to the American debt. Some government-funded programs create enough revenue to not only pay for themselves, but produce a profit as well. An example would be government assistance to farmers to grow their businesses, which gives farmers the opportunity to sell more of their product, and eases U.S. dependence on imported food. Assisting citizens will ensure that they are better able to produce larger profits, which will then filter back into United States' income. The more productive America is as a country, the better able it will be to reduce deficit spending, and pay off the national debt.

To provide the necessary services to keep up with changing societal needs, the United States government has needed to spend more money each year. However, Democrats are also more willing to require increases in revenue from the American people, in the form of taxes on Americans in the highest tax brackets. If Americans can pay for things themselves, they will not need to borrow from outside sources. The services mentioned above require a large federal government to maintain those services, and enough government workers to ensure those services are being coordinated correctly. This has become an increasingly expensive bureaucracy to fund. However, Democrats tend to believe that the United States should be able to pay for increasing costs with increased revenue from the profitability of some services and a small tax increase on some of the wealthiest Americans.

Republicans claim that U.S. support for these services has become unsustainable. The revenue brought in through services and taxation will not be enough to balance the budget anymore, forcing the United States to borrow more and increase the debt limit. Perhaps the most divisive example of expansion of services promised to Americans is the recently passed Affordable Care Act. Republicans claim that this will become too costly for Americans to pay for on their own, and that the United States will need to take on more debt to pay for such a service. Reducing funding for entitlement programs like Medicaid and TANF (Temporary Assistance for Needy Families) that primarily benefit the poor have become a common stipulation for Republicans when it comes time to approve increasing the debt ceiling. They have also tried to link passing a debt ceiling increase to repealing the Affordable Care Act. Democrats, who are backed by the impartial Congressional Budget Office, state that the Affordable Care Act will ultimately be a cost-saving service (Stone 2014), which will help curtail the national debt. They argue that Republicans are taking the American people hostage by demanding unfair spending cuts, and using the ticking clock of reaching the debt limit as leverage (Caldwell 2013).

Republicans on the Debt Ceiling

Republicans have become quite vocal about the need to stop raising the debt ceiling. While the 2012 Republican Party Platform does not use the phrase "debt ceiling" specifically, it does mention the nation's "unsustainable debt produced by a big government entitlement society," and that the interest on this debt is taking up "an ever-increasing portion of the country's wealth" (Republican National Committee 2012). When discussing the need for debt reduction, the first culprit has become increased government spending, specifically in the areas advocated by Democrats. Rhetoric like "elected officials have overpromised and overspent, and now the bills are due" (Republican National Committee 2012) is common in Republican statements. The typical Republican response to lowering the national debt has been to decrease what they deem to be unnecessary social services spending, and to reduce future spending on promised benefits, such as Social Security and Medicare, commonly referred to as entitlements. This is proposed through the creation of long-term spending caps and reduction of the size of government departments (U.S. Congress, Joint Economic Committee 2013, 26).

Many Republicans agree that some entitlements are necessary and cannot be funded through the private sector, but disagree on current funding levels and programs. Texas Representative Kevin Brady described the proposed cuts as "merely asking this 500-pound federal government to lose 10 pounds" (U.S. Congress, Joint Economic Committee 2013, 59–60). The GOP argument is that government has become so bloated that huge sums of tax revenue are collected and distributed for government services and entitlements that are simply unnecessary, and some argue the American people would not miss those services. In fact, Republicans believe that reducing government programs, and therefore the taxes needed to fund them, will increase private income saved in this country. They imagine a more productive workplace, where the private sector is free to spend their money on their own needs. The now smaller government would be able to use the tax money that was previously used for government services to pay down the national debt. This would produce a budget that never comes close to the current debt ceiling.

In the past, Republicans have been more tolerant of increasing national spending, and the eventual need to raise the debt ceiling, especially when debts went to pay for increased defense spending. There was enough Republican support for the debt limit increases over the years that President Bush spent billions of dollars in the name of national defense and the "War on Terror." However, as the party shifted further to the right, the more conservative Republicans became less tolerant of adding to the national debt without also cutting current and future spending, even in matters of national defense.

Many Republicans share similar political philosophies, but differ in the intensity of their ideology. More moderate Republicans advocate for spending cuts and a smaller government, but they are willing to concede that allowing the United States government to default on their loans is more dangerous to the American economy than finding long-term solutions to cut spending. More conservative members of the Republican Party, now led by the Tea Party Movement, feel that reducing wasteful government spending, and therefore shrinking the burden on the individual taxpayer is the most important aspect of their job as legislators, even if it means putting the debt ceiling vote on hold, forcing the government to default on their loans, and dealing with the inevitable fallout of that decision. They believe that any more debt accumulated by the United States is inherently harmful to the nation's stability, and that raising the debt ceiling without a plan to reduce government spending gives Democrats permission to continue what they see as reckless spending (Paul 2015). Conservative Republicans gained a lot of political power when they first took office in 2010, which allowed them to merge the issue of raising the debt ceiling with balancing the budget. Some even went so far as to call for the introduction of a balanced budget amendment to the Constitution during the 2011 debate to raise the debt ceiling. However, after the political turmoil their demands created in 2011 and 2013, members of the conservative wing of the Republican Party have lost some of their political influence of congressional decision making, allowing more room for compromise.

Grace Allbaugh

Further Reading

Caldwell, Leigh Ann. 2013. "What Do Shutdown and Debt Limit Have to Do with Obamacare?" *CNN.* September 24. Accessed September 3, 2015. http://www.cnn.com/2013/09/24/politics/shutdown-debt-limit-obamacare-difference/.

Cohen, Tom, Greg Botelho, and Holly Yan. 2013. "Obama Signs Bill to End Partial Shutdown, Stave off Debt Ceiling Crisis." *CNN.* October 17. Accessed October 4, 2015. http://www.cnn.com/2013/10/16/politics/shutdown-showdown/.

Frank, Ellen. 2004. *The Raw Deal: How Myths and Misinformation about Deficits, Inflation, and Wealth Impoverish America.* Boston: Beacon Press.

Herszenhorn, David M. 2015. "Congress Strikes a Budget Deal with President." *New York Times,* October 26. Accessed November 12, 2015. http://www.nytimes.com/2015/10/27/us/politics/congress-and-white-house-near-deal-on-budget.html.

Hulse, Carl, and Helene Cooper. 2011. "Obama and Leaders Reach Debt Deal." *New York Times,* July 31. Accessed November 4, 2015. http://www.nytimes.com/2011/08/01/us/politics/01FISCAL.html?_r=0.

Maltsev, Yuri, and Roman Skaskiw. 2013. *The Tea Party Explained: From Crisis to Crusade.* Chicago: Open Court.

Paul, Rand. 2015. "Floor Speech: Sen. Rand Paul Speaks Out against Budget Agreement." *Rand Paul.* October 29. Accessed November 3, 2105. http://www.paul.senate.gov/news/press/floor-speech-sen-rand-paul-speaks-out-against-budget-agreement.

Republican National Committee. 2012. "We Believe in America: 2012 Republican Platform." GOP.com. Accessed November 14, 2015. https://www.gop.com/platform/.

Stone, Chad. 2014. "Obamacare Is (Still) Fiscally Responsible." *U.S. News and World Report,* June 20. Accessed October 3, 2015. http://www.usnews.com/opinion/economic-intelligence/2014/06/20/cbo-confirms-obamacare-reduces-deficits.

U.S. Congress. Joint Economic Committee. 2013. *The Economic Costs of Debt-Ceiling Brinkmanship: Hearing before the Joint Economic Committee, Congress of the United States, One Hundred Thirteenth Congress, First Session, September 18, 2013.* S. Hrg. Vol. 113–127. Washington, DC: U.S. Government Printing Office.

Defense Spending

At a Glance

Republicans consistently support increasing or maintaining high levels of military spending. At various points the party presides over some cuts in spending, but these moments are infrequent. During the last few decades, Republicans supported higher spending levels during the "War on Terror" and opposed government efforts to cut military budgets.

Democrats also support high levels of military spending historically, although at times they also push for reductions in such appropriations. The party consistently voices its support for the U.S. military and for preserving U.S. national security. Democrats also believe that changing political conditions at times necessitate reductions in such spending, for example, following the end of the Cold War and during periods when deficit spending is perceived to be growing out of control.

Many Republicans . . .

- Support extended military conflicts that are fought in the name of keeping Americans safe from foreign threats
- Traditional support large military budgets, whether in peacetime or during periods of conflict such as the "War on Terror" and the Cold War
- Oppose any cuts in military spending

Many Democrats . . .

- Support large military budgets, tempered by concern with cutting spending when it is seen as excessive or unnecessary
- Are apprehensive about fighting extended foreign conflicts, particularly if they are seen as too costly and if the outcomes are seen as uncertain
- See reductions in the defense budget as legitimate in overall efforts to control government spending

———————

Overview

U.S. military spending in the modern era is marked by a general bipartisan consensus that commits a large percentage of tax revenues to the national defense. Modest differences between the parties have emerged over the years, as spending levels fluctuated during the 1990s, 2000s, and 2010s, depending on the political party in power. Despite changes in spending, however, the United States has consistently played the role of world leader in military funding allocations. In 2014, U.S. military spending accounted for 46 percent of the world's total military spending, significantly more than any other country (Taylor 2015).

Large defense budgets are not without controversy. Perhaps the most famous historical criticism of military spending was expressed by Republican President Dwight Eisenhower, who warned against the growth of the "military industrial complex." This reference was meant to draw attention to a system of spending that was institutionalized after the Second World War. Eisenhower feared that military spending would build up inertia of its own, fueled by private economic interests that profited from defense contracts, and officials would become dependent on campaign support from military contractors (Eisenhower 2011). Decades after Eisenhower's warning, recent research suggests that military contractors do indeed exercise significant influence over congressional defense allocations via their prominent role in creating jobs, promoting economic growth, and in granting campaign contributions to political officials (Thorpe 2014).

Military budgets are allocated to a variety of different programs. The largest categories include spending on military personnel and housing, weapons and procurement contracts for military hardware, wartime operations, research and development for new weapons and equipment, and funding for nuclear programs, and for constituting and preserving nuclear warheads. Department of Defense spending is broken down into five main categories, including pay for veterans, soldiers on active duty, pay for those serving as reserve personnel and those serving in the National Guard, and civilian pay for those employed at the Pentagon and elsewhere.

U.S. defense allocations varied significantly in the last half century. From the 1950s through the 2010s, military spending fluctuated from a low of just under $400 billion a year, to a high of over $700 billion a year, in inflation-adjusted 2013 dollars. Spending was cyclical, including peaks and valleys, occurring almost every decade. Periods characterized by significant increases, or even spikes in military spending, included the early 1950s, the late 1960s, the mid-1980s, and the entire 2000s. Periods marked by significant cuts in spending included the mid-1960s, the mid-1970s, the mid-1990s, and the mid-2010s. These figures suggest that both American political parties have presided over significant levels of spending over time, including the Cold War era (1950s through 1980s), the post-Cold War era (the 1990s), and during the "War on Terror" (2001 onward).

Both Democrats and Republicans preside over a national political system that prioritizes military spending as one of its top three funded programs. Defense spending accounted for 18 percent of the federal budget in 2014, compared to Social Security, which accounted for 24 percent of the budget, and Medicare, Medicaid, child health insurance, and "Obamacare" health care subsidies, which comprised 24 percent of the budget (Center on Budget and Policy Priorities 2015). U.S. leaders have long voiced support for the United States playing a leading role in world affairs, and military interventions are a staple of U.S. foreign policy. Both parties have engaged in military interventions involving ground troops, as seen in actions initiated during Republican administrations—including the invasion of Grenada (Ronald Reagan, 1983), the invasion of Panama (George H. W. Bush, 1989), the war in Iraq (George H. W. Bush, 1991), the war in Afghanistan (George W. Bush, 2001), and the invasion of Iraq (George W. Bush, 2003). Similarly, Democratic administrations initiated or intensified conflicts involving ground troops in Korea (Harry Truman, 1950), Vietnam (John Kennedy, 1961, and Lyndon Johnson, 1964), and Afghanistan (Barack Obama, 2009). Other Democratic military initiatives could be included for discussion—such as U.S.-led bombing campaigns in Yugoslavia (Bill Clinton, 1995), Libya (Obama, 2011), and against Islamic fundamentalists in Iraq and Syria (Obama, 2014)—although these conflicts did not include use of ground troops. In many of the above-mentioned conflicts, however, U.S. military action was strongly supported—at least at the outset—by both Republicans and Democrats, irrespective of the party affiliation of the occupant of the Oval Office. In sum, Democrats and Republicans have engaged in numerous foreign conflicts, while committing large sums of money to fund the military to fight these conflicts and provide for security at home.

In the last few decades, military spending fluctuated depending on the priorities of presidents and Congress, and also based on whether or not the United States was involved in sustained conflicts throughout the world. During the 1990s, and following the end of the Cold War between the United States and the former Soviet Union, military spending generally remained high under President George H. W. Bush, averaging nearly $500 billion a year in 2013 inflation-adjusted dollars in the early 1990s, and during the U.S. conflict with Iraq. Spending, however, began to decline under Bush, and fell to below $400 billion a year during the Clinton era, when no major military conflict was occurring between the United States and another country. After the September 11, 2001, terrorist attacks, however, U.S. conflicts in Afghanistan and Iraq were accompanied by significant spikes in military spending. Annual military appropriations increased from over $400 billion a year in the early 2000s to more than $700 billion by the late 2000s. The "War on Terror" never formally came to an end, and military spending reached over $700 billion a year continued during President Barack Obama's first term in office, amounting to approximately 20 percent of all federal spending per year.

During the 2010s, Republicans and Democrats have engaged in conflicts over military spending, during a period generally marked by significant cuts in such allocations. In 2011, both congressional Democrats and Republicans, and Democratic President Barack Obama agreed to a "Budget Control Act" that committed the government to cutting more than $1 trillion dollars in federal spending over the next decade, with nearly half the cuts scheduled to come from reduced military spending. These cuts were referred to as the "sequester," and provoked significant controversy in Congress at a time when many political leaders in both parties were seeking to shield the military from significant spending reductions.

Despite both political parties promoting cuts in military spending in 2011, Democratic and Republican leaders later reversed course, declaring support for rolling back their previous efforts to cut spending that became known as the "sequestration." Military cuts are often seen as unpopular with the American public, so vocal Democratic opposition to the sequester cuts was predictable. Not wanting to be seen as failing to support the troops, and seeking to avoid a negative public backlash, Democratic President Barack Obama announced in 2015 that his budget would include "increases in our defense funding . . . if Congress does nothing to stop the sequestration, there could be serious consequences for our national security, at a time when our military is stretched on a whole range of issues" (Obama 2015). Obama insisted that Republican efforts to raise military spending, while avoiding increased spending for infrastructure, was a non-starter for the federal budget: "I will not accept a budget that severs the vital link between our national security and our economic security. I know there's some on Capitol Hill who would say, well, we'd be willing to increase defense spending, but we're not going to increase investments in infrastructure, for example, or basic research. Well, those two things go hand in hand. If we don't have a vital infrastructure, if we don't have broadband lines across the country, if we don't have a smart grid, all that makes us more vulnerable. America can't afford being shortsighted, and I'm not going to allow it" (Obama 2015). Obama's comments suggested that the president viewed funding for infrastructure and military spending as inextricably linked and both necessary to promoting American national security.

Despite their votes to force spending cuts via the sequester, Republicans expressed concern about the impact of the sequester on military readiness. Republican House Majority Leader John Boehner criticized Democrats because they opposed increases in military spending if funding for domestic programs was still going to be cut because of the sequestration. In arguing for increased military spending, Boehner stated: "Whatever our troops need to get the job done, they should get it, and the House [of Representatives] has acted to provide just that . . . . With all the threats our troops face and the sacrifices they make, Democrats opposition to this defense bill is in face indefensible." Boehner's comments suggest that U.S. national security was automatically equated with spending more on the military. Efforts to cut military spending were assumed to produce an inevitable decline in citizens' security.

The Republican battle with Democrats to increase spending for the military, Boehner argued, was "about whether you support our men and women in uniform." Speaking for the entire Republican rank and file in the House of Representatives, Boehner announced in preparation for the fall 2015 budget battle with Democrats that "there is overwhelming support in our conference for providing additional resources to protect our national security." Boehner's statement was consistent with longstanding Republican rhetoric that associates hawkish Republican positions on spending with supporting the troops and with a strong national defense.

Republicans on Defense Spending

Republicans have long been the more "hawkish" party on military spending. In other words, they are usually more likely to support the use of force to resolve U.S. disputes with other countries, and are more likely to support increased military budgets and oppose significant cuts to such spending. Hawkish behavior is not universally observed, however, within the party. During his tenure, President George H. W. Bush implemented a 17 percent cut in spending from the military budget he inherited from Republican President Ronald Reagan (Korb et al. 2011). Still, by the 1990s, high-profile Republican criticisms of Democratic President Bill Clinton's budget cuts were common place. Clinton's focus on budget cuts was eventually rolled back, as the Republican Party introduced large increases in military spending during the 2000s under President George W. Bush.

The Republican Party led the charge for increased military spending during the 2000s. September 11, 2001, proved to be a pivotal historic event that provided the impetus for large military budgets. Spending increased dramatically during the early, mid, and late 2000s. Just nine days after the September 11 attacks, President George W. Bush officially declared a "War on Terror" in a national speech that committed the United States to a path of action that included wars in multiple countries. Bush announced that "our war on terror begins with Al Qaeda, but it does not end there. It will not end until every terrorist group of global reach has been found, stopped, and defeated" (Bush 2001). Whether or not one agreed that the United States was capable of eliminating all global terrorist groups, Bush's declaration of a "War on Terror" demanded a sizable monetary commitment, as the large increases in military budgets following September 11 suggested. Furthermore, the president's speech suggested that his global war may have no end in sight for the foreseeable future: "Our response [to September 11] involves far more than instant retaliation and isolated strikes. Americans should not expect one battle but a lengthy campaign, unlike any other we have ever seen. . . . Every nation, in every region, now has a decision to make. Either you are with us, or you are with the terrorists. From this day forward, any nation that continues to harbor or support terrorism will be regarded by the United States as a hostile regime." By describing any state in which terrorists might reside as a potential U.S. target, President Bush was committing to a potentially massive and extended military campaign (Bush 2001).

In implementing his "War on Terror," President Bush undertook two wars—in Afghanistan and Iraq—in the wake of the September 11 attacks. Both wars—which estimates suggest cost in total between $4 to 6 trillion—were defended via claims that they were vital fronts in the global campaign to eliminate terrorism. Military spending—on both wars and other defense related programs—increased markedly between 2002 and 2009. President Bush's fourth-year military budget represented a 34 percent increase from his first year budget. Military spending had increased by 48 percent from Bush's first- to sixth-year budgets, and by 56 percent from his first- to eighth-year budgets (Jaffe 2015). Bush's second term budgets were significantly larger than those seen during the presidencies of other Republicans, including George H. W. Bush, Ronald Reagan, Richard Nixon, and Dwight Eisenhower (Jaffe 2015).

By the end of President Bush's second term, Republican officials had begun to warn against potential cuts in military spending. These warnings coincided with Republican attacks on Democratic presidential candidate Barack Obama, who had indicated in 2008 his support for a phased withdrawal from Iraq. Republican opinions of Obama were mixed, however, by late-2009, as the president sent tens of thousands of additional troops to Afghanistan, and committed tens of billions in additional dollars per year to the war effort. The funding increases were large, as total war spending doubled in two years from $60 billion in 2009 to $105 billion in 2010 and $118 billion in 2011 (Riley 2011). Republican officials in Congress agreed with the president that the additional funds and troops were necessary to roll back the growing power of the Taliban and prevent Al Qaeda's re-emergence in the country. Specifically, they supported President Obama's December 2009 troop escalation, although they opposed his announced plan for a gradual, phased U.S. withdrawal from Afghanistan.

Throughout the 2010s, Republicans have acted in (at times) contradictory ways regarding military spending, although they have generally indicated a commitment to increasing spending. The tension in Republican actions was apparent with the party's initial agreement to cut hundreds of billions from military spending as part of the 2011 Budget Control Act, when contrasted with their denunciations of Obama for being (allegedly) responsible for the cuts. Such claims were not historically accurate, however, considering that Republicans and Democrats in Congress joined with the president to sign into law the Budget Control Act and subsequent sequester cuts in spending. While Republican attacks appeared largely self-serving in the run-up to congressional and presidential elections, they also reflected a meaningful policy position, considering that the party actively promoted and passed legislation seeking to reverse the "sequester" military cuts. For example, the 2015 House military budget called for $612 billion in defense spending for fiscal year 2016, despite the Budget Control Act mandating a cap of no more than $523 billion in spending (Parker 2015). This proposal represented a proposed 17 percent increase in military spending beyond that permitted under previous legislation. Democrats in the Senate blocked proposed Republican spending increases for 2016, suggesting a significant divide between the two parties regarding the military budget.

Democrats on Defense Spending

The Democratic Party has demonstrated a significant commitment to military spending, despite pursuing both cuts and increases in spending at various times in recent history. During the 1990s, President Bill Clinton promoted sustained cuts in military spending, based on the justification that the end of the Cold War imposed new realities on the country. In commenting to reporters in July 1993, Clinton stated, "Now that the Cold War is over, we see the opportunity around the world and in this country to reduce defense spending rather dramatically and to devote our attention to rebuilding our country here at home." He also warned that the cuts would significantly affect defense contractors and employees of those firms, "reduced defense spending means reduced spending on defense contracts. And people, therefore, who work in defense plants are affected by it." Clinton claimed, however, that "difficult and painful" steps were needed to serve U.S. foreign and domestic "interests" in an era marked by a "greatly reduced threat" to the U.S. and its allies following the fall of the Soviet Union (Clinton 1993b).

The attacks of September 11, 2001, resulted in a significant prioritization of increased military allocations. This increase coincided with the creation of the Department of Homeland Security and its mandate to intercept terrorist threats, and the wars that began in Afghanistan (2001) and Iraq (2003). As the minority party in the House and Senate from 2002 through 2006, Democrats were junior partners in making decisions regarding U.S. foreign policy. After September 11, President Bush was recognized as leading the "War on Terror," although Democrats played an important role in foreign policy by supporting the president, and agreeing to sizable increases in military spending. For example, in the year following September 11, 2001, Democrats in the House and Senate consistently voiced support for President Bush's military budgets, although they at times took issue with specific provisions of laws. Democratic voting against the president on military items was minimal during his time in office. General support for spending, mixed with pragmatic criticisms of the types of spending included in military appropriations, was evident, for example, in the comments of House Democratic Minority Leader Dick Gephardt, who announced in a 2003 vote on the military budget that, "This legislation will allow us to wage war effectively in the year ahead," while also complaining about Republican efforts "to close down" extended debate on specific issues like military-base closings, nuclear weapons policy, and other issues deemed "critical to the American people" (Loven 2002). Such challenges, however, were relatively minor in the larger picture of Democratic support for growing military budgets.

Democrats became increasingly antagonistic toward President Bush in the late-2000s, as the party began to push for a withdrawal from the Iraq war, despite Republican opposition to setting a timetable for reducing U.S. troops. Still, the election of Democratic President Barack Obama coincided with Democratic majorities in the House and Senate that continued the high levels of military appropriations allocated in the late-Bush years. President Obama supported a drawdown of troops in Iraq, an increase of troops in Afghanistan, and military spending budgets comparable to those seen during Bush's years. During Obama's first term in office, the military budget remained at or near $700 a billion a year, which was essentially unchanged from the spending levels in President Bush's last two years in office, when Democrats held the majority in both congressional chambers

(Jaffe 2015). Large military allocations were encouraged by Obama's military escalation in Afghanistan, as he sent tens of thousands of troops in 2009 in an effort to reverse the Taliban's military successes in asserting control over large areas of that country. In general, Obama framed high levels of spending as necessary for keeping Americans safe. Specifically, he spoke of his "responsibility to our armed forces—giving them the resources and equipment and strategies to meet their missions. We need to keep our military the best-trained, the best-led, the best equipped fighting force in the world." These comments suggest a commitment to continuing the "War on Terror" that was declared by President Bush (Obama 2009).

While President Obama's first term was marked by higher levels of military spending, the national political debate turned toward government spending cuts from 2011 onward. With the Budget Control Act of 2011, both parties and the president agreed to legislation mandating $1 trillion in cuts to the military within a decade. These cuts were part of the "austerity" agenda that emerged by 2011, with President Obama and congressional Republicans agreeing to budget cuts across government programs. Mandated cuts in spending were to reduce yearly military appropriations by hundreds of billions from the early-to-late 2010s. Republican efforts to reverse mandated cuts to Congress were met with opposition from Democratic officials and President Obama. Democratic officials complained that it was unacceptable to reverse military cuts mandated by the Budget Control Act, while advancing spending cuts for domestic programs mandated under that very same act (Huetteman and Parker 2015). A determined Democratic minority in the Senate blocked a final vote on reversing military cuts in June of 2015, sending a clear message that previously mandated military cuts would move forward. Although President Obama later criticized military cuts as they went into effect, his party had taken a clear stance in favor of military cuts—a stance that would define U.S. military spending through the remainder of Obama's second term (Obama 2015).

The 2000s and 2010s were polarizing times in American politics, with growing dissent among the American public and the Democratic Party regarding the wars in Afghanistan and Iraq. Large military budgets, however, continued to grow steadily after September 11 in light of Republican support for both wars, and Republican control of the White House (2001–2009) and Congress (2001–2007). Republican officials, including the president, regularly spoke of the need to remain in, and fund the wars in Afghanistan and Iraq, to fight the Al Qaeda terrorist threat. Democrats have supported this "War on Terror," although they also supported significant cuts to military spending during the 2010s.

Anthony DiMaggio

Further Reading

Bush, George W. 2001. "Address to a Joint Session of Congress and the American People." The White House. September 20. Accessed October 1, 2015. http://georgewbush -whitehouse.archives.gov/news/releases/2001/09/20010920-8.html.

Center on Budget and Policy Priorities. 2015. "Policy Basics: Where Do Our Federal Tax Dollars Go?" *Center on Budget and Policy Priorities*. March 11. Accessed October 1, 2015. http://www.cbpp.org/research/policy-basics-where-do-our-federal-tax-dollars-go.

Clinton, William J. 1993a. "The President's Radio Address." *The American Presidency Project*. April 3. Accessed October 1, 2015. http://www.presidency.ucsb.edu/ws/index.php?pid=46401&st=defense&st1=.

Clinton, William J. 1993b. "Remarks Announcing the Defense Conversion Plan and an Exchange with Reporters." *The American Presidency Project*. July 2. Accessed October 1, 2015. http://www.presidency.ucsb.edu/ws/index.php?pid=46793&st=Remarks+Announcing+the+Defense+Conversion+Plan+and+an+Exchange+with+Reporters&st1=.

Eisenhower, Dwight D. 2011. "IKE's Warning of Military Expansion, 50 Years Later." *National Public Radio*. January 17. Accessed October 1, 2015. http://www.npr.org/2011/01/17/132942244/ikes-warning-of-military-expansion-50-years-later.

Huetteman, Emmarie, and Ashley Parker. 2015. "Democrats Balk at Sparing Only Military Spending from Mandated Cuts." *New York Times*, May 14. Accessed October 1, 2015. http://www.nytimes.com/2015/05/15/us/politics/democrats-balk-at-sparing-only-military-spending-from-mandated-cuts.html.

Jaffe, Greg. 2015. "Obama Budget's Boost for Military Spending Points to Brewing National Security Debate." *Washington Post*, February 1. Accessed October 1, 2015. http://www.washingtonpost.com/politics/obama-budgets-boost-for-military-spending-points-to-brewing-national-security-debate/2015/02/01/914c5030-a967-11e4-a2b2-776095f393b2_story.html.

Korb, Lawrence J., Laura Conley, and Alex Rothman. 2011. "A Historical Perspective on Defense Budgets." *Center for American Progress*. July 6. Accessed October 1, 2015. https://www.americanprogress.org/issues/budget/news/2011/07/06/10041/a-historical-perspective-on-defense-budgets/.

Loven, Jennifer. 2002. "House Prepares to Pass $383 Billion Bill Authorizing 2003 Defense Spending." *Associated Press*, May 9.

Obama, Barack. 2009. "Remarks by the President at the Veterans of Foreign Wars Convention." The White House. August 17. Accessed October 1, 2015. https://www.whitehouse.gov/the-press-office/remarks-president-veterans-foreign-wars-convention.

Obama, Barack. 2015. "Remarks by the President on the FY 2016 Budget." The White House. February 2. Accessed October 1, 2015. https://www.whitehouse.gov/the-press-office/2015/02/02/remarks-president-fy2016-budget.

Parker, Ashley. 2015. "House Passes Military Bill After Fight on Budget Cuts." *New York Times*, May 15. Accessed October 1, 2015. http://www.nytimes.com/2015/05/16/us/house-passes-military-spending-bill-after-fight-on-cuts.html.

Riley, Charles. 2011. "Troop Drawdown Won't Stop Spending Machine." *CNN.com*. June 22. Accessed October 1, 2015. http://money.cnn.com/2011/06/22/news/economy/afghanistan_war_costs/.

Taylor, Adam. 2015. "Chart: U.S. Defense Spending Still Dwarfs the Rest of the World." *Washington Post*, February 11. Accessed October 1, 2015. https://www.washingtonpost.com/news/worldviews/wp/2015/02/11/chart-u-s-defense-spending-still-dwarfs-the-rest-of-the-world/.

Thorpe, Rebecca U. 2014. *The American Warfare State: The Domestic Politics of Military Spending*. Chicago: University of Chicago Press.

Deficits and Balanced Budgets

At a Glance

In general both Republicans and Democrats favor balancing the budget and reducing the national deficit. However, they differ significantly in the specifics of how to obtain these policy goals.

Many Republicans . . .

- Describe the deficit as a long-term threat to the prosperity of the United States
- Say that immediate action should be taken to reduce it
- Believe the deficit was created by decades of poor decision making on the part of elected officials in both major political parties
- Support a three-question test for authorizing any new federal spending: (1) Is it constitutional, (2) Is it likely to be effective, and (3) Is it absolutely necessary?
- Favor requiring the use of market-based policies to restructure key entitlement programs like Medicare to reduce spending
- Oppose raising taxes to reduce the deficit
- Support major tax cuts, most of which would go to the wealthiest Americans

Many Democrats . . .

- See the deficit as in part a result of taxation policies that favor wealthy Americans over the middle-class
- Favor pay-as-you-go budgeting where any new federal spending must be offset by federal costs savings or new revenues
- Support raising new revenue to reduce the deficit by increasing the taxes paid by the wealthy, closing corporate tax-loopholes, and introducing new taxes on the financial transactions of high volume traders
- Favor limiting CEO pay as part of a broader package of reforms to reduce rising income inequality in the United States

Overview

Among the many large advertisements in and around New York City's Times Square is a digital billboard on 6th Avenue listing a real-time count of the United States' national debt. Those not in New York City can visit www.usdebtclock.org to obtain an up-to-date count of the growing U.S. national debt, as well as ratios displaying total United States' per-citizen and per-taxpayer costs. As of this writing, the country's total national debt stands at over $18 trillion. That national debt refers to the total amount of money the United States owes its creditors as a result of borrowing. The mere presence of debt, however, is not necessarily problematic. In fact, the United States borrowed to finance a portion of the cost of the Revolutionary War, meaning the national debt is as old as the country itself. What is potentially problematic, and a focus of this chapter, is the means by which the national debt grows: deficit spending.

Public sector budgeting is a complex exercise by which the executive and legislative branches of government draft and vote on a piece of legislation authorizing the expenditure of public funds to pay for public programs and operations. A variety of administrative officials, including federal employees, agency heads, and the non-partisan Congressional Budget Office, handle much of the logistics of budgeting. However, it is elected officials who ultimately make the decision on how to prioritize government spending. Budgeting is about priorities, and the allocation of limited government funds to programs and services is the formal mechanism by which government officials state their priorities and policy preferences.

Ideally, the amount of money collected by the federal government from taxes and fees would equal the amount of money required to fund the priorities of legislators. The reality of budgeting, however, is much more complex. One reason for this is different political parties often lead the executive and legislative branches of the federal government. These parties, as demonstrated throughout this edited volume, often disagree on key policy issues. The reality of split government begs the question, how can a federal budget reflect the priorities of elected officials who are plagued by internal disagreement over those very same priorities?

A more practical concern is the variations in projected public revenues and expenditures created by factors beyond the control of elected officials. For example, in difficult economic times, such as the recent recession, federal tax revenues fall short of budgeted expenditures. Or, federal government spending can often be higher than budgeted amounts due to natural disasters, armed conflicts, increased demand for the federal social safety net, cost overruns for capital projects, and any number of other reasons. In either scenario, the federal government faces a shortfall in the amount of revenue required to cover promised expenditures. This shortfall is called a budget deficit.

The United States experienced a budget deficit from 1970 to 1997, and every year since 2002. In the years between 1998 and 2001, the federal government experienced a surplus, meaning federal government revenues exceeded expenditures.

During these years Democrats controlled the executive branch, and Republicans controlled both the Senate and House of Representatives. Thus, neither political party holds a monopoly on creating deficits or surpluses.

Elected officials generally have three options to deal with a budget deficit. First, officials may cut government spending to eliminate the deficit. This option is often politically unpopular and/or practically impossible because budgeted costs are often sunk into infrastructure projects, human capital, or "sum-sufficient" programs from which funding cannot be easily cut ("sum-sufficient" programs are ones in which funding is guaranteed even if costs run higher than budgeted appropriations). Second, elected officials may increase government revenues by increasing tax-rates. This option too, is often politically unpopular if not impossible, and often logistically difficult given the time lag between a change in tax policy and actual revenue collections. The third option for addressing a budget deficit is to borrow money to balance the budget.

The federal government borrows money by issuing bonds that may be purchased by United States citizens and financial institutions, as well as foreign governments, citizens, and financial institutions. All of these entities purchase United States debt as an investment, as the United States government must pay back these loans with interest. Under federal law there is a debt ceiling that limits the total amount of allowable federal government debt. Because hitting the debt ceiling removes the ability for the United States to borrow additional funds, Congress can and frequently does raise the debt ceiling.

The importance of balancing the budget and limited deficit spending is a subject of disagreement among politicians and pundits. Though there is general bipartisan agreement that a balanced budget is a laudable goal, efforts to pass a constitutional amendment requiring a balanced budget have repeatedly failed. Some argue that deficit spending is a necessary tool to stimulate the economy during difficult economic times and that government borrowing is akin to personal borrowing and is not inherently problematic. Others see deficit spending as an irresponsible practice that will hurt future generations of Americans. It is clear, however, that the United States more often than not does not have a balanced federal budget, and that deficit spending leads to a steadily increasing national debt on which the United States government, through its taxpayers, must pay interest.

Democratic Position on Deficits and Balanced Budgets

Democratic United States President Franklin D. Roosevelt, despite originally campaigning in favor of a balanced budget, famously initiated a major campaign of deficit spending on an array of jobs programs, social programs, and infrastructure improvements known collectively as The New Deal. Roosevelt's spending policies were in-line with British Economist John Maynard Keynes's economic theory of pump-priming, where increased government spending, even if it contributes to the national debt, can stimulate the economy in ways that improve the economy over time. Though historians and economists still debate the extent to which the New Deal, as opposed to World War II itself, stimulated the economy, the United States did experience a post-World War II economic boom.

More recently, the nearly $800 billion economic stimulus package offered by President Barack Obama, known as the American Recovery and Reinvestment Act of 2009, demonstrated that the theory of pump-priming in general, and deficit spending specifically, was still in the Democratic arsenal as a possible policy response to an economic recession. However, the Democratic Party today has also made clear that balancing the budget and reducing the national deficit are policy priorities. The 2012 Democratic Party Platform outlined several specific positions related to deficits and balanced budgets.

First, Democrats support the implementation of pay-as-you-go budgeting where "new spending and tax cuts must . . . be offset by savings or revenue increases" (Democratic National Committee 2012). In other words, the Democratic position is that the federal government cannot increase its current level of deficit spending. While the overall deficit may continue to grow based on the current level of deficit spending, it will not increase exponentially. Second, and more broadly, the Democratic Party stated as part of its 2012 presidential platform that its goal was to lower the overall deficit by more than $4 trillion dollars over a 10-year period.

The favored methods by which these reductions might be realized are a series of changes to the tax code that Democrats claim will improve the economy and ensure a fair tax burden on United States citizens. First, Democrats favored cutting or maintaining the current level of tax burden for families whose total annual income is less than $250,000. Second, Democrats supported raising taxes on the wealthiest 2 percent of Americans. The Democratic Party specifically favored the Buffett Rule where "no millionaire pays a smaller share of his or her income in taxes than middle class families do" (Democratic National Committee 2012, 7). Third, Democrats support a series of nuanced changes to the corporate tax code, including a reduction in tax rates for companies headquartered in the United States, tax incentives for companies that place research and development and manufacturing activities in the United States, and finally removing tax incentives for companies that increase their number of employees based outside of the United States. Last, Democrats are supportive of policies that assist individual states in eliminating their budget deficits.

In 2015, the ranking Democrat on the House of Representative Budget Committee, Chris Van Hollen, unveiled what he called an action plan listing the budgeting priorities of Democrats. Broadly the plan calls for changes that "raise revenue to lower deficits and help put [the United States] on a sustainable fiscal course" (Van Hollen 2015). First, the plan introduces limits on chief executive officer (CEO) pay for purposes of reducing income inequality in the United States. Second, the plan calls for reducing the $640 billion dollars currently spent annually on the military and national defense. Third, the action plan calls for the creation of a high-roller fee that targets high-volume stock market traders by placing a new fee on financial transactions made in the United States.

The overall position of the Democratic Party in regards to balanced budgets and deficits can be summed up in three key principles. The first principle is a desire to eliminate the deficit and annually balance the budget. This position is not dissimilar to the Republican position, meaning there is agreement across party lines on the value of balancing the budget and lowering the national debt. However, the means by which Democrats favor balancing the budget differ from those favored by Republicans.

This leads to the second key principle, a commitment to targeting tax increases on specific audiences. As stated earlier, the Democratic Party favors raising the overall tax burden on the wealthiest American citizens, corporations that engage in outsourcing and/or relocating facilities outside of the United States, and financial institutions that engage in high-volume stock trading. Implicit in these policy ideas is the belief that the federal deficit is in part created by tax policies that favor high-income Americans and private corporations at the expense of middle-class citizens.

The second principle leads directly to the third, which is the packaging of financial policies described as balancing the budget and reducing that national debt with policies designed to address social inequities in American society. Alone, policies such as the maintenance of the middle-class tax code and the reduction in CEO pay do nothing to improve the budget situation of the United States because neither change raises new revenue or reduces overall spending. However, both policies are paired with policies, like tax increases for higher income Americans and the closing of tax loopholes that do address the country's budgetary challenges directly by raising additional revenue.

The linking of financial goals with social goals demonstrates the Democratic Party's commitment to using fiscal policies to address social and income inequalities in the United States. President Barack Obama perhaps best articulated this commitment in a 2013 interview, when he stated, "My goal is not to chase a balanced budget just for the sake of balance. My goal is how do we grow the economy, put people back to work, and if we do that we are going to be bringing in more revenue" (Stephanopoulos 2013). In other words, Democrats desire a balanced budget, but only to the extent to which it allows competing core policy goals to be achieved.

Republican Position on Deficits and Balanced Budgets

On April 21, 1981, President Ronald Reagan released his Program for Economic Recovery, which consisted of a series of tax cuts and spending reductions that he argued would grow the economy in ways that would allow him to balance the United States budget by the year 1984 (Reagan 1981b). Reagan explicitly rejected the idea of immediately balancing the federal budget through increases in taxes, instead stating that both tax cuts and reductions in the deficit were obtainable through policies encouraging growth. In reality, Reagan would never actually balance the federal budget during his eight years in office; however his stated commitment to addressing the country's budget challenges through economic growth remain the foundation of the Republican position on deficits and balanced budgets.

The official Republican platform for the 2012 presidential election, "We Believe in America," emphasized the Republican position that deficits are a severe problem threatening the future prosperity of the United States. In their party platform Republicans place blame on a history of irresponsible short-term decisions made by members of both parties, concluding that "Elected officials have overpromised and overspent, and the bills are due" (Republican National Committee 2012). The official Republican position is that federal spending is currently at an unsustainable level, and the national debt threatens future generations through increasing debt-service costs. What then, is the Republican plan to deal with the nation's budgetary challenges?

First, Republicans argue for hyper-vigilance, proposing a three-question test before any new federal activity is approved by the legislature. One, is the new federal activity constitutional? Two, is the new federal activity likely to be effective, and it is it necessary? Three, is the proposed activity important enough to justify the incurrence of additional debt? Implicit in this test is the belief that increased transparency created by consideration of these three questions will reduce the activities, and therefore the expenditures, of the federal government.

The Republican platform also emphasizes the need to reduce government expenditures as part of any effort to balance the federal budget. Specifically, Republicans propose a general reduction in entitlement spending, the restructuring of the welfare state through the use of market-based reforms such as Medicaid vouchers, and increased use of technology to create new efficiencies in federal government programs. The Republicans also stress the need to pair spending cuts with increased transparency in the budgetary process, and the creation of a super-majority requirement that makes it more difficult for the legislature to raise taxes. Unlike the Democrats, the Republicans oppose both the pairing of budgetary policies with policies designed to redistribute wealth, and targeted tax increases on wealthy Americans.

The more recent Fiscal Year 2015 Budget Resolution proposed by the Republican House of Representatives, entitled *The Path to Prosperity,* provides additional insight into the Republican position on balanced budgets and deficits. The proposal articulates the importance Republicans place on solving the country's budgetary challenges, stating, "The growing probability of a debt crisis is the most urgent challenge we face today" (House Budget Committee 2014, 86). Accordingly, the Republican plan proposes to cut spending by $5.1 trillion dollars over the next 10 years to stop the growth of the national debt, and reduce it in the future. Under the plan the federal budget will be balanced by the year 2024. However, several Republic proposals, including those to end Obamacare and reduce the overall tax burden, could increase the federal deficit. The general rationale of House Republicans is clear in their claims, "A balanced budget will foster a healthier economy and help create jobs" (House Budget Committee 2014, 5).

Paul Ryan on the Deficit and Spending

United States Congressman Paul Ryan is a Republican representing Wisconsin's First Congressional district who in the fall of 2015 became Speaker of the House in the U.S. House of Representatives. Ryan was born and currently resides in Janesville, Wisconsin, a largely blue-collar community of 63,575 people in south central Wisconsin. Prior to holding elected office Ryan earned degrees in economics and political science at Miami University in Oxford, Ohio, and served as a staffer for then U.S. Senator and current Kansas Governor Sam Brownback.

Ryan was first elected to Congress in 1999 at the age of 28. Over time he solidified himself as a leading Republican on budgetary issues, first by serving as the Chairman of the House Budget Committee, and then as the Chairman of the powerful House Ways and Means Committee. In these leadership roles Ryan has proposed several alternative budget plans representing the dominant Republicans positions on debt, entitlement reform, and deficit spending. As a result, he has become one of the most prominent of the GOP's deficit "hawks," although critics assert that during the George W. Bush years he repeatedly supported bills that increased the deficit, such as Bush's prescription drug coverage expansion in Medicare. Democrats also insist that tax cut proposals championed by Ryan over the years would also explode the size of the deficit.

Representative Ryan gained increased national exposure as Mitt Romney's running mate in the 2012 presidential elections. As a vice presidential candidate, Ryan voiced a strong opposition to President Barack Obama's stimulus package, advocated for a reduction in the national deficit, spoke in favor of entitlement reforms, and articulated a strong general commitment to principles of limited government. Today he continues to be the key national spokesman for Republic positions on budgeting and debt.

Sources

"Biography of Congressman Paul Ryan." 2015. Accessed May 14, 2015. http://paulryan.house. gov/biography/#.VVzBBOtgbbg.

Chait, Jonathan. 2012. "The Legendary Paul Ryan." *New York*, April 29.

Overall, the position of the Republican Party in regard to balanced budgets and deficits can be distilled in three basic principles. First, deficit spending and the failure to balance the federal budget are viewed potentially as a mortal threat to the future prosperity of the United States. As such, Republicans do not favor waiting to act on the deficit, but rather propose substantial changes to the nature and structure of federal spending to balance the budget in a defined time frame.

Second, the failure to balance the federal budget is in part the result of a lack of accountability and transparency in regards to government spending. The basic ideological position articulated by Ronald Reagan in the early 1980s, that the federal government is too large and inefficient, is imbedded in the Republic platform for fixing the country's budgetary challenges. While Republicans do place importance on economic growth as a means of addressing the national deficit, a substantial part of their approach is reducing spending through policies that bring to light instances of government waste.

Third, in contrast to the Democratic Party's platform, Republicans do not pair their policy proposals for addressing the deficit with policies designed to redistribute income and/or address social inequities. Rather, the Republicans broadly see a balanced budget as a necessity for a level of economic growth that ensures a strong middle-class. Crucial to this idea is the concept of fairness, that is, that tax adjustments singling out subsets of American citizens and companies are in violation of America's founding values of freedom and fairness.

In summary, much like Democratic Party leaders, Republicans view a balanced budget and the elimination of the national debt as important policy goals. Arguably Republicans contrast with Democrats in that they feel the threat posed by an unbalanced budget is more immediate, unlikely to be addressed through economic growth alone, and an overall byproduct of a lack of accountability and transparency in federal government.

Michael R. Ford

Further Reading

Democratic National Committee. 2012. "Moving America Forward: 2012 Democratic Platform." Accessed May 2, 2015. http://www.presidency.ucsb.edu/papers_pdf/101962.pdf.

House Budget Committee. 2014. "The Path to Prosperity: Fiscal Year 2015 Budget Resolution." April. Accessed May 12, 2015. https://budget.house.gov/uploadedfiles/fy15_blueprint.pdf.

Reagan, Ronald. 1981a. Address to the Nation on the Economy. Simi Valley, CA: Ronald Reagan Presidential Library & Museum. Accessed November 16, 2015. https://catalog.archives.gov/id/7450170?q=radio%20OR%20address%20OR%20broadcast.

Reagan, Ronald. 1981b. "President Ronald Reagan's Speech to a Joint Session of Congress on the Program for Economic Recovery." April 28. Accessed April 14, 2015. http://www.pbs.org/wgbh/americanexperience/features/primary-resources/reagan-recovery/.

Republican National Committee. 2012. "We Believe in America—Restoring the American Dream, Rebuilding the Economy and Creating Jobs: 2012 Republican Platform." GOP.com. Accessed May 4, 2015. https://cdn.gop.com/docs/2012GOPPlatform.pdf.

Stephanopoulos, George. 2013. "President Obama Won't Balance Budget 'Just for the Sake of Balance.'" ABCNews.com. March 12. Accessed May 12, 2015. http://abcnews.go.com/blogs/politics/2013/03/president-obama-wont-balance-budget-just-for-the-sake-of-balance/.

Van Hollen, Chris. 2015. "An Action Plan to Grow the Paychecks of All, Not Just the Wealth of a Few." U.S. House of Representatives Committee on the Budget. January 12. Accessed May 1, 2015. http://democrats.budget.house.gov/sites/democrats.budget.house.gov/files/documents/Action%20Plan%20-%20PDF.pdf.

Earmarks

At a Glance

When the use of earmarks—congressional instructions within legislative bills for government funds to be spent on a specific project—came under increased scrutiny in the 21st century, the strongest support for their use came from senior members of both the Democratic and Republican Parties. Their support for earmarks was based on Article I of the U.S. Constitution that gives Congress the sole power to authorize spending of U.S. Treasury funds. Any threat to this authority was seen as a loss of legislative power.

The strongest opposition to earmarks came from newly elected conservative legislators who aligned themselves with the Tea Party wing of the Republican Party. Their commitment to reducing government spending and the overall size of the federal government led to their vocal opposition to earmarks. Ultimately, they generated enough political pressure for the passage of a ban on the practice, with results are that are continuing to be hotly debated.

Many Democrats . . .

- See earmarks as part of Congress' constitutional responsibility to supervise and direct federal spending
- Defend earmarks as a tool to provide funding for valuable local projects that would otherwise go unfunded
- View earmarks as useful in facilitating compromise among legislators and speeding the passage of legislation
- Acknowledge that earmarks are sometimes wasteful of taxpayer dollars
- Criticize earmarks that are indicative of political corruption

Many Republicans . . .

- See earmarks as a legitimate facet of Congress' "power of the purse"
- Believe that irresponsible use of earmarking eroded Americans' trust in the federal government
- Assert that earmarks resulted in wasteful spending of taxpayer dollars on unnecessary projects and programs

- Contend that earmarking sometimes led to instances of political corruption
- Acknowledge that earmarking could be useful in facilitating the passage of proposed laws

---

Overview

Earmarking, a practice sometimes described pejoratively by critics as the ultimate in "pork barrel" politics, has a long history in American politics. Earmarks were funds members of Congress obtained for their home districts or for businesses they favored by inserting language that directed funds to specific programs or projects into federal appropriations or authorization bills. The term "earmark" derived from marks placed on the ears of domestic farm animals, such as cattle or sheep, to show ownership (Pulick 2010). The term "pork barrel" had its roots in the pre-civil war custom of distributing salt pork out of barrels to hungry slaves who rushed to snatch it (Clemmitt 2006). Legislators often acquired earmarks to please constituents or increase political support within their districts.

Article I of the Constitution grants Congress "the power of the purse," bestowing the sole responsibility of appropriating all expenditures from the U.S. Treasury to the legislative branch. This appropriations power allows Congress to prohibit executive branch agencies from spending more money than is appropriated to them. Although most of the U.S Treasury funds are allocated to federal agencies, prior to the ban of earmarks in 2011, the remainder was available to Congress.

Earmarking allowed legislators to circumvent the executive branch's standard bidding process where money is allocated to programs on the basis of expert professionals' peer reviews of projects' merits (Dizikes 2009). In contrast, earmarks were usually inserted into the fine print of legislation or at the last minute, so they underwent little public scrutiny or legislative debate.

Beginning with the 109th Congress (2005–2006), both houses adopted rules to increase the transparency of the appropriations process. Then, during the 110th Congress (2007–2008), both houses enacted rules and legislation that increased the transparency of the earmarking process. Transparency involved requiring members to post earmark requests on their websites with an explanation of why they are valuable, with the aim of exposing the inappropriate use of earmarks.

In 2010, both parties took steps to distance themselves from earmarks in response to several highly publicized scandals and public protests, such as the "Bridge to Nowhere," a proposed $398 million bridge intended to replace a ferry connecting the 8,900-person town of Ketchikan, Alaska, with its airport on the sparsely populated Island of Gravina (Cowan 2012). The day after Democrats on the House Appropriations Committee announced a ban on corporate earmarks, House Republicans announced a unilateral, one-year ban on all earmarks (Chaddock 2010). Congress banned earmarks permanently in 2011.

President Bush's 2008 Executive Order on Earmarks

Executive Order 13457, "Protecting American Taxpayers from Government Spending on Wasteful Earmarks," was signed by President George W. Bush, on January 29, 2008, to curtail the use of legislative earmarks. Following are excerpts from Bush's order:

Section 1. *Policy*. It is the policy of the Federal Government to be judicious in the expenditure of taxpayer dollars. To ensure the proper use of taxpayer funds that are appropriated for Government programs and purposes, it is necessary that the number and cost of earmarks be reduced, that their origin and purposes be transparent, and that they be included in the texts of bills voted upon by the Congress and presented to the President. For appropriations laws and other legislation enacted after the date of this order, executive agencies should not commit, obligate, or expend funds on the basis of earmarks included in any non-statutory source, including requests in reports of committees of the Congress or other congressional documents, or communications from or on behalf of Members of Congress, or any other non-statutory source, except when required by law or when an agency has itself determined a project, program, activity, grant, or other transaction to have merit under statutory criteria or other merit-based decision-making.

Section 2. *Duties of Agency Heads*. (a) With respect to all appropriations laws and other legislation enacted after the date of this order, the head of each agency shall take all necessary steps to ensure that:

(i) agency decisions to commit, obligate, or expend funds for any earmark are based on the text of laws, and in particular, are not based on language in any report of a committee of Congress, joint explanatory statement of a committee of conference of the Congress, statement of managers concerning a bill in the Congress, or any other non-statutory statement or indication of views of the Congress, or a House, committee, Member, officer, or staff thereof;

. . .

(b) An agency shall not consider the views of a House, committee, Member, officer, or staff of the Congress with respect to commitments, obligations, or expenditures to carry out any earmark unless such views are in writing, to facilitate consideration in accordance with section 2(a)(ii) above. All written communications from the Congress, or a House, committee, Member, officer, or staff thereof, recommending that funds be committed, obligated, or expended on any earmark shall be made publicly available on the Internet by the receiving agency, not later than 30 days after receipt of such communication, unless otherwise specifically directed by the head of the agency, without delegation, after consultation with the Director of the Office of Management and Budget, to preserve appropriate confidentiality between the executive and legislative branches.

. . .

Section 3. *Definitions*. For purposes of this order. . .

(b) the term "earmark" means funds provided by the Congress for projects, programs, or grants where the purported congressional direction (whether in statutory text, report language, or other communication) circumvents otherwise applicable merit-based or competitive allocation processes, or specifies the location or receipt, or otherwise curtails the ability of the executive branch to manage its statutory and constitutional responsibilities pertaining to the funds allocation process.

Source

U. S. President. Executive Order 13457 of January 29, 2008. "Protecting American Taxpayers from Government Spending on Wasteful Earmarks." *Federal Register* 73, no. 22 (February 1, 2008): 6417–6418.

Supporters of earmarks claim that in their absence, valuable local projects go unfunded if lawmakers don't intentionally direct funds to them. They view earmarks as a good way to get money, resources, programs, and infrastructure to people who need it. Advocates of earmarks maintain that members of Congress know their districts, and the needs of their districts, far better than federal bureaucrats (Zelizer 2014).

On the other hand, critics of earmarks don't believe it is the federal government's role to fund local projects, which in their opinion, should be funded by local tax dollars. Opponents of earmarks argue that earmarked federal dollars spent on local programs diverted money from federal programs (Clemmitt 2006; Heaser 2009). Congress first sets an overall budget cap before any separate agency appropriations are considered, so the more earmarks there are, the more dollars are taken from other items. Opponents also charge earmarks divert legislators' attention away from important policy questions and congressional duties and functions, such as oversight. Furthermore, they charge that pork barrel spending creates inequities because some members get more funds than others based on seniority or committee assignment, rather than the actual level of need in their district (Dizikes 2009).

Furthermore, critics of earmarks maintain they breed corruption. Preceding the ban, multiple members of Congress were investigated in response to charges they had traded earmarks in the form of government contracts for campaign contributions (*Wall Street Journal* 2010). Many analysts believed earmarks are particularly vulnerable to corruption. If someone attempts to bribe a legislator to support a bill, there is opposition on the other side of the issue that must be dealt with. However with earmarks, no one is arguing the other side of the issue, which makes it appear that the payment will yield the desired outcome. Under these circumstances, the likelihood of bribery of officials increases because people are more willing to pay someone for a "sure thing" and are less willing to pay someone for a "maybe" (Clemmitt 2006, 534).

According to many political observers, however, the earmark ban has intensified legislative gridlock. They point out that historically, earmarks have facilitated the passage of national legislation by providing congressional leaders with a tool to influence members—namely, by trading funding for local projects for members' votes (Clemmitt 2006). Republican Representative Steven La Touretta of Ohio noted that if a member of Congress supports 90 percent of a bill and is only uncomfortable with a small portion of it, an earmark that benefits his or her district can make up for the last 10 percent (Cowan 2012). Many significant pieces of legislation would not have come to fruition without presidential use of earmarks. For example, President Franklin Roosevelt generated support for his New Deal legislation by providing key Northern legislators with major public works programs in their home districts. Likewise, President Lyndon Johnson used earmarks to overcome the Senate filibuster over the Civil Rights Act of 1964 (Zelizer 2014).

Some analysts think restoring earmarks would move Congress beyond its current dysfunctional state of legislative gridlock (Zelizer 2014). Steve Ellis, Vice President for Taxpayers for Common Sense, a non-partisan budget watchdog organization, cites legislative gridlock as the major impetus influencing lawmakers to consider rescinding the earmark ban. Many members of Congress believe reinstating earmarks is the only way to resolve the gridlock (Cowan 2012). Economics professor Thomas Stratmann agreed, "If earmarks are used to generate compromise, then you're taking away another tool for lawmakers to use to prevent gridlock. Someone has to give and to the extent that earmarks grease the wheel, they are beneficial" (Montopoli 2010).

There is debate over whether earmarks increased the total amount of federal spending or simply affected the allocation of federal dollars. Prior to their ban, earmarks amounted to 1 to 2 percent of the discretionary federal budget. Earmarks comprised such a small percentage of the federal budget that most analysts believe the ban had little impact on the total amount of federal spending. For example, Senate Republican leader, Mitch McConnell of Kentucky asserted, "You could eliminate every congressional earmark and you would save no money" (Bendavid 2010). In contrast, Republican Senator Tom Coburn of Oklahoma characterized earmark spending as "the gateway drug to spending addiction in Washington" (Hook 2010).

Democrats on Earmarks

There was widespread support for earmarks throughout the Democratic Party, particularly among senior members of Congress. The remarks of Senate Democratic Leader, Harry Reid of Nevada, one of the most outspoken supporters of the use of earmarks, are symbolic of Democrats' views. Senator Reid stated, "I have been a fan of earmarks since I got here the first day" (Newsmax 2014). Senate Democratic leaders tend to believe elected representatives are more in tune with local needs than bureaucrats in the executive branch, so members of Congress better understand how to spend money in their districts (Miller 2009).

Despite their support for earmarks, Democrats reluctantly agreed to an earmark ban following defeats in the 2010 congressional elections and after President Obama threatened to veto bills filled with them. Obama's actions were the fulfillment of his campaign promise to reform congressional earmarking.

Obama's ban on earmarks sparked considerable dissension in his party. Senate Democratic Leader Harry Reid of Nevada publicly clashed with the President over this issue, at one point telling him to "back off" (Wong 2011). Senator Ben Nelson of Nebraska made a counter threat to Obama that if the Senate wasn't allowed to earmark money for its projects, it would not allow the President to spend the money in areas he preferred. Senator Mary Landrieu of Louisiana explained why she thought the earmark ban was a mistake, saying "I think it's a shortsighted policy, and it's going to be very hurtful to Louisiana and a lot of states" (Raju 2011).

Congressional Democrats even questioned whether earmarking fell under the President's constitutional jurisdiction. The late Democratic Senator Daniel Inouye of Hawai'i (1963–2012), then chair of the Senate Appropriations committee, commented, "I don't believe that this policy or ceding authority to the executive branch on any spending decisions is in the best interests of the Congress or the American people" (Chaddock 2010). There is concern among congressional Democrats that the earmark ban tipped the balance of power away from the legislative branch and toward the executive branch (Stein and Grim 2014). Senator Harry Reid maintained the ban "takes power away from the legislative branch of government . . . it only gives the President more power. He's got enough power already" (Raju 2011).

Party leaders such as Senators Reid and Durbin see earmarking as a legitimate negotiating tool that could help unite the gridlocked Congress. Senator Durbin ruminated that earmarking "was the glue that held everything together, Democrats and Republicans were working for a common goal" (Newsmax 2014).

Although Democrats are generally in favor of earmarks, they acknowledge the political reality Congress faces. As Washington Senator Patty Murray, chairwoman of the Democratic Senatorial Campaign Committee noted, "We're being pragmatic about it this year, but we also [believe] strongly that as members of Congress, we have to represent our states and fight for them" (Wong 2011).

Republicans on Earmarks

The Republican Party is more divided on the issue of earmarks than the Democratic Party (Cowan 2012). Although Republicans present a fairly united stance against earmarks, some Republicans privately share Democrats' support for earmarks, but are afraid to acknowledge this publicly (Zelizer 2014). Their reluctance may be related to Democrats' 2006 congressional election victories that observers partially blame on former House Majority Leader Tom DeLay's abuse of earmarks (*Wall Street Journal* 2014). Republican opposition also stems from the importance they place on reducing government spending. Senator Tom Coburn of Oklahoma highlighted this concern, "Our long-term budget challenges are so great that we cannot afford to spend time, much less taxpayer dollars, securing earmarks" (Dinan 2011).

Opposition to earmarks is greatest among the more conservative wing of the Republican Party, and is strongest among legislators affiliated with the Tea Party.

Many of the Republicans swept into office during the 2010 election landslide, including Senators Mike Lee of Utah, Mark Kirk of Illinois, and Rand Paul of Kentucky, and Representative Marco Rubio of Florida campaigned against earmarks. Shortly after their election, lawmakers aligned with the Tea Party flexed their newly acquired political clout by reforming earmarking. Senior Republicans who supported and practiced earmarking throughout their political careers agreed to an earmark ban to avoid antagonizing the Tea Party. Formerly staunch advocates of earmarks such as Senate Republican Leader Mitch McConnell reluctantly ceded to the ban. "I know the good that has come from projects I have helped support throughout the state," he said. "I don't apologize for this. But there is simply no doubt that the abuse of this practice has caused Americans to view it as a symbol of the waste and out-of-control spending that every Republican in Washington is determined to fight" (Bendavid 2010).

Republicans' opposition to earmarking also reflects public disapproval of the practice. House Majority Leader John Boehner stated, "This earmark ban shows the American people we are listening and we are dead serious about ending business as usual in Washington" (Montopoli 2010). Republican Senator Tom Coburn of Oklahoma echoed Boehner's views, "We'll never be trusted to be the party of less spending while we're rationalizing more spending through earmarks" (Hook 2010).

However, a minority of Republicans continue to defend the use of earmarks. They tend to believe Congress has a constitutional right to direct spending and lawmakers know which projects in their districts and states are most worthy of funding. These lawmakers tout earmarking as "necessary to exercise control over President Obama's bureaucrats" (*Wall Street Journal* 2014). To them, ceding spending authority to the executive branch represents a dereliction of their constitutional responsibility.

Although supportive of the ban, House Speaker John Boehner acknowledged in 2012 that the loss of earmarking made his job more difficult. He noted that previous transportation bills moved through Congress more smoothly, receiving bipartisan support, because lawmakers could insert funding for pet projects beneficial to—and popular with—voters in their home districts and states (Cowan 2012).

Gardenia Harris

Further Reading

Bendavid, Naftali. 2010. "Tea Party Wins GOP Vow to Ban Earmarks." *Wall Street Journal* (Eastern Edition), November 16. Accessed September 28, 2015. http://www.wsj.com/articles/SB10001424052748703326204575616911269710850.

Chaddock, Gail Russell. 2010. "House Republicans Besting, Democrats Will Ban All Earmarks." *The Christian Science Monitor*, March 11. Accessed September 30, 2015. http://www.csmonitor.com/USA/Politics/2010/0311/House-Republicans-besting-Democrats-will-ban-all-earmarks.

Clemmitt, Marcia. 2006. "Pork Barrel Politics: Do Earmarks Lead to Waste and Corruption?" *CQ Researcher* 16 (23): 529–552.

Cowan, Richard. 2012. "House Republicans Discuss Reviving Earmarks." *Reuters.com*. March 30. Accessed September 25, 2015. http://www.reuters.com/article/2012/03/30 /us-usa-congress-earmarks-idUSBRE82T10F20120330.

Dinan, Stephen, 2011. "Senate Democrats Ban Earmarks: Spending Bills Will Not Include Pork Requests." *The Washington Times*, February 1. Accessed September 29, 2015. http:// www.washingtontimes.com/news/2011/feb/1/senate-democrats-bow-earmarks/.

Dizikes, Cynthia. 2009. "Congressional Earmarks: Pros and cons—and Minnesota's cut." *MinnPost*, March 4. Accessed August 18, 2015. http://www.minnpost.com/politics -policy/2009/03/congressional-earmarks-pros-and-cons-and-minnesotas-cut.

Heaser, Jason. 2009. "Pulled Pork: The Three Part Attack on Non-statutory Earmarks." *Journal of Legislation* 35 (1): 32–47.

Hook, Janet. 2010. "A New Push to Ban Earmarks in Senate." *Wall Street Journal* (Eastern Edition), November 9, A5. Accessed September 28, 2015. http://www.wsj.com /articles/SB10001424052748703957804575602930038132758.

Miller, S. A. 2009. "Democrats Brand Earmarks as Good." *The Washington Times*, March 9. Accessed September 28, 2015. http://www.washingtontimes.com/news/2009/mar/09 /top-democrats-cite-earmarks-as-worthy-projects/?page=all.

Montopoli, Brian. 2010. "House Republicans Adopt Earmarks Ban in New Congress." *CBS News*. November 18. Accessed September 27, 2015. http://www.cbsnews.com/news /house-republicans-adopt-earmarks-ban-in-new-congress/.

Newsmax. 2014. "Harry Reid, Democrats: Earmarks Could Ease Gridlock." *Newsmax. com*. May 7. Accessed September 29, 2015. http://www.newsmax.com/Politics/Harry -Reid-pork-earmarks-Congress/2014/05/07/id/570021/.

Pulick, Kimberly S. 2010. "Bringing Home the Bacon: A Two-Pronged Approach to Transparent and Effective Congressional Earmarking." *University of the District of Columbia Law Review* 13 (Spring): 115–136.

Raju, Manu. 2011. "Obama Earmark Threat Flusters Dems." *POLITICO*. January 26. Accessed September 29, 2015. http://www.politico.com/story/2011/01/obama-earmark -threat-flusters-dems-048208.

Stein, Sam, and Ryan Grim. 2014. "Harry Reid Wants to Revive Earmarks and Says a Top House Republican Does Too." *Huffington Post*: Politics. June 26. Accessed September 29, 2015. http://www.huffingtonpost.com/2014/06/26/harry-reid-earmarks_n_5531388 .html.

Wall Street Journal. 2010. "Earmarks Forever; The House Ignores Nancy Pelosi's Board of Outside Ethics Watchdogs." *Wall Street Journal (online)*, March 6. Accessed November 9, 2015. http://www.wsj.com/articles/SB10001424052748703862704575099832389 494288.

Wall Street Journal. 2014. "A GOP Earmark Statement: The House Majority Defeats and Effort to Restore the Pork Habit." *Wall Street Journal*, November 18. Accessed September 30, 2015. http://www.wsj.com/articles/a-gop-earmark-statement-1416269355.

Wong, Scott. 2011. "Senate Dems Give in on Earmark Ban." *POLITICO*, February 2. Accessed September 29, 2015. http://www.politico.com/story/2011/02/senate-dems -give-in-on-earmark-ban-048623.

Zelizer, Julian. 2014. "Is There Anything Wrong with a Little Pork Barrel Spending?" *CNN.com*. May 12. Accessed September 25, 2015. http://www.cnn.com/2014/05/12 /opinion/zelizer-the-case-for-earmarks/.

Energy Policy

At a Glance

Views on energy policy in the United States vary by factors including political party, geographic location, energy type, and global prices and conflicts. This means there is rarely one partisan position on energy prices or choice of energy source. Both Democrats and Republicans support natural gas development through hydraulic fracturing, but differ on how the federal government should regulate it. They also agree on offshore drilling in the Atlantic Ocean, but disagree on the permitting process or which environmental safeguards should be implemented.

One of the most recent debates centers on the extent to which the government should support development of renewable energy. Advocates, primarily Democrats, argue federal support through tax breaks, subsidies, and research and development funding is essential to make renewable energy financially competitive. Opponents, primarily Republicans, support renewable energy technologies, but believe the private sector should drive this development. Renewable energy is an important issue when looking at U.S. energy policy, but natural gas exploration known as fracking, oil drilling, and nuclear power will be the focus of this chapter.

Many Democrats . . .

- Believe the Alaskan National Wildlife Refuge (ANWR) should remain off-limits for oil drilling
- Assert that climate change is a growing human-caused problem
- Support pursuing renewable energy technologies to grow the economy, address climate change, and reduce U.S. dependence on foreign energy sources
- Favor expansion of natural gas drilling, as long as activity is carefully regulated by federal agencies to ensure any damaging environmental effects are minimized
- See renewable energy sources as far more environmentally friendly than fossil fuels.

Many Republicans . . .

- Say that reducing dependence on foreign oil by drilling in ANWR should be one of our primary energy goals
- Favor approval of the Keystone XL pipeline, which they describe as an important job creator and way to transport oil across the country
- Believe that the private sector is best able to regulate energy development including natural gas, oil, and coal exploration
- Complain that environmentalists exaggerate the impact of fossil fuel exploration, development, and consumption on the natural world and public health

---

Overview

Energy policy in the U.S. evolves as new energy sources are discovered. When development of oil fields in East Texas started in 1930, oil became a critical resource for the U.S. economy as it emerged from the Great Depression. Nuclear energy came online in the 1940s with the first commercial nuclear power plant station beginning operation in the early 1950s. With the advent of commercial nuclear power, demand declined for wind turbines and most were shut down.

In 1960, the global oil market changed when several countries in the Middle East and Venezuela created the Organization of the Petroleum Exporting Countries (OPEC). OPEC's self-described purpose is "to co-ordinate and unify petroleum policies among Member Countries, in order to secure fair and stable prices for petroleum producers; an efficient, economic and regular supply of petroleum to consuming nations; and a fair return on capital to those investing in the industry" (Organization of the Petroleum Exporting Countries 2015). OPEC plays a leading role in the global oil supply with its ability to control prices and influence the market.

In 1968, oil was discovered in Alaska's North Slope, at Prudhoe Bay, setting up a debate between industry, Alaskan Natives, and environmentalists over drilling in the sensitive ecosystem. The Alaska Native Claims Settlement Act (ANCSA) was passed in 1971 to create 12 Native-owned corporations and authorize them to select 44 million acres of federal land in the state. Under Section 17 (d) (2) of the ANCSA, the Secretary of the Interior also withdrew 80 million acres of land from development for later designation as a national park, wildlife refuge, wild and scenic river, or forest. These "d-2" lands became the focus of the 1971 Alaska National Interest Lands Conservation Act (ANILCA) as the state and federal government tried to reach a compromise between growing development needs of oil, preserving Native lifestyles, and environmental protections. ANILCA protected 100 million acres, expanded the national park and refuge system and protected the existing wilderness (National Parks Conservation Association 2011). With these laws, the federal government owned 60 percent of Alaska, with most of this land off-limits for development, 70 million acres of land was left 'open" in the state ("Modern Alaska" 2015).

Under the Department of Energy Organization Act, Congress created the Cabinet-level Department of Energy in 1977. This statute consolidated energy programs scattered throughout the federal government into one federal agency. Until the 1970s, energy was relatively cheap and managed by the private sector without a cohesive federal policy to regulate energy prices. As a result of the oil embargo by OPEC and rising gas prices, American interest in wind power increased at this time. During this decade, the Natural Gas Policy Act (U.S. Energy Information Administration 1978) and Public Utility Regulatory Policies Act (PURPA 1978) were passed and the federal government began expanding its energy policy into natural gas and requiring utilities to buy a percentage of their electricity from renewable energy sources, respectively. Subsequent conflicts and embargoes in the Middle East continued to put pressure on the federal government to pursue alternatives to oil from OPEC members, from renewable energy sources to domestic oil, coal, and gas deposits.

Major Energy-Related Laws and Court Decisions Since the 1970s

- **Natural Gas Policy Act (1978):** The NGPA authorized the Federal Energy Regulatory Commission to regulate interstate and intrastate natural gas production. It also established a type of natural gas pricing category that could obtain what the EIA calls unregulated market-determined prices in a three-stage system of price ceilings.
- **Public Utility Regulatory Policies Act (1978):** Congress enacted PURPA during the energy crisis of the 1970s with the purpose of reducing dependence on foreign oil, promote alternative energy sources, improve energy efficiency, and diversify the electric power industry by requiring public utilities to buy a percentage of their electricity from renewable energy sources. This purchase requirement played a critical role in promoting the development of renewable energy in the United States.
- **Energy Policy Act (1992):** The EPA's two main purposes were to reduce U.S. dependence on foreign oil and improve air quality through alternative fuels, renewable energy, and energy efficiency. It also established regulations that required some federal, state, and local fleets to build an inventory of alternative fuel vehicles.
- **Energy Policy Act (2005):** Put forth by the George W. Bush administration, this statute amended the Energy Policy Act of 1992 and focused on energy production from the following: (1) energy efficiency; (2) renewable energy; (3) oil and gas; (4) coal; (5) Tribal energy; (6) nuclear matters and security; (7) vehicles and motor fuels, including ethanol; (8) hydrogen; (9) electricity; (10) energy tax incentives; (11) hydropower and geothermal energy; and (12) climate change technology. It also provided relief from federal royalties for leases over a five-year period.

- **Energy Independence and Security Act (2007):** The three main provisions of EISA are the Corporate Average Fuel Economy Standards, the Renewable Fuel Standard, and the appliance/lighting efficiency standards. This statute reinforced federal energy goals put forth in Executive Order 13423.
- **American Recovery and Reinvestment Act (2009):** Also known as the "stimulus package," the ARRA passed in response to the financial crisis in 2008. It included the following three goals: Create new jobs and save existing ones, spur economic activity and invest in long-term growth, and foster unprecedented levels of accountability and transparency in government spending. Under this statute, the Department of Energy received over $31 billion to support a range of initiatives including clean energy products, subsidies, tax breaks, among others.
- *Utility Air Regulatory Group v. Environmental Protection Agency* **(2014):** In this Supreme Court case, the Utility Air Regulatory Group challenged the Environmental Protection Agency's (EPA) interpretation of the Clean Air Act provisions used by the agency to regulate stationary sources to have a Title V permit on the sole basis of the source's greenhouse gas emissions. Justice Scalia delivered the opinion in which the Court upheld the EPA's interpretation requiring emitting sources to have a permit and comply with "best available control technology" of greenhouse gas emissions.

Commercial natural gas production from shale through hydraulic fracturing ("fracking") started in 1947 and large-scale development of the Barnett Shale in Texas began in 2000. It went largely unregulated for several years and the 2005 Energy Policy Act exempted fracking from Environmental Protection Agency regulatory authority and most major environmental laws including § 1421(d) of the Safe Drinking Water Act (SDWA) regulating the Underground Injection Control program (Council on Foreign Relations 2015). From 2011–2013, fracking reduced the country's energy imports by one-third. More than half of the increase in modern-day shale gas production is from the Haynesvile and Marcellus formations. Generation of natural gas is dependent on competing prices with existing coal plants and renewable energy. It is also strongly influenced by world energy prices. The Energy Information Administration's (EIA) *Annual Energy Outlook 2015* (AEO2015) projects that natural gas will be 42 percent of total energy generation in the United States by 2040. This would make it the leading source of energy.

Based on the AEO2015 report, renewable energy sources provided 13 percent of U.S. electricity in 2013 with wind and solar power comprising two-thirds of growth in renewable energy. By 2040, the EIA projects wind to be the largest source of renewable energy and overtaking hydropower as the largest source of renewable energy generation. Currently, the EIA reports that the United States produces more electricity from wind than any other country in the world.

Democrats on Energy Policy

In their 2012 campaign platform, Democrats expressed support for reducing dependence on foreign fossil fuels by increasing the domestic energy supply through oil production, natural gas technologies such as fracking, "clean coal," and expanding renewable energy technologies. They proposed achieving these goals through federal environmental regulations. The Obama Administration has pursued an "all of the above" energy policy that incorporates the 2012 platform. Green subsidies and renewable energy are discussed in greater depth in the Green Energy Subsidies chapter.

Fracking

To increase domestic energy supplies, the Obama Administration supports expansion of natural gas exploration. From FYs 2009–2013, lease revenue from oil and natural gas accounted for $48 billion in revenue (Government Accountability Office 2015). Representative John Delaney (D-MD) said, "It's a huge business opportunity for the country" and Senator Sheldon Whitehouse (D-RI) stated, "I'm willing to defer cracking down on natural gas, because the economic benefits to the nation have been so great" (Harder 2014). Democrats in New England who have historically advocated for climate-friendly sources of energy are expressing similar hopes for expansion of natural gas. Senator Chris Murphy (D-CT) remarked, "It's always a difficult issue because there are always people who don't want a pipeline in their backyard, but I'm convinced that natural gas is going to be this bridge fuel that gets us to renewables" (Colman 2014).

In 2012, the Bureau of Land Management (BLM) proposed a rule to regulate fracking, effective June 24, 2015. Provisions include a required demonstration of integrity for all wells, stricter requirements for trade secret exemption claims, greater protections for fluids recovered and contained during fracking operations, more information available to the public about hydraulic operations, and cooperation between the BLM, states, and tribes to improve efficiency and lower administrative expenses.

As concerns grow over the lack of regulations and environmental issues resulting from fracking, divisions within the Democrat party are emerging as some state and local officials oppose President Obama's policy on natural gas. In 2014, Governor Andrew M. Cuomo of New York announced a state ban on hydraulic fracturing over concerns that risks to public health outweighed the economic benefits (Kaplan 2014). Based on a November 2013 poll of New York voters, 63 percent of self-identified liberals opposed fracking and 52 percent of surveyed conservatives opposed it. Governor Cuomo faced a closer partisan split upstate where the Marcellus Shale, and a likely location of future fracking operations, is located: 41 percent supported fracking and 53 percent of respondents opposed (Marist 2013).

Oil Drilling

A major component of President Obama's policy has been expanding offshore drilling exploration, but the 2010 Deepwater Horizon disaster off the coast of

Louisiana raised issues of safety management within the Minerals Management Service (MMS). Following this incident that killed 11 people and spilled an estimated 3.2 billion barrels of oil, the Department of the Interior (DOI) divided and restructured the MMS into two new bureaus and one new office: Bureau of Ocean Energy Management, Bureau of Safety and Environmental Enforcement, and the Office of Natural Resources and Revenue (Monroe 2011).

As part of President Obama's "all of the above" energy strategy, the DOI announced plans to open federal waters off the Atlantic seaboard for oil and gas drilling and sell leases for drilling in federal waters from 2017–2022, receiving support from the Republican Party and criticism from environmental groups who have historically supported Democrats. The DOI also plans to open new areas of the Gulf of Mexico for drilling while banning drilling in parts of the Arctic. Secretary of Interior Sally Jewell described the decisions as follows, "This is a balanced proposal that would make available nearly 80 percent of the undiscovered technically recoverable resources, while protecting areas that are simply too special to develop" (Davenport 2015).

Nuclear Energy

High construction costs, market forces, storing spent fuel, and public opinion make nuclear energy a controversial issue with political risk. In 2010, President Obama fulfilled a 2008 campaign promise in Nevada to cancel funding for the Yucca Mountain nuclear waste depository while also strongly supporting nuclear power and providing $8.3 billion in government loan guarantees for development of two new nuclear reactors in Georgia (Debusmann 2010).

After the 2011 Fukushima disaster in Japan, support for nuclear power shifted, putting pressure on the Obama administration and nuclear regulatory authorities to reconsider nuclear power and dangers of on-site nuclear waste storage. In New York, Governor Andrew Cuomo vowed to shut down the Indian Point nuclear power plant in 2011, but public support near the plant was divided. Forty-nine percent of surveyed residents in the area opposed closing the plant and 40 percent supported keeping it open (Marist 2011). It remained open as of 2015.

Republicans on Energy Policy

In their 2012 campaign platform, Republicans advocated expansion of natural gas production through fracking, increased domestic oil production, specifically in the Arctic National Wildlife Refuge and the Keystone XL pipeline, and conservation efforts managed by the private sector and free market rather than the federal government (Republican National Committee 2012). While some of the party's goals are similar to the Democrats' proposals, significant differences exist in each party's implementation strategy and the preferred level of government oversight.

Fracking

At the request of Vice President Dick Cheney, a provision in the Energy Policy Act of 2005 under President George W. Bush specifically exempts fracking activities from the Safe Drinking Water Act (SDWA), Clean Air Act, and Clean Water Act provisions. This is referred to as the "Halliburton loophole" because of Vice President Cheney's prior tenure as CEO of the Halliburton oil company, a player in the fracking industry. Many Republicans argued states could best regulate fracking operations. Subsequent attempts to close the loophole have failed in Congress.

Oil and gas companies contributed over $70 million dollars to candidates in the 2012 election cycle, with 90 percent of this funding going to the Republican Party, reflecting an increasingly conservative focus from the industry when compared to 2010 funding levels. Senators John Cornyn (R-TX), Mary Landrieu (D-LA), and Cory Gardner (R-CO) were the top recipients from 2013–2014 (Center for Responsive Politics 2015).

In response to a citizen-led attempt to ban fracking in Denton, Texas, Republican Governor Greg Abbott signed a law on May 18, 2015, prohibiting a city or town from imposing an ordinance prohibiting fracturing or other natural gas activities. Governor Abbott argued he was protecting private property interests from "the heavy hand of regulation" (Associated Press 2015). On May 29, 2015, Republican Governor Mary Fallin of Oklahoma signed a similar ban into state law, preventing towns or cities from choosing whether they want oil and gas operations in their jurisdiction. Under the legislation, the state's all-Republican Oklahoma Corporation Commission retains decision-making authority over oil and gas drilling operations in the state (Murphy 2015).

Oil Drilling

As stated in the party's 2012 platform, Republicans tend to believe in pursuing on and offshore oil resources and oppose any moratoriums on permitting development in the Outer Continental Shelf (OCS). Republican leaders criticized President Obama's veto of the Keystone XL Pipeline, which would have connected Canadian and American oil with U.S. refineries, arguing this is an important distribution system that would have also created jobs. The Republican Party also believes in opening the OCS for energy exploration and opening the coastal plain of ANWR for both oil and natural gas exploration.

In January 2015, the debate over opening ANWR's coastal plain intensified after President Obama asked Congress to designate the area as a wilderness, prohibiting all commercial development including oil exploration. Alaskan Senator Lisa Murkowski stated in an interview about the proposed designation: "We are a state that has been providing oil to the country for decades now and doing so in an environmentally sound and safe way. But what the president is proposing has the potential to thwart any development there. All of a sudden, it's a one-two-three kick to Alaska. . . . What we are faced with right now is a different battle than we had in 1995 when Clinton vetoed the opening of ANWR to limited exploration and development. What we're faced with now is not a situation where we're trying to get votes to open it to limited access. We're trying to keep this area from being locked up permanently, indefinitely, forever to anything. And keep in mind that what the president has started is a process that would move toward a wilderness designation. But it is ultimately and only the Congress that can make that determination. I can almost guarantee that this Congress will not approve placing ANWR into wilderness status. So the president is pushing something in the Congress that it will not endorse" (Murkowski 2015).

The Republican-led House of Representatives' proposed budget for FY 2016 states, "the United States is on track to become energy independent within the next 10 years. . . . This budget encourages further exploration of oil and natural gas both onshore and offshore in North America on both private and public lands" (Fisher 2015). The budget echoes a similar sentiment to the 2012 campaign platform with its support for domestic energy sources and reducing regulations the party feels are burdensome for industry.

Nuclear Energy

With no new nuclear power plants built or licensed in 30 years, Republicans want the Nuclear Regulatory Commission to process new reactor applications in a timelier manner. They also emphasize the importance of the federal government addressing the problem of storage and disposal of spent nuclear fuel after President Obama canceled plans for the Yucca Mountain storage site. Many Republicans are concerned that the continued lack of a federal depository poses additional financial burdens on the state and taxpayers.

Elizabeth Wheat

Further Reading

American Recovery and Reinvestment Act, 26 U.S.C. § 1 (2009). Accessed June 1, 2015. http://www.recovery.gov/arra/About/Pages/The_Act.aspx.

Associated Press. "New Texas Law Bans Cities from Banning Fracking, Drilling." KXAN-TV. Accessed June 1, 2015. http://kxan.com/2015/05/18/new-texas-law-bans-cities-from-banning-fracking-drilling/.

Center for Responsive Politics. 2015. "Oil & Gas." Accessed June 1. https://www.opensecrets.org/inudstries/indus.php?ind=E01.

Colman, Zack. 2014. "New England Democrats Seek More Natural Gas." *Washington Examiner*, April 25. Accessed June 1, 2015. http://www.washingtonexaminer.com/new-england-democrats-seek-more-natural-gas/article/2547657.

Council on Foreign Relations. 2015. "Hydraulic Fracturing (Fracking)." CFR Backgrounders. Accessed June 1. http://www.cfr.org/energy-and-environment/hydraulic-fracturing-fracking/p31559.

Davenport, Coral. 2015. "Obama's Plan: Allow Drilling in Atlantic, but Limit It in Arctic." *New York Times*, January 27. Accessed June 1, 2015. http://www.nytimes.com/2015/01/28/us/obama-plan-calls-for-oil-and-gas-drilling-in-the-atlantic.html?ref=topics.

Debusmann, Bernd. 2010. "Obama, Politics and Nuclear Waste." *Reuters*. Accessed June 1, 2015. http://blogs.reuters.com/great-debate/2010/03/05/obama-politics-and-nuclear-waste/.

Energy Policy Act, 42 U.S.C. § 13201 (2005). Accessed May 15, 2015. http://www2.epa.gov/laws-regulations/summary-energy-policy-act.

Fisher, Joe. 2015. "Republican Budget Embraces Shale Oil/Gas, Spurns Renewables." NGI Natural Gas Intelligence. Accessed June 1. http://www.naturalgasintel.com/articles/101697-republican-budget-embraces-shale-oilgas-spurns-renewables.

Government Accountability Office. 2015. "Oil and Gas Resources: Interior's Production Verification Efforts and Royalty Data Have Improved, but Further Actions Needed." Doc. No. GAO-15-39. Accessed June 1. http://www.gao.gov/products/GAO-15-39.

Harder, Amy. 2014. "Democrats Increasingly Backing Oil and Gas Industry." *Wall Street Journal*, August 11. Accessed June 1, 2015. http://www.wsj.com/articles/democrats-increasingly-backing-oil-and-gas-industry-1407790617.

Kaplan, Thomas. 2014. "Citing Health Risks, Cuomo Bans Fracking in New York State." *New York Times*, December 18. Accessed June 1, 2015. http://www.nytimes.com/2014/12/18/nyregion/cuomo-to-ban-fracking-in-new-york-state-citing-health-risks.html?ref=topics&_r=0.

Marist. 2013. *Nature of the Sample: WSJ/NBC 4 NY/Marist Poll of 817 New York State Adults*. n.p.: Marist/*Wall Street Journal*/NBC 4 New York. Accessed June 1, 2015. http://maristpoll.marist.edu/wp-content/misc/nyspolls/NY131118/Cuomo/Complete%20November%202013%20The%20Wall%20Street%20Journal_NBC%20New%20York_Marist%20Poll%20NYS%20Tables%20.pdf#page=25.

Marist. 2011. "8/16: Nearly Half of Residents near Indian Point Want to Keep Power Plant Open." Marist Poll. Accessed June 1, 2015. http://maristpoll.marist.edu/816-radioactive-dummy-post/.

"Modern Alaska ANILCA." 2015. Alaska History and Cultural Studies. Last modified 2015. Accessed June 1, 2015. http://www.akhistorycourse.org/articles/article.php?artID=256.

Monroe, Leila. 2011. "Restructure and Reform: Post-BP Deepwater Horizon Proposals to Improve Oversight of Offshore Oil and Gas Activities." *Golden Gate University Environmental Law Journal* 5 (1): 61–85. Accessed June 1, 2015. http://digitalcommons.law.ggu.edu/cgi/viewcontent.cgi?article=1069&context=gguelj.

Murkowski, Lisa. 2015. "Murkowski Critical of Proposal for Arctic National Wildlife Refuge." Interview. *Morning Edition*. NPR. January 27. Accessed June 1, 2015. http://www.npr.org/2015/01/27/381783164/sen-murkowski-critical-of-proposed-plan-for-arctic-national-wildlife-refuge.

Murphy, Sean. 2015. "Oklahoma Joins Texas with Law Preventing Cities, Towns from Banning Oil and Gas Operations." *U.S. News*, May 29. Accessed June 1, 2015. http://www.usnews.com/news/business/articles/2015/05/29/oklahoma-is-latest-state-to-prevent-local-fracking-bans.

National Parks Conservation Association. 2011. "Alaska National Interest Lands Conservation Act." Alaska National Interest Lands Conservation Act. Accessed June 1, 2015. http://www.npca.org/news/media-center/fact-sheets/anilca.html.

Office of the Historian. 2015. "MILESTONES: 1969–1976 Oil Embargo, 1973–1974." United States Department of State. Accessed June 1, 2015. https://history.state.gov/milestones/1969-1976/oil-embargo.

Oil and Gas; Hydraulic Fracturing on Federal and Indian Lands, 80 Fed. Reg. (Mar. 26, 2015) (to be codified at 43 C.F.R. pt. 3160). Accessed June 1, 2015. https://www.federalregister.gov/articles/2015/03/26/2015-06658/oil-and-gas-hydraulic-fracturing-on-federal-and-indian-lands.

Organization of the Petroleum Exporting Countries. 2015. "Brief History." *OPEC.org*. Accessed June 1. http://www.opec.org/opec_web/en/about_us/24.htm.

Public Utility Regulatory Policies Act, 16 U.S.C. § 2601 (1978). Accessed June 1, 2015. http://www.usbr.gov/power/legislation/purpa.pdf.

Republican National Committee. 2012. "We Believe in America—America's Natural Resources: 2012 Republican Platform." Accessed June 1, 2015. https://www.gop.com/platform/americas-natural-resources/.

U.S. Energy Information Administration. 1978. "Natural Gas Policy Act of 1978." Accessed June 1, 2015. http://www.eia.gov/oil_gas/natural_gas/analysis_publications/ngmajorleg/ngact1978.html.

Estate Tax

At a Glance

With few exceptions, support for maintaining a strong estate tax lies within the Democratic Party. Although many leaders of the Democratic Party remain open to the idea that the wealth levels of an estate at which the estate tax is activated ought to be raised, advocates of a strong estate tax argue just the opposite. They contend that a strong estate tax is not only healthy for America's democracy, encouraging public philanthropy, it is also one element of obtaining income for the government to be used for programs promoting the overall welfare of all citizens.

Most opposition to the estate tax, up to and including calls to abolish it altogether, comes from the Republican Party. Oppositional rhetoric originating the libertarian wing of the Republican Party quickly is echoed among mainstream Republicans as well. Among those who advocate abolition of the estate tax, the claim is that it is confiscatory, that it discourages capital accumulation, and that in a philosophical sense there is something simply anti-American about the idea of imposing one final tax on a person after death (hence the ubiquitous reference to the estate tax as the "death tax" among abolitionists).

Many Democrats . . .

- Feel the estate tax creates a more even playing field in each generation
- See the estate tax as supportive of democracy by diminishing intergenerational wealth accumulation
- Feel the estate tax encourage estate planning that supports public philanthropy and giving to federally recognized charities
- Support taxing capital gains income that would otherwise be completely untaxed
- See the estate tax as an important generator of revenue for government programs and projects
- Emphasize that the estate tax applies to only a very small fraction of wealthy Americans

Many Republicans . . .

- Criticize the death tax as an unneeded and unnecessary intrusion of the government into the private economy
- Assert that the death tax applies to many more people than just the super-wealthy
- Criticize the death tax for discourages capital accumulation, the heart of the U.S. economic system
- See the death tax as philosophically and morally out of line with American values
- Frame the death tax as fundamentally unfair since it targets a specific sector of the population only
- Describe the death tax's confiscatory rates as staggeringly high and aimed mainly at wealth redistribution
- Have called for outright abolishment of the death tax, a position that they claim is supported by most Americans

---

Overview

The estate tax, also commonly referred to as the inheritance tax in the documents of individual states, is one of a number specialized taxes outlined in the Federal Tax Code dealing with the transfer of wealth across generations. Taxes on inheritance are a common practice among nations, and in the United States dates back to the earliest days of the country (Jacobson 2007). Although all estates must be accounted for in the process of legal inheritance, only a very small number of those require an estate tax filing with the Internal Revenue Service.

As with any section of the federal tax code, the estate tax stipulations are complicated and nothing said in this short article should be considered expert advice. But for purposes of highlighting political and policy aspects, it can be said simply that when a person whose cumulative wealth is above a specified level dies, the estate tax is triggered and a specified percentage of that person's gross estate must be paid to the IRS in the process of transferring the estate to designated heirs. Included in a gross estate are "real estate, cash, stocks, bonds, businesses, and decedent-owned life insurance policies. Deductions are allowed for administrative expenses, indebtedness, taxes, casualty loss, and charitable and marital transfers. The taxable estate is calculated as gross estate less allowable deductions" (Internal Revenue Service 2015). Variability occurs in the triggering level and percentage of the estate that must be paid. The triggering level has risen over the years, and in 2015 stands at $5.43 million for individuals, and is double that for couples. According to *Americans for Tax Fairness*, based on statistics for 2012, only about 0.2 percent of estates (approximately 3,300 overall) end up paying any portion of the estate tax (Americans for Tax Fairness 2015). The tax applies only to that portion of the estate above the $5.43 million exemption threshold.

The parameters of the estate tax apply to the deceased person's estate at the time of death. There are many recognized and established means to reduce the size of an estate before death occurs, and thus the prospect of the estate tax serves as a motivating force to take advantage of such means during a person's lifetime. These include the establishment of trusts for offspring, but also and most importantly donations to federally recognized charities, public and private institutions, and other forms of public philanthropy.

For most of the 20th century there was a basic working agreement among the political parties that a tax on the right to inherit wealth is an acceptable element of the American economic system. This consensus began to break down in the closing decades of the century, sparked by the ideas of Milton Friedman (1912–2006, 1976 Nobel Prize Laureate in Economics). Friedman taught economics at the University of Chicago for some thirty years, then he became a policy adviser for the Reagan Administration. With his wife Rose, he published the best-selling book, *Free to Choose* (Friedman 1980), arguably the most influential book in economics in the last 50 years or more. Echoing Friedman's unabashed celebration of free market capitalism, new voices in social and policy discussions began to be heard challenging more or less every instance of government "interference" in the course of free market capital accumulation. While for decades those who would seriously question the bipartisan consensus on the legitimacy of taxing the right to inheritance were relegated to the extreme margins, such challenges increasingly have been taking center stage in policy discussions since at least the 1990s, initially emanating only from the nascent "libertarian" corners of the Republican Party, but by now also from those firmly within the Republican mainstream.

Liberal and Conservative Policy Experts Debate the Estate Tax

In a position paper published by the progressive Center for Budget and Policy Priorities, updated March 2015, Chye-Ching Huang and Brandon DeBot outline ten points of fact in favor of the estate tax:

. . . Roughly two of Every 1,000 Estates Face the Estate Tax
. . . Taxable Estates Generally Pay Less Than One-Sixth of Their Value in Tax
. . . Large Loopholes Enable Many Estates to Avoid Taxes
. . . Only a Handful of Small, Family-Owned Farms and Businesses Owe Any Estate Tax
. . . The Largest Estates Consist Mostly of "Unrealized" Capital Gains That Have Never Been Taxed
. . . The Estate Tax Is a Significant Revenue Source
. . . Repeal Would Likely Leave Less Capital for Investment
. . . Compliance Costs Are Modest
. . . The United States Taxes Estates More Lightly Than Comparable Countries
. . . The Estate Tax Is the Most Progressive Part of the U.S. Tax Code

Republicans, meanwhile, have their own favorite policy studies that paint the estate tax as harmful, such as this Republican staff study for the Joint Economic Committee, updated July 2012:

> The estate tax has reduced the amount of capital stock in the economy as described in previous Joint Economic Committee studies in 1998 and 2006. As of 2008, the estate tax has cumulatively reduced the amount of capital stock in the U.S. economy by roughly $1.1 trillion since its introduction as a permanent tax in 1916, equivalent to 3.2 percent of the total capital stock.
>
> The estate tax is an overwhelming cause of the dissolution of family businesses. The estate tax is a significant hindrance to entrepreneurial activity because many family businesses lack sufficient liquid assets to pay estate tax liabilities.
>
> The estate tax does not reduce income and wealth inequality. Perversely, the estate tax creates a barrier to income and wealth mobility. Economic inefficiencies due to the distortionary effects of the estate tax are burdensome, and the costs of compliance associated with the estate tax add to the paperwork and time necessary to comply with other taxes.
>
> The estate tax raises a negligible amount of revenue. Since its inception nearly 100 years ago, the estate tax has raised just under $1.3 trillion in total revenue; by comparison, that is equivalent to the U.S. federal deficit for fiscal year 2011 alone.
>
> Many studies have indicated that abolition of the estate tax would actually increase overall federal tax revenue in at least two ways: (1) the estate tax robs additional federal tax revenues from the collection of other taxes like the income tax, and (2) a larger total capital stock could increase income tax revenue.

Sources

Huang, Chye-Ching, and Brandon DeBot. 2015. "Ten Facts You Should Know About the Federal Estate Tax." *Center for Budget and Policy Priorities.* March 15. http://www.cbpp.org/research/ten-facts-you-should-know-about-the-federal-estate-tax.

Joint Economic Committee Republicans. 2012. "Costs and Consequences of the Federal Estate tax." July 25. http://www.jec.senate.gov/republicans/public/?a=Files.Serve&File_id=bc9424c1-8897-4dbd-b14c-a17c9c5380a3.

The recent controversy over the estate tax reached a high point when in 2001, under the administration of George W. Bush, a strongly Republican controlled congress voted to phase it out over a 10-year period. However, they establish its elimination in the law, the Obama Administration reintroduced it in 2011. Only one year, 2010, had a zero estate tax. Approaching the national elections of 2016, the debate over estate tax policy is no longer one of political horse-trading concerning acceptable thresholds and taxing percentages, but is clearly now a philosophical argument divided between those (almost exclusively Republicans) who claim the tax itself is illegitimate and should be abolished, and those (almost exclusively Democrats) who see continuing social value in the tax.

Democrats on the Estate Tax

In the current political climate, it is very difficult to speak from the stump on raising taxes of any kind, and thus it is difficult to find clear examples of Democrats who must face popular elections making specific statements in favor of retaining the estate tax. The Democratic Platform of 2012, *Moving America Forward*, is a good example of the way Democrats deal with estate tax policies. The platform mentions tax *cuts* as often as possible, and the general philosophy represented in the document is one of tax cuts and credits for the hard-pressed middle class Americans and small businesses, and removing tax breaks and loopholes for the super wealthy and large corporations. Thus support for a strong and continuing estate tax is implied more than directly stated.

This is underscored by the fact that the estate tax was revived, with a top rate of 40 percent, under the Obama Administration. Making specific statements in support of the estate tax is complicated for Democrats seeking popular election by the fact that, depending on how the question is asked, as high as 70 percent of Americans indicate support for abolishing the estate tax altogether (Luntz 2007). This reflects high levels of public ignorance about the tax—data suggests that nearly half of the people think the estate tax applies to "most" families, and studies do suggest that when people are corrected about the facts support of the policy increases considerably (Sides 2011).

Nevertheless, the facts are not easily translated into sound-bites, and there is even some evidence that the strongest supporters of abolishing the estate tax are unswayed by statistics about who is subject to the tax (Krupnikov 2006). In light of these difficulties, it is no wonder Democratic politicians prefer to confine their stump speeches to those areas is which they can employ the rhetoric of tax cuts and credits, rather than include areas in which the phrase "tax increase" might have to appear. Luckily, however, in their white papers and other publications, pundits, academic economists, and the denizens of Democratic leaning think tanks do not have to be so reticent.

One of the points in favor of a robust estate tax among Democrats is the argument that accumulated wealth across generations in practice significantly distorts the American ideal of a level playing field for all. As Americans we cling to the concept that in at least some of the most salient areas our social hierarchy reflects the results of talent and ability (our revered meritocracy) and not simply that the rich get richer. In this regard, former Secretary of the Treasury Robert Rubin wrote: "Our nation has always held itself out as a meritocracy and a land of opportunity, and an estate tax helps avoid accumulation of inherited economic and political power that is antithetical to this historical vision of our society" (Rubin 2010).

Another of the points by Democratic supporters is that the policy favors democracy by diminishing intergenerational wealth accumulation. A wide range of research now suggests that the unprecedented gap between the super wealthy and the rest of society is not only unhealthy for the economy, but also is dangerously detrimental to our democratic system of governance as well (Hartmann and Sacks 2012). A number of pundits and analysts now unapologetically use the term oligarchy to characterize the current system (Cassidy 2014). This arguably rhetorical claim was recently underscored by hard evidence in a study completed by two highly respected scholars, Martin Gilens (Princeton University) and Benjamin Page (Northwestern University). Their extensive research on legislation and policies actually enacted demonstrates clearly that in the current atmosphere, in which legislators must rely on campaign contributions from extremely wealthy individuals and the PACS representing their interests, actual policies and legislation always conforms to the interests of the economic elite (Gilens and Page 2014). In an article titled "No to Oligarchy" published *The Nation* magazine, Vermont Senator Bernie Sanders (an Independent who caucuses with the Democrats) gives voice to this concern. Sanders outlines the reasoning in his proposal, the Responsible Estate Tax Act (S.3533). Among a number of arguments in its favor, Sanders concludes: "This legislation must be passed because . . . the United States must not become an oligarchy in which a handful of wealthy and powerful families control the destiny of our nation. Too many people, from the inception of this country, have struggled and died to maintain our democratic vision. We owe it to them and to our children to maintain it" (Sanders 2010).

One of the long-term effects of a hefty estate tax, supporters say, is that it motivates the super wealthy to pursue avenues for significantly reducing the net value of their estate before they die. As is seen in the countless public libraries, public and university buildings, and hospital wings, to highlight only a few, that are "named" for or by the wealthy donors to these institutions, a hefty estate tax also provides incentives for large gifts targeted for the public benefit. This is actually welcomed by many among the super wealthy as an opportunity to "give back" to a society that provided much of the social capital that allowed the accumulation of great wealth in the first place. Here, for example, is a statement by Richard Rockefeller, great-grandson of John D. Rockefeller and heir to that family's great wealth: "The Rockefeller fortune could never have been created without the foundation of public laws, public education and infrastructure which undergirded American industry . . . far from resenting our tax system, which allows this infrastructure to remain strong, I believe that a strong estate tax makes perfect sense" (Rockefeller 2013).

A significant portion of the wealth of the super-rich in America consists of unrealized capital gains, which are subject to taxation only when sold (realized). Such capital gains passed along to heirs would then be subject to taxation based on the amount of their worth at the time of transfer, not at the time of the original investment. The estate tax, supporters suggest, is the main mechanism by which such capital gains are fairly taxed. Jonathan Tasini, labor consultant and President of the *Economic Future Group,* expressed this view when he wrote: "The estate tax is an important complement to our income tax system. Inherited wealth is one of the only forms of income that is entirely excluded from income taxation . . . The estate tax makes up for this inequity . . . without the estate tax, a substantial portion of income would go entirely untaxed at any point under the current system . . . capital gains income on assets that are not sold during the owner's lifetime are never subject to any tax . . . the estate tax at least ensures that some tax is paid on capital gains for the wealthiest estates. For estates worth more than $100 million for example, these unrealized capital gains constitute 55 percent of their value" (Tasini 2015).

Supporters of a strong estate tax generally emphasize that it applies to only a handful of the wealthiest estates (estimates range from 2 percent at the higher end, and 0.2 percent on the lower end). Nevertheless, because of the gross amount that is recouped from these extremely wealthy estates, the overall addition to government revenue, and the programs supported by that revenue, is noteworthy. Here again is Robert Rubin, Treasury Secretary during the Clinton Administration: "Our country is on an unsustainable fiscal path. A progressive state tax can . . . fund deficit reduction, additional public investment or added assistance to those affected by the economic crisis" (Rubin 2010).

These and many other similar statements can be cited among those (which overwhelmingly lean toward the Democratic Party) supporting the retention and enhancement of strong and significant estate and inheritance tax policies.

Republicans on the Estate Tax

Among the first declarative policy statements in the document "We Believe in America," the Republican Party Platform for the 2012 election, is "End the Death Tax" Much as Democratic politicians facing popular election have shied away from explicit public statements on estate tax policy, statements that quoted in isolation could be easily framed as favoring "high taxes," on the Republican side of things politicians and pundits alike seem almost to compete with each other in casting aspersions on what they ubiquitously refer to as the "death tax." Republican pollster Frank Luntz, in fact considers this substitution of the term death tax as one of his most significant contributions to current Republican rhetoric. Luntz notes that his research indicated the highest levels of support for abolition of the tax when it was described as a "death tax." This terminology quickly was adopted universally by estate tax opponents (Luntz 2007).

While this might be seen as a rhetorical move only, it can also be confusing in places when trying to nail down specific Republican proposals and arguments other than blanket abolition. Thus Curtis Dubay, Research Fellow for the Heritage Foundation (a leading Republican-leaning think tank) differentiates between the "death tax," suggesting that it can and should be abolished, but replaced by a beefed up version of the existing "inheritance tax" (Dubay 2010). Most every other source on both sides of this issue (including the IRS code, which covers all of this under the umbrella of Estate and Gift Taxes, and speaks in both cases of "a tax on the right of to transfer property within the US at death") conflates estate tax and inheritance tax and use these terms interchangeably.

Dubay does present cogently, however, a widespread and major Republican point in favor of abolishing the estate tax; that it is an unneeded and unnecessary intrusion of the government into the private economy. Dubay writes: "The death tax slows economic growth, destroys jobs, and suppresses wages *because it is a tax on capital and on entrepreneurship*. Capital is any source that individuals or businesses use to generate income. Like anything else, when the income accruing to capital is taxed, its price rises and less of it is purchased. Less capital means slower productivity growth, lower wages and fewer jobs. As such, taxes on capital should be minimal or nonexistent" (emphasis added) (Dubay 2010).

While Democratic arguments for a strong estate tax repeatedly emphasize the very small number of estates to which the tax applies, perusing Republican arguments against it reveals an exact opposite point. Here the emphasis is on the large numbers of "family farms and small businesses" that are caught up in the jaws of the estate tax, and this literature is replete with anecdotes of miserable people losing their means of living because they have to sell out in order to pay these taxes. The 2014 campaign advertisement of Senate Leader Mitch McConnell (R-Kentucky) is paradigmatic in this regard, featuring a hard-pressed Kentucky farmer, John Mahan of Bourbon County, lamenting that the "death tax" makes it difficult for family farmers to pass along their farms to their children. Says Mahan, "As a farmer there's good years and bad. The last thing we need is Washington making it harder on us. The death tax makes it harder for us to hand our farm on to our kids. Mitch McConnell has been fighting to end the death tax to help us keep our Kentucky family farms. For our family farms to survive, we've got to get in this fight. I signed [McConnell's] petition to end the death tax" (Contorno 2014).

Another point often made by opponents of the estate tax is that it motivates the wealthy to squander their wealth while they are still alive. Writing for the conservative think tank *Tax Foundation*, David Block and Scott Drenkard, suggest: "the estate tax has since its inception decreased capital stock by $1.1 trillion due to discouragement of savings and the taxing of intergenerational transfers, which are perhaps the largest source of aggregate capital in the economy. The estate tax discourages savings by promoting a "die broke" mentality, as untaxed consumption becomes relatively cheaper than savings for those who intend to build wealth and bequeath a gift to inheritors, such as children or grandchildren" (Block and Drenkard 2012).

Many commentators express outrage at what in their view is the staggeringly confiscatory rate of the estate tax, whose underlying purpose is not much more sophisticated than stealing rightful wealth from one in order to give to someone else. Gayle Trotter of the *Independent Women's Forum* states that view rather succinctly: "the death tax has nothing to do with raising revenue. . . . So why have a death tax at all? When it comes right down to it, the tax is about social engineering and confiscatory wealth redistribution. Death-tax proponents support confiscatory taxation of lifetime earnings in the interest of wealth redistribution. And what's not to like about wealth redistribution? . . . In the short run, it's certainly not good for the person whose property is taken away. Nor is it good for that person's heirs. And, in the long run, it's not good to reduce the rewards of hard work and increase the benefits of idleness, which is exactly what happens "when you spread the wealth around." In any case, since when is it fair to take one person's rightful property and give it to someone else?" (Trotter 2012).

As is clear already from the points against the estate tax already outlined, on the abolitionist side of the debate there is less concern specifically with the nuts and bolts of the policy, which theoretically could be tweaked this way and that to improve its implementation. On this side of the debate "over, under, around and through" there is an unmistakable and pervasive sense of moral indignation about the very idea of the estate tax itself; that the estate tax is, in fundamentally a philosophical and moral sense, out of line with basic America values. In "Grave Robbers: The Moral Case Against the Death Tax," Edward J. McCaffery, a University of California professor of law writes that "We especially don't have to tax wealthy individuals who go to their graves leaving behind a store of capital unspent on their own personal whims. These are perfectly good and noble Americans, and it is little short of a sin that their distant Uncle Sam should be dancing on their graves. In short and in sum, for moral reasons above all, it high time to kill the death tax" (McCaffery 1999).

There is no disagreement on the facts about the estate tax that could not be cleared up easily by use of scientific investigative methods. The fundamental disagreement is on the level of philosophy and moral world view. One side looks at a set of facts and declares it good and desirable, while the other side encounters this same set of facts and declares it malevolent and odious. The estate tax debate is unfortunately now paradigmatic of our habit in American politics of each side talking past the other.

Daniel Liechty

Further Reading

Americans for Tax Fairness. 2015. "99.8 Percent of Estates Do Not Pay the Estate Tax." Accessed April 21. http://www.americansfortaxfairness.org/files/ATF-Fact-Sheet-99.8 -Percent-Of-Estates-Do-Not-Pay-The-Estate-Tax-1.pdf.

Block, David and Scott Drenkard. 2012. "The Estate Tax: Even Worse Than Republicans Say." *Tax Foundation,* September 4. Accessed April 21, 2015. http://taxfoundation.org /article/estate-tax-even-worse-republicans-say.

Cassidy, John. 2014. "Is America an Oligarchy?" *The New Yorker*, April 18. Accessed April 21, 2015. http://www.newyorker.com/news/john-cassidy/is-america-an-oligarchy.

Contorno, Steve. 2014. "Pro-McConnell Group Says the Estate Tax Makes It Hard for Family Farms to Survive." *PolitiFact*, April 3. Accessed October 21, 2015. http://www .politifact.com/truth-o-meter/statements/2014/apr/03/kentucky-opportunity-coalition /pro-mcconnell-group-says-estate-tax-makes-it-hard-/.

Democratic National Committee. 2015. "Moving America Forward: 2012 Democratic Platform." Accessed April 21. http://www.presidency.ucsb.edu/papers_pdf/101962.pdf.

Dubay, Curtis. 2010. "The Economic Case Against the Death Tax." *Backgrounder Published by the Heritage Foundation* 2440, 1–8.

Friedman, Milton, and Rose Friedman. 1980. *Free to Choose: A Personal Statement.* New York: Harcourt Brace and Company.

Gilens, Martin, and Benjamin Page. 2014. "Testing Theories of American Politics: Elites, Interest Groups, and Average Citizens." *Perspective on Politics* 12 (3), September, pp. 564–581.

Hartmann, Thom, and Sam Sacks. 2012. "Danger Ahead: The Oligarchs Don't Understand That Economic Collapse Happens When They Get All the Money." November 12. Accessed April 21, 2015. http://www.alternet.org/economy/danger-ahead-oligarchs -dont-understand-economic-collapse-happens-when-they-get-all-money.

Internal Revenue Service. 2015. "SOI Tax Stats—Estate Tax Statistics." Accessed April 21. http://www.irs.gov/uac/SOI-Tax-Stats-Estate-Tax-Statistics.

Jacobson, Darien B., Brian G. Raub, and Barry W. Jacobson. 2007. "The Estate Tax: Ninety Years and Counting." Summer. *Statistics of Income Bulletin.* Accessed April 21, 2015. http://www.irs.gov/pub/irs-soi/ninetyestate.pdf.

Krupnikov, Yanna, et al. 2006. "Public Ignorance and Estate Tax Repeal: The Effect of Partisan Differences and Survey Incentives." *National Tax Journal* LIX (September): 425–437.

Luntz, Frank. 2007. *Words That Work: It's Not What You Say, It's What People Hear.* New York: Hyperion.

McCaffery, Edward J. 1999. "Grave Robbers: The Moral Case Against the Death Tax." *Cato Institute Policy Analysis* 353. October 4. Accessed April 22, 2015. http://object.cato.org /sites/cato.org/files/pubs/pdf/pa353.pdf

Rockefeller, Richard. 2013. Quoted in "Estate Tax Quotes." *United for a Fair Economy.* September 8. Accessed April 21, 2015. http://faireconomy.org/enews/estate-tax-quotes.

Rubin, Robert. 2010. Quoted in "Estate Tax Quotes." *United for a Fair Economy.* Accessed April 21, 2015. http://faireconomy.org/enews/estate-tax-quotes.

Sanders, Bernie. 2010. "No to Oligarchy." *The Nation,* July 22. Accessed April 21, 2015. http://www.thenation.com/article/37889/no-oligarchy#.

Shaper, Alexander, and William Stewart. 2014. *Estate and Gift Tax Guide 2014.* eBook Kindle Editions.

Sides, John. 2011. "Stories, Science, and Public Opinion about the Estate Tax." George Washington University, July. Accessed April 21, 2015. http://home.gwu.edu/-jsides /estatetax.pdf.

Tasini, John. 2015. "Three Reasons for Tax Fairness." *Working Life,* March 26. Accessed April 21, 2015. http://www.workinglife.org/2015/03/26/three-reasons-for-the-estate-tax/.

Trotter, Gayle. 2012. "Put the Death Tax Six Feet Under." *The Daily Caller,* December 12. Accessed April 21, 2015. http://dailycaller.com/2012/12/18/put-the-death-tax-six-feet -under.

Financial Industry Regulation

At a Glance

Since the turn of the 20th century, most Republicans have worked to undermine Democrats' efforts to expand the federal government's role in the financial system. Despite this resistance, eleven regulatory organizations and coordinating forums currently oversee American banks, credit unions, securities and derivatives markets, and other financial service providers (Murphy 2013, 2). Most Democrats view regulators as publically spirited guardians of citizens' savings and investments. In contrast, many Republicans see regulatory organizations as collections of unaccountable self-serving bureaucrats who often lack the expertise and information necessary to effectively regulate an increasingly complex financial industry.

Republicans argue that banks and financial markets are the most efficient, stable, and beneficial to the real economy when they are the least burdened by federal rules and enforcement. They do not deny the existence of bad actors within the financial sector, but they have greater confidence in the ability of the marketplace to punish individuals and firms who act irresponsibly. In contrast, Democrats insist that in the absence of federal oversight, the financial marketplace is plagued by instability, crisis, fraud, and opportunism. They believe that market forces within the financial sector do not always punish bad behavior and may even encourage it.

Particularly when the economy is growing and the public is not paying attention, both parties are receptive to financial industry lobbying. In times of crisis, both parties respond to popular anger and agree to reform in principle.

Many Republicans . . .

- Feel that government intervention in the financial industry undermines economic growth and stability
- Charge that regulators lack expertise and are concerned primarily with increasing their own power and resources
- Contend that attempts to limit risk taking within the financial sector reduce the supply of credit to new firms and small businesses
- Claim that government involvement in housing finance was the primary cause of the Financial Crisis of 2008

Many Democrats . . .

- Believe that crises in the financial industry are primarily the result of reckless industry behavior, the inherent instability of financial markets, and inadequate government oversight
- Assert that regulators possess sufficient knowledge to act effectively and are primarily concerned with protecting the interests of everyday financial consumers and investors
- Argue that the social and economic benefits of financial regulation are far greater than the total compliance costs paid by the financial industry

---

Overview

The U.S. system of financial regulation seeks to protect three groups of market actors: depositors who place their surplus income in banks and other depository institutions; ordinary borrowers who receive loans from banks and other lenders; and investors who provide money to companies in exchange for those companies' securities. The other goal of financial regulation is *crisis prevention*. Known in policy circles as systemic risk management, this regulatory goal is not concerned with preventing the failure of individual firms, but about ensuring the stability of the financial system as a whole. Historically, lawmakers utilized financial policy to pursue other social and economic goals such as the stabilization of agricultural commodity prices, debt relief for agricultural producers, urban development, and the promotion of home ownership. Democrats typically show a greater willingness to use financial regulation as a tool of social policy. Republicans argue that the mixing financial regulation with broader social policy goals plants the seeds of future crisis.

Scholars have identified clear cyclical patterns in financial growth and regulation (Green 2012, 137–140). During periods of economic stability and growth, individuals accumulate debt and use larger portions of their income for investments. Eventually, economic expectations change causing steep drops in the prices of financial assists. If the decline in the value of investments is substantial, it can lead to financial crisis, recession, or even the Great Depression. Partisan and regulatory politics shadow this pattern (McDonnell 2013). During good times, both Democrats and Republicans share investors' optimism regarding the efficiency and stability of financial markets. This leads them to be more responsive to the financial industry's call for less regulation. The public, enjoying the upswing in asset prices, typically pays little attention to industry's deregulatory push. As a result, both parties accept more permissive rules, less intrusive monitoring and disclosure, and more forgiving enforcement. Differences between the parties are less severe when stock markets are high and credit is plentiful. Democrats prefer limited and gradual deregulation during good times while Republicans prefer deregulation that is rapid and far-reaching.

Following crisis or crash, these political dynamics reverse. A temporarily attentive and indignant public demands that politicians "do something" to prevent another crisis. The reputation of the financial industry is tarnished making its lobbying less effective. Politicians of both parties recognize these pro-reform political winds and agree to reform in principle. Nearly every major regulatory reform in U.S. history passed following a crisis. The legislative push that eventually culminated in the Federal Reserve Act of 1913 began in large part because of the 1907 Knickerbocker Banking Panic. The Securities and Banking Acts of the 1930s were a direct response to the Stock Market Crash of 1929 and the Great Depression. The Financial Institutions Reform, Recovery and Enforcement Act of 1989 was a response to the widespread failures of savings and loan associations during the 1980s. Perhaps the two clearest examples of the role of crises in facilitating reform are the deposit insurance provisions within the Banking Act of 1933 and the Sarbanes–Oxley Act of 2002. Although passed in different political contexts, both acts demonstrate that electoral pressures can force politicians of *both* parties to back away from their initial policy positions or even their closely-held ideological commitments.

Democrats on Financial Industry Regulation

The 1933 Banking Act created the Federal Deposit Insurance Corporation as an independent agency designed to prevent bank runs by reimbursing depositors if they lose their savings due to a bank failure. Although deposit insurance passed with wide bipartisan support, the deposit insurance provisions of the 1933 Banking Act were initially met with deep skepticism and resistance from the banking industry, Democratic congressional leaders, President Franklin Delano Roosevelt (1933–1945), and his Republican treasury secretary (Flood 1992, 51–56). Lawmakers of both parties witnessed the failures of state run systems of deposit insurance and were concerned that a federal deposit guarantee could put an unbearable fiscal burden on the federal government in times of crisis. Their other major argument against deposit insurance was moral hazard. Experts from both sides suggested that if depositors know that their deposits are insured, they have little incentive to discriminate between well-run prudent banks and poorly-run excessive risk-taking banks. If bank customers fail to reward responsible banks for their prudence, all banks have incentives to take greater risks than they would in the absence of deposit insurance—a clear example of moral hazard. Despite their initial reservations, the Democratic majority in Congress and President Roosevelt caved to their panicked constituents and passed a nationwide system of government operated but privately financed deposit insurance.

The stock market crash of 1929 convinced many Democrats that "excessive" risk-taking and weak investor protections within securities markets could threaten the stability of the entire financial system. In response, Democrats passed the Securities Act of 1933 with minimal Republican opposition. A year later, public anger toward financial elites waned. As a result, the Exchange Act met stiff resistance from the financial industry and emboldened Republicans.

The proposed 1934 Securities and Exchange Act aimed to bring greater transparency to the circulation of securities after their initial sale, reduce stock price manipulation, and outlaw insider trading. The law established a framework for regulating the operation of stock exchanges; limited the use of debt to fund securities trading; defined the content of corporate accounting statements; and sought to protect ordinary investors from the fraud and opportunism of corporate executives, stockbrokers, and other investment intermediaries. All of these tasks were given to a new regulatory agency, the Securities and Exchange Commission (SEC). Democrats asserted that by protecting the interests of small investors, the SEC would play an indispensable part in restoring the public's confidence in the financial industry. Exchange Act proponents also believed that financial sector self-regulatory organizations such as stock exchanges could not be trusted to supervise and discipline their members without close government supervision. Therefore, Democrats gave the SEC the power to force industry organizations to adopt particular trading, disclosure, and conflict of interest rules. Overall, Democrats believe that the financial industry should be encouraged or even coerced into respecting the interests of the small investor (McCraw 2009, 153–209).

Democrats argue that the 2008 financial crisis was caused by financial industry irresponsibility; a lack of transparency within markets for mortgage backed securities and other derivatives; weak consumer protections for mortgage borrowers; and a lack of bureaucratic capacity to monitor systemic risk and manage the failure of large financial institutions. In response to public anger over widespread mortgage defaults and the massive bailouts received by Wall Street firms, Democrats passed the Dodd-Frank Wall Street Reform and Consumer Protection Act of 2010. Despite bipartisan agreement that reform was needed, the bill faced nearly unanimous Republican opposition. The Democrats' bill imposed restrictions on the investment activities of banks and increased the minimum reserve capital requirements for certain types of financial institutions. Democrats also adjusted corporate governance rules so that shareholders have a greater influence over CEO compensation and boards of directors are more independent of senior managers. Due to Dodd-Frank, the originators of certain securities and participants in swaps and derivatives markets will face new disclosure and registration requirements.

The two most controversial reforms within Dodd-Frank were the creation of the Consumer Financial Protection Bureau (CFPB) and the Financial Stability Oversight Council (FSOC). The CFPB is authorized to protect everyday borrowers and consumers of a wide variety of financial services. The Bureau is charged with regulating certain features of credit card contracts and the terms of automobile, student, payday, and home loans. In addition, the CFPB oversees financial institutions compliance with consumer protections, investigates consumer complaints, and punishes abusive lenders and financial service providers. The FSOC brings together the Treasury Secretary and officials from over 10 regulatory bodies and is designed to give the government a more holistic view of the risks within the U.S.

President Obama Defends Dodd-Frank

President Obama said the following in support of the Dodd-Frank Wall Street Reform and Consumer Protection Act of 2010:

> Over the past two years, we have faced the worst recession since the Great Depression. . . . It was a crisis born of a failure of responsibility from certain corners of Wall Street to the halls of power in Washington. For years, our financial sector was governed by antiquated and poorly enforced rules that allowed some to game the system and take risks that endangered the entire economy.
>
> Unscrupulous lenders locked consumers into complex loans with hidden costs. Firms like AIG placed massive, risky bets with borrowed money. And while the rules left abuse and excess unchecked, they also left taxpayers on the hook if a big bank or financial institution ever failed. . .
>
> . . . So, all told, these reforms represent the strongest consumer financial protections in history. And these protections will be enforced by a new consumer watchdog with just one job: looking out for people—not big banks, not lenders, not investment houses . . . And that's not just good for consumers; that's good for the economy.
>
> Now, beyond the consumer protections I've outlined, reform will also rein in the abuse and excess that nearly brought down our financial system. It will finally bring transparency to the kinds of complex and risky transactions that helped trigger the financial crisis. Shareholders will also have a greater say on the pay of CEOs and other executives, so they can reward success instead of failure.
>
> And finally, because of this law, the American people will never again be asked to foot the bill for Wall Street's mistakes. There will be no more tax-funded bailouts— period. If a large financial institution should ever fail, this reform gives us the ability to wind it down without endangering the broader economy. And there will be new rules to make clear that no firm is somehow protected because it is "too big to fail."

Source

Obama, Barack. 2010. "Remarks by the President at Signing of Dodd-Frank Wall Street Reform and Consumer Protection Act." Accessed April 14, 2015. https://www.whitehouse.gov/the -press-office/remarks-president-signing-dodd-frank-wall-street-reform-and-consumer -protection-act.

---

financial system. In addition, Democratic authors gave the FSOC the authority to designate particular firms as systemically important financial institutions (SIFIs). Since the failure of a SIFI can threaten the entire financial system, they are subject to more stringent regulation and oversight by the Federal Reserve. Finally, SIFIs must develop "resolution" plans that outline their financial relationships with other firms and how their assets should be managed in the event of their failure. Overall, Democrats argue that the FSOC makes financial regulation more coherent, bailouts less likely, and systemic risk more manageable.

Republicans on Financial Industry Regulation

The modern Republican Party consistently sides with senior executives against the federal government's efforts to regulate the inner workings of corporate firms. However, after highly publicized accounting frauds and auditing failures at Enron, WorldCom, Global Crossing, and Tyco, public outrage caused many Republicans to reconsider the political costs and benefits of adhering to their ideological commitments. Fearing loses in a quickly approaching midterm election, House Republican leadership and Republican President George W. Bush (2001–2009) joined Democrats in passing the Sarbanes-Oxley Act of 2002 (Cioffi 2010, 97–139). The act transformed corporate America's accounting, auditing, and boardroom practices. Despite the considerable financial contributions they receive from corporate executives, Republicans sided with an angry public and supported what many conservative commentators consider to be some of the most intrusive and costly corporate governance regulations in U.S. history (Romano 2005, 1544–1564).

Although the previous two sections demonstrated the ability of crisis and public anger to push both parties toward regulatory reform, policy disagreement often remains. Two of the more contentious regulatory policy debates are discussed below.

Republicans were deeply divided over the specifics of the 1934 Act. Progressive and populist Republicans of the Great Plains and west attacked the financial sector with an almost religious fervor and joined their Democratic counterparts in supporting the bill (Carney 2011, 26–27). In contrast, Northeastern Republicans were far more receptive to the complaints of the financial sector and joined industry in making dire predictions that the new regulations would drive companies away from American stock markets, reduce investment, and prevent economic recovery. Many non-western Republicans were deeply suspicious of the expansion of the Federal government's power over what they viewed as the lynchpin of the free enterprise system: the decision making autonomy of corporate managers. In their eyes, the SEC was just another example of the Roosevelt administration's policy overreach, and the Agency's bureaucratic meddling would serve only to starve rather than stabilize the stock market. Northeastern Republicans joined corporate elites in arguing that the Exchange Act's registration and disclosure requirements encroached on what should be the strictly private affairs and trade secrets of corporate firms. Overall, many Republicans preferred a private system of industry self-regulation and therefore opposed giving the SEC much power over stock markets' and broker-dealer associations' practices of rulemaking and discipline (McCraw 2009, 160–200).

In line with some of today's most economically conservative Republicans, many 1930s congressional Republicans and former Herbert Hoover administration (1929–1933) officials believed that the occasional financial market downturn actually served a constructive purpose; market downturns eliminate the unsuccessful investments of unsophisticated and irresponsible investors who entered the market during financial booms. Furthermore, they assumed that the financial losses of the unlucky and unwise would allow economic resources to be reallocated to more efficient purposes accelerating the inevitable recovery. Overall, industry allied Republicans asserted that the struggling economy did not need more federal bureaucracy or intervention by the Federal Reserve, it simply needed time to recover (DeLong 1990, 3–9).

While sharing the Democrats' strong disapproval of Wall Street excess, Republicans identify government intervention in mortgage markets and the incompetence of regulatory agencies as the dual causes of the 2008 Financial Crisis. Republicans did support Fannie Mae and Freddie Mac's efforts to promote homeownership during the 1990s and early 2000s. However, current Republicans argue that these Government Sponsored Enterprises (GSEs) fueled the housing bubble by giving

The Conservative Republican Perspective on Dodd-Frank

Republican Alabama Senator Richard Shelby spoke for many in the GOP when he made the following statement in opposition to the Dodd-Frank Wall Street Reform and Consumer Protection Act of 2010:

> Nearly two years ago, the financial crisis exposed massive deficiencies in the structure and culture of our financial regulatory system . . . Decades of insulation from accountability distracted regulators . . . Instead of acting to ensure safe . . . markets, they primarily became focused on expanding the scope of their bureaucratic reach.
>
> Congress could have written a bill to streamline regulation and eliminate the gaps that firms exploit in a race to the regulatory bottom. This bill does the opposite by making our financial regulatory system even more complex. . . In fact, most of the existing regulators that so recently failed us have been given expanded power and scope. . .
>
> . . . The actual provisions in the bill will benefit big Wall Street institutions because they substantially increase the amount and cost of financial regulation. Only large financial institutions will have the resources to navigate the new laws and regulations that this legislation will generate. As a result, this bill disproportionately will hurt small and medium-sized banks which had nothing to do with the crisis. . . . Therefore, this bill will result in higher fees, less choice, and fewer opportunities to responsibly obtain credit for blameless consumers. While a consumer protection agency may sound like a good idea, the way it is constructed in this bill will slow economic growth and kill jobs by imposing massive new regulatory burdens on businesses—small and large. It will stifle innovation in consumer financial products and reduce small business activity. It will lead to reduced consumer credit and higher costs for available credit . . .
>
> This bill serves only to expand the federal bureaucracy and government control of private sector activities. It will impose large costs on American taxpayers and businesses without creating one new private sector job. It will lower the availability of credit, raise costs, and hinder economic growth.

Source

Shelby, Richard. 2014. "Dodd-Frank Not Real Reform, Just More of the Same." Accessed April 14, 2015. http://www.shelby.senate.gov/public/index.cfm/2010/7/shelby-dodd-frank -not-real-reform-just-more-of-the-same.

risky (i.e., low income) borrowers greater access to home loans for houses they could not afford. Furthermore, the two GSEs originated mortgage-backed securities that turned out to be far riskier than advertised increasing levels of panic and uncertainty once the crisis arrived. In short, Republicans agree with conservative financial scholars that the federal government's attempt to mix the social policy of home ownership promotion with financial regulation inflated the housing bubble that eventually caused the crisis (Calomiris and Haber 2014, 203–282). Republicans also argued that the complexity of financial regulatory system makes each regulator more concerned with protecting its bureaucratic turf than in managing risk within its area of responsibility.

When the Dodd-Frank Act was introduced, congressional Republicans insisted that the bill's thousands of new rules and requirements would increase compliance costs to the disadvantage of small financial firms and community banks, stifle innovation, and drive businesses to countries where executive compensation is not the subject of government regulation. They maintained that higher reserve requirements do not eliminate systemic risk but instead reduce the supply of credit available to consumers and business owners (Calomiris and Haber 2014, 4–5). Given their view of the pre-crisis regulatory regime as overly complex, Republicans fought fiercely against the creation of the CFPB. They feared and continue to argue that the CFPB lacks accountability to Congress and paternalistically interferes with individuals' rights to purchase financial services on whatever terms they deem appropriate. Republicans also strongly objected to the creation of the FSOC. Rather than preventing future government rescues of distressed financial firms, Republicans believe the FSOC institutionalizes bailouts and creates moral hazard. They argue that the FSOC's SIFI designation is equivalent to a public admission that a particular firm is "too big to fail." Republicans also insist that firms will interpret their SIFI status as an implicit federal guarantee and take larger risks than they would have had they never gained the designation. For the reasons outlined above, the 2012 Republican Platform explicitly declares the Party's intention to repeal the entirety of the Dodd-Frank Act.

Lucas Lockhart

Further Reading

Calomiris, Charles W., and Stephen H. Haber. 2014. *Fragile by Design: The Political Origins of Banking Crises and Scarce Credit*. Princeton: Princeton University Press.

Carney, Richard. 2011. "The Domestic Political Origins of Global Financial Standards: The Agrarian Roots of American Securities Regulations." *Business and Politics* 13 (3): 1–39.

Cioffi, John W. 2010. *Public law and private power: corporate governance reform in the in the age of finance capitalism*. Ithaca: Cornell University Press.

DeLong, J. Bradford. 1990. *"Liquidation" Cycles: Old-Fashioned Real Business Cycle Theory and the Great Depression*. Working paper 3546. Washington DC: National Bureau of Economic Research. Accessed April 4, 2015. http://www.nber.org/papers/w3546.pdf.

Flood, Mark D. 1992. "The great deposit insurance debate." *Federal Reserve Bank of St. Louis Review* 74, 51–77.

Green, David. 2012. "Political Capture and the Regulatory Cycle: How Should It Be Addressed." In *Making Good Financial Regulation: Towards a Policy Response to Regulatory Capture,* ed. Stefano Pagliari. Surrey, UK: Grosvenor House Publishing.

McCraw, Thomas K. 2009. *Prophets of regulation.* Cambridge: Harvard University Press.

McDonnell, Brett. 2013. "Dampening financial regulatory cycles." *Florida Law Review* 65, 1602–1608.

Murphy, Edward V. 2013. *Who Regulates Whom and How? An Overview of US Financial Regulatory Policy for Banking and Securities Markets.* CRS Report No. R43087. Washington, DC: Congressional Research Service.

Romano, Roberta. 2005. "The Sarbanes-Oxley Act and the Making of Quack Corporate Governance." *Yale Law Journal* 114 (7): 1544–1564.

Flat Tax

At a Glance

Most support for the flat tax in the United States lies within the Republican Party. Advocates contend that simplicity is one of the most significant benefits of the flat tax, which would eliminate deductions and require all taxpayers to pay the same fixed percentage of their income. One tax rate makes for easy computation by both the taxpayer and the Internal Revenue Service (IRS), which could be greatly reduced in size (or perhaps eliminated altogether) as a result. Advocates also argue that a flat tax increases the incentive to work, since workers would not pay higher tax rates on higher levels of income as they do under the current progressive income tax.

Most opposition to the flat tax comes from Democrats who hold that such a tax code would place an unfair burden on lower income families and further widen the economic gap between rich and poor in America. They argue that the flat tax penalizes low-income citizens, who must spend a greater proportion of their income on necessities than do the higher income groups. They further contend that the flat tax benefits corporations at the expense of individuals. In addition, they warn that institution of a flat tax would lead to diminished services from the federal government because revenue to the U.S. Treasury would decline dramatically under most Republican flat tax proposals.

Many Democrats . . .

- Contend that a flat tax would further shift the tax burden to poor
- Assert that flat tax schemes eliminate deductions that are vital to low- and middle-income families
- Observe that flat tax plans reduce overall government revenue, which would necessitate cuts to beneficial social programs
- Complain that flat tax plans exempt investment and inheritance income that mostly goes to the wealthy
- Assert that imposition of a flat tax would further widen the gap between rich and poor

Many Republicans . . .

- Say a flat tax would be easy for taxpayers to understand and follow
- Feel that a flat tax would reduce the size of the federal government
- Contend that institution of a flat tax would encourage business investment
- Assert that flat tax plans increase incentives to work and save for retirement
- Argue that a flat tax would reduce political favoritism by eliminating tax loopholes and exemptions that benefit select groups

---

Overview

The United States currently employs a progressive or graduated tax system that features different rates of taxation for different income levels and a wide range of special tax deductions and exemptions. Under a flat tax, every taxpayer pays the same fixed percentage of income, with no income brackets and few if any exemptions. In some respects, it is similar to the funding structure for Social Security. The Social Security tax is a flat tax for most Americans, because the payroll tax that funds the program is levied only on a certain amount of annual income ($117,000 in 2014). But there are limitations to this comparison. Not only do wealthy Americans escape Social Security withholding on earned income above that cap, they also pay no Social Security tax at all on things like interest, capital gains, or investment income.

For corporations, a flat tax would apply to the difference "between sales of goods and services on the one hand and the sum of wages, pension contributions, material costs and capital investments on the other" (Gale 1996). The flat tax would apply to both incorporated and unincorporated businesses and would allow businesses to deduct their annual capital investments. According to flat tax advocates, these changes would spark much greater levels of investment and drive overall economic growth.

A flat tax on income in America was first enacted during the Civil War, when President Abraham Lincoln signed the Revenue Act of 1861 into law. This measure assessed a 3 percent tax rate on all income above $800. Since the federal government lacked an Internal Revenue Service at the time, however, this revenue was never collected. The next attempt to impose a flat tax came with the economic crisis of 1893. Congress passed the Wilson-Gorman Tariff Act in 1894, which included a flat tax of 2 percent on all income over $4,000 (Cherry 2011). The purpose of the income tax was to make up for revenue that would be lost by tariff reductions. The Senate added so many amendments to the bill, however, that its reforms were nullified.

In 1983 two Stanford economists, Robert Hall and Alvin Rabushka, revived the flat tax in their book *Low Tax, Simple Tax, Flat Tax*. The flat tax scheme championed by Hall and Rabushka would replace the current personal income and corporate income tax structure with a two-level tax designed to tax all income exactly once, and at the same rate.

A Prominent Republican's Case for the Flat Tax

Republican Dick Armey has been one of the foremost flat tax advocates of the past quarter-century. In 1994 Armey, who was a Texas Congressman from 1985 to 2003 (and House Majority Leader from 1995 to 2003), made his case for such a reform:

> I am convinced that the Flat Tax is in America's future. Here is how it works. Rather than tinkering, we scrap the entire tax code, corporate and personal, and replace it with one flat rate that applies to all Americans. We leave just one exception, a generous family allowance to ensure that every family has the first claim to its own income sufficient to support itself. . . . No deductions. No loopholes. No tax breaks. No tables. No schedules. No nothing.

Source

Armey, Dick. 1995. "United We Stand Conference." August 12. http://www.ontheissues.org /Tx/Dick_Armey_Tax_Reform.htm.

In the early 1990s, Republican Congressman Dick Armey proposed a flat tax that would have fundamentally revised the current tax system. His proposal never made it through the U.S. Congress, but conservative proponents of the flat tax took heart in encouraging developments overseas. In post-Communist Eastern and Central Europe, more than a dozen countries adopted a flat tax, including Russia (which approved a 13 percent flat tax on personal income in January 2001), Romania (which adopted a 16 percent flat tax on personal income and corporate profits beginning in 2005), and the Czech Republic (which in 2008 instituted a 15 percent individual tax rate).

Back in the United States, meanwhile, support for a flat tax continued to gain traction in conservative political circles. In today's Republican party, it is a widely held belief that government should spend money only to enforce contracts, maintain basic infrastructure and national security, and protect citizens against criminals. Republican policymakers, economists, and pundits favor reducing taxes for businesses to allow businesses to grow and thus hire more employees.

Flat tax proposals have thus garnered significant attention in Republican presidential primaries. In 2012, for example, Republican candidate Rick Perry touted a single flat tax rate of 20 percent as a way to unleash the U.S. economy and balance the federal budget at the same time. Another candidate in the 2012 Republican presidential primaries, Herman Cain, proposed a "9-9-9" flat tax consisting of 9 percent income tax, a 9 percent corporate income tax, and a 9 percent sales tax. A third candidate, Newt Gingrich, proposed an optional 15 percent flat tax on personal income (Scherer 2011). The eventual Republican nominee that year, Mitt Romney, also stated that flat tax proposals had merit, but his own proposed economic package touted lower and simpler taxes rather than an outright flat tax.

Since Romney's defeat in 2012 at the hands of Democratic incumbent Barack Obama, flat tax support has remained strong among some Republicans. In a 2014 appearance before the Conservative Political Action Conference (CPAC), prominent Republican Ben Carson gave a ringing endorsement to the flat tax. That same year, the libertarian-leaning Reason Foundation conducted a poll asking Americans if they would support or oppose changing the federal tax system to a flat tax. The organization reported that 62 percent of respondents favored the flat tax and 33 percent were opposed. When asked where they would set the flat tax, the average response was 15 percent. Respondents who support small government and who believe that the free market can better solve problems than a strong government favored a flat tax by a margin of nearly 50 points (roughly 72 to 25 percent) (Ekins 2014).

Opponents of the flat tax, primarily Democrats, staunchly oppose these sentiments. They argue that the flat tax places a higher burden on low- and middle-income citizens not only by removing deductions for things such as home mortgages, but by forcing them to shoulder a higher percentage of the overall tax burden than they do under the current progressive tax system, which taxes a higher percentage of wealthy people's income.

As this debate rages on at the national level, several states have already turned to the flat tax. Illinois, for example, charges a flat 5 percent state income tax. That means that regardless of the amount of money earned, all income is taxed at 5 percent. In Iowa, a 2013 proposal would have allowed residents the option of paying a flat 4.5 percent tax rate or staying with the current system that allows deductions. This bill did not pass. In October 2014, a measure was introduced into the Iowa Senate advocating a 23 percent flat tax. The Democrat-controlled body did not call the proposal for a vote, but it is predicted that flat taxes will be a key item in the 2015 legislative session in Iowa if Republican majorities win the state House and Senate.

Elsewhere, North Carolina Republican Governor Pat McCrory signed into law a modified flat tax system in 2013. The governor described the change as an opportunity to recruit new businesses to the state and to create jobs. Under the North Carolina bill, the individual income tax rate will be 5.8 percent in 2014 and fall to 5.75 percent in 2015. It is not, however, a pure flat tax—individuals are still required to pay taxes on investments and it still allows several tax breaks (Sadahi 2013). Other states like California use the flat tax for corporations but a progressive income tax for individuals.

As of 2015, seven states maintain flat tax systems for personal income: Colorado (4.63 percent), Illinois (5 percent), Indiana (3.4 percent), Massachusetts (5.3 percent), Michigan (4.35 percent), Pennsylvania (3.07 percent), and Utah (5 percent). Complicating the scene in some of these states is that the flat tax does not bring in enough revenue to cover pension obligations. This had led to underfunded pension systems in states like Illinois, which in turn has prompted accusations that these states are taking retirement income from pensioners or pushing their financial obligations onto future generations.

Democrats on the Flat Tax

The majority of current Democrats stand in opposition to the flat tax. In a 2011 *Wall Street Journal* poll, for example, Democrats opposed the flat tax by a wide margin, 52 percent to 19 percent (Brady and Frisby 2011). A poll conducted by *Princeton Survey Research Associates* in March 2014 found that self-identified Democrats are more likely to oppose the flat tax (43 percent) compared to Republicans (29 percent) and Independents (29 percent) (Ekins 2014).

Democrats see the flat tax as punishing the poor because the percentage of the tax represents much more of their usable income. For example, if you make $1,000 and there is a flat tax of 6 percent, that leaves you with $940 for living expenses. If you make $10,000, the flat tax leaves you $9,400 for living expenses. Obviously, the person that makes more is not as affected by the tax because they have so much more disposable income left after taxes.

Another conviction held by many Democrats is that the flat tax is a cynical "backdoor" maneuver by Republicans to drastically cut social services and other government programs because under such a system, working-class and middle-class taxpayers would face higher taxes to fund the federal government at current levels. Big cuts would be the only politically realistic option under such a scenario.

Democrats also argue that enforcing a flat tax is actually more complicated than it initially appears. For example, in the case of wealthier taxpayers, who often get a substantial portion of their money from stock dividends or capital gains, it is difficult to pinpoint precisely when that income occurs and thus when it should be taxed. Businesses, too, point out that they need some mechanism in the tax code that will allow them to deduct their expenses to be fairly taxed on their actual profits. There is also the complex question of how to deal with the tax components of imports and exports under a flat tax system. Another criticism by Democrats is that one uniform tax rate prevents the government from using tax advantages as incentives to engage in socially positive behavior, as is currently done with the home ownership mortgage deduction. Wielding these various arguments, Democrats have thus far warded off the various flat tax proposals made by Republican political leaders.

Not all Democrats, however, oppose the flat tax. Karen Bass, the Democratic Speaker of the House in California, pushed a recommendation in 2013 that the state adopt a flat income tax. According to Joe Mathews of the nonpartisan New America Foundation, Bass and some other liberal-leaning California legislators realized "they need a tax base that doesn't count on a large slice of revenue from taxes on a relatively small number of wealthy residents who can flee the state or who are themselves vulnerable to losing a substantial portion of income in a recession" (Mathews 2009). The plan favored replacing the six tax brackets with a single flat tax. The plan would also eliminate corporate and sales taxes and replace them with a business net receipt tax. The mainstream of the state's Democratic Party argues that the tax system needs to be progressive to protect low- and middle-income families and people on fixed incomes.

Some advocates of a flat tax have tried to alleviate such concerns. They insist that a system could be crafted that would not increase the financial burden of lower-income families. For example, Rabushka proposed that the flat tax would not apply to family incomes of less than $16,000. An appropriate threshold for a flat tax, or reduced tax rates for lower incomes, must be determined.

During his time in office, President Obama has expressed support for streamlining and simplifying the U.S. tax code, but he has consistently opposed the flat tax, which he claims has severe shortcomings. In a 2010 speech in Buffalo, for example, he discussed a hypothetical flat tax of 10 percent. "That means [billionaire] Warren Buffett is paying 10 percent. It means the construction worker is paying 10 percent. It means somebody who has got a minimum-wage job is paying 10 percent. And the question is does that 10 percent take a bigger bite out of the cashier at the supermarket than it does out of Warren Buffett? Because she is paying more of her income in food and rent and just basic necessities, and so does it make sense for Warren Buffett to be paying a little bit more? . . . to have a flat tax that was revenue-neutral, that didn't add to the deficit, it'd have to be a pretty substantial tax, but it would mean a huge tax break for Warren Buffett. And so the question is, is there a way of achieving simplification, but still having some element of progressivity and some element of fairness in the tax system? That's part of what makes it complicated" (Obama 2010).

Republicans on the Flat Tax

In 2011, several Republicans proposed a flat tax in the U.S. House of Representatives. Labeled the "Freedom Flat Tax Act," H.R. bill 1040 would have amended the Internal Revenue Code to authorize an individual or a person engaged in business activity to make an irrevocable election to be subject to a flat tax (in lieu of the existing tax provisions) of 19 percent for the first two years after such an election was made, and 17 percent thereafter. The bill also included language to require a two-thirds vote of the House of Representatives or the Senate to increase the aforementioned flat tax rate, or to reduce the standard deductions or business-related deductions allowed by the act. It was referred to the Committee on Ways and Means and to the Rules Committee but the 112th Congress adjourned before taking action on the bill. The Freedom Flat Tax Act was reintroduced in the 113th Congress as well, but as of November 2014 it awaited action from the House Rules Committee.

The murky prospects of the Freedom Flat Tax Act in the GOP-controlled House, however, have been largely a reflection of political realities rather than diminished party enthusiasm for a flat tax. Republicans know that such an act would not pass a Democrat-controlled Senate or be accepted by Obama, so there is little incentive to press for House passage.

Mitt Romney and the Flat Tax

Republican Mitt Romney was a strong opponent of the flat tax in 1996. A supporter of eventual Republican nominee Bob Dole, Romney made several arguments against the flat tax proposals of fellow candidate Steve Forbes. Romney thought the tax relief the flat tax provided to the wealthy by the Forbes plan couldn't be justified—politically or substantively. Romney told the *Boston Globe* that "the problem with the Forbes flat tax is that it isn't flat at all—it's a zero tax on the wealthy and a 17 percent tax on working Americans . . . The Forbes flat tax is a gimmick, a phony, and not what it pretends to be. . . . There are a number of flat tax proposals around that would be better than the tax system we have now. But if all we talk about is the Steve Forbes proposal we'll just cement in people's minds the notion that the Republican Party is the party of the rich. . . . The middle class should be the priority for a tax cut. Those are the people struggling to pay college tuitions and make families work."

When Romney ran for president in 2012, Democrats accused him of flip-flopping on the flat tax after the candidate said that the flat tax "has positive features." Defenders of Romney note, however, that Romney added that whatever other merits a flat tax might have, "you have to make sure it doesn't raise taxes on middle income Americans." According to *Slate*'s John Dickerson, Romney has actually been consistent on the flat tax since 1996, when he slammed the Forbes flat tax scheme. In Romney's view, wrote Dickerson, "taxes should be flat but without hurting the middle class, which means retaining some of the trinkets and loopholes in the current code, such as the mortgage interest deduction. Flat-tax purists say that's not really a flat tax, which is why Romney and others talk about a 'flatter tax.'"

Sources

Dickerson, John. 1995. "Flip-Flop Flopped: Actually, Mitt Romney Hasn't Changed His Mind about the Flat Tax." *Slate.com,* August 12. http://www.slate.com/articles/news_and_politics/politics/2011/10/mitt_romney_on_the_flat_tax_he_s_not_a_flip_flopper_.html.

Kaczynski, Andrew. 1995. "When Concerned Citizen Mitt Romney Hated the Flat Tax." *Buzzfeed*, August 12. http://www.buzzfeed.com/andrewkaczynski/when-concerned-citizen-mitt-romney-hated-the-flat.

Nonetheless, many Republicans remain sympathetic to flat tax goals. In 2012, for example, the official GOP platform unveiled by the Republican National Committee (RNC) called for comprehensive tax reform that would create a "simpler, transparent, flatter, and fairer" system. The RNC emphasized the party's widely held belief that the government's role should be limited and that government spending needed to be reduced. So while the GOP's official party platform did not specifically call for the implementation of a flat tax, it did advocate for reforms compatible with flat tax goals: "We reject the use of taxation to redistribute income, fund unnecessary or ineffective programs, or foster the crony capitalism that corrupts both politicians and corporations."

The GOP's 2012 platform also emphasized tax simplification, another pillar of the flat tax argument. "The current IRS code is like a patchwork quilt, stitched together over time from mismatched pieces, and is beyond the comprehension of the average citizen," stated the platform. This statement takes advantage of the fact that there exists considerable popular appeal to the idea of replacing thousands of pages of the current U.S. tax code, which multiply in number each year to add new tax treatments or exemptions for special interests and require armies of lawyers and accountants to interpret. This is a policy goal, according to Republicans, that differentiates them from their Democratic counterparts.

In light of these views, conservative enthusiasm for a flat tax system seems unlikely to dissipate any time soon. In 2014, for instance, Republican businessman (and 1996 presidential candidate) Steve Forbes wrote that "the federal tax code is beyond redemption. We should kill it and institute a flat tax. My flat-tax proposal calls for a 17 percent tax rate for all, with generous deductions for individuals and families (a family of four would owe no federal income tax on their first $46,000). And that's it—no tax on savings and no death tax. The federal corporate tax rate would be dropped to 17 percent, and capital investments would be expensed immediately" (Forbes 2014).

Even among flat tax enthusiasts, however, broad disagreements exist about where the flat tax should be set. Republican Senator Rand Paul of Kentucky asserted that, "the Church never asked for more than 10%. I don't understand why the government should get any more" (Paul 2014). Paul argued that under his flat tax plan, the tax system would be greatly simplified. Everyone would just record their income, multiply by 10 percent and send their tax to the federal government on a postcard. If the resulting revenue did not cover the cost of government services, he would reduce the size of government. "According to the IRS, individuals and businesses spend more than 1.6 billion hours a year complying with the filing requirements and responding to filings or audits," said Paul. "This time spent complying with tax laws is equivalent to the work put in by three million full-time workers and costs the economy hundreds of billions of dollars annually" (Paul 2014).

Self-proclaimed Tea Party members, a key constituency of the Republican base, are more supportive of the flat tax than are Republicans in general. They see the flat tax as an opportunity for wealthy Americans to save money and to cut back on the size of government. They generally subscribe to the belief that lower taxes will spur increased economic activity and hence an increase in overall revenue, a central tenet of so-called Reaganomics.

Nancy S. Lind

Further Reading

Armey, Dick. 1995. "United We Stand Conference." August 12. Accessed October 17, 2014. http://www.ontheissues.org/Tx/Dick_Armey_Tax_Reform.htm.

Brady, David, and Tammy Frisby. 2014. "Do Americans Favor a Flat Tax." Accessed October 22. http://www.hoover.org/research/do-americans-favor-flat-tax.

Cherry, Matt. 2011. "America's History with the Flat Tax." *CNN Radio*. November 21. Accessed October 24, 2014. http://politicalticker.blogs.cnn.com/2011/11/21/americas -history-with-the-flat-tax/.

Dickerson, John. 2011. "Flip-Flop Flopped: Actually, Mitt Romney Hasn't Changed His Mind about the Flat Tax." *Slate.com*, October 24. Accessed October 28, 2014. http:// www.slate.com/articles/news_and_politics/politics/2011/10/mitt_romney_on_the_flat _tax_he_s_not_a_flip_flopper_.html.

Ekins, Emily. 2014. "62 Percent of Americans Say They Favor a Flat Tax." *Reason.com*, April 15. Accessed October 19, 2014. http://reason.com/poll/2014/04/15/62-percent -of-americans-say-they-favor-a.

Forbes, Steve. 2014. "The Tax Code: Make It Flat." *Forbes*. March 7. Accessed October 27. http://www.forbes.com/sites/steveforbes/2014/03/07/the-tax-code-make-it-flat/.

Gale, William. 1996. "Business Taxes and the Flat Tax." Brookings Institute. March 7. Accessed October 27, 2014. http://www.brookings.edu/research/opinions/1996/03/07taxes-gale.

Hall, Robert, and Alvin Rabushka. 1983. *Low Tax, Flat Tax, Simple Tax*. New York: McGraw-Hill.

Kaczynski, Andrew. 2012. "When Concerned Citizen Mitt Romney Hated the Flat Tax." *Buzzfeed.com*. January 19. Accessed October 28, 2014. http://www.buzzfeed.com /andrewkaczynski/when-concerned-citizen-mitt-romney-hated-the-flat.

Mathews, Joe. 2009. "Democrats for a Flat Tax." *Wall Street Journal*. July 11,. Accessed October 25, 2014. http://newamerica.net/publications/articles/2009/democrats_flat _tax_15711.

Obama, Barack. 2010. "Remarks by the President on the Economy." WhiteHouse.gov. May 10. Accessed October 28, 2014. http://www.whitehouse.gov/the-press-office/.

Paul, Rand. 2014. "Expanding Economic Opportunity." Accessed October 23. http://www .paul.senate.gov/?p=issue&id=57.

Sadahi, Jeanne. 2013. "North Carolina's Republican tax experiment." *CNN Money*. August 8. Accessed October 22, 2014. http://money.cnn.com/2013/08/08/pf/taxes/tax-reform -north-carolina/index.html.

Scherer, Ron. 2011. "Which GOP Flat Tax Plan Is Fairest of them all?" *The Christian Science Monitor*, October 26. Accessed October 23, 2014. http://www.csmonitor.com/USA /Politics/2011/1026/Which-GOP-flat-tax-plan-is-fairest-of-them-all.

Williams, T. Christopher. 2011. "Rand Paul on Flat Tax: The Church Never Asked for More than 10%." *RepublicanRedefined.com*, April 15. Accessed October 23, 2014. republicanredefined.com/2011/04/15/rand-paul-on-flat-tax-the-church-never-asked -for-more-than-10/.

Food Stamps/SNAP

At a Glance

The food stamp program, now known as Supplemental Nutrition Assistance Program (SNAP), provides millions of Americans with access to food they otherwise could not afford. It is the largest and most expensive food assistance program in the United States ("Supplemental Nutrition Assistance Program: Overview" 2014) and is a hotly contested issue between Democrats and Republicans.

Democrats believe that SNAP is an important safety net that allows individuals who lack a stable source of food to feed themselves and their families during times of economic hardship. They tend to believe that the focus of the program should remain broad to help as many people in need as possible, but they have made recent concessions that indicate they have become concerned with the sudden increases in cost. Democrats tend to believe that the program should be maintained to the extent possible, even while making cuts to the program to keep it manageable.

Republicans assert that any successful welfare program must be targeted at helping only those who are truly in need. It must also focus not only on providing benefits but also on helping people get back on their feet and off public assistance. As a result, Republicans argue that SNAP should limit who receives benefits and that benefits be tied to work requirements. They argue that this would help to ensure that nutritional aid gets to those who need it most, but prevent people from becoming dependent on this aid. This would help keep costs down in a program Republicans feel costs far too much.

Many Republicans . . .

- Say that SNAP benefits should be restricted to only those who absolutely need it
- Support tying SNAP benefits to work requirements
- Support cuts to the SNAP budget

Many Democrats . . .

- Argue that SNAP provides an important safety net
- Feel that SNAP eligibility requirements should be broad
- Oppose cuts to the SNAP budget

———————

Overview

The SNAP program is a central feature in the U.S. welfare system. In 2014 alone, it provided a nutritional safety net to over 46 million disadvantaged Americans, allowing them a level of nutrition they otherwise would not have been able to achieve. Given the high number of people receiving SNAP assistance, the program requires billions of dollars in federal funding and has become a contentious issue between Democrats and Republicans.

The first food stamp program began in 1939 and is largely credited to then Secretary of Agriculture Henry Wallace and Milo Perkins, the program's first administrator. The program was created in response to high unemployment rates and widespread poverty that was commonplace in America as a result of the Great Depression. The food stamp program was designed to get surplus food products produced on American farms to those in need of them elsewhere in the country. The program had what is called a purchase requirement that meant that people had to first buy into the program before they could receive benefits from it. Though successful, the program eventually came to an end in 1943 when the conditions that gave rise to it receded.

It would be another 20 years before a permanent food stamp program was established. In the 1960s, the rise of the Civil Rights Movement as well as publication of Michael Harrington's, *The Other America*, a widely read book detailing the prevalence of poverty in American society, the issue of poverty once more took center stage in American politics (Matthews 2014). In an effort to address it, the Johnson Administration launched an anti-poverty initiative, "The War on Poverty," that eventually led to the establishment of a variety of welfare programs including the Food Stamp Act of 1964 that established a permanent food stamp program. Interestingly, the Food Stamp Act was passed as part of the Farm Bill. This was done to secure the support of congressmen located in urban districts, who favored the Food Stamp Act as part of farm legislation they otherwise might have voted against (Weiner 2013). Since then, the Farm Bill and the Food Stamp Act have been linked.

The new program was to be much larger in scope than its predecessor 20 years earlier. While the first food stamp program only reached about half the counties in the United States, the new program was to be nationwide. It was to be administered by the states, which would be responsible for setting up the infrastructure needed for the program to operate at the state level, while the federal government would provide the majority of funding. Any person meeting federal and state qualifications would be able to acquire food stamps by paying "an amount commensurate with their normal expenditures for food and receiving an amount of food stamps representing an opportunity . . . to obtain a low-cost nutritionally adequate diet" ("Supplemental Nutrition Assistance Program: A Short History" 2014). In other words, just like the first program, this one also had a purchase requirement. Food stamps were not meant to fully cover an individual's food expenses but rather only supplement them.

Over the next few years the program grew in both size and cost and by 1974 the food stamp program was operating nationwide. It was during this time that the current debate over the program began to take root. This debate centered around three key issues. The first issue was program accessibility: who should receive food assistance and who should not? The second issue concerned how the program was administered: how much freedom should states have in deciding how to run their individual programs? How can the program be made more efficient in getting assistance to those who need it while cutting down on fraudulent activity? The final issue concerned the cost of the program: how much money should be spent on food stamps?

A simplified analysis of food stamp legislation from 1970 to the modern day reveals legislative attempts to address these questions. For example, in 1977, an effort was made to expand accessibility to the program. The Food Stamp Act of 1977 removed the purchase requirement and a month later participation increased by 1.5 million people. However, in the 1990s the question of accessibility was revisited and this time accessibility was restricted. This changed again in the early 2000s when program accessibility was expanded. The analysis reveals legislators constantly revisiting the issue of accessibility. Administration and funding were also reevaluated in a similar manner.

While our current food stamp program may look very different from the one established in 1964—the old name has been thrown out in favor of a new hip one and paper stamps have been replaced with an electronic system—the same questions that were debated 50 years ago are still debated today and they continue to shape food stamp policy.

Democrats on Food Stamps/SNAP

The Democrats tend to view SNAP as an important safety net to keep people who are in poverty from going hungry during tough economic times. Democrats have historically advocated maintaining or increasing spending on social programs such as SNAP. Democrats argue that significant reductions in the food stamp program will prevent families from maintaining consistent access to adequate food. Advocates for SNAP claim that hunger is often a hidden problem, affecting primarily working poor families, children, and the disabled. Many working class families have to skip meals and ration food to make ends meet, and benefits from food stamps typically only last for two weeks of the month (Cass and Jalonick 2013).

The Democratic Party Platform proclaims that there is far too much poverty in the United States, and that it is the government's responsibility to expand social welfare programs such as the SNAP program. They profess that SNAP allows the impoverished to make sure they put enough food on the table, which will allow them to pursue better opportunities (Democratic National Committee 2012).

Democrats have worked to expand the program by lowering the eligibility hurdle to allow more people to participate during tough economic times when unemployment rises. They supported wide expansions to SNAP during the economic hardships of 2002 and 2008, which allowed many more Americans to participate by opening the program to individuals who do not have children or dependents, allowing people living in the United States but who are not citizens to receive benefits, and reducing the stigma behind paying for food with food stamps by creating a system where beneficiaries can pay with a debit card.

SNAP has become increasingly controversial in recent years due to its increased cost. With the program expansions in 2002 and 2008, and the challenges that the Great Recession in 2008 presented, the number of people claiming SNAP benefits has increased so markedly that the cost of the program has doubled. As a result of this, Democrats have battled Republicans in an attempt to minimize cuts to the program (Resnikoff 2014).

The American Recovery and Reinvestment Act of 2009, passed by Democrats and signed by President Obama to mitigate the damage of the Recession, allowed

---

A Progressive Defense of Expanding SNAP during the Great Recession

Liberal groups and lawmakers strongly defended the decision by the Obama administration to expand the federal food stamp program in response to the Great Recession. Here is a representative assessment of SNAP from Stacy Dean, vice president for Food Assistance Policy with the progressive Center on Budget and Policy Priorities:

> What's disturbing is that so many Americans are poor, not that the share that receive food assistance is about the same as the share who live in poverty. SNAP has grown substantially in recent years. But that is primarily because of the deepest economic downturn since the Depression, and because—as a result of bipartisan reforms—the program does much better than it used to in reaching people eligible for the program, especially the working poor.

Source

Dean, Stacy. 2012. "Opposing View: Don't Cut Food Assistance." *USA Today*, July 4. Accessed September 17. http://usatoday30.usatoday.com/news/opinion/story/2012-07-04/food-stamps-SNAP-deficit/56020104/1.

many states to opt out of many of the requirements that are normally in place for the program. This increased the cost of the SNAP, as many who would not otherwise be eligible have suddenly been allowed to apply for benefits.

Recently, the Democrats reluctantly conceded to cuts in SNAP aid amid controversy that it has become too expensive. In 2013, a stimulus bill was allowed to expire that reduced SNAP benefits by approximately 5 percent. A family receiving $350 worth of benefits could see their monthly benefits decrease by $29 (Stolber 2013).

Democrats and Republicans jointly cut $8.7 billion from SNAP in a bill passed in 2014. The cut affects approximately 850,000 households and will reduce these households' food budgets by about $90 per month. These savings were obtained by eliminating state "Heat and Eat" policies. SNAP allows for extra benefits if the recipient also has to pay to heat their home in winter months. Some states were allowing their residents to claim a one dollar heating bill, even if there was no true heating bill, so that they could claim the additional benefit. The 2014 Farm Bill had the support of many Democrats, but they were also unwilling to make further cuts to the program that the Republicans had requested. The households affected by these changes could lose $90 a month on average (Resnikoff 2014).

Automatic cuts to SNAP eligibility and funding are also being allowed to occur, as the United States recovers from the Great Recession. The lowered requirements offered by the American Recovery and Reinvestment Act no longer apply to many states, and many governors are not opting in. Additionally, automatic cuts will be taking place in coming years.

Republicans on Food Stamps

To understand the Republican position on SNAP it is necessary to examine Republican views on welfare programs overall. Republicans often argue that welfare programs are wasteful and that far too much money is thrown into programs that only serve to breed dependency on government handouts. The Republican platform maintains that the success of a welfare program should not be measured in terms of how much money is spent to help the poor, but rather in how many of those in poverty are able to achieve economic independence (Republican National Committee 2012). Toward this end, the GOP argues that welfare programs should only give temporary assistance to those individuals who truly need it.

This underlying attitude toward welfare is reflected in the Republican position regarding SNAP. Republicans believe that SNAP assistance should be directed toward individuals who actually require it, not simply want it. Therefore, accessibility to the program should be restricted. For example, individuals with no children who are not looking for work should not be eligible to receive benefits. In addition, Republicans often push for work requirements to be tied to any assistance. Republicans argue that requirements like these help get people off SNAP assistance, both empowering those on the program and cutting program costs. On the basis of these positions Republicans view many parts of SNAP as wasteful and often advocate cutting funding for the program.

Some of the more recent legislation passed regarding SNAP clearly represents these themes in the Republican position. The Personal Responsibility and Work Opportunities Reconciliation Act of 1996 (PRWORA), a major overhaul of the welfare system and a "bill largely written on Republican terms" (Harris and Yang 1996) restricted legal immigrants from participating in the program and set limits on how long someone could be on the program if they were not actively looking for work or enrolled in a work program. The desire to restrict accessibility to the program as well as the provision of incentives for those wishing to receive benefits to seek work is evident.

Additional evidence of the above themes in the Republican position on food stamps is demonstrated by Republican President George W. Bush's approval of a 2002 law that once again restored benefits to legal immigrants, which resulted in his administration coming under attack by congressional Republicans who criticized the move. House Republicans offered their own proposal that would have only restored benefits to immigrants that could show they had worked in the U.S. for five years. The rationale given for this was that without the five-year work stipulation, immigrants would take advantage of the system and have reduced incentives to work (Barrett 2002). Once again, the House bill represented a desire to restrict access to the program as well as a Republican concern that a program that was too accessible might lead to people growing dependent on public assistance.

More recently in 2013 when the renewal of the Food Stamp Act again came up for debate, the themes of restricted access and a push for work requirements surfaced again in the Republican position, although this time the debate also included funding cuts. In response to the rising cost of SNAP, Republicans repeatedly backed

---

USA Today Endorses Cuts to SNAP

On July 4, 2012, the editorial board of USA Today expressed agreement with conservative Republican complaints about the size and scope of America's SNAP program, making special note of the fact that the number of people enrolled in the program had jumped from 17 million in 2000 to 46 million in 2012:

> People in need obviously should not be left without food. But numbers like these erode people's faith in the fairness of government anti-poverty programs. These numbers . . . have come about at a time when Americans—particularly those on the lower-income rungs—are struggling with obesity.

Source

USA Today Editorial Board. 2012. "Food Stamps Expansion Driven by Politics." USA Today, July 4. Accessed September 17, 2015. http://usatoday30.usatoday.com/news/opinion/editorials/story/2012-07-04/SNAP-farm-bill-food-stamps/56020262/1.

legislation to drastically cut spending. In 2013 House Republicans voted to cut the SNAP budget by $40 billion and attempted to separate the legislation regarding the program from the rest of the Farm Bill. The hope was that a bill on SNAP alone, rather than farm subsidies and SNAP, would fail. In addition to budget cuts, the Republican bill also placed stricter work requirements on adults without children and limited the length of time individuals could stay on the program (Nixon 2013). Though this bill failed to pass given heavy opposition to it in the Senate and by President Obama, the bill that was passed in 2014 nonetheless contained substantial funding cuts. The themes of the Republican position toward SNAP were contained in the House bill with a focus on stricter work requirements, cuts in funding, and limits on the access of some individuals, namely adults with no dependent children, to program benefits. This is largely consistent with the Republican position in 1996 and 2002.

These examples demonstrate that the Republican position on SNAP is largely formed by their views toward welfare programs in general. Access to a welfare program should be limited to only those who need it most. Aside from providing limited assistance, program funding should also be expended on initiatives that empower people and get them off public assistance. Finally, Republicans tend to believe that welfare programs overall cost too much and there should be cuts in these programs. These themes are present in recent Republican-backed food stamp legislation, and are likely to resurface in political debates over SNAP in the foreseeable future.

Christopher Farrer and
Jason Hochstatter

Further Reading

Barrett, Ted. 2002. "House GOP at Odds with Bush on Food Stamps Issue." CNN. April 23. http://www.cnn.com/2002/ALLPOLITICS/04/23/congress.foodstamps/index.html.

Cass, Connie, and Mary Clare Jalonick. 2013. "Food Stamps Again a Vivid Symbol in Poverty debate." *USA Today*, September 21. Accessed September 14, 2015. http://www.usatoday.com/story/money/personalfinance/2013/09/21/food-stamps-poverty/2847719/.

DeHaven, Tad. 2015. "Food Stamps Growth Has Bipartisan Roots." *Cato Institute*. Accessed September 15. http://www.cato.org/blog/food-stamps-growth-has-bipartisan-roots.

Democratic National Committee. 2012. "Moving America Forward: 2012 Democratic Platform." Accessed October 23, 2015. https://www.democrats.org/party-platform.

"Food Stamps Expansion Driven by Politics." 2012. *USA Today*, July 4. Accessed September 15, 2015. http://usatoday30.usatoday.com/news/opinion/editorials/story/2012-07-04/SNAP-farm-bill-food-stamps/56020262/1.

Harris, John F., and John E. Yang. 1996. "Clinton to Sign Bill Overhauling Welfare." *Washington Post*, August 1. Accessed September 15, 2015. https://www.washingtonpost.com/wp-srv/politics/special/welfare/stories/wf080196.htm.

Herszenhorn, David M., and David Stout. 2008. "Defying President Bush, Senate Passes Farm Bill." *New York Times*, May 15. Accessed September 15, 2015. http://www.nytimes.com/2008/05/15/washington/15cnd-farm.html?_r=0.

Matthews, Dylan. 2014. "Everything You Need to Know About the War on Poverty." *Washington Post*, January 8. Accessed April 20, 2016. http://www.washingtonpost.com/news/wonkblog/wp/2014/01/08/everything-you-need-to-know-about-the-war-on-poverty/.

Nixon, Ron. 2013. "House Republicans Pass Deep Cuts in Food Stamps." *New York Times*, September 19. Accessed July 16, 2014. http://www.nytimes.com/2013/09/20/us/politics/house-passes-bill-cutting-40-billion-from-food-stamps.html.

"Opposing View: Don't Cut Food Assistance." 2012. *USA Today*, July 4. Accessed September 17, 2015. http://usatoday30.usatoday.com/news/opinion/story/2012-07-04/food-stamps-SNAP-deficit/56020104/1.

Republican National Committee. 2012. "We Believe in America—Renewing American Values: 2012 Republican Platform." *GOP.com*. Accessed November 11, 2015. https://www.gop.com/platform/renewing-american-values/.

Resnikoff, Ned. 2015. "Food stamp benefit cut may force a million people into 'serious hardship.'" *Al Jazeera*, January 6. Accessed September 15, 2015. http://america.aljazeera.com/articles/2015/1/6/report-one-millionpeoplecouldlosefoodstampbenefitsinnextyear.html.

Resnikoff, Ned. 2014. "Bipartisan Farm Bill Deal to Cut over $8 billion in Food Stamps." *MSNBC*. January 28. Accessed August 8, 2015. http://www.msnbc.com/msnbc/congress-set-cut-billions-food-stamps.

"SNAP—Statewide Able Bodied Adults Without Dependent (ABAWD) Waivers Effective Immediately for Eligible States." 2009. U.S. Department of Agriculture. February 25. Accessed September 15, 2015. http://www.fns.usda.gov/sites/default/files/022509.pdf.

Stolber, Sheryl Gay. 2013. "On the Edge of Poverty, at the Center of a Debate on Food Stamps." *New York Times*, September 4. Accessed October 23, 2015. http://www.nytimes.com/2013/09/05/us/as-debate-reopens-food-stamp-recipients-continue-to-squeeze.html?_r=0.

"Supplemental Nutritional Assistance Program (SNAP): National Level Annual Summary." 2015. U.S. Department of Agriculture. Last Modified August 7. Accessed October 4, 2015. http://www.fns.usda.gov/pd/supplemental-nutrition-assistance-program-snap.

"Supplemental Nutrition Assistance Program (SNAP): Overview." 2014. U.S. Department of Agriculture Economic Research Service. Last modified March 10. Accessed November 1, 2015. http://www.ers.usda.gov/topics/food-nutrition-assistance/supplemental-nutrition-assistance-program-%28snap%29.aspx.

"Supplemental Nutrition Assistance Program (SNAP): A Short History." 2014. U.S. Department of Agriculture. Last modified November 20. Accessed November 11, 2015. http://www.fns.usda.gov/snap/short-history-snap.

Weiner, Rachel. 2013. "The Fight over Food Stamps Explained." *Washington Post*, July 11. Accessed November 17, 2015. http://www.washingtonpost.com/news/the-fix/wp/2013/07/11/the-fight-over-food-stamps-explained.

Free Trade

At a Glance

U.S. economic history shows that for many years, the Republican Party championed highly protectionist policies by building walls of tariff through presidential and congressional acts (Lighthizer 2008). The Republican Party's dominance of presidential and congressional politics provided the party a platform to adopt protectionist policies culminating in the infamous Smoot-Hawley tariff of 1930. However, Republicans in the modern era have shed their long-held protectionist positions to embrace free trade (Nzelibe 2014).

For most of the 20th century, the Democratic Party was more supportive of free trade as it branded itself the party of prosperity, which the party argues could be further achieved by promoting open markets. By the late 1960s, and especially during the 1970s and 1980s, Democrats had moved toward protectionism because free trade and globalization have failed to deliver the material benefits to ordinary Americans, and particularly to American workers, one of the party's major constituencies (Cassidy 2015). More recently, Democrats have shown an inclination to support trade more than Republicans (Pew Research Center 2015).

Many Republicans . . .

- Promote free trade, with the U.S. setting the standards
- Favor the restoration of presidential Trade Promotion Authority
- Support imposing countervailing duties against China on intellectual property and currency violations
- Assert that free trade practices give America a competitive advantage in the global economy

Many Democrats . . .

- Support opening new markets to American products with new trade agreements
- Advocate for the removal of barriers to free, fair, and balanced trade

- Support investigation into China's workers' abuses and currency manipulation
- Favor incorporating measures to protect the environment and workers' rights into trade agreements

———————————

Overview

Any general review of free trade policy in the United States should at the onset clarify that, within the limits imposed by popular sentiments and political needs, both parties have had difficulty maintaining a consistent position on free trade.

An examination of U.S. trade policy following the passage of the 1934 Reciprocal Trade Agreements Act (RTAA) documents the course of U.S. efforts to increase trade openness. The goal of the RTAA as its opening line stated was "for the purpose of expanding foreign markets for the producers of the United States" (Berglund 1935). The RTAA permitted the President to conclude bilateral, reciprocal trade agreements with a view toward reducing the tariffs of mutual interest to the United States and specific trade partners (United States International Trade Commission, n.d.).

Bedeviled by soaring unemployment, plummeting economic activity, widespread fears about the future, and other fallout from the Great Depression, the Franklin Roosevelt administration saw free trade as an important component of its broad efforts to revive the global economy and create good jobs for all Americans. During the Roosevelt administration, congressional Democrats made tremendous efforts to eliminate protectionism; an effort that would ultimately not only break down the Smoot-Hawley Tariff, but would also pave the way for the creation of the multilateral global economy (Woolner 2011). With the signing of the RTAA into law, FDR saw the opening up of the world's economy as a positive measure that would help alleviate poverty, improve the lives of workers, reduce tensions among nations, and help usher in a new age of peace and prosperity. Inspired by this vision, the Roosevelt administration also championed the 1944 Bretton Woods Accords, which set up the International Monetary Fund, and the World Bank.

In seeking to avoid economic inequities that some have argued contributed to the beginning of World War II, Democratic President Truman sought to promote broad international economic collaboration through the 1941 Atlantic Charter and other economic policies of his administration. In calling for the renewal of the RTAA in 1945, President Truman argued that the purpose of the whole effort was to eliminate economic warfare, to make practical international co-operation effective on as many fronts as possible, and to lay the economic basis for the secure and peaceful world (Jackson 1969).

In furtherance of the potential of free trade to create and sustain employment in the U.S., and lay groundwork for peace around the world, Republican President Dwight Eisenhower pushed for the extension of the RTAA in 1958. Other aspects of his administration's trade policies included the revision of customs regulations to remove procedural obstacles to profitable trade; doing whatever government properly can to encourage the flow of private American investment abroad; and receiving from the rest of the world, in equitable exchange for what the U.S. supplies, greater amounts of raw materials which the country did not have in adequate quantities.

For his part, President John F. Kennedy linked the advancement of freedom with trade, inspiring the Kennedy Round of world trade talks, which led to significant tariff cuts and trade expansion. "A vital expanding economy in the free world is a strong counter to the threat of the world Communist movement," said Kennedy after signing the 1962 Trade Expansion Act. Democratic President Johnson believed that a world without war could be achieved through the free movement of men, goods, and ideas across every border and every boundary. To advance this vision, he urged Congress to extend the RTAA that would give U.S. trading partners competitive access to U.S. markets, while doing the same for the United States.

President Nixon's rise to power coincided with the economic rise of Japan and Germany, with Japan showing more nationalist behavior with a series of trade barriers against the United States. Rather than follow suit, Republican President Nixon competed with Japan with "no economic warfare." He was of the view that tariffs were just another entitlement that weakened incentives (Nixon 1992).

In his State of the Union message to Congress in 1978, President Jimmy Carter reiterated the need for fair and balance trade agreements lowering barriers to trade to enable the U.S. to increase its export potentials. And although President Ronald Reagan's position on free trade was on par with those before him, he was compelled, despite opposition from free traders, to impose import quotas on Japanese cars in 1985 to save the big three car manufacturers in the United States.

Republican President George H. W. Bush favored continued trade expansion and signing of new trade agreements but like his predecessor Reagan, he was forced to depart from his free trade principles when in 2002, he imposed tariffs of 8 to 30 percent on most steel imports for three years in an effort to shore up the long-declining domestic industry. After a flurry of international disapproval and criticism from his domestic conservative supporters, his administration began approving exemptions (Allen 2003).

Two years later, in 1994, Democratic President Bill Clinton praised the culmination of the so-called Uruguay Round, a pivotal round of multilateral trade negotiations conducted within the framework of the General Agreement on Tariffs and Trade (GATT), a major trade agreement which had been established after World War II. The Uruguay Round, negotiations for which had actually begun in 1986 under the direction of the Reagan administration, ultimately included 123 participating countries and made possible the creation of the World Trade Organization (WTO). Under the manifesto "A New Agenda for the New Decade," President Clinton made efforts to use the WTO to write new rules for the global economy.

Common Ground on Free Trade

On February 22, 1996, Senator Robert Dole, the 1996 Republican presidential nominee, made the following remarks at the Hudson Chamber of Commerce in defense of free trade and open markets:

> We can choose to leave our country with a trade system that exports jobs rather than products or we can put our trade partners on notice that free trade means their free ride is over. My friends, in each case, the choice is clear. We must choose the future rather than the past. We must free America from deficits. We must free America from unreasonable taxation. We must free America from excessive regulation. And we must insist on the freedom to compete in a fair international marketplace.
>
> By fighting for these four freedoms of economic security, we will put our economy back on track, and we will put Americans back to work.

On September 19, 2011, Thomas Daschle, former Democratic Senate majority leader, made the following remarks on how to revive U.S. trade policy in an interview at the Council on Foreign Relations.

> It's also clear that we're falling behind on trade, while other countries are pushing ahead. The only way we're going to grow this economy is to recognize that our economic strength lies not only with our own productivity, but also with our ability to apply that productivity worldwide.
>
> . . . We need to have an active trade policy, one that's focused on opening the overseas markets for a more competitive U.S. goods and services strategy, to bring the benefits of trade to more Americans with higher incomes and additional jobs.

Sources

Dole, Robert. 1996. "Remarks at Hudson Chamber of Commerce." February 22, *The American Presidency Project*. Accessed May 29, 2015. http://www.presidency.ucsb.edu/ws/?pid=85188.
Daschle, Thomas. 2011. "How to Revive U.S. Trade Policy." *Council on Foreign Relations*, September 19. Accessed May 29, 2015. http://www.cfr.org/trade/revive-us-trade-policy/p25905.

Clinton notably steered the Democratic Party toward a less-protectionist bent and worked with Republicans to secure passage of the North American Free Trade Agreement (NAFTA).

Throughout his career in politics, whether as a Democratic senator in the U.S. Congress, a candidate running for the presidency, or as president of the United States, President Barack Obama has shown strong support for free trade, but with a proviso that such agreements must be fair and contain adequate protections for the environment and workers. Along this line, he has committed to ensuring fair trade by enforcing existing trade agreements. President Obama believes any trade agreement must have real, tangible benefits for U.S. business and workers and will work to enforce the trade agreements on the books.

Republicans on Free Trade

Two polls conducted by the *Wall Street Journal* and National Broadcasting Corporation (NBC) (2007 and 2015) show much higher skepticism in Republican support for free trade. Though the Republican Party traditionally defends the principles of free trade and open markets, in the most recent poll, 36 percent of Republicans said free trade has hurt the U.S economy. This sentiment was higher in 2007, when 6 in 10 Republicans agreed with a statement that free trade has been bad for the U.S. and said they would agree with a Republican candidate who favored tougher regulations to limit foreign imports (Seib 2015). In a related poll conducted by Gallup in 2015, Republican's optimism about free trade is flat at 51 percent, while Democrats has increased slightly, to 61 percent.

At a very general level, pro-business constituencies in the Republican Party seek to build an innovative, globally competitive economy through free and fair trade. International trade, according to many in the party, has become the world's most powerful economic force, and as such proposes to act globally, regionally, and bilaterally to negotiate new trade agreements and enforce existing trade commitments. The party discusses the importance of free trade agreements to the U.S. economy since President Reagan's trailblazing pact with Israel in 1985. Against this background, the 1996 Republican Party Platform stood for a vigorous enforcement of the trade agreements the United States already had on the books. "Republicans will enforce United States trade laws, including antidumping laws, and will use the Super 301 investigations that give the President authority to challenge foreign barriers to our exports and we will use the Export Enhancement Program to boost American farm exports. To advance economic freedom, we insist that United States foreign aid, whether bilateral or through the World Bank and the International Monetary Fund promote market reforms, limit regulation, and encourage free trade" (Republican National Committee 1996).

The 2012 Republican platform emphasized a new and ambitious round of multilateral negotiations on opening markets. To achieve this goal, the party said it was committed to the restoration of presidential Trade Promotion Authority (TPA). This authority, the party argues, ensures up or down votes in Congress on any new trade agreements, without meddling by special interests. TPA was commonly referred to as Fast Track authority through the 1990s. This authority enabled the president to negotiate international trade agreements that could then be presented to Congress for approval. The most recent iteration of Trade Promotion expired in 2007. In 2015, the Obama Administration went before Congress asking for such authority to negotiate trade agreements with 11 other countries in the Pacific region (Republican National Committee 2012).

Republicans aspire for full parity in trade with China, and state they are ready to impose countervailing duties against China on intellectual property and currency manipulation to achieve it. To this end, they insist on commercial discrimination in kind; aggressively stopping the importation of counterfeit goods to the U.S.; and encouraging victimized private firms to raise legal claims in both U.S. courts and at the World Trade Organization. In addition, the Republican platform used its 2012 campaign document to address the exclusion by China of American products from government purchases and regulations and standards designed to keep out foreign competition: "the United States government will end procurement of Chinese goods and services unless China abides by the World Trade Organization Government Procurement Agreement" (Republican National Committee 2012).

By securing America's competitive advantage and preventing other countries from erecting barriers to innovation, the Republican Party's 2012 platform claimed that it would place the U.S. in a dominant trade position. Along this line, it expressed a desire to negotiate reductions in tariffs on U.S. industrial goods so that U.S. autos, heavy machinery, and textiles could make deeper inroads in foreign markets. It also proposes within this frame of action to advance Free Trade Area of the Americas to take advantage of the burgeoning markets at its doorstep. It further stated its support for a Trans-Pacific Partnership (TPP), a proposed new trade agreement that proponents say will open rapidly developing Asian markets to U.S. products (Republican National Committee 2012).

Democrats on Free Trade

Recent polling shows that the Democratic Party has a generally favorable stance toward free trade, in part because organized labor, traditionally among the most skeptical of foreign trade deals, constitute a much smaller percentage of both the Democratic base and the overall American workforce, then they were back in the union heyday of the 1950s and 1960s. In a 2015 poll conducted by the *Wall Street Journal* and NBC, only 26 percent of Democrats said free trade has hurt the country. This marks a considerable change from 2007, when a *Wall Street Journal*/NBC poll showed that 54 percent of Democratic voters said free trade agreements have hurt the United States, compared with 21 percent who said they have helped (Seib 2015). In another related poll conducted by Gallup, 61 percent of Democrats see trade more as an opportunity for economic growth than as a threat to the domestic economy from imports. For Republicans, that number is 51 percent—barely a majority (Mandel 2015).

The Democratic platform conveys a general message of using trade to strengthen the American economy and create more American jobs, while laying a foundation for democratic, equitable, and sustainable growth around the world. Accordingly, the party states that it is dedicated to designing and implementing smart, strong and fair trade policies to achieve these broad goals. The party pledges to negotiate free trade agreements that open markets for American products, while ensuring that other countries not only play by the same rules, but also agree to include enforceable international labor and environmental standards that are consistent and fair (Democratic National Committee 2012).

Along this line, President Obama signed into law new trade agreements with South Korea, Colombia, and Panama, with a commitment to reaching more agreements like the Trans-Pacific Partnership between the United States and eight countries in the Asia-Pacific region.

The Democratic platform also emphasizes the importance of knocking down barriers to free, fair, and balanced trade. "We must continue to work to lower foreign trade barriers; insist that foreign companies play by fair rules at home and abroad; strengthen rules that protect the global economy from fraud and dangerous instability; advance American commercial interests abroad; and ensure that the new global economy is directly beneficial to American working families. As we work to open new markets, we must negotiate to guarantee that all trade agreements include standards to protect children, workers, public safety, and the environment" (Democratic National Committee 2012).

The Democratic Party also states that it will review all existing trade agreements and particularly, investigate Chinese rights abuses. "We will aggressively enforce our trade agreements with a real plan that includes a complete review of all existing agreements; immediate investigation into worker's rights abuses and currency manipulation" (Democratic National Committee 2012). This benchmark will also be used to amend the North American Free Trade Agreement with Canada and Mexico so that it works better for all signatories to the agreement. The party also tends to believe in working with other countries to achieve a successful completion of the Doha Round Agreement that would increase U.S. exports.

As part of its strategy to use international trade to boost the U.S. economy, the Democratic platform states an intention to move ahead with "open skies agreements" in the Americas to expand opportunities for commercial aviation to bring people and businesses together. An open skies agreement is an arrangement under which two or more countries allow unrestricted overflight and landing rights—especially commercial aviation—to one another.

Osaore Aideyan

Further Reading

Allen, Mike. 2003. "President to Drop Tariffs on Steel, Bush Seeks to Avoid a Trade War and Its Political Fallout." *Washington Post*, December 1, p. A.

Allessi, Christopher, and Robert McMahon (eds.). 2012. "U.S. Trade Policy." *Council on Foreign Relations*. March 14. Accessed May 20, 2015. http://www.cfr.org/trade/us -trade-policy/p17859.

Bartlett, Bruce. 1998. "The Truth about Trade in History." *Cato Institute*, July 1. Accessed May 25, 2015. http://www.cato.org/publications/commentary/truth-about-trade-history.

Berglund, Abraham. 1934. "Reciprocal Trade Agreement Act of 1934," *The American Economic Review* 25 (3): 411–425.

Buchanan, Patrick. 2004. *Where the Right Went Wrong: How Neoconservatives Subverted the Reagan Revolution and Hijacked the Bush Presidency.* New York: Thomas Dunne Books.

Cassidy, John. 2015. "R.I.P., Free-Trade Treaties?" *The New Yorker,* June 16. Accessed November 10, 2015. http://www.newyorker.com/news/john-cassidy/r-i-p-free-trade-treaties.

Clinton, William Jefferson. 1996. *Between Hope and History.* New York: Random House, 1996.

Democratic National Committee. 2012. "Moving America Forward: 2012 Democratic Party Platform." *The American Presidency Project.* September 3. Accessed May 28, 2015. http://www.presidency.ucsb.edu/ws/?pid=101962.

Jackson, H. John. 1969. *World Trade and the Law of GATT.* Indianapolis: Bobbs-Merrill Co., Inc.

Lighthizer, Robert. 2008. "Grand Old Protectionists." *New York Times,* March 6. Accessed May 25, 2015. http://www.nytimes.com/2008/03/06/opinion/06lighthizer.html.

Mandel, Seth. 2015. "Is the GOP Really the Party of Free Trade? Not Exactly." *Commentary Magazine,* April 22. Accessed May 29, 2015. https://www.commentarymagazine.com/2015/04/22/is-the-gop-really-the-party-of-free-trade-not-exactly/.

Nixon, Richard M. 1992. *Seize the Moment: America's Challenge in a One-Superpower World.* New York: Simon and Shuster.

Nzelibe, Jide. 2014. "The Elusive Free Trade Constitution." *Yale Law School,* March 25. Accessed May 26, 2015. http://www.law.yale.edu/documents/pdf/LEO/leo_Nzelibe.pdf.

Pew Research Center. 2015. "Free Trade Agreements Seen as Good for U.S., But Concerns Persist." *Pew Research Center,* May 27. Accessed November 10, 2015. http://www.people-press.org/2015/05/27/free-trade-agreements-seen-as-good-for-u-s-but-concerns-persist/.

Republican National Committee. 1996. "Republican Party Platform of 1996." *The American Presidency Project.* August 12. Accessed May 28, 2015. http://www.presidency.ucsb.edu/ws/?pid=25848.

Republican National Committee. 2012. "We Believe in America: 2012 Republican Platform." Accessed May 11, 2015. https://cdn.gop.com/docs/2012GOPPlatform.pdf.

Seib, Jerry. 2015. "Populist Sentiment Against Free Trade Found in Both Parties." *Wall Street Journal,* May 12. Accessed May 20, 2015. http://blogs.wsj.com/washwire/2015/05/12/populist-sentiment-against-free-trade-found-in-both-parties-wsjnbc-news-poll/.

United States International Trade Commission. 2015. "U.S. Trade Policy Since 1934." In *History of the U.S. Trade Policy Since 1934.* United States International Trade Commission website. Accessed May 10. http://www.usitc.gov/publications/332/us_trade_policy_since1934_ir6_pub4094.pdf.

Uslaner, M. Eric. 2000. *"The Democratic Party and Free Trade: An Old Romance Restored."* Paper presented for the Conference on The United States and the Future of Free Trade in the Americas. March 25. Edwin L. Cox School of Business, Southern Methodist University, Dallas, TX.

Woolner, David B. 2011. "FDR's Comprehensive Approach to Freer Trade." *The Roosevelt Institute,* October 13. Accessed May 20, 2015. http://www.nextnewdeal.net/fdrs-comprehensive-approach-freer-trade.

Green Energy Subsidies

At a Glance

From 2002–2008, the federal government provided $72.5 billion in subsidies for fossil fuels contrasted with $29.0 billion for renewables. A majority of these ($16.8 billion) are designated for corn-based ethanol (Environmental Law Institute 2009). The Overseas Development Institute estimates the return on a fossil fuel subsidy is 1.4 dollars of investment for every one dollar subsidy compared with a return of $2.50 for every one dollar of renewable subsidy (Frangoul 2004).

In 2009, green energy subsidies entered the national debate when President Barack Obama advocated for their inclusion in the American Recovery and Reinvestment Act (ARRA). Electricity-related subsidies increased from $11.7 billion in FY 2010 to $16.1 billion in FY 2013, primarily due to solar and wind energy and Section 1603 grants through the Department of Treasury. Wind energy received the most direct subsidies from the federal government (37 percent of electricity subsidies) (U.S. Energy Information Administration 2015). Partisan positions on government subsidies vary depending on whether they are for renewable or fossil fuels.

Many Democrats . . .

- See green energy subsidies as critical to expanding renewable energy use in the United States
- Believe that the United States must invest in renewable energy to reduce the effects of climate change and support the research and development of otherwise cost-prohibitive technologies

Many Republicans . . .

- Assert that subsidies for renewable energy cost taxpayers more than they generate in revenue or jobs
- Say that the federal government should not finance green energy subsidies at the expense of fossil fuel subsidies

Overview

Wind and solar power receive tax credits, rebates, and subsidies at the federal, state, and local levels of government. In 1992 Congress passed the Energy Policy Act (EPACT) that changed utility laws to expand clean energy use and established the Production Tax Credit (PTC) renewable power subsidies (Miller 2013). Senator Chuck Grassley, a Republican from Iowa, wrote the legislation creating the wind production tax credit that President George H. W. Bush signed into law in 1992 and President George W. Bush renewed in 2005 (Leber 2015). Congress repeatedly extended the subsidies through statutes including the ARRA and Tax Increase Prevention Act of 2014 until their expiration on December 31, 2014. On July 21, 2015, the Senate Finance Committee restored the wind power tax credit, but partisan differences over energy policy and an upcoming election make its future uncertain (Kerr 2015). The constantly changing status of the PTC credit for wind made it challenging for the wind industry to make long-term plans because investments in technology dropped as each expiration date approached. This led to President Obama asking for a permanent extension in February 2015 as part of his FY 2016 presidential budget (Martin 2015).

President Obama's FY 2016 budget calls for $48 billion in tax incentives over 10 years for green energy projects including subsidies for building alternative fuel vehicles and energy-efficient homes. The proposal to make the tax credits for electricity production from wind and solar sources permanent is the most expensive provision in the budget, with a cost of $31.5 billion over 10 years. The Obama administration proposes this provision be offset by eliminating tax preferences for fossil fuel companies (Bastasch 2015a).

The Department of Energy (DOE) administers most federal renewable energy incentive programs. The U.S. Department of the Treasury operates the Section 1603 grant program and the Department of Agriculture (DOA), the Department of the Interior (DOI), the Department of Labor (DOL), and Department of Housing and Urban Development (HUD) are responsible for other energy-related programs. The solar rebate varies by program and state, but usually covers a maximum of 30 percent of the cost of a solar power system through an investment tax credit (ITC). The purpose of this type of program is to encourage consumers to switch to renewable energy and lower their energy usage.

Democrats on Green Energy Subsidies

During his 2008 campaign, then-candidate Barack Obama estimated five million new green jobs could be created by greater investment in renewable energies, particularly in solar power, through a combination of tax credits, grants, subsidies, and guaranteed loans (Hollingsworth 2015). When advocating for an end to tax subsidies for oil and gas companies in favor of tax benefits and subsidies for renewable energy, Obama said, "You can either stand up for oil companies, or you can stand up for the American people. You can keep subsidizing a fossil fuel that's been getting taxpayer dollars for a century, or you can place your bets on a clean-energy future" (Bastasch 2013).

Clean Energy Investment in the American Recovery and Reinvestment Act

The massive economic stimulus package known as the American Recovery and Reinvestment Act, which was passed in 2009 by President Obama and congressional Democrats over the opposition of the GOP, contained major financial support for clean energy programs and businesses. In 2010 journalist Michael Grunwald summarized the goals of these green energy initiatives:

> The Recovery Act is the most ambitious energy legislation in history, converting the Energy Department into the world's largest venture-capital fund. It's pouring $90 billion into clean energy, including unprecedented investments in a smart grid; energy efficiency; electric cars; renewable power from the sun, wind and earth; cleaner coal; advanced biofuels; and factories to manufacture green stuff in the U.S. The act will also triple the number of smart electric meters in our homes, quadruple the number of hybrids in the federal auto fleet and finance far-out energy research through a new government incubator modeled after the Pentagon agency that fathered the Internet. . . .
>
> The Recovery Act's clean-energy push is designed not only to reduce our old economy dependence on fossil fuels that broil the planet, blacken the Gulf and strengthen foreign petro-thugs but also to avoid replacing it with a new economy that is just as dependent on foreign countries for technology and manufacturing. Last year, exactly two U.S. factories made advanced batteries for electric vehicles. The stimulus will create 30 new ones, expanding U.S. production capacity from 1% of the global market to 20%, supporting half a million plug-ins and hybrids. The idea is as old as land-grant colleges: to use tax dollars as an engine of innovation . . . . "They won't all succeed." [green energy executive Matt] Rogers says. "But some will, and they'll change the world."

Source

Grunwald, Michael. 2010. "How the Stimulus Is Changing America." *Time*, August 26. Accessed April 21, 2015. http://content.time.com/time/magazine/article/0,9171,2013826,00.html

In 2009, Congress passed the ARRA as part of a broader effort to stimulate the country's recession-wracked economy. President Obama advocated investments in renewable energy to help fulfill his campaign promises. The ARRA included three main programs: (1) payment-in-lieu-of-tax-credits (1603); (2) manufacturing tax credits (48C); and (3) loan guarantees. The 1603 credits have been disbursed to more than 44 states and more than 500 projects, creating 10,000 construction jobs and 2,000 operation and maintenance jobs. As part of the 48C credit program, more than $2 billion in tax credits have been given to 43 states for 183 clean energy projects. Finally, $2 billion in conditional or closed loan guarantees have been made for renewable energy projects to expand clean power generating capacity and reduce CO_2 emissions (White House n.d.). Rhone Resche, the president and CEO of the Solar Energy Industries Association (SEIA) said, "These programs just level the playing field for

---

The Obama White House and Clean Energy

After first taking office in 2009, Democratic President Barack Obama made clean energy a priority of his administration. On March 29, 2012, the president discussed his position on energy subsides in the White House Rose Garden:

> I think it's curious that some folks in Congress, who are the first to belittle investments in new sources of energy, are the ones that are fighting the hardest to maintain these giveaways for the oil companies.
>
> . . . We should be using that money to double-down on investments in clean energy technologies that have never been more promising—investments in wind power and solar power and biofuels; investments in fuel-efficient cars and trucks, and energy-efficient homes and buildings. That's the future.
>
> . . . We're going to keep investing in clean energy like the wind power and solar power that's already lighting thousands of homes and creating thousands of jobs. We're going to keep building more homes and businesses that waste less energy so that you're in charge of your own energy bills.
>
> . . . They can either vote to spend billions of dollars more in oil subsidies that keep us trapped in the past, or they can vote to end these taxpayer subsidies that aren't needed to boost oil production so that we can invest in the future. It's that simple.
>
> . . . And as long as I'm President, I'm betting on the future. And as the people I've talked to around the country, including the people who are behind me here today, they put their faith in the future as well. That's what we do as Americans. That's who we are. We innovate. We discover. We seek new solutions to some of our biggest challenges. And, ultimately, because we stick with it, we succeed.

Source

Obama, Barack. 2012. "Remarks by the President on Oil and Gas Subsidies," March 29. Accessed October 23, 2015. https://www.whitehouse.gov/the-press-office/2012/03/29 /remarks-president-oil-and-gas-subsidies.

---

what oil and gas and nuclear industries have enjoyed for the last 50 years. Do you have to provide more policy support and funding initially? Absolutely. But the result is more energy security, clean energy and domestic jobs" (Lipton and Krauss 2011).

In July 2015, President Obama announced an executive initiative to install 300 megawatts of solar power in public housing by 2020 in addition to providing assistance for local governments installing the power. HUD, DOE, DOA, and the Environmental Protection Agency (EPA) are responsible for implementation. The DOE is also starting the National Community Solar Partnership to establish neighborhood solar power systems for housing units instead of only individual units. Public housing authorities in over 20 states have committed to 260 solar projects, primarily for low-income residents with another $520 million in money designated. The Federal Housing Authority updated its second-mortgage program to allow homeowners to borrow money for energy-efficient improvements to their property. A White House press release noted, "Last year [2014], the United States brought online as much solar energy every three weeks as it did in all of 2008, and the solar industry added jobs 10 times faster than the rest of the economy. And since the beginning of 2010, the average cost of a solar electric system dropped by 50 percent" (White House 2015).

Also during the summer of 2015, the Obama administration announced its 15-year Clean Power Plan with a 2030 deadline. The goal is to reduce carbon emissions by requiring utilities to use renewable sources to produce electricity. It will also help renewable energy industries such as solar and wind by creating greater demand for their services. The ITC to the solar industry is set to be reduced 20 percent in 2017 and the lengthy timeframe for the Clean Power Plan will help lessen that financial shock. Chief Executive Officer of SunPower Corp. Tom Werner remarked, "It gives new hope to a different approach. Abrupt change is rarely good for industry" (Goom 2015). Werner adds that this tax credit has helped his solar industry become competitive with fossil fuels in one-third of U.S. states.

Hillary Clinton, 2016 presidential candidate, supports renewable energy growth and her platform calls for the United States to obtain one-third of its electricity from renewable sources such as wind and solar by 2027, with a 700 percent increase in solar capacity. In a campaign video Clinton said, "On day one as president, I will set two ambitious national goals that will test our capacities. First, I will ensure we hit a target of having more than a half-billion solar panels installed across the country by the end of my first term. We'll set a 10-year goal of generating enough renewable energy to power every single home in America" (Kirby 2015). Senator Bernie Sanders, another 2016 Democratic presidential candidate, proposed the Low Income Solar Act in July 2015 to help low-income families receive loans for installing solar panels and offset the upfront costs (Phillips 2015).

Republicans on Green Energy Subsidies

Support for energy subsidies varies within the Republican Party. In a 2013 hearing before the House Committee on Science, Space, and Technology, Representative Cynthia Lummis of Wyoming stated, "Government should work to ensure that Americans have access to abundant, affordable, reliable energy, and target taxpayer resources to fundamental research that could one day enable these [renewable] technologies to compete without expensive subsidies or mandates. Doing so would not only help bring energy independence and grow our economy, but it would bring revenue to the treasury" (U.S. House of Representatives 2013). In contrast, Representative Mike Pompeo of Kansas argued, "Companies should have customers, not political patrons. The last thing we can afford during our dire financial straits is giving taxpayer-backed subsidies to companies that don't need them in markets that can't sustain them" (Bastasch 2013). Pompeo later introduced a bill, H.R. 259, to eliminate all energy tax credits (Bastasch 2015a).

One Conservative Republican's Criticisms of Green Energy Subsidies

U.S. Senator Jeff Flake of Arizona has been a staunch fiscal conservative in Washington ever since he was first elected to the U.S. House of Representatives. In May 2014 he delivered a Senate floor speech in which he harshly criticized the Obama administration's enthusiasm for subsidizing the clean energy industry as fiscally irresponsible:

> In 1992, the PTC was temporarily established to promote development of renewable energy—electricity, particularly. This was for the then-fledgling wind power industry.
>
> . . . In reality, the Federal Government's financial commitment extends well beyond the 10-year period considered in the JTC's initial estimate. The government will still likely be passing out these credits in 2027 and beyond.
>
> . . . That is a long commitment for a technology that former Energy Secretary Steven Chu said was mature in 2009. In fact, he projected that wind would be cost competitive with other forms of energy without subsidies by the end of this decade.
>
> . . . Wind power generation is no longer an infant industry. It is no longer in need of Federal support. By the end of last year, more than 61,000 megawatts of wind power capacity had been installed around the U.S., which is 15 times the amount that existed in 2001. In 2012, wind power was the top source of new generating capacity, beating out additional capacity from natural gas.
>
> . . . The production tax credit distorts the market by having the government favor one source of energy over another.
>
> . . . Instead of extending an energy subsidy that picks winners and losers and creates market inefficiencies, Congress should eliminate the PTC and support an energy policy that encourages entrepreneurs to satisfy demand by providing consumers with alternative sources of energy.

Source

Flake, S. J. 2014. Senate Session [Video]. May 14, 2014. Accessed October 30, 2015. http://www .c-span.org/video/?319306-1/us-senate-legislative-business.

The current Republican platform highlights companies such as Solyndra that declared bankruptcy in 2011 after receiving $535 million in subsidies. It argues the Obama Administration has played favorites by giving subsidies to the renewable energy industry and "publicly threatened to bankrupt anyone who builds a coal-powered plant" (Republican National Committee 2012).

Several 2016 presidential hopefuls have commented on the subsidies while on the campaign trail. Former Florida Governor Jeb Bush stated he would cut subsidies for both fossil fuels and renewable energy if elected. "I think we should phase out, through tax reform, the tax credits for wind, for solar, for the oil as gas sector, for all that stuff . . . I don't think we should pick winners and losers. I think tax reform ought to be to lower the rate as far as we can and eliminate as many of the subsidies, all of the things that impede the ability in a more dynamic way to get where we need to get, which is low-cost energy that is respectful of the environment" (Kerr 2015). Republican Senator Ted Cruz of Texas also opposes the tax credit saying, "Look, I think wind is terrific. As you know Texas and Iowa are one and two in the country in wind production, but once again I don't think it should be the federal government dictating that" (Leber 2015).

Wind energy opinions also vary. Joining Senator Lamar Alexander of Tennessee, Arizona Senator Jeff Flake said, "Neither of us is saying there is no place for wind energy. There is an important place for it . . . but it's time for the federal subsidy to end." However, former Senator Chuck Grassley of Iowa supported the wind credit and argued, "Opponents of the renewable energy provisions want to have this debate in a vacuum, without regard for the many incentives and subsidies that exist for other sources of energy and are permanent law. . . . If one energy provision is on the table for removal, all should be on the table and judged on the merits. Singling out one provision is unfair and distorts the debate" (Cox 2014). Senator Grassley wanted the Senate to approve subsidies that would pay wind producers 2.3 cents per kilowatt hour over 10 years for the energy they generate or allow operators of wind farms to take a 30 percent investment tax credit instead of power payments. With the third largest installed wind power capacity in the U.S. and the first state to have over 20 percent of its power from wind, Iowa greatly benefits from both wind and solar subsidies (Bastasch 2015b).

Solar power is criticized for producing a small amount (0.5 percent) of U.S. electricity. The Department of Energy's goal is for solar power to comprise 14 percent of all electricity by 2030 and 27 percent by 2050. The Taxpayers Protection Alliance argues the cost of solar power is several times greater than traditional power and that the subsidies are a waste of taxpayer money (Hollingsworth 2015). In response to President Obama advocating the solar and wind power subsidies partially at the expense of ending fossil fuel subsidies, Jack Gerard, president of the American Petroleum Institute (API) stated, "Historically, raising taxes on energy raises costs for consumers. We create well-paying jobs, build infrastructure with private dollars, generate billions of dollars in government revenue, support retirees, and help businesses grow with affordable and reliable energy. The president's annual call to raise taxes on U.S. oil and natural gas development would hurt job creation, infrastructure investment, the federal deficit, seniors on fixed incomes and domestic manufacturing" (Bastasch 2015a). From 1990–2014, the API has been a large contributor to Republican candidates and Democrat candidates in oil and gas dependent states such as Louisiana, spending $1.35 million in political contributions and over $89 million in lobbying (OpenSecrets n.d.).

Elizabeth Wheat

Further Reading

Bastasch, Michael. 2013. "CBO: Most Energy Tax Subsidies Go toward Green Energy, Energy Efficiency." *Daily Caller*, February 2. Accessed August 5, 2015. http://dailycaller.com /2013/03/14/cbo-most-energy-tax-subsidies-go-toward-green-energy-energy-efficiency/.

Bastasch, Michael. 2015a. "Obama 2016 Budget Includes $48 Billion in 'Green Energy' Subsidies." *Daily Caller*, February 2. Accessed August 5, 2015. http://dailycaller.com /2015/02/02/obama-2016-budget-green-energy/.

Bastasch, Michael. 2015b. "Senate May Revive Expired Green Energy Tax Subsidies." *Daily Caller*, July 20, 2015. Accessed August 5. http://dailycaller.com/2015/07/20/senate -may-revive-expired-green-energy-tax-subsidies/.

Cox, Ramsey. 2014. "GOP Senators: It's Time to End Wind Energy Subsidy." *The Hill*. Last modified May 14. Accessed August 5, 2015. http://thehill.com/blogs/floor-action/senate /206138-gop-senators-its-time-to-end-wind-energy-subsidy.

Environmental Law Institute. 2009. "Energy Subsidies Black, Not Green." Environmental Law Institute. Last modified September. Accessed August 5, 2015. http://www.eli.org /sites/default/files/docs/Energy_Subsidies_Black_Not_Green.pdf.

Frangoul, Anmar. 2004. "It's Not Easy Being Green: Fossil Fuel Subsidies." CNBC. Last modified December 19. Accessed August 5, 2015. http://www.cnbc.com/2014/12/19 /its-not-easy-being-green-fossil-fuel-subsidies.html.

Groom, Nichola. 2015. "Green Energy Sees Secure Future from Obama's Climate Plan." *Business Insider*, August 3. Accessed August 5, 2015. http://www.businessinsider.com /r-green-energy-sees-secure-future-from-obamas-climate-plan-2015-8.

Hollingsworth, Barbara. 2015. "Despite $39B in Annual Gov't. Subsidies, Solar Produced 0.5% of Electricity in US." CSN News. Last modified February 17, 2015. Accessed August 5. http://cnsnews.com/news/article/barbara-hollingsworth/despite -39b-annual-govt-subsidies-solar-produced-05-electricity.

Kerr, Jacob. 2015. "Jeb Bush Wants to Cut All Energy Subsidies." *Huffington Post*, July 23. Accessed August 5, 2015. http://www.huffingtonpost.com/entry/jeb-bush-energy-sub sidies_55b0f682e4b0a9b94853c851?.

Kirby, David. 2015. "Hillary Clinton Has a Plan to Cover America in Solar Panels." *Takepart*. Last modified July 29. Accessed August 15, 2015. https://www.takepart.com /article/2015/07/29/hillary-clinton-wants-put-half-billion-solar-panels-american-roofs.

Leber, Rebecca. 2015. "Republicans' Flip Flop on Wind Energy Could Hurt Them in 2016." *New Republic*, July 20. Accessed August 5, 2015. http://www.newrepublic.com /article/122331/republicans-flip-flop-wind-energy-could-hurt-them-2016.

Lipton, Eric, and Clifford Krauss. 2011. "A Gold Rush of Subsidies in Clean Energy Search." *New York Times*, November 11. Accessed August 5, 2015. http://www.nytimes .com/2011/11/12/business/energy-environment/a-cornucopia-of-help-for-renewable -energy.html?_r=0.obama-administration-finds-new-way-to-push-solar-energy/.

Martin, Chris. 2015. "Wind Power without U.S. Subsidy to Become Cheaper than Gas." *Bloomberg Business*, March 12. Accessed August 5, 2015. http://www.bloomberg.com /news/articles/2015-03-12/wind-energy-without-subsidy-will-be-cheaper-than-gas-in -a-decade.

Miller, John. 2013. "How Effective Are U.S. Renewable Power Policies?" *Energy Collective*. Last modified December 3. Accessed August 5, 2015. http://www.theenergycollective .com/jemillerep/311406/how-effective-are-us-renewable-power-policies.

OpenSecrets. 2015. "American Petroleum Institute Profile for 2014 Election Cycle." Accessed November 14. https://www.opensecrets.org/orgs/summary.php?id=D000031 493&cycle=A.

Phillips, Ari. 2015. "Bernie Sanders Plan to Make Solar Power More Accessible." *Climate Progress*. Last modified July 7. Accessed August 5, 2015. http://thinkprogress.org /climate/2015/07/07/3677745/bernie-sanders-introduces-solar-legislation/.

Republican National Committee. 2012. "We Believe in America—America's Natural Resources: 2012 Republican Platform." GOP.com. Accessed August 5, 2015. https://www.gop.com/platform/americas-natural-resources/.

Solar City. 2015. "Solar Energy Tax Credits and Rebates." Solar City. Accessed August 5. http://www.solarcity.com/residential/solar-energy-tax-credits-rebates.

U.S. Department of Energy. 2015. "Renewable Electricity Production Tax Credit (PTC)." Accessed August 5. http://energy.gov/savings/renewable-electricity-production-tax-credit-ptc.

U.S. Energy Information Administration. 2015. *Analysis & Projections—Direct Federal Financial Interventions and Subsidies in Energy in Fiscal Year 2013.* U.S. Energy Information Administration. Accessed August 5, 2015. http://www.eia.gov/analysis/requests/subsidy/.

U.S. House of Representatives. 2013. *Federal Financial Support for Energy Technologies: Assessing the Costs and Benefits: Hearings Before the Committee on Science, Space, and Technology* (statement of Cynthia Lummis). Committee on Science, Space and Technology. Hearing before the Subcommittee on Energy. Accessed November 11, 2015. http://www.gpo.gov/fdsys/pkg/CHRG-113hhrg79931/pdf/CHRG-113hhrg79931.pdf.

The White House, Office of the Press Secretary. 2015. "FACT SHEET: Administration Announces New Initiative to Increase Solar Access for All Americans." White House Office of the Press Secretary. Last modified July 7. Accessed November 14, 2015. https://www.whitehouse.gov/the-press-office/2015/07/07/fact-sheet-administration-announces-new-initiative-increase-solar-access.

The White House. 2015. "Promoting Clean, Renewable Energy: Investments in Wind and Solar." *The Recovery Act.* Accessed August 5. https://www.whitehouse.gov/recovery/innovations/clean-renewable-energy.

Health Care

At a Glance

For nearly a century, Democrats have advocated making quality and afford-able health care available to all Americans. Supporters argue that ensuring quality, affordable health care for every single American is essential to chil-dren's education, workers' productivity, and businesses' competitiveness, and that it is a moral responsibility as well.

Republicans say that they support health care reforms that will lower costs, ensure quality care, and end lawsuit abuse. But they assert that the United States can improve on what they already describe as the best health care sys-tem in the world by increasing opportunities for individuals to manage their own health care needs without interference from government bureaucrats.

Many Democrats . . .

- See affordable health insurance for everyone as a policy priority
- Support ending coverage discrimination based on pre-existing conditions
- Advocate for extending the coverage that members of Congress enjoy to all Americans
- Support policies to end disparities in health care due to income, gender, race, or location
- Favor empowerment and support of older Americans and people with disabilities

Many Republicans . . .

- Advocate for giving individuals tools to manage their own health needs
- See protecting individuals with pre-existing conditions as a legitimate policy goal
- Favor providing health care through free market principles, where compe-tition drives costs down
- See frivolous lawsuits as a problem in American health care
- Contend that maintaining high-quality and accessible health care options for seniors and disabled individuals will only be possible by reining in escalating Medicare costs

Overview

Health care policy has been one of the most hotly debated issues in U.S. history. Efforts to achieve national health insurance have been very complicated. For example, attempts to get government to take the leading role in health care have been met with conservative opposition and concern about "socialized medicine or care" (Hoffman 2009). In addition, public support for such efforts has declined when reforms have included requirements for individuals to contribute more to the costs. Despite these complications, opinion polls dating back to the 1930s have generally supported guaranteed access to health care, health insurance for all, and a government role in financing (Hoffman 2009). While short of providing national health insurance, major health reforms have been enacted in the past eighty-five years through Medicare, Medicaid, the Children's Health Insurance Program, and the Patient Protection and Affordable Care Act, often referred to as "Obamacare."

In 1912, after serving as a progressive Republican president, Theodore Roosevelt rallied his Bull Moose Party to make the first national attempt to guarantee access to health care and health insurance. The inability to create a state-based system of compulsory health insurance caused this effort to fall short. Democratic President Franklin Roosevelt became a champion for national health insurance in 1935, during the Great Depression. Although reducing unemployment, and providing security for the aged made national health insurance a lower priority for Roosevelt's administration, matching funds were provided to states to expand public health and maternal and child health services. By the end of World War II, Democratic President Harry Truman resurrected the idea of a national health insurance program as part of his "Fair Deal" agenda, calling on Congress to pass legislation to ensure the right to medical care. A single insurance system was proposed to cover all Americans with public subsidies to assist the poor. Truman's effort was thwarted by the American Medical Association, which denounced the plan as a step toward socialized medicine (Dominowski 2012).

The election of Republican Dwight D. Eisenhower as president in 1953 signaled a marked departure from previous administrations. Eisenhower had campaigned against national health insurance in 1952. As president, however, he recognized the burden faced by families and the rising costs of health care. Eisenhower proposed to address these issues through use of private insurance plans. He proposed a federal reinsurance for any private company as protection against heavy losses resulting from health insurance. After the first five years, the program was to become self-financing with money from premiums paid by the insurance companies. Eisenhower's plan (H.R. 8356) was strongly opposed by the AMA who expressed concern that the program would lead to socialized medicine and government control of doctors. Organized labor representatives also opposed the bill stating that it would not be sufficient to provide comprehensive coverage for Americans with insurance and because it could not provide protection to those without it (*CQ Almanac* 1954). Once the bill was introduced, the House voted 238 to 134 in support of recommitment, essentially killing the bill. The *New York Times* reported that the "bill simply had been caught up in a crossfire by the conservative wings of both parties from one direction and by New Deal and Fair Deal Democrats from the other" (Morris 1954). The Senate bill never came up for debate and died on the Senate calendar.

In the 1960 presidential race, health care for seniors was a major campaign issue for Democratic candidate John F. Kennedy. As president, Kennedy supported legislation (Medicare) in 1962 for hospital coverage for seniors. He made the decision not only to advocate for his proposal with legislators, but also to build public pressure to force members of Congress to act (Dickerson 2013). The legislation was strongly opposed by the American Medical Association (AMA) as well as Southern Democrats and Republicans in the Senate. As a result, the bill was blocked in a 52 to 48 vote (Centers for Medicare and Medicaid Services 2015). In 1964, following a landslide victory at the polls along with a large liberal democratic majority in Congress, Democratic President Lyndon B. Johnson made national health care the centerpiece of his "Great Society" program. In July 1965 the Medicare (health needs of the elderly) and Medicaid (for the poor) programs were signed into law as part of the Social Security Act.

In 1974 Republican President Richard Nixon joined Democratic Senator Edward Kennedy of Massachusetts in proposing a universal health coverage plan. Kennedy favored a single-payer plan, with a national health budget, no consumer cost sharing, to be financed through payroll taxes. Nixon's plan (Comprehensive Health Insurance Plan) included universal coverage, voluntary employer participation, and a separate program for the working poor and unemployed to replace Medicaid. Despite the high degree of bipartisan support, progress toward legislation was interrupted by the Watergate scandal. Efforts by Republican President Ford to revive the health reform plans of Nixon and Kennedy failed due to lack of committee consensus in Congress.

Democratic President Jimmy Carter also tried to revive a comprehensive health plan in 1977. He proposed that businesses provide a minimum package of benefits, public coverage for the poor and aged would be expanded, and a new public corporation would be created to sell coverage to everyone else. Like earlier measures, this plan also failed to gain congressional support. Senator Edward Kennedy (D-Massachusetts), a long-time health care advocate, was strongly opposed to Carter's 1978 comprehensive health care bill. Kennedy had campaigned for comprehensive National Health Insurance (NHI) that promoted a single payer, compulsory system that would be open to all. The AFL-CIO supported the NHI proposal. Carter endorsed NHI in his candidacy to win the support of the UAW but was not prepared to embrace the scale of reform that Kennedy sought (Stanley 2010). The proposal Carter put forth focused heavily on hospital cost-containment that was intended to reduce the cost of medical bills.

Kennedy opposed the bill because it did not include comprehensive coverage and concern that the cost-containment package was considered likely to raise the price of health care as costs might be increased in other areas to cover loss in revenues. Kennedy also opposed the provision that any future programs would be run by private insurers with no "public option" for consumers to buy insurance from the government (Stanley 2010). Kennedy's opposition diminished liberal support for the bill in Congress.

Although he denounced government involvement in health care as "socialist" in his first term, Republican President Ronald Reagan signed the Consolidated Omnibus Reconciliation Act (COBRA), into law in 1986. COBRA represented an initiative that allowed some workers to keep employer provided health insurance for a period of time if they lost their jobs. In 1988, President Reagan also signed into law a major expansion to Medicare that, for a price, gave seniors access to prescription drug benefits and catastrophic care (Dominowski 2012).

Republican President George H. W. Bush's response to spiraling health care costs in 1988 was to call for reforms to the health insurance market, a personal mandate for middle class workers, and health insurance credit for low-income families. Bush's plan met the same fate as many prior plans.

In 1993, with Hillary Clinton playing a leading role, Democratic President Bill Clinton revived efforts to develop a national health insurance plan. The proposed Health Security Act required businesses to cover their workers while everyone else would be mandated to have health insurance. Bitter opposition from Republicans and President Clinton's low approval rating before the 1994 midterm elections led to the act's failure in the Senate. Clinton was, however, able to sign bipartisan legislation in 1997 creating a federally subsidized program for state provided health coverage for families of low-income children who were unable to qualify for Medicaid.

Republican President George W. Bush's efforts in healthcare reform included obtaining congressional support to add the Reagan prescription-drug coverage plan to Medicare. Assistance provided through this legislation represented a "major new federal entitlement for Medicare beneficiaries" (Oliver et al. 2004).

Rather than have the executive branch craft the bill that would later be introduced in Congress as had been done in the failed efforts by President Clinton 15 years earlier, President Obama laid out the broad principles and goal of what he wanted in a health reform law, and left it to the House and Senate to provide the legislative details (Herszenhorn and Calmes 2009). Filibuster-proof Democratic majorities in Congress, rapidly escalating healthcare costs, and the increasing numbers of uninsured Americans created the opportunity to pass healthcare reform legislation.

The Patient Protection and Affordable Care Act (ACA) of 2010 mandates that everyone must purchase health insurance and help pay for it and that no one may be turned down due to pre-existing conditions.

Democrats on Health Care

A review of the national platform hearings of the Democratic Party shows that many Democrats are united around a commitment that every American be guaranteed affordable, comprehensive health care (Democratic National Committee 2008). They believe that covering everyone is not just a moral imperative, but is also the foundation of individual achievement and economic prosperity. In the same way, affordable health care for every single American is essential to children's education, workers' productivity and businesses' competitiveness.

There continues to be strong support among Democrats for a single-payer healthcare system. Many proposals have been made for a single-payer healthcare system, including one that has been put forward every year since 2003 by Representative John Conyers (D-Michigan) in *The United States National Health Care Act* (Health Care). Advocates of a single-payer system, such as Democratic presidential candidate Bernie Sanders, view health care as a human right that should be guaranteed to all Americans. Many Progressives are convinced that the single-payer is the way to both insure access to health care and to control costs (Sparer, Brown, and Jacobs 2009).

Democrats tend to believe that health care should be a shared responsibility between employers, workers, insurers, providers, and government. All Americans, they argue, should have coverage they can afford; employers should have incentives to provide coverage to their workers; insurers and providers should ensure high quality affordable care; and the government should ensure that health insurance is not only affordable, but provides meaningful coverage (Democratic National Committee 2008).

As part of its strategy to strengthen and improve the healthcare system for all Americans, the Democratic platform states that it is committed to ensuring that there is no arbitrary insurer cancellation and refusal to insure children and women because of pre-existing medical conditions or gender (Democratic National Committee 2012).

Intrinsic to the goal to cover all Americans and provide real choices of affordable health insurance options, the Democratic platform aspires to give families and individuals the option of keeping the coverage they have or choosing from a wide array of health insurance plans, including private health insurance options and a public plan. The platform states that those who do not get insurance at work will be able to shop in new exchanges and be eligible for new tax credits.

The platform also discusses the importance of prevention to reduce the nation's overall health care spending. This component of the party's healthcare goals seeks to promote healthy lifestyles, disease prevention and management, especially with health promotion programs at work and physical education in schools. Through these means, the development of chronic conditions, such as obesity, diabetes, heart disease, and hypertension can be prevented. To further the prevention and wellness reform goal, the Democratic Party states its intention to support public health and research. The party argues that it will ensure that Americans benefit from healthy environments that allow them to pursue healthy choices. Additionally Democrats promise to work to ensure healthy environments in schools to reduce the rates of childhood obesity.

The Democratic platform emphasizes the importance of a modernized system that lowers the cost and improves the quality of care for Americans. On one hand, these goals can be advanced through an aggressive effort to cut costs and eliminate waste from the country's health system, which the party estimates will save the typical family up to $2,500 per year. On the other hand, the adoption of state-of-the-art information technology systems, privacy-protected electronic medical records, reimbursement incentives, and an independent organization that reviews drugs, devices, and procedures can ensure that people get the right care at the right time. Another end goal of these reform measures is reduction of lawsuits related to medical errors.

As an addition to the above described reform initiatives, the Democratic Party's platform contends that increased competition in the insurance and drug markets can lower costs of care in the United States. For example, drug costs can be lowered if the Medicare program is allowed to bargain for lower prices. The Democrats tend to favor permitting the importation of safe medicines from other developed countries, creating a generic pathway for biologic drugs, and increasing the use of generics in public programs as additional options for lowering drug costs. The Democratic Party's platform also states an intention to building a strong health care workforce through training and reimbursement incentives for those who are committed to training as nurses and primary care physicians as well as direct care workers.

Other core Democratic strategies for achieving affordable, quality healthcare coverage for all Americans include: building strong partnerships with states, local governments, tribes and territories; protecting the reproductive healthcare choices of women; and providing assistance to those recovering from traumatic, life altering injuries and illnesses as well as those with mental health and substance abuse use disorders (Democratic National Committee 2008).

Democrat Nancy Pelosi Praises the Affordable Care Act

On March 25, 2015, House minority leader, Democrat Nancy Pelosi, issued the following remarks marking the fifth anniversary of the ACA:

The Affordable Care Act has provided newfound health security to millions of children, women, workers and families. Thanks to this historic law, more than 16 million previously uninsured Americans have finally secured quality, affordable coverage for themselves and their families. No longer do 105 million Americans live under the threat of an annual or lifetime limit on their health care. No longer can the 130 million Americans with pre-existing conditions be denied health coverage. And no longer is being a woman considered a pre-existing condition.

Over the last few years, health care spending has been growing at the slowest rate in more than half a century. Since the Affordable Care Act, we have extended the solvency of the Medicare Trust fund by more than a decade. We have helped save taxpayers $116 billion through new Medicare efficiencies. More than 9 million seniors have saved more than $15 billion on prescription drugs, an average savings of $1,598 per senior. We are ensuring that no senior is forced to choose between paying for medicine and a meal.

Five years later, as more Americans enjoy affordable, quality health coverage, we know that the ACA works. Yet, House Republicans continue their obsession with destroying this law and the health security it is providing millions and millions of American families. After fifty-six votes to repeal or undermine the Affordable Care Act later, it is time for Republicans to seek help for their fixation, and join with us in celebrating the health and economic security that this landmark law affords every American.

Source

Pelosi, Nancy. 2015. "Pelosi Statement on Fifth Anniversary of Affordable Care Act," Press Release, March 23. Accessed May 13, 2015. http://pelosi.house.gov/news/press-releases /pelosi-statement-on-fifth-anniversary-of-the-affordable-care-act.

With support from the Pharmaceutical Research and Manufacturers of America, the American Medical Association, AARP, and many unions, the U.S. House of Representatives on November 9, 2009, by a vote of 220 to 215, passed a health care reform bill (Affordable Health Care for America Act), with the Senate passing an almost similar version of a health care reform bill (Patient Protection and Affordable Care Act) on December 24, 2009, by a margin of 60 to 39 votes. These bills enjoyed almost unanimous support from Democrats, but the only Republican in either house of Congress to vote for passage was freshman Representative Ahn "Joseph" Cao of Louisiana. In March 2010, both the Senate and the house versions of the healthcare reform bills were reconciled through the Health Care and Education Reconciliation Act of 2010, and signed into law by President Obama on March 23, 2010.

The Affordable Care Act (ACA) that focuses largely on expanding the number of people with health insurance in the United States has the following key features:

With few exceptions requires everyone to have health insurance (individual mandate)

Provides that insurance companies provide coverage for people with pre-existing conditions

Provides for young adult coverage under their parents policies until the age of 26

Provides access to health care through a health insurance marketplace

Provides prescription discounts for seniors as well as free preventive care for all

Holds insurance companies accountable by making them justify any premium increase of ten percent or more before the rate takes effect (U.S. Department of Health and Human Services 2015).

Republicans on Health Care

Republican commitment to healthcare reform is based on the creation of opportunities that come with having the "best medical resources in the world" (Republican National Committee 2015). For many conservatives, the key to reform is to give control of the healthcare system to patients and their healthcare providers, not to government bureaucrats or businesses. Republicans tend to support using the private market place to provide health care to Americans, and oppose "socialized medicine" in the form of a government-run universal healthcare system or a public option (i.e., health coverage managed by the government as an option to health insurance that is privately owned).

Senator Charles Grassley of Iowa, a senior member of the Senate Finance Committee, described Republican concerns as healthcare costs rising at three times the inflation rate and the large number of uninsured Americans, with millions more fearing the loss of their insurance in a weak economy or because of pre-existing conditions (Grassley 2009). Grassley also pointed to physicians' readiness to leave medicine because of high malpractice insurance costs and low government reimbursement rates. Republicans fear both the major expansion of Medicaid and the federal mandate for coverage backed by the enforcement authority of the Internal Revenue Service. Instead, they advocate applying free market principles and reducing governmental control over what they see as a matter of personal decision making and personal responsibility (Grassley 2009).

Within its platform, the Republican Party communicates its intent to repeal the Patient Protection and Affordable Care Act (ACA). For Republicans, the ACA (also known as Obamacare), represents an attack on the U.S. Constitution because of its requirement (individual mandate) that citizens purchase health insurance. The ACA is perceived as a strategy for expanding government control over one-sixth of the U.S. economy that healthcare spending represents, rather than providing assistance to Americans who are in need of a more effective health care system (Republican National Committee 2012).

Ironically, major components of the ACA were directly inspired by Republican Mitt Romney's Health Care legislation, *An Act Providing Access to Affordable, Quality, Accountable Health Care* ("RomneyCare"), enacted in Massachusetts in 2006. RomneyCare included systematic health insurance market reform, a mandate on individuals to purchase insurance, subsidies to make insurance affordable, and an insurance exchange to connect people with coverage. It was identified as one of the models for consideration at a meeting of key stakeholders convened in 2008 by staff of the U.S. Senate Committee on Health, Education, Labor, and Pensions (HELP). The purpose of the meeting was to begin working on a legislative effort to enact national health care reform in Congress in 2009. Committee chair, Senator Edward M. Kennedy, asked that key system stakeholders be brought together to see whether they could find consensus on a path to reform (McDonough, 2011). The stakeholders included representatives and leaders of consumer protection, disease advocacy, business, insurance, physicians, hospitals, labor, and pharmaceutical organizations. The group was presented with three options for consensus: (a) a radical shift from the current employer provided insurance toward a single-payer system; (b) an incremental approach that would include federal government support provided to state high-risk pools to cover those with pre-existing conditions and subsidize lower income individuals; and (c) reform based on the key elements of the near-universal coverage law enacted in Massachusetts in 2006 under the leadership of Republican Governor Mitt Romney (McDonough, 2011). The stakeholders chose to develop consensus around the third option that became the template for national health care reform.

Republicans assert that they are committed to saving Medicaid and Medicare by taking measures to modernize both programs. The party tends to favor block grants to Medicaid and other payments to states while limiting federal requirements on both private insurance and Medicaid. Although the programs are different in terms of intent and participants served, both are seen as being unsustainable if measures are not taken to restructure them. Republicans point to rapidly increasing Medicare and Medicaid rolls and inflexible bureaucracy as taking funding away from other essential government functions.

Republicans hold that states should be maintained as the local regulators of insurance markets and as providers of care for the needy, and state officials should carefully consider the increased costs of medical mandates that may be pricing low-income families out of the insurance market. The Republican platform holds that all patients would be assisted, including those with pre-existing conditions through reinsurance and risk adjustment. In identifying a need for "fostering personal responsibility in taking care of one's health," the Republican platform emphasizes the high percentage of chronic diseases, "many attributable to lifestyle," that are driving more than 75 percent of U.S. healthcare spending. The Republican response is to reduce demand and lower health care costs by increasing preventative services to promote healthy lifestyles. Republicans also express belief in Americans having better access to affordable, coordinated, quality health care that includes behavioral health care.

Republicans express concerns about perspectives on healthcare needs and mandates. For example, the GOP disagrees with abortion as being a form of health care, arguing instead that abortion endangers the health and well being of women. Further, the Republican Platform holds the position that no healthcare professional or organization should ever be required to perform, provide for, withhold, or refer to a medical service against their conscience.

The Republican Party claims it is invested in a healthcare system that provides higher quality care at a lower cost while protecting the patient-physician relationship. It seeks to increase healthcare options and simplification of the system for both patients and providers. Republicans would also support an end to what they see as tax discrimination against the individual purchase of insurance and allow consumers to purchase insurance across state lines.

RNC Chairman Reince Priebus Denounces the Affordable Care Act

On March 23, 2015, Reince Priebus, Republican National Committee Chairman released the following statement on the fifth anniversary of the ACA.

Today is an anniversary most Americans would rather forget. Five years ago, ObamaCare was forced on the American people after being sold on a series of lies. President Obama and his fellow Democrats broke their promise to make health care more affordable. They broke their promise to reduce premiums. They broke their promise that you could keep your doctor and keep your plan. And they broke their promise that they wouldn't raise taxes on the middle class.

ObamaCare has been a burden for families and small businesses, and as rates continue to rise, that burden is not going away. Today is a reminder that America needs a patient-centered health care system. The Obama-Clinton approach to health care has only produced broken promises. It's time for Democrats to come to terms with that reality.

Source

Republican National Committee.2015. "RNC Statement on ObamaCare Anniversary." *GOP.com*. Accessed May 12, 2015. https://www.gop.com/rnc-statement-on-obamacare-anniversary/?

Republicans affirm patient privacy and ownership of health information. Patients have the right to consent to medical and behavioral health care treatment, drug treatment, and treatment involving pregnancy, contraception, and abortion. The platform also supports legislation that would require parental consent to transport girls over state lines for abortions.

The Republican approaches for managing health care costs include a strong focus on consumer choice. There is support for price transparency with the belief that if consumers know the actual cost of treatments before receiving them, they will be less likely to over-utilize services. There is also support for reducing costs through tort reform to help avoid the practice of defensive medicine, having small businesses form purchasing pools to expand coverage to the insured, and encouraging the private sector to rate competing insurance plans.

Osaore Aideyan and
Kathryn Conley Wehrmann

Further Reading

Centers for Medicare and Medicaid Services. 2015. *Tracing the History of CMS Programs: From President Theodore Roosevelt to President George W. Bush.* Accessed November 10. https://www.cms.gov/About-CMS/Agency-Information/History/Downloads/President CMSMilestones.pdf.

Conyers, John Jr. 2015. "Health Care." Accessed November 13. https://conyers.house.gov /issues/health-care.

Democratic National Committee. 2015. "Health Care." *Democrats.org*. Accessed May 12. http://www.democrats.org/issues/health-care.

Democracy National Committee. 2008. "Renewing America's Promise—Affordable, Quality Health Care Coverage for All Americans: 2008 Democratic Platform" (pp. 9–13). Accessed May 11, 2015. http://www.p2012.org/issues/platformhc.html.

Dickerson, John. 2013. "50 Years Before Obamacare, JFK's Own Health Care Debacle." *Slate*. Accessed November 5, 2015. http://www.slate.com/articles/news_and_politics /history/2013/11/john_f_kennedy_s_health_care_failure_jfk_and_barack_obama_s _tough_fights.2.html.

Dominowski, Michael. 2012 "Health Care Policy in America—A Political History." Slive. com, July 8. Accessed May 7, 2015. http://www.silive.com/opinion/columns/index.ssf /2012/07/health_care_policy_in_america.html.

Grassley, Chuck. 2009. "Health Care Reform: A Republican View." *The New England Journal of Medicine* 361 (25). Accessed May 25, 2015. http://www.nejm.org/doi/full/10.1056 /NEJMp0911111.

"Health Reinsurance." 2015. *CQ Almanac 1954* 10, 04-215-04-217. Accessed November 5. http://library.cqpress.com/cqalmanac/cqal54-1357935.

Herszenhorn, David, and Jackie Calmes. 2009. "Despite Major Plans, Obama Taking Softer Stands." *New York Times*, April 18. Accessed November 9, 2015. http://www.nytimes .com/2009/04/19/us/politics/19lobby.html?_r=0.

Hoffman, Catherine. 2009. "National Health Insurance—A Brief History of Reform Efforts in the U.S." *Focus on Health Reform* #7871. The Henry J. Kaiser Family Foundation. Accessed May 29, 2015. https://kaiserfamilyfoundation.files.wordpress.com/2013/01 /7871.pdf.

McDonough, John E. 2011. *Inside National Health Reform*. Oakland: University of California Press.

Morris, John D. 1954. "Eisenhower Plan for Health Funds Rejected in House." *New York Times*, July 14, 1. Accessed November 7, 2015. http://query.nytimes.com/gst/abstract .html?res=9902EEDA1438E23BBC4C52DFB166838F649EDE.

Oliver, Thomas R., Phillip R. Lee, and Helene Lipton. 2004. "A Political History of Medicare and Prescription Drug Coverage." *The Milbank Quarterly* 82 (2). Accessed May 24, 2015. http://www.ncbi.nlm.nih.gov/pmc/articles/PMC2690175/?report=reader.

Pelosi, Nancy. 2015. "Pelosi Statement on Fifth Anniversary of the Affordable Care Act." Democratic Leader Nancy Pelosi. Accessed May 13. http://pelosi.house.gov/news/press -releases/pelosi-statement-on-fifth-anniversary-of-the-affordable-care-act.

Republican National Committee. 2012. "We Believe in America: 2012 Republican Platform." Accessed May 24, 2015. https://www.gop.com/platform/.

Republican National Committee. 2015. "ObamaCare." Accessed May 12. https://gop.com /issue/obamacare/canonical/.

Sparer, Michael S., Lawrence D. Brown, and Lawrence R. Jacobs. 2009. "Exploring the Concept of Single Payer." *Journal of Health Politics, Policy and Law* 34: 447–451. doi 10.1215/03616878-2009-0110.

Stanley, Timothy. 2010. "Memo to Jimmy Carter: Ted Kennedy Didn't Sabotage Healthcare Reform." *George Mason University History News Network*. September 20. Accessed November 4, 2015. http://historynewsnetwork.org/article/131473#sthash.CVu1D49R .bkEPSsRZ.dpuf.

U.S. Department of Health and Human Services. 2015. "Health Care." Accessed November 9. http://www.hhs.gov/healthcare/.

Immigration

At a Glance

In 1903, Emma Lazarus's 1883 poem entitled "The New Colossus" was engraved on a plaque within the Statue of Liberty in New York City. The poem's often quoted line, "Give me your tired, your poor / Your huddled masses yearning to breathe free" welcomes tourists and visitors to the statue by painting a picture of the history of United States immigration as being open and welcoming to those who sought freedom. However, today political debates and policies regarding the issue of immigration paint a very different, and more complex, picture than that of the past.

The history of migration to the United States can be traced back to the earliest days as many immigrants, primarily European settlers, came to the United States seeking religious freedom, economic opportunity, or an escape from the famines and insufferable conditions of their homelands. Today, the greatest numbers of immigrants come from Mexico, India, China, and the Philippines to the United States, considered to be one of the most desirable destinations among prospective immigrants worldwide. The percentage of immigrants living in the U.S. has continued to grow in recent decades. In 1970, immigrants comprised roughly 5 percent of the U.S. population. Today, immigrants make up 13 percent of the U.S. population (Zong and Batalova 2015).

At the core of the Republican Party's stance on immigration is the necessity of abiding by the rule of law, the notion that a nation should be governed by the law rather than by the rules set forth by individual government representatives. Furthermore, no individual is above the law and everyone is subject to the law. For this reason, many Republicans assert that all immigrants must follow the legal channels throughout the immigration process.

The Republican Party's 2012 platform stressed that throughout the country's history, legal immigrants have contributed to the growth of the nation's economy. However, at the same time, illegal immigrants stand to hinder the accomplishments and future employment of legal residents and citizens.

The Democratic Party's 2012 platform argued that we are a nation of immigrants and that immigration reform should be widespread and focus on fostering a thriving economy while also supporting the immigrants that helped develop that economy. Further, the platform stipulates that policy should produce a means to reunite families (National Network for Immigration and Refugee Rights 2015).

Many Republicans . . .

- Favor strict and extensive border control measures to protect the country from illegal immigrants
- Reward the "rule followers" by granting them permanent residency and political equality
- Would like to deny amnesty to and reserve the right to deport those who do not adhere to the rule of law when immigrating
- Support protecting legal workers' jobs through the use of status verification systems
- Favor the use of verification programs to determine whether or not an immigrant's status and documents qualify him or her for government benefits

Many Democrats . . .

- Support policies that provide law-abiding undocumented immigrants with the opportunity to earn citizenship
- Favor policies to keep children who are undocumented immigrants with their families
- Focus on deporting undocumented immigrants that threaten the nation's security rather than those that are of no threat
- Support legislation that encourages undocumented youth to contribute to society and become legal residents and citizens

---

Overview

The earliest immigrants were welcomed via an uncontrolled immigration policy, producing the American "melting pot." During the 17th century, immigrants came primarily from England, yet others came from Germany, France, Ireland, and the Netherlands. Since the U.S.'s founding, the country has transitioned through distinct eras of immigration policy: "It is widely accepted that there have been five eras of immigration policy in the New World. Four of these eras have occurred since the advent of the United States and are labeled the open door era, the era of regulation, the era of restriction, and the era of liberalization" (Jaggers, Gabbard, and Jaggers 2014, 4).

Toward the end of the 18th century and the beginning of the 19th century, the Industrial Revolution spread across Europe, ushering in new manufacturing practices. European farmers and artisans were forced to either adapt their skill sets to the needs of an industrializing society or search for new opportunities elsewhere. Many departed for America, reputed to be a land of opportunity, social and religious freedom, and cheap land.

With the establishment of the Naturalization Act of 1790, legislators issued citizenship status exclusively to white immigrants deemed to be of "good character." As a measure of character, citizenship was only granted once a qualified immigrant had been living in the U.S. for two years. The law largely limited citizenship based on race, ethnicity, and, at times, gender.

The American belief in Manifest Destiny emerged in the 19th century. Believing that Americans had an instinctive right to territorial expansion, settlers aggressively encroached on territories beyond the nation's boundaries. Following the U.S. victory in the Mexican-American War of 1846 to 1848, the United States significantly expanded its territory by acquisitioning two-fifths of Mexico's territory.

Until the late 1800s, state governments attempted to regulate immigration within their borders. However, in 1875, the U.S. Supreme Court ruled that immigration thenceforth is a federal matter, no longer governed by the states. Shortly thereafter, Congress passed the Immigration Act of 1891. The Immigration Act gave the federal government the sole authority to regulate immigration by instituting the Office of the Superintendent of Immigration, an office overseen by the Department of Treasury. In 1892, Ellis Island opened as the nation's first federal immigration inspection station. Similarly, the Angel Island Immigration Station opened in San Francisco Bay in 1910 and served as a detention facility for primarily Asian immigrants, the majority specifically from China. At this time, the U.S. government labeled Chinese immigrants as "undesirable" and perceived them as being the greatest threat to the American way of life. This led to the 1882 Chinese Exclusion Act, which explicitly banned the immigration of Chinese laborers for a period of 10 years, but continued to be imposed until 1943. It was one of the most prominent immigration laws introduced to restrict immigration for a particular race or ethnic group, and it ushered in an era of strict immigration regulation.

The early 20th century ushered in America's "Great Wave" of immigration. Between 1900 and 1920, approximately 24 million immigrants came to the United States (Center for Immigration Studies n.d.). In response, Congress solidified a national quota system in 1924, ushering in an era of immigration restriction: "The quota provided immigration visas to two percent of the total number of people of each nationality in the United States as of the 1890 national census. It completely excluded immigrants from Asia" (U.S. Department of State n.d.). That same year, Congress founded the United States Border Patrol. The year 1965 marked the beginning of the second great wave of immigration, the passing of the 1965 Immigration Act, and the start of a more liberalized immigration policy. As a part of the 1965 Immigration Act,

---

The Case of *Yick Wo v. Hopkins*

Immigration law has taken various steps forward and backwards in United States history. One such forward leap was *Yick Wo v. Hopkins* (1886). This case involved an ordinance passed by the City of San Francisco that mandated all laundries operating in non-brick and stone buildings were required to obtain a city permit for business. The vast majority of laundries in San Francisco were owned and operated by Chinese immigrants. Most laundries in San Francisco were made of wood and therefore fell under the permitting process. The Board of Supervisors was given full discretion in choosing who qualified for a permit and not one permit was given to a Chinese business owner. Yick Wo was not extended a permit and continued to operate his laundry. He was fined $10 for operating a laundry without a permit. After refusing to pay the fine, Yick Wo was arrested and placed in prison. Wo sued the sheriff (Hopkins) arguing that application of the fine and enforcement were a violation of his 14th Amendments rights under the equal protection clause.

The California Supreme Court and the U.S. Court of Appeals felt the law was written in such a way that was non-discriminatory. After Wo lost in the California Supreme Court and the U.S. Court of Appeals, the case was appealed to the U.S. Supreme Court. The U.S. Supreme Court granted certiorari and found that regardless of the non-discriminatory language, the biased enforcement violated Wo's 14th Amendment rights under the equal protection clause.

This landmark case codified into federal law that a city may not enforce ordinances in an arbitrary and racially discriminatory manner. While the law itself was written in a manner to reduce the risk of fire in wooden laundries, its application only targeted Chinese immigrants. Laws can and have been written in ways that look fair on the surface but in practice are racially discriminatory. Justice Matthews wrote the decision for the Court, which ruled unanimously for the defendant.

Source

"*Yick Wo v. Hopkins*, 118 U.S. 356 (1886)." *Justia*. Accessed August 20, 2015. https://supreme
   .justia.com/cases/federal/us/118/356/case.html.

Congress increased the yearly number of immigrants that could be admitted into the country. Contrary to the Chinese Exclusion Act and the previous quota system, this law permitted the immigration of people of all races and ethnicities and changed the focus of the immigration system to help reconnect previous immigrants with their families. At this time, most immigrants came from Latin America.

In 1986, Congress passed the Immigration Reform and Control Act (IRCA). The IRCA provided many illegal immigrants with the opportunity to go through the naturalization process. Specifically, this opportunity was available to the following:

1. Illegal immigrants who immigrated before and lived within the U.S. since 1982; and
2. Illegal immigrants who worked as seasonal agricultural workers.

The IRCA also structured employer verification requirements for hiring new employees. In 1996, Congress initiated the Illegal Immigrant Reform and Immigrant Responsibility Act (IIRIRA). The IIRIRA served to increase border control and strengthen and improve the agencies responsible for monitoring the visa process (Cornell University Law School n.d.).

After the terrorist attacks of September 11, 2001, the nation as a whole searched for answers as to how to reduce the vulnerability that existed in protecting its borders from attack. As a result, the USA PATRIOT Act was implemented in 2001 to develop preventative measures and instruments to deter terrorism. Shortly thereafter the 2002 Homeland Security Act was passed, establishing the Department of Homeland Security (DHS), which merged the Immigration and Naturalization Service with 21 other agencies.

Republicans on Immigration

Since the terrorist attacks of September 11, 2001, protecting the country from security threats has remained a key element of the Republican stance on immigration. Many Republicans strongly assert the importance of tightening up America's borders to protect citizens from potential terrorist attacks. They argue that the growing population of undocumented immigrants makes it difficult to monitor for potential terrorists. To support their argument, Republicans often draw attention to the fact that the September 11 terrorist attacks included "a total of 20 foreign-born terrorists . . . 19 that took part in the attack that caused 2,974 civilian deaths. The terrorists had entered the country on tourist or student visas. Four of them, however, had violated the terms of their visas and become illegal aliens" (Center for Immigration Studies 2015).

Republicans tend to argue that cracking down on immigration policies could prevent such acts of terrorism in the future. They contend that borders must be more secure; visa distribution, verification, and renewal should be more closely monitored; and that only legal immigrants should be welcomed in the country. They strongly oppose giving amnesty to illegal immigrants for two main reasons: (1) it rewards illegal immigrants for breaking the law, and (2) it only serves to encourage others to illegally immigrate rather than go through the required channels of legal immigration. Republicans tend to believe that illegal immigrants should face strict punishments, which may serve as a deterrent for those considering illegal immigration. Simultaneously, they emphasize that legal immigrants should be rewarded via permanent residency and political equality because they followed the law.

Republicans also frequently argue that illegal immigrants consume more in social services than they pay in taxes, and that they take job opportunities that would otherwise be available to citizens. For the latter reason, some lawmakers in the GOP have stated that employers should be required to verify the immigration status of applicants so as to give legal residents and citizens the advantage in the employment process. Thus, they support the use of the E-verify program, an Internet-based program that according to the Department of Homeland Security, "compares information from an employee's Form I-9, Employment Eligibility Verification, to data from U.S. Department of Homeland Security and Social Security Administration records to confirm employment eligibility" (U.S. Citizenship and Immigration Services 2015a, 2015b). They believe that the E-verify program can help facilitate a fairer hiring process nationwide.

The Republican Party also supports the use of the Systematic Alien Verification for Entitlements (S.A.V.E.) program and demands that it be nationally implemented. The S.A.V.E. program uses an Internet-based program to verify an applicant's immigration status to determine whether the applicant qualifies for the government benefit he or she has applied to receive. This then can help prevent unqualified applicants from gaining access to benefits that they are not legally entitled to receive. Although the S.A.V.E. program itself does not determine whether an individual qualifies for a particular benefit, it gives government entities and their employees information pertaining to immigration status so that they can determine whether or not the individual is qualified (American Immigration Council 2011).

Compared with the Democratic Party, the Republican Party has taken a hardline approach to its stance on policymaking pertaining to illegal immigrants already living in the country. Historically, the party has supported deportation. More recently, the 2012 Republican presidential nominee Mitt Romney stressed the importance of "self-deportation." The premise behind this approach is to restructure immigration policy to reduce illegal aliens' abilities to be successful in the U.S. so that they choose to leave the country and return only through legal channels. Romney articulated that programs such as E-verify could help make "self-deportation" a successful means of reducing the population of illegal aliens currently living within the United States. Since 2012, it has been largely argued that Romney's "self-deportation" proposal likely hindered his performance in the 2012 presidential elections: "Democratic President Barack Obama, who was reelected in 2012, won 71 percent of the Hispanic vote to Republican challenger Mitt Romney's 27 percent" (Cooney 2014). Furthermore, the Republican Party as a whole has faced difficulties in presenting a uniform and consistent stance on this issue. At times even, the party has appeared to be disjointed in this regard as it tries to gain support from Latino voters while remaining true to its base.

On the individual level, Republicans each have their own views on how best to fix the current immigration system. These views vary among politicians and candidates. The 2016 Republican presidential candidates put these differences into perspective. For example, Jeb Bush has been largely labeled as a moderate concerning his views on immigration. In April 2014, for example, Bush stated that "[illegal immigrants] crossed the border because they had no other means to work, to be able to provide for their family, yes, they broke the law, but it's not a felony. It's an act of love, it's an act of commitment to your family" (Cooney 2014). In running for his party's 2016 presidential nomination, however, Bush presented a more conservative approach to immigration reform, advocating for greater border control and the need to "identify and send home the people who are entering the

United States and overstaying their visas or otherwise violating the terms of their admission" (Jeb2016.com 2015).

Another GOP presidential candidate, businessman and television personality Donald Trump, saw a significant growth in Republican support of his candidacy largely as a result of his brazen anti-immigrant stance on immigration policy reform. Most notably, Trump contends that a wall must be built across the U.S.–Mexico border and that Mexico should be responsible for financing the project (Donaldjtrump.com 2015). As these candidates illustrate, Republicans within the party have their own understanding and interpretation of the Republican Party's stance on immigration. The Republican National Committee (RNC) asserts that it respects these differences but that the party as a whole is continuously working to improve its standing with Latino voters while still remaining committed to its base.

Democrats on Immigration

The contemporary Democratic Party has placed the issue of immigration front and center in its party platform. Comprehensive immigration reform took center stage in the 2012 Democratic Party Platform and it looks to be a focus in 2016. Issues such as support for the DREAM Act and constructing a path to citizenship for undocumented immigrants leading productive lives in the United States are among its greatest priorities. The Obama administration has taken extraordinary steps in the area of immigration reform and signed multiple executive actions that have led to increased tensions between the Democratic and Republican parties. For example, on November 20, 2014, the president announced a series of executive actions to crack down on illegal immigration at the border, prioritize deporting felons not families, and require certain undocumented immigrants to pass a criminal background check and pay taxes to temporarily stay in the U.S. without fear of deportation.

These initiatives include:

- Expanding the population that is eligible for the Deferred Action for Childhood Arrivals (DACA) program to people of any current age who entered the United States before the age of 16 and lived in the United States continuously since January 1, 2010, and extending the period of DACA and work authorization from two years to three years.
- Allowing parents of U.S. citizens and lawful permanent residents to request deferred action and employment authorization for three years, in a new Deferred Action for Parents of Americans and Lawful Permanent Residents program, provided they have lived in the United States continuously since January 1, 2010, and pass required background checks.
- Expanding the use of provisional waivers of unlawful presence to include the spouses and sons and daughters of lawful permanent residents and the sons and daughters of U.S. citizens.
- Modernizing, improving, and clarifying immigrant and nonimmigrant visa programs to grow our economy and create jobs.

- Promoting citizenship education and public awareness for lawful permanent residents and providing an option for naturalization applicants to use credit cards to pay the application fee.

These executive actions are part of the overall Democratic Party position on immigration. Today, Democrats tend to emphasize that the government needs to continue to work on controlling the nation's borders as a homeland security measure and to lessen the frequency of illegal immigration in the future. They also claim the U.S. needs to more heavily monitor businesses and employers to ensure that immigrants are not being taken advantage of and undermined within their workplace. This pertains especially to undocumented workers but the impact of this exploitation also disadvantages American workers who are searching for fair employment opportunities. Before gaining the opportunity to apply for citizenship, undocumented immigrants must admit to breaking the law and "must get right with the law" (Democratic National Committee 2012). Additionally, many Democrats are working to reduce the threat of deportation for minor offenses. Lastly, Democrats aim to reform the Immigration and Naturalization Service (INS) to make it more efficient. Currently, the citizenship application process can take years to complete because of the present backlog of applications. Democrats believe that reform could reduce the waiting time to a matter of months.

Currently, many Democrats agree for the most part on the necessity of a path to citizenship. Some Democrats have supported building a fence along the U.S.–Mexico border and others have argued for continued mass deportations of undocumented immigrants. For example Hillary Clinton supports a pathway to citizenship but as a senator voted for H.R. 6061—Secure Fence Act of 2006, which authorized the construction of a fence along the U.S.–Mexico border. In comparison with many in the Republican Party, Democrats tend to agree on more issues regarding immigration and have held similar positions over the last few party platforms. The Democratic Party has made significant electoral strides in the Latino community and this has prompted a continued effort to recruit Latino voters and Latino candidates. Long-range Democratic electoral planning focuses on this growing voting block to put states like Texas and Arizona into play.

Erik T. Rankin and
Katelyn Schachtschneider

Further Reading

American Immigration Council. 2015. "The Systematic Alien Verification for Entitlement (SAVE) Program: A Fact Sheet." Accessed August 10. http://www.immigrationpolicy.org/just-facts/systematic-alien-verification-entitlements-save-program-fact-sheet.

Center for Immigration Studies. 2015. "Historical Overview of Immigration Policy." Accessed June 15. http://cis.org/ImmigrationHistoryOverview.

Cooney, Peter. 2014. "Jeb Bush Says Illegal Immigration Often 'An Act of Love.'" *Reuters* (Washington, DC), April 6. Accessed April 11, 2015. http://www.reuters.com/article /2014/04/06/us-usa-politics-bush-idUSBREA350 P620140406.

Cornell University Law School. 2015. "Illegal Immigration Reform and Immigration Responsibility Act." Accessed July 15. https://www.law.cornell.edu/wex/illegal_immigration _reform_and_immigration_responsibilityact.

Democratic National Committee. 2012. "Moving America Forward: 2012 Democratic Platform." Accessed November 11, 2015. https://www.democrats.org/party-platform# american-community.

Donaldjtrump.com. 2015. "Immigration Reform that Will Make America Great Again." *Trump: Make America Great Again!* Accessed November 12, 2015. https://www.donaldjtrump .com/positions/immigration-reform.

Jaggers, Jeremiah, W. Jay Gabbard, and Shanna J. Jaggers. 2014. "The Devolution of U.S. Immigration Policy: An Examination of the History and Future of Immigration Policy." *Journal of Policy Practice* 13: 3–15.

Jeb2016.com. 2015. "Border Security." *Jeb 2016.* Accessed November 3, 2015. https:// jeb2016.com/border-security/?lang=en.

Lazarus, Emma. 2002. "The New Colossus." In *Emma Lazarus: Selected Poems and Other Writings*, edited by Gregory Eiselein, 233. Canada: Broadview Press Ltd.

National Network for Immigration and Refugee Rights. 2015. "Republican and Democratic Party 2012 Immigration Platform Comparison." Accessed June 24, 2015. http:// www.nnirr.org/~nnirrorg/drupal/sites/default/files/republican-democratic_ immigration _platform_chart.pdf.

Progressives for Immigration Reform. 2015. "U.S. Immigration History," *United States Immigration Policy—Environmental Impact Statement.* Accessed July 2, http://www .immigrationeis.org/about-ieis/us-immigration-history.

Republican National Committee. 2015. "RNC Statement Commemorating National Hispanic Heritage Month." Press Releases. Accessed September 25, 2015. https://www .gop.com/rnc-statement-commemorating-national-hispanic-heritage-month/.

U.S. Citizenship and Immigration Services. 2015a. "Executive Actions on Immigration." Accessed August 20. http://www.uscis.gov/immigrationaction.

U.S. Citizenship and Immigration Services. 2015b. "Origins of the Federal Immigration Service." Accessed June 15. http://www.uscis.gov/history-and-genealogy/our-history /agency-history/origins-federal-immigration-service.

U.S. Department of Homeland Security, U.S. Citizenship and Immigration Services. 2015a. "Our History." Accessed August 13. http://www.uscis.gov/about-us/our-history.

U.S. Department of Homeland Security, U.S. Citizenship and Immigration Services. 2015b. "What is E-Verify?" Accessed August 1. http://www.uscis.gov/e-verify/what-e-verify.

U.S. Department of State, Office of the Historian. 2015. "Milestones: 1866–1898. Chinese Immigration and the Chinese Exclusion Acts." Accessed June 15. https://history.state .gov/milestones/1866-1898/chinese-immigration.

U.S. Department of State, Office of the Historian. 2015. "Milestones: 1921–1936. The Immigration Act of 1924 (The Johnson-Reed Act)." Accessed June 17. https://history .state.gov/milestones/1921-1936/immigration-act.

"U.S. Immigration History." 2015. *United States Immigration Policy—Environmental Impact Statement.* Accessed July 2. http://www.immigrationeis.org/about-ieis/us-immigration -history.

U.S. Library of Congress. "Bill Summary & Status 99th Congress (1985–1986) S. 1200 All Information." Thomas. Accessed July 2, 2015. http://thomas.loc.gov/cgi-bin/bdquery /z?d099:SN01200:@@@L&summ2=m&%7CTOM:/bss/d099query.html.

Yick Wo v. Hopkins, 118 U.S. 356. (1886). *Justia*. Accessed August 20, 2015. https://supreme. justia.com/cases/federal/us/118/356/case.html.

Zong, Jie, and Jeanne Batalova. 2015. "Frequently Requested Statistics on Immigrants and Immigration in the United States." *Migration Policy Institute*, February 26. Accessed March 3, 2015. http://www.migrationpolicy.org/article/frequently-requested-statistics -immigrants-and-immigration-united-states.

Income Inequality

At a Glance

In the United States there is a substantial gap between the richest and poorest Americans. For example, the top 20 percent of income generating households earn more than 12 times as much as the bottom 20 percent. This is a much higher gap than reported in other developed countries (Joint Economic Committee 2014). The implication of this gap was explored in a 2013 United Nations report entitled, *Inequality Matters*, where it was concluded that income inequality was responsible not only for slowing global economic growth, but also increasing political instability in the United States.

Republicans and Democrats agree that income inequality has grown over the past several decades, but they differ in how much and what the government should do to address it. In a 2014 Pew Research survey, only 45 percent of Republicans believed that the government should do something about the increasing income gap, compared to 90 percent of Democrats (Pew Research Center 2014). The partisan debate does not end there. Republican solutions to income inequality center on encouraging economic growth through: lowering taxes for the wealthy and for corporations, as well as reducing business regulations that discourage entrepreneurship. They argue that by doing so, a premium is placed on higher education, as well as, advanced training, allowing American workers the opportunities to improve their families' economic standing. By comparison, Democrats tend to favor redistribution solutions in the form of increasing taxes on the wealthiest Americans and expanding programs for the poor.

Many Republicans . . .

- See income inequality as largely a result of individual choices and capabilities
- Believe that governmental solutions to income inequality hinder national economic growth, and instead favor business solutions, which encourage entrepreneurship
- Oppose governmental efforts to modify market outcomes or to redistribute wealth via government programs and policies
- Oppose increasing the federal minimum wage

Many Democrats . . .

• Charge that income inequality is created by unfair social systems
• Believe that government has a legitimate role to play in reducing the wealth gap
• Support expansion of the federal minimum wage and social benefits for the poor

---

Overview

In his book, *The Politics of Income Inequality in the United States,* Nathan Kelly described income inequality as the question of "Who gets what?" (Kelly 2011). In answering this question, we find that the gap between the rich and the poor in the U.S. continues to widen. According to the GINI Coefficient (created in 1912 by sociologist Corrado Gini), which is the most commonly used inequality measurement, American income inequality increased significantly between the mid-1980s and 2012 (Organization for Economic Co-Operation and Development 2014). For example, the top 1 percent of earners increased their income 86.1 percent between 1993 and 2012 while the bottom 99 percent's income growth was 6.6 percent in the given period time (Saez 2013).

Income inequality is apparent in the middle classes as well as the lower classes. Current middle-class households make less money than their 1989 counterparts. However, earning less money is not the only reason behind the financial crisis of the middle class. Substantially higher living expenses plague many middle-income households, including medical expenditures and school tuition. Moreover, middle class wage earners are finding that stable and well-paid job opportunities are not as plentiful as in past years (Joint Economic Committee 2014).

From an international perspective, the news is not any better. Analyses conducted by the Organization for Economic Co-Operation and Development (OECD), an international organization made up of eighteen European countries plus the United States and Canada created in the 1960s to study international economic development, suggest that income inequality is greater in the United States than in any other democratic nation (Organization for Economic Co-Operation and Development 2014). For example, according to the OECD data, an average American makes $123 compared to the $100 average a person in other OECD countries makes. However, this story does not apply to those at the bottom of the economic structure. The poorest 10 percent in the U.S. make only $0.73 for every dollar of their OECD counterparts.

The division between the top wage earners and the lowest wage earners illustrates patterns of disparity. In 2012, an estimated 15 percent of the entire population was determined to be living under the poverty line; these data indicate that nearly 50 million Americans live beneath the poverty threshold. Certain groups are highly visible in the impoverished population. For example, nearly 22 percent of children and 28 percent of those with disabilities are under the poverty line in 2012 (Joint Economic Committee 2014). The differences between household incomes show greater discrepancies between racial groups within the country as well. For example, according to Census Bureau data in 2013, median income for a white household was $58,270 compared with $40,963 for Hispanics and $34,598 for blacks.

One explanation of the wage gap is that Hispanics and blacks find themselves over-represented in the bottom rungs of the occupational ladder. Although the Civil Right Act of 1964 made it illegal to blatantly discriminate based on race or gender, disparities remain. Blacks and Hispanics are more likely to work in blue collar and service jobs, rather than professional and executive managerial jobs where whites and Asian Americans are concentrated (Campbell and Kaufman 2006). The failure of the minimum wage to keep up with inflation also contributes to income inequality. In his 2014 State of the Union address, President Obama called again on Congress to raise the national minimum wage, this time from $7.25 to $10.10 an hour. In sum, Republicans and Democrats both acknowledge that there are all sorts of tools that lawmakers can use to reduce inequality; however, disagreements arise over whether they should and what form the intervention should take.

Republicans on Income Inequality

Republican solutions to income inequality tend to revolve around providing opportunities for economic growth, which they frame as drivers of employment and wage growth for the working and middle classes. Republicans also tend to believe that individual differences, such as gaps in capacities, skills, and characters, lead people into different socioeconomic statuses and contribute to income inequality. For example, Pew Research results suggest that nearly 6 in 10 Republicans say that hard work has more to do with a person's wealth than any advantages they may have had in life (Pew Research Center 2014). From their perspective, reducing the income gap is up to individuals, who must put forth more effort to achieve more success (Zolt 2013). Because equality is about opportunity, education provides equal access to that opportunity. For this reason, Republicans put a premium on higher education as a solution to income inequality.

To make the point that providing opportunities for economic growth can benefit the American economy, Republicans point to the link between earnings and education. In 1980, an American with a college education earned only about 30 percent more than a person who had graduated from high school. Today that college graduate earns 70 percent more. Graduate degrees show even greater returns (Becker and Murphy 2007). This trend has contributed greatly to the growth in income inequality in the United States, but also shows that the potential to improve one's employment prospects through higher education is great and that this opportunity today extends beyond both racial and gender lines.

For these reasons, one Republican solution to income inequality is to increase educational opportunities for people of all socioeconomic backgrounds, thereby giving them the means to improve their own lives. Support for this position comes from Gary Becker and Kevin Murphy, economists from the University of Chicago, who argue that instead of lamenting the increased earning gap, policymakers should focus attention on how to address American youth left behind, rather than trying to interfere directly with inequality (Becker and Murphy 2007). In 2001, Republican President George W. Bush, rolled out his federal program, entitled *No Child Left Behind*, which is indicative of a recent national effort to level the educational playing field. While the program has fallen short of its goals to reduce gaps across race, geography, and economic circumstances, it has illustrated the idea that by modifying the future marketability of American employees through skill-building and knowledge, income inequality may be solved by those willing to take the opportunity (Commission on No Child Left Behind 2007).

Republicans generally equate democracy with freedom and a free market economy. For this reason, many Republicans vehemently oppose proposals to redistribute income in a way that benefits the poor more than the rich. Becker and Murphy (2007, 27) critiqued the idea of raising taxes on the rich, asking: "Would these same individuals advocate a tax on going to college and a subsidy for dropping out of high school in response to the increased importance of education?" They argued that raising taxes on the rich would have such an effect. These neoliberal beliefs assert that governmental solutions that modify market outcomes or redistribute wealth run counter to democratic principles.

Republican hopefuls for the 2016 presidential nomination engaged in debate on income inequality in the early months of their candidacy announcements. For example Jeb Bush, a candidate for the Republication presidential nomination, gave a speech in Detroit titled, "Restoring the Right to Rise in America," addressing the rapidly increasing inequality in the United States, touting the problem not as income inequality, but as opportunity inequality. While the Democrats have tagged this move as disingenuous, *National Review's* Ramesh Ponnuru claimed the motivation behind the Republican dialogue is to fix the damaged reputation of the Republicans as being a party that "only cares about the economic interest of the rich" before the 2016 presidential race (Ponnuru 2015).

Democrats on Income inequality

When thinking about inequality, many Democrats appreciate the sentiments attributed to U.S. Supreme Court Justice Louis Brandeis: "We can have democracy in this country, or we can have great wealth concentrated in the hands of a few, but we cannot have both" (Dilliard 1941). For Democrats, the very existence of an increasing income gap suggests that inequality stems from unfair social structures, including limited opportunities for the poor. Economist James Kurth explained that the wealth of the rich is never simply the product of free enterprise and free market, but comes by exploiting a network of governmental supports, such as licenses, regulations, subsidies, and contracts (Kurth 2006). Of most concern are the reductions of taxes on wealth (i.e., estate taxes) and on income from wealth (i.e., capital-gains taxes). By stacking the deck through governmental support and then reducing the taxes paid on that gained wealth, a vicious cycle ensues whereby the rich get richer and the poor get poorer.

Because Democrats believe the process is biased, it is no surprise to them that the inequality unfavorably impacts women and minorities. Following Obama's election in 2012, he signed the Lilly Ledbetter Fair Pay Act to address the wage gap. The legislation restored the protection against pay discrimination that was stripped away by the Supreme Court ruling in the *Ledbetter v. Goodyear* (2007) case. Although millennial women have closed the gender wage gap from previous generations, given that women today make, on average, 77 cents for every dollar paid to man, it appears that closure mostly applies to entry level positions. Men still outrank and out-earn women as they move up the ladder toward a glass ceiling,

---

Obama Administration Efforts to Reduce Income Inequality

President Barack Obama has made significant efforts to reduce the income gap between the wealthy and the impoverished during his presidency through three major initiatives: (1) the Lilly Ledbetter Fair Pay Restoration Act, (2) the National Equal Pay Enforcement Task Force, and (3) an Executive Order to increase the minimum wage for federal workers.

Lilly Ledbetter was a female employee who worked for twenty years at Goodyear Tire & Rubber Co. During her employment, she earned less than her male colleagues doing equivalent work but remained unaware of the discrimination in pay. When she retired from the company in 1998, she decided to sue. Her case reached the Supreme Court and, due to the fact that the 180-day statutory charging period—which is a limited amount of time to file a legal charge of discrimination—had passed, Ledbetter's suit was rejected. President Obama signed the Lilly Ledbetter Fair Pay Restoration Act to address this loophole. Most importantly, the law makes clear that pay discrimination claims on the basis of sex, race, national origin, age, religion, and disability are unacceptable. In the bill, President Obama wrote the below statements:

> That making our economy work means making sure it works for everyone. That there are no second citizens in our workplaces, and that it's not just unfair and illegal—but bad for business—to pay someone less because of their gender, age, race, ethnicity, religion, or disability. And that justice isn't about some abstract legal theory, or footnote in a casebook—it's about how our laws affect the daily realities of people's lives: their ability to make a living and care for their families and achieve their goals.

The Lilly Ledbetter Act of 2009 was a substantial step forward for income equality and for supporting the founding principle of the United States that all citizens are created equal and deserve a chance to pursue happiness.

To better enforce this law, the National Equal Pay Enforcement Task Force was established. The Task Force cooperates with the following governmental agencies, the Equal Employment Opportunity Commission (EEOC), the Department of Justice (DOJ), the Department of Labor (DOL), and the Office of Personnel Management (OPM), to achieve the following five goals: (1) investigation of unfair payment at work places, (2) data collection for monitoring and tracking income discrimination, (3) offering educational programs for both employers and employees, (4) providing solutions with respect to the specific problems, and (5) enforcement of the existing fair payment laws.

According to the U.S Department of Labor Wage and Hour Division, President Obama signed Executive Order 13658 in February 12, 2014. This raised the minimum wage to $10.10 per hour for federal workers, starting January 1, 2015, with additional increases planned in 2016. While the Executive Order only applies to federal workers, several states led by Democratic lawmakers have followed Obama's lead and increased their minimum wage.

These national endeavors also affected private businesses; some companies including Costco, Gap, IKEA, and Disney agreed to raise their minimum wage in accordance with the new law. These Democratic actions may bring a ripple effect to the U.S., benefiting low-income workers, fighting poverty, and boosting the nation's economy.

Sources

Obama, Barack. 2009. "Remarks of President Barack Obama on the Lilly Ledbetter Fair Pay Restoration Act Bill Signing," January 29. Accessed August 1, 2015. https://www .whitehouse.gov/the-press-office/remarks-president-barack-obama-lilly-ledbetter-fair-pay -restoration-act-bill-signin.

The White House. 2015. National Equal Pay Enforcement Task Force. Accessed August 3, 2015. https://www.whitehouse.gov/sites/default/files/rss_viewer/equal_pay_task_force.pdf.

U.S. Department of Labor, Wage and Hour Division. 2015. "Worker Rights Under Executive Order 13658." Accessed August 5, 2015. http://www.dol.gov/whd/regs/compliance/posters /mw-contractors.pdf.

the term used to describe the barriers women face as they move up the corporate ladder. Democrats argue that greater family medical leave and benefits may help to close this gap. The U.S. is one of the few countries that does not guarantee paid maternity leave. As a result, women's wages suffer as they interrupt their careers to care for their children. Of course, many critics argue that the legislation, while symbolic, does little to change the plight of women, as the protections afforded in the legislation are rarely utilized.

Democrats tend to believe that the political system contributes to the perpetuation of this inequality. Pointing to research that suggests that the most substantial political contributions come from the most affluent strata, and that donations from this elite strata tend to tilt strongly Republican, the Democrats argue that the wealthy buy politicians and public figures, therefore even further stacking the deck in favor of tax cuts for the rich. Three-quarters of Democrats believe that the economic system unfairly favors the wealthy (Pew Research Center 2014). Democrats bemoan the lack of fairness in the United States tax code that allows the wealthy to dodge taxes, as well as blocking funding, campaign finance, and support for policies that would alleviate the gap, such as paid maternity leave, raising the minimum wage, and increased spending on programs for the impoverished.

Democrats believe that it is the government's responsibility to do something about this cycle. From their perspective, the income gap can be reduced by the government's direct actions, such as tax reform and redistribution policies that take money from the very wealthy and redistribute it to the impoverished via social welfare programs. To do this, the American tax system must be overhauled. One solution is to apply the estate tax to estates at the $7 million dollar mark, rather than the current $10.24 million mark. By expanding the estates that will pay taxes, those revenues will be redistributed to the impoverished and needy through the expansion of social insurance and programs for vulnerable populations, such as Supplementary Security Income (SSI), public assistance, Medicaid, educational assistance, housing subsidies, and food stamps (Democratic National Platform 2012).

Income inequality was one of the issues that President Obama ran on in his first term. In his 2012 State of the Union Address, President Obama argued taxing the rich helped the economy as a whole, "here's the kicker: We created a lot of millionaires, too. The economy, when you look back on American history, always works best when the middle class is doing well" (The White House 2012). Income inequality remained a theme in his second term as well, when he stated "let's close the loopholes that lead to inequality by allowing the top 1 percent to avoid paying taxes on their accumulated wealth" (Obama 2015). The issue of income inequality is also expected to be a centerpiece of Democratic campaign strategies in the races for state governorships, House and Senate seats, and the White House itself in 2016.

Cara E. Rabe-Hemp and
JiHye Park

Further Reading

Becker, Gary S., and Kevin M. Murphy. 2007. "The Upside of Income Inequality." *The American*, May/June, 20–23.

Campbell, L., and R. Kaufman. 2006. "Racial Differences in Household Wealth: Beyond Black and White." *Research in Social Stratification and Mobility* 24: 131–152.

Commission on No Child Left Behind. 2007. *Beyond No Child Left Behind: Fulfilling the Promise to Our Nation's Children.* Washington, DC: Aspen Institute.

Democratic National Committee. 2012. "Moving America Forward: 2012 Democratic Platform." Presented at the Democratic National Convention, Charlotte, North Carolina. Accessed November 16, 2015. http://www.nytimes.com/interactive/2012/09/04/us/politics/20120904-DNC-platform.html?_r=0.

Dilliard, Irving. 1941. *Mr. Justice Brandeis, Great American; Press Opinion and Public Appraisal.* Saint Louis, MO: The Modern View Press.

Joint Economic Committee (JEC). 2014. *Income Inequality in the United States.* Washington, DC: JEC Democratic Staff.

Kelly, Nathan J. 2011. *The Politics of Income Inequality in the United States.* New York: Cambridge University Press.

Kurth, James. 2006. "The Rich Get Richer." *The American Conservative.* September 25, 6–11.

Ledbetter v. Goodyear Tire and Rubber Company, 550 U.S. 618 (2007).

Nolan, Brian, Wiemer Salverda, and Timothy Smeeding. 2009. *The Handbook of Economic Inequality.* New York: Oxford University Press.

Obama, Barack. 2015. State of the Union Address. January. Accessed November 16, 2015. https://www.whitehouse.gov/photos-and-video/video/2015/01/20/president-obamas-2015-state-union-address.

Organization for Economic Co-Operation and Development (OECD). 2014. *United States: Tackling High Inequalities Creating Opportunities for All.* Paris: OECD Paris.

PEW Research Centre (PRC). 2014. *Most See Inequality Growing, but Partisans Differ over Solutions.* January 23. Accessed November 11, 2015. http://www.people-press.org/2014/01/23/most-see-inequality-growing-but-partisans-differ-over-solutions/.

Ponnuru, Ramesh. 2015. "Let's Not Mention Inequality," *National Review.* February 9.

Republican National Committee. 2012. "We Believe in America: 2012 Republican Platform." Presented at the Republican National Convention, Tampa, Florida. Accessed November 1, 2015. http://www.cnn.com/interactive/2012/08/politics/rnc.schedule/.

Saez, Emmanuel. 2013. "Striking It Richer: The Evolution of Top Incomes in the United States." University of California, Berkeley, September.

Tollerson, Earnest. 1996. "The Flat-Tax Candidate Subordinates Himself to His Economic Message." *New York Times*, February 26. Accessed July 15, 2015. http://www.nytimes.com/1996/02/27/us/politics-steve-forbes-flat-tax-candidate-subordinates-himself-his-economic.html.

United Nations. 2015. *Inequality Matters.* Accessed July 15. http://www.un.org/esa/socdev/documents/reports/InequalityMatters.pdf.

Washington Post. 2015. "The CNN Democratic Debate Transcript, Annotated." *Washington Post*, October 13. Accessed November 3, 2015. https://www.washingtonpost.com/news/the-fix/wp/2015/10/13/the-oct-13-democratic-debate-who-said-what-and-what-it-means/.

The White House, Office of the Press Secretary. 2012. Remarks by the President and First Lady at a Campaign Event in Dubuque, IA, August 15. Accessed July 3, 2015. https://www.whitehouse.gov/the-press-office/2012/08/15/remarks-president-and-first-lady-campaign-event-dubuque-ia.

Zolt, Eric M. 2013. "Inequality in America: Challenges for Tax and Spending Policies." *Tax Law Review* 68: 641.

Income Tax

At a Glance

Income generally includes compensation for services, gain from sale of goods or other property, interest, dividends, rents, royalties, annuities, and pensions. An income tax, then, is a levy imposed on an individual's income by government used as a source of revenue to fund federal programs or state programs as the income tax is a tool used by both levels of government to raise revenue. The federal income tax is allowed by an amendment to the U.S. Constitution while states decide for themselves whether or not to have an income tax. As of 2015, 43 states and the District of Columbia impose individual income taxes.

When the Sixteenth Amendment to the U.S. Constitution was ratified, making the federal income tax constitutional, few could have predicted the resulting revenues. The potential of the income tax to produce federal revenue, coupled with the complicated current tax structure, has made the income tax one of the more debated partisan issues of the 21st century.

Republicans tend to argue not only that the progressive structure of the current taxation system punishes talent, hard work, and entrepreneurship, but that it is overly complicated and unwieldy. The current Internal Revenue Service Code subsection on income taxes, found in the U.S. Code Title 26 Subtitle A, is five chapters in length. Adding to the code's complexity, individuals do not pay a single tax rate on the entirety of income, but instead tax brackets dictate the tax rate for one's income amount. For example, a single person who earned $15,000 in 2014 was taxed at the rate of 10 percent of $9,075 of his or her income (the first bracket). His or her remaining income of $5,925 was taxed at 15 percent, so the tax owed was $1,796.25. This scenario does not include an individual's potential deductions, exemptions, and credits, which makes the amount owed less (U.S. Department of Treasury 2014).

Many Republicans assert that the majority of the income tax burden falls upon the highest earners, which acts as a punishment for an individual's financial success. While some dissension exists as to the extent of tax inequity and tax burden and whether the tax code should be revised, generally

Republicans favor supply-side economics and reinvestment tax policy, and disagree with what they perceive as restrictions to the free market. These factors equate to a push for lower income taxes on those considered the most burdened: the rich. This is because many Republicans associate democracy with a free market economy and perceive interference with the free market as potentially damaging to the economy, as well as to the democratic principles of the nation.

In contrast, Democrats tend to argue that income tax produces revenues necessary to fund the federal government, especially social programs like Medicaid, Medicare, and Social Security. Many Democrats believe in strongly supporting these and other social programs, which reflect their conviction that assisting those in need is a key role of a democratic government. For this reason, Democrats assert that the current tax system favors the ultra-rich and argue that the rich should be taxed at a higher rate than the working class. Democrats often assert that loopholes in the current tax code that primarily benefit the wealthiest should be closed or tightened to better ensure that all individuals, regardless of income level, pay their share of taxes.

Many Republicans . . .

- Believe that income taxes are too high and impede economic activity
- Assert that state and federal governments should only levy taxes to pay for essential functions
- Support changes to the tax code to benefit corporations and the wealthy, on the theory that such reforms help businesses to grow, resulting in job creation
- Say that cutting income taxes allow individuals to retain more of their earned income, resulting in a net gain of disposable income, a key to economic expansion and vitality

Many Democrats . . .

- Emphasize that income taxes help fund governmental operations at the local, state, and federal level that provide a wide range of vital services and programs
- Insist that the rich should be taxed at a higher rate than middle- and working-class Americans

---

Overview

The United States initially did not allow federal taxation. In fact, in 1895 the Supreme Court ruled the income tax unconstitutional under Article I of the

Constitution. Later, though, a variety of historical, political, and social changes prompted the adoption of the Sixteenth Amendment to the Constitution. Why this shift in public sentiment?

The economic hallmark of this era was the great disparity between the ever-wealthier, capitalist industrialists, who were growing richer, and agricultural workers and the cities' working class who were growing poorer. During the country's early history, the tax code allowed the wealthy to largely avoid a tax burden. Instead of income tax, federal revenues came from import and export tariffs on as well as an excise tax on alcohol and cigarettes. Eventually there was a growing sense among the middle and working class that they were shouldering more than their fair share of the tax burden. In response, in 1913, Congress ratified the Sixteenth Amendment to allow the federal government to "lay and collect taxes on incomes, from whatever source derived, without apportionment among the several states, and without regard to any census or enumeration," based on the argument that income tax should be collected both as a necessary source of revenue and a tool for social justice ("16th Amendment to the U.S. Constitution: Federal Income Tax" 1913)..

The U.S. faced a period of high unemployment causing a sharp recession in 1920–1921, during which unemployment briefly exceeded 11 percent (Carter 2006). The share of U.S. wealth controlled by its richest citizens increased rapidly to perhaps the highest level in history. After its ratification, though, the federal income tax became an important source of revenue for the running of government programs. From this point forward, top tax rates and overall tax revenue steadily grew, and at several points in the 20th century—during World War I, the Great Depression, and World War II—the top income tax rates exceeded 75 percent. The trend since 1950, however, has been a gradual diminishment in top tax rates.

By 2010, the federal government collected about 90 percent of its revenue from taxes, of which 42 percent came from the personal income tax. Despite the importance of income tax revenue to federal funding, many economists feel that the current tax system is overly complex, unfair, and inefficient (Burnham 2011). While the income tax serves as the primary source of federal revenue, it no longer raises enough revenue to support the government's current level of spending. In the past decade increased federal spending has resulted in an increasing gap between legislated taxation levels and federal spending. For example, in 2015, the federal government collected about $3.3 trillion in revenues, but spent $3.7 trillion, leaving a deficit of $426 billion dollars (Congressional Budget Office 2015). The Congressional Budget Office argues the reason for the deficit is that relative to the size of the economy, federal revenues are currently at their lowest point in 60 years. Despite this concern, the deficit has shrunk the last seven years, since reaching an all-time high in 2007, leaving some to suggest that the U.S. is headed in a positive fiscal trajectory while others lament the long-term picture that includes funding the upcoming retirement of the baby boomers (Congressional Budget Office 2015). Republican and Democratic opinions on whom to tax and where best to spend U.S. revenues differ dramatically.

Republicans on Income Taxes

Republicans tend to assert they favor taxes only to the extent necessary to fund essential functions of government. Beyond what they consider an essential level, Republicans believe increasing taxes on the wealthy will damage the health of the economy, ultimately resulting in downturns in economic activity that hurt all Americans. In Stanford University's *Policy Review*, Kip Hagopian (2011) argued that the progressive income tax system punishes hard work, a common refrain from GOP lawmakers. Within the current tax code, high-income families pay the larger percentage of income tax by virtue of falling into a higher tax bracket. Republicans point to unfairness in the tax code with examples such as this: in 2013, individuals with adjusted gross incomes of $250,000 or higher accounted for only 2.4 percent of tax returns filed; however, these individuals were responsible for 48.9 percent of all income taxes paid for the year (Desilver 2015). Republicans regularly refer to the tax code as a penalty for working, instead advocating additional types of taxes to gain revenue, arguing that states that levy additional sales taxes, for instance, display greater economic growth (Sinquefield 2015a, 2015b).

Rand Paul's "Fair and Flat" Tax Plan

One of the flat tax's most vocal supporters, Republican Rand Paul was born in Pennsylvania in 1963, the third of five children born to Ron Paul, U.S. congressman and 2012 Republican presidential candidate. Paul attended Baylor University and then Duke University for medical school. After his ophthalmology residency at Duke, Rand moved to Bowling Green, Kentucky, to start a medical practice.

Rand entered the political arena in 1994 when he founded Kentucky Taxpayers United, a watchdog group tracking taxation and spending issues in the Kentucky state legislature. In 2008, he became active in the nationwide anti-tax movement known as the Tea Party and announced his interest in running for U.S. Senate. In 2010 Paul won a Senate seat with help from the endorsements of several high-profile conservatives, including Sarah Palin and James Dobson. In April 2015, Rand announced he would run for President in 2016 on a platform that included a "Fair and Flat" tax plan. Under this plan touted by Rand, income tax levels would be set at a flat 14.5 percent for everyone and most deductions currently in the tax code would be eliminated. Rand argued that his tax plan would reduce the role of government in American society and trigger tremendous economic expansion.

Source

"Rand Paul." *Biography*. Accessed November 13, 2015. http://www.biography.com/people/rand
-paul-588472.

Thorndike, Joseph. 2015. "Rand Paul's Flat Tax Plan May Be Radical, But It's Not Impossible."
Forbes, June 26. Accessed November 23, 2015. http://www.forbes.com/sites/taxanalysts
/2015/06/26/rand-pauls-tax-plan-may-be-radical-but-its-not-impossible/.

The age and complexity of the U.S. tax code is at the center of many Republican arguments calling for reform. Some conservative Republicans contend the Internal Revenue System is corrupt and favors special interest groups. Stephen Moore, a senior fellow at The Heritage Foundation, a conservative think tank, argued, "the only people who benefit from a complicated, barnacle-encrusted 70,000-page tax code are tax attorneys, accountants, lobbyists, IRS agents and politicians who use the tax code as a way to buy and sell favors" (Moore 2015, 2).

While Republicans as a whole tend to favor changes in the federal tax code, the Pew Research Center identifies a distinct separation between moderate/liberal Republicans and their conservative counterparts' opinions on taxation. Conservative Republicans support a tax code overhaul by a vast majority of 72 percent, while moderate and liberal Republicans (admittedly a smaller percentage of the overall Republican Party) support tax code changes, but only at a slight majority of 53 percent. The distinction between factions does not end there. When asked whether they feel the wealthy fail to pay their fair share of taxes, 38 percent of conservative Republicans argue this is true compared to 64 percent of moderate and liberal Republicans (Pew Research Center 2014)

These distinctions are illustrated in tax reforms proposed by 2016 Republican presidential candidates. Ben Carson, Ted Cruz, Lindsay Graham, and Rick Santorum endorsed variations of a flat income tax, while Mike Huckabee advocated a "Fair Tax" solution eliminating income, payroll, gift, and estate taxes in favor of a single consumption tax. Senator Rand Paul proposed to combine tactics, repealing the existing IRS tax code, eliminating many federal taxes, and implementing a flat 14.5 percent income tax on individuals and businesses (Rand 2015). Candidates Chris Christie and Marco Rubio both favored a progressive income tax, but with far fewer brackets. In a proposal developed with Republican Senator Mike Lee of Utah, the Rubio-Lee Tax Reform Plan, Rubio criticized the current tax code as "stacked against those who are working hard and playing by the rules, while the system seems rigged for insiders who don't" (Lee and Rubio 2015). If implemented, their plan would reduce the number of brackets to two, eliminate most itemized deductions, and creates a child tax credit (Schuyler and McBride 2015). Many Republicans consider tax reform at the heart of their 2016 platform.

Democrats on Income Tax

A 2013 *Washington Post* poll revealed a majority of Democrats view the tax code in a positive light (Cillizza and Sullivan 2014). One reason is that Democrats see benefits to revenues produced by the income tax and see social detriment occurring without the existence of programs and services supported by income tax revenue. Due to the income tax's unpopularity with Republicans and Republicans' rhetoric around taxation, raising the income tax remains very controversial among the public since citizens perceive an approaching upper limit to the burden government can impose on its citizens. Many Democrats argue when the Treasury is deprived of revenue from income tax, it becomes difficult to fully fund important federal programs such as Social Security.

The debate about income tax has raised critical questions about income inequality or disparity in the United States. Democrats point out today's working and middle class pay a bigger portion of income in taxes than they did 30 years ago. Between the 1940s and 1980, the highest earners were taxed at approximately 70 percent, while today that number is 35 percent. Democrats argue the rich pay a far lower share of income in tax, the lowest share since World War II when the ultra-wealthy were taxed at almost 94 percent.

One Democratic proposal to increasing federal revenues is to raise taxes on the rich. President Obama and financial strategist Warren Buffett have been among the most vocal proponents on the merits of this strategy. In August of 2011, Buffett made his case in the *New York Times* using his personal tax situation as an example:

> Last year my federal tax bill—the income tax I paid, as well as payroll taxes paid by me and on my behalf—was $6,938,744. That sounds like a lot of money. But what I paid was only 17.4 percent of my taxable income—and that's actually a lower percentage than was paid by any of the other 20 people in our office. Their tax burdens ranged from 33 percent to 41 percent and averaged 36 percent (Buffett 2011, 1).

Bernie Sanders and Progressive Views on Tax Policy

Bernie Sanders has been widely influential in shaping the Democratic Party's platform on taxation. Born in 1941, the younger of two sons of Jewish immigrants from Poland, Sanders grew up in Brooklyn where his father worked as a paint salesman. Sanders attended Brooklyn's James Madison High School, going on to Brooklyn College before transferring to the University of Chicago where Sanders became involved in the civil rights movement. Eventually Sanders returned to the east coast, where he started his political career as mayor of Burlington, Vermont. From there, he won a seat in the U.S. House of Representatives, becoming the U.S.'s longest-serving Independent member of Congress (1991–2007). In 2007 and again in 2012, Sanders was elected to the U.S. Senate.

In 2015, he announced his intention to run for President as a Democrat. A central issue of his platform is income tax reform. Sanders favors tax reform through increasing rates for the wealthy, famously stating that he would consider taxing the wealthiest Americans at 90 percent if he became president in a 2015 interview with CNBC's John Harwood (Harwood 2015).

Sources

"Bernie Sanders." *Biography.com*. Accessed November 13, 2015. http://www.biography.com /people/bernie-sanders.

Harwood, John. "Bernie Sanders Questions Morality of US Economy." *Speak Easy with John Harwood, CNBC*, May 26, 2015. Accessed November 13, 2015. http://www.cnbc.com/2015 /05/26/bernie-sanders-questions-morality-of-us-economy.html.

Billionaire Buffett's work on the issue of tax equality has led to the creation of the so-called "Buffett Rule," a principle based on the notion everyone should pay their fair share of tax. Buffett famously points out his effective tax rate is lower than his secretary's because he can afford to hire tax attorneys highly trained to ferret out every possible deduction. Democrats argue that today's tax code benefits the wealthy who can employ specialists to find legal methods to lessen an individual's tax liability. These loopholes allow the ultra-wealthy to enjoy a comparatively light tax burden, say Democrats, while the poor and working- and middle-class Americans shoulder much of the tax burden.

Many Democrats argue that one pathway to greater tax equity is to close loopholes in the current tax code that utilized almost exclusively by the wealthiest Americans. Another is to raise tax rates on the top 1 percent of American households. Not surprisingly, then, they have been critical of the tax cuts for the wealthy that President George W. Bush and Republicans in Congress passed during the early 2000s. Those "tax cuts that went to every millionaire and billionaire in the country," declared Democratic President Barack Obama, will "force us to borrow an average of $500 billion every year over the next decade" (Scherer 2011, 1). Obama's tax reform ideas include: "cutting tax preferences for high-income households; eliminating special tax breaks for oil and gas companies; closing the carrier interest loophole for investment fund managers; and eliminating benefits for those who buy corporate jets" (Office of Management and Budget 2011, ii).

In his May 2015 interview with CNBC's John Harwood, Democratic Senator Bernie Sanders of Vermont, candidate for the 2016 Democratic presidential nomination, made headlines when he stated he could back a 90 percent top marginal tax rate. The highest current rate is 39 percent, although in reality most pay less than that. Currently the U.S. adheres to the 2012 bipartisan American Taxpayer Relief Act that raised the tax rate on the highest incomes from 35 percent to 39 percent.

Democrats largely support the argument made by Robert Reich, former U.S. Secretary of Labor under President Clinton, who argues, "the only way America can reduce the long term budget deficit, maintain vital services, protect Social Security and Medicare, invest more in education and infrastructure, and not raise taxes on the working middle class is by raising taxes on the superrich" (Reich 2011, 9).

Cara E. Rabe-Hemp and
Cassandra Dodge

Further Reading

Buffett, Warren. 2011 "Stop Coddling the Super Rich," *New York Times,* August 14. Accessed November 13, 2015. http://www.nytimes.com/2011/08/15/opinion/stop-coddling-the-super-rich.html?_r=0.

Burnman, Lee. 2011. "Tax Reform Is Essential, Inevitable, and Impossible." *The Christian Science Monitor,* October 21. Accessed November 13, 2015. http://www.csmonitor.com/Business/Tax-VOX/2011/1021/Tax-reform-is-essential-inevitable-and-impossible.

Carter, Susan, Scott Sigmund Gartner, Michael Haines, Alan Olmsted, Richard Sutch, and Gavin Wright. 2006. *Historical Statistics of the United States: Millennial Edition.* Cambridge: Cambridge University Press. Accessed November 13, 2015. http://hsus.cambridge.org/.

Cillizza, Chris, and Sean Sullivan. 2013. "Who Likes Taxes? Democrats and No One Else." *Washington Post,* April 10. Accessed November 13, 2015. http://www.washingtonpost.com/news/the-fix/wp/2013/04/10/who-likes-taxes-democrats-and-no-one-else/.

Congressional Budget Office. 2015. "Outlook for the Budget and the Economy." Accessed November 13, 2015. https://www.cbo.gov/topics/budget/outlook-budget-and-economy.

Department of Treasury. 2015. "Your Federal Income Tax for Individuals, 2014." *Internal Revenue Service.* Accessed November 13, 2015. www.irs.gov/publications/p17/index.html.

Desilver, Drew. 2015. "High-Income Americans Pay Most Income Taxes, but Enough to Be 'Fair'?" *Pew Research Center*, March 24. Accessed November 13, 2015. http://www.pewresearch.org/fact-tank/2015/03/24/high-income-americans-pay-most-income-taxes-but-enough-to-be-fair/.

Drenkard, Scott, and Joseph Henchman. 2014. "2015 State Business Tax Climate Index." *Tax Foundation.* October 28. Accessed November 13, 2015. http://taxfoundation.org/article/2015-state-business-tax-climate-index.

Hagopian, Kip. 2011. "The Inequity of the Progressive Income Tax." *Hoover Institution*, April 1. Accessed November 14, 2015. http://www.hoover.org/research/inequity-progressive-income-tax.

Hall, Thomas E. 2014. *Aftermath: The Unintended Consequences of Public Policies.* Washington, DC: CATO Institute.

Herigstad, Sally. 2015. "How Tax Brackets Work: Examples and Myth Busting." *Tax Act.* Accessed November 13, 2015. http://blog.taxact.com/how-tax-brackets-work/.

Lee, Mike, and Marco Rubio. 2015. "Economic Growth and Family Fairness Tax Reform Plan." Accessed November 13, 2015. http://www.rubio.senate.gov/public/index.cfm/files/serve/?File_id=2d839ff1-f995-427a-86e9-267365609942.

Moore, Stephen. 2015. "Remember the Flat Tax?" *The Weekly Standard*, May 4. 1–3. http://www.weeklystandard.com/articles/remember-flat-tax_928682.html.

Office of Management and Budget. 2011. "Message of the President." *Living Within Our Means and Investing the Future: The President's Plan for Economic Growth and Deficit Reduction.* Office of Management and Budget, September, i–ii.

Paul, Rand. 2015. "Blow Up the Tax Code and Start Over." *RandPaul.com.* Accessed November 13. https://randpaul.com/news/rand-pauls-fair-and-flat-tax.

Pew Research Center. 2014. "Inequality, Poverty Divide Republicans More than Democrats," January 29. Accessed November 13, 2015. http://www.pewresearch.org/fact-tank/2014/01/29/inequality-poverty-divide-republicans-more-than-democrats/.

Reich, Robert. 2011. "Deficit Won't Budge Without Raising Taxes on the Rich," *The Christian Science Monitor,* April 5. Accessed November 13, 2015. http://www.csmonitor.com/Business/Robert-Reich/2011/0405/Deficit-won-t-budge-without-raising-taxes-on-the-rich.

Scherer, Michael. 2011. "In Debt Speech, Barack Obama Fires 2012 Warning Shots." April 13. Accessed November 14, 2013. http://swampland.time.com/2011/04/13/in-debt-speech-barack-obama-fires-2012-warning-shots/.

Schuyler, Michael, and William McBride. 2015. "The Economic Effects of the Rubio-Lee Tax Reform Plan." *Tax Foundation*, March 9. Accessed November 13, 2015. http://taxfoundation.org/article/economic-effects-rubio-lee-tax-reform-plan.

Sinquefield, Rex. 2015a. "Governor LePage Leads the Charge to Eliminate Income Tax by 2020." *Forbes*, May 15. Accessed November 13, 2015. http://www.forbes.com/sites /rexsinquefield/2015/05/15/governor-lepage-leads-the-charge-to-eliminate-income -tax-by-2020/.

Sinquefield, Rex. 2015b. "The States Compared, No Income Tax States Winning Across the Board—Is Rauner's Illinois Next?" *Forbes*, February 23. Accessed November 13, 2015. http://www.forbes.com/sites/rexsinquefield/2015/02/23/the-states-compared-no -income-tax-states-winning-across-the-board-is-rauners-illinois-next/.

"16th Amendment to the U.S. Constitution: Federal Income Tax." 1913. *Our Documents Initiative*. Accessed November 13, 2015. http://www.ourdocuments.gov/doc.php?flash =true&doc=57.

Inflation

At a Glance

Republicans and Democrats have vastly different views of the effect inflation has on the United States. Neither political party disputes that high inflation negatively impacts the American economy, but Democrats appear more tolerant of the existence of inflation than Republicans. The United States economy is complicated, with many variables affecting its overall health. This makes it difficult to determine if one party's actions are actually making a difference, so there is a lot of room for disagreement between Republicans and Democrats.

Most Democrats see some inflation as an inevitable byproduct of an increased standard of living, and the natural compromise for healthy levels of employment. They believe that a carefully managed inflation rate can be healthy for the U.S. economy. Some inflation, typically 1 to 2 percent, is an appropriate rate of inflation in the eyes of many Democrats, and they trust the Federal Reserve Board, the institution in charge of monetary policy, to preserve an appropriate inflation rate.

Republicans on the other hand, tend to view inflation as inherently harmful to the economy. They consider it to be a hidden tax, forced on Americans without consent. Republicans try to ensure that inflation rates stay as close to zero as possible, which they believe can best be maintained by allowing natural supply and demand in the marketplace to control the economic value of goods. There has been a push among more radical Republicans, who have become distrustful of the Federal Reserve, to tie the value of the American dollar to a fixed material like gold or silver.

Many Democrats . . .

- Believe that controlled inflation can be healthy for the United States' economy
- Say that control of inflation should be left to the Federal Reserve Board
- Support steady increases in the wages of Americans to meet the demands of inflation

Many Republicans . . .

- View inflation as a hidden, unwanted tax on the American people
- Believe the inflation rate would be much lower, if the value of materials were left up to the natural supply and demand of the market
- Assert that tying the dollar to the value of a material with a relatively fixed value will stabilize the economy in ways that Federal Reserve policies cannot

Overview

Inflation is defined as the sustained increase in the average price of goods over time, or the decreasing value of currency. One can buy fewer goods with the same amount of money as prices of purchasable items inflate (Board of Governors of the Federal Reserve 2014). Inflation that rises too rapidly will limit the goods that consumers can purchase, as their uninflated income would not be valuable enough to pay the increased prices. However, deflated prices can also cause economic distress if the value of goods depreciates enough so that suppliers cannot make a profit. Uncontrolled inflation or deflation of the dollar's value would affect not just the U.S. economy, but the economies of most countries in the world. Because the American dollar is used as a baseline for the value of international goods and other countries use it to measure the value of their own currency, an aggressively unstable dollar would destabilize the global economy.

The inflation rate is tied to the general health of a nation's economy, and as such, is an important economic characteristic to monitor, no matter the political party affiliation. What divides Republicans and Democrats on this issue is how the government should go about controlling inflation. Republicans, who tend to focus on lowering consumer costs, focus on how to stop rising prices. Democrats, who focus on increasing employment, are much more tolerant of inflation. For Democrats, small amounts of inflation are an acceptable consequence of high employment, as some economists argue that increased employment rates also cause increased inflation.

The organization tasked with actually monitoring the United States economy, and therefore controlling the inflation rate, is the Federal Reserve Board (Fed) led by its chairperson. To manage inflation, the Fed is in charge of the national banking system, and therefore controls the supply of money in the United States (Axilrod 2009, 5). They do this by increasing or decreasing the interest rates charged to other banks, purchasing or selling American debt, and changing the required percentage of consumer's deposits that need to be kept in banks. All of these actions help the Federal Reserve control the amount of available American money there is in the country, which then affects the dollar's relative value compared to goods.

The Fed was not always as powerful as it is today. From 1935, when the modern Federal Reserve was created, until the mid-1950s, the Fed had little real control over economic stability in the United States. The United States tied the value of its currency to the price of gold, a material with a relatively unchanging value, so the Federal Reserve had little control over the economy. However, this changed in later decades. As the American economy became more internationally focused in the 1960s and the 1970s, the U.S. removed its ties to gold as a measurement of the dollar's value, and inflation rose to record highs, becoming increasingly volatile in the process.

Now referred to as America's "Great Inflation," the instability of the 1960s and 1970s is a good example of how devastating the negative effects of runaway inflation can be on a country. Rapidly increasing prices meant that citizens never knew how much they would need to spend on essential goods and services, which could be as cheap as an item at the grocery store, or as expensive as a semester's tuition for college. This made paying bills, maintaining long-term savings, or reducing loans extremely difficult. Citizens felt their lives were no longer in their control. This also meant that the nation's confidence in its leaders also diminished, as citizens lost faith in their government's ability to control the economy (Samuelson 2008, 3–18). However, this crisis gave the Federal Reserve chairs the opportunity to accept more responsibility over the dollar, as they attempted to manipulate the dollar's value to bring down the inflation rate. Several chairmen tried to reduce inflation before President Jimmy Carter appointed Paul Volcker as chair of the Federal Reserve in 1979. Through manipulation of interest rates, selling American securities, and tightening the amount of money in circulation, Volker brought inflation down to a single digit rate (Axilrod 2009, 13, 91–95). The new responsibilities taken on by the Federal Reserve gave the institution much more control over American economic policies so that they would be able to prevent or mitigate future crises from occurring.

In 1987, Volker retired and Alan Greenspan's tenure as head of the Federal Reserve began. A conservative economist, Greenspan was appointed by President Ronald Reagan with the intent to maintain low inflation rates through open and robust markets, rather than through government control of the dollar. This was also quite successful, and led to several years of an inflation rate that was very close to zero. Republicans prefer Greenspan's watchful approach, whereas Democrats prefer a more active Federal Reserve Chair, like Paul Volker (Axilrod 2009, 13).

Ben Bernanke followed Greenspan as Chair of the Federal Reserve in 2006, and he served until Janet Yellen took over in 2014. Both Bernanke and Yellen prefer a mix of monitoring the markets and government intervention. For the last decade, the Fed has worked to maintain an inflation rate of about 1 or 2 percent, and it has been more or less successful at achieving this goal (Board of Governors, 2014). Even throughout the period of economic instability in 2007–2008, the inflation rate never got to 3 percent, and avoided falling into deflation altogether (U.S. Department of Labor 2015a). However, the fear of future economic instability and a loss of faith in government institutions have pushed some Republicans to advocate going back to the fixed exchange system, rather than relying on the whims of the international economy and the controls put in place by the Fed. A fixed exchange system would tie the American economy to a tangible material, which some argue would keep inflation lower and more stable than the current floating exchange system. Some conservatives argue that the instability of the mid-2000s would have been prevented if currency were tied to a fixed material. In contrast, most Democrats have confidence in the Federal Reserve Board's ability to keep the value of the dollar stable, even during times of economic instability.

Republicans on Inflation

For the most part, Republicans follow what is called supply-side economic theory. Made famous during the Reagan administration, supply-side economics is marked by a preference for a steady supply of goods within an economy and keeping income in the hands of the consumers who have earned it. According to this theory, with a plentiful supply of purchasable goods on the market, demand for those goods decreases and suppliers must compete to see who can sell their goods for the least expensive price. Supply-side economists believe that this open-market economy is best for economic growth, because it naturally creates low prices and incentivizes productivity and creativity in the workplace. Lower prices leave Americans with more disposable income, allowing them to purchase more goods and improve their quality of life. Inflation undermines this philosophy, and therefore supply-side economists advise reducing inflation rates. Inflated prices limit the amount of goods that can be purchased by consumers, competition is reduced, and money is kept out of the free market. Fewer purchases translate to employers not making profits and having to reduce the size of their companies, putting many Americans out work.

Republicans also tend to see inflation as "a forcible confiscation of wealth" by the government (Frank 2004: 128). Republicans believe that citizens understand their own needs better than the bloated, bureaucratic government. Republicans believe citizens should be able to choose how to spend their own money, and not have to hard-earned dollars to the government beyond the income needed to fund the small number of necessary services offered by that government. Forcing Americans to give up more of their income to compensate for the growing cost of goods directly goes against this philosophy. Republicans see the Federal Reserve's current practice of maintaining an inflation rate of 2 percent as deliberately taking money away from consumers. The official Republican Platform calls inflation a "hidden tax on the American people" (Republican National Committee 2012), implying that not only is inflation a tax which provides nothing to Americans, but it is pushed on citizens without their explicit knowledge. Not only does the federal government have mechanisms in place that deliberately takes income away from citizens, they are doing so without the permission of the American citizens, which places Republicans squarely against positive inflation rates.

Republicans typically respond to inflation by attempting to reduce government manipulation of the economy, as they feel that more government interaction causes economic instability, including more aggressive inflation rates. To limit government involvement, Republicans have tried to shorten the reach of the Federal Reserve. For example, the Republican Party Platform calls for an annual audit of the Federal Reserve's activities and congressional oversight over the Fed's actions (Republican National Committee 2012). Congressional involvement will allow Republicans to pass legislation to take away the mechanisms the Federal Reserve uses to keep inflation at their preferred 2 percent. Some Republicans have also made attempts in the last few years to draft legislation that would create a commission to "consider the feasibility of a metallic basis for U.S currency" (Republican National Committee 2012). In other words, go back to something like the Gold Standard, when the Federal Reserve had few mechanisms to influence monetary policy or inflation. If Republicans succeeded in bringing a fixed exchange rate back to the United States, the Federal Reserve would not be able to artificially inflate or deflate the value of money. Substances like gold or silver have relatively unchanging monetary values attached to them, so the Fed would be forced to also increase or decrease the amount of gold or silver held in reserve to match the new currency value, and there is not enough available gold or silver accommodate those changes.

Some Republicans share a similar goal to Libertarians, who want to eliminate the Federal Reserve altogether, leaving the value of goods and services entirely up to the open marketplace. Libertarians believe that the government has no business controlling an individual's money at all. Prominent Libertarian Congressman Ron Paul published a book, *End the Fed* (2009), which charged that Federal Reserve policies work against the American people, and that the body should be eliminated. Paul asserted that the Federal Reserve was a creator of inflation rather than a controller of it, and that the American people would be better off if the value of the dollar was left completely up to the natural balance of supply and demand (Paul 2009, 14). The majority of Republicans still agree that the Federal Reserve should continue to exist in a more limited capacity, but a small but vocal minority has expressed support for ending the Fed altogether.

Democrats on Inflation

When making economic decisions, Democrats have historically followed the philosophy of John Maynard Keynes, an early 20th century economist who advocated government intervention in the economy in order to keep it stable. Keynes believed leaving the economy entirely in the hands of the free market and the private sector would lead to erratic and dangerous changes in economic circumstances and behavior. He maintained it is the government's responsibility to intervene and help stabilize the economy by increasing or decreasing the money in circulation.

Modern Keynesian economists believe that to maintain such control over the American dollar, the United States needs to maintain what is called a floating exchange-rate system of currency. The value of the dollar comes from the relative value of itself against other international currencies. In order to balance the changing international value system, the Fed can either deflate or inflate the value of the dollar by increasing or decreasing the number of bills in circulation. Controlling the dollar in this way also gives the government some advanced notice for when the economy starts to slow. It is then better prepared in the event of some sort of financial crisis. With a steady inflation rate, the Federal Reserve will already have mechanisms in place to help mitigate falling prices, if it occurs.

Democrats also accept some amount of inflation because they want to keep as much of the country employed as possible. This goal is evident in the Democratic Party Platform, where ensuring employment opportunities for every American is brought up throughout the document (Democratic National Committee 2012). This also reflects a Keynesian perspective. Keynes advocated that a government work to have near full employment in order to maintain a stable economy. Full employment means that anyone who wants to find work is able to do so—and to receive adequate compensation as well. Those who are out of work are changing jobs or going through some sort of life transition; they are not permanently unemployed. However, in order to achieve full employment, Americans must accept inflated prices, because Keynesian economists also argue that inflation is a natural byproduct of a country working toward full employment.

Democrats accept the connection between employment and inflation because of the work of A. W. H. Phillips, a British economist and a contemporary of Keynes. Phillips discovered that when employment increased in his country inflation rates also increased, and thus came to the conclusion that inflation is a byproduct of high employment. The graphical representation of that research is now called a Phillips Curve. Other economists agreed with his conclusions and continue to argue that inflation and employment are connected. Because of Phillips' research, modern Democrats argue that when citizens are employed they have more disposable income, and will be able to purchase more goods. The demand for those goods increases, which also increases the value of those goods, and therefore would decrease the value of the dollar, otherwise known as inflation.

Democrats are tolerant of some inflation, but only at a manageable rate that can be countered by an equally increasing income from the consuming workforce to keep pace with price increases. If prices rise while Americans' paychecks remain the same then the buying power of those paychecks is lowered, and many Democrats see this as the biggest concern regarding the issue of inflation. This is why the current Democratic Party Platform states the intention to adjust the minimum wage for inflation, to protect those being paid the minimum wage and ensure they are appropriately compensated for their work so they are able to purchase goods (Democratic National Committee 2012). This is the only direct mention of inflation in this platform, and one can infer inflation on its own is not necessarily a major priority for most Democrats. Their priority is to ensure that the gradually rising inflation rate is also met with a gradually rising income for citizens to match the rising costs of goods and services, as this has not been the case in recent years (U.S. Department of Labor 2015b). To the disappointment of most Democrats, however, the federal minimum wage has not been increased since 2009 due to GOP opposition to a hike. It has stayed at $7.25 since that last increase. In order to have kept up with even recent modest inflation rates, economists estimate that it should be closer to $10–$15 in today's economy (U.S. Department of Labor 2015c). Democrats have made it a legislative priority to increase the minimum wage, and they are expected to make it a centerpiece of their political campaign strategies in the years ahead.

Grace Allbaugh

Further Reading

Axilrod, Stephen H. 2009. *Inside the Fed: Monetary Policy and its Management, Martin through Greenspan to Bernanke.* Cambridge: MIT Press.

Board of Governors of the Federal Reserve. 2014. "Current FAQs." Last modified November 3. Accessed June 3, 2015. http://www.federalreserve.gov/faqs/allfaq.htm.

Democratic National Committee. 2012. "Moving America Forward: 2012 Democratic Platform." Accessed January 21, 2015. http://www.democrats.org/democratic-national-platform.

Frank, Ellen. 2004. *The Raw Deal: How Myths and Misinformation about Deficits, Inflation and Wealth Impoverish America.* Boston: Beacon Press.

Paul, Ron. 2009. *End the Fed.* New York: Grand Central Pub.

Republican National Committee. 2012. "We Believe in America: 2012 Republican Platform." Accessed January 21, 2015. https://www.gop.com/platform/.

Samuelson, Robert J. 2008. *The Great Inflation and Its Aftermath: The Past and Future of American Influence.* New York: Random House.

U.S. Department of Labor. 2015a. "Databases, Tables & Calculators by Subject." Accessed July 20. http://data.bls.gov/timeseries/CUUR0000SA0L1E?output_view=pct_12mths.

U.S. Department of Labor. 2015b. "History of Federal Minimum Wage Rates Under the Fair Labor Standards Act, 1938–2009." Accessed May 5. http://www.dol.gov/whd/minwage/chart.htm.

U.S. Department of Labor. 2015c. "Minimum Wage Mythbusters." Accessed May 2. http://www.dol.gov/minwage/mythbuster.htm.

Job Creation Programs

At a Glance

Republicans and Democrats both emphasize their desire for policies and programs that expand job opportunities for American workers, but the parties differ widely on how such programs should be developed and financed. Generally speaking, Democrats are more favorably disposed toward public spending for job creation programs either at the state/local level or at the federal level. Democrats tend to view job creation projects as beneficial to large segments of the population and view federal stimulus projects as a particularly good way to shore up employment in troubled economic times. Republicans have been less enthusiastic about federally sponsored job creation programs, especially during the Obama administration. Many modern Republicans see federal job creation programs as "big government" interventions that should be avoided in favor of letting the private sector and free market operate unfettered. Republicans tend to argue that the best path to developing a robust U.S. economy with plentiful employment opportunities is to lower business taxes and do away with "burdensome" government regulations that hinder business growth.

Many Democrats . . .

- Believe job creation programs give the unemployed opportunities to do productive work, earn an income, and pay taxes
- Support investing in America through transportation and infrastructure projects
- See job creation programs as helpful to the U.S. economy because they keep struggling households afloat (and buying goods and services) until their economic circumstances improve

Many Republicans . . .

- See job creation programs as irresponsible spending of taxpayer dollars
- Criticize job creation programs as ineffective in stimulating economic growth

- Charge that job programs artificially lower unemployment only as long as federal money funds the jobs
- Support major expenditures for some infrastructure needs such as roadways, but are less supportive of spending bills aimed at other infrastructure development and repairs.

Overview

When the subject of government job creation is considered, the Great Depression of the late 1920s and 1930s comes to mind. Prior to this time, job creation efforts were most often undertaken at the local level by cities or by individual states, rather than by the national government. For example, during such times of economic crisis as the depressions of 1857, the 1870s, and the 1890s, cities such as New York, Boston, and Philadelphia developed municipal programs to aid the poor and unemployed. Some of the same questions that face politicians today were present in the mid-to late 19th century. Should the local government be involved in "relief work"? Or did such projects slowly lead the city into the dreaded path of socialism (Sautter 1991)? Beyond the social and philosophical questions, the administration and financing of such programs presented major problems for cities. These difficulties led to proposals for state governments or the federal government to assume the responsibility for work relief programs. In 1873 Democratic reformers pressed Republican President Rutherford B. Hayes to put the jobless to work constructing railroads at federal expense. Hayes and fellow conservatives strongly opposed public works programs. In 1893, labor leader Samuel Gompers, at an American Federation of Labor convention, convinced delegates to pass a resolution in favor of public works. In 1894, Coxey's Army, a large group of unemployed workers, demonstrated in Washington, D.C., demanding work on road construction and similar public programs. Despite the range of nineteenth century job creation proposals, though, none produced state or federal action.

In the early decades of the 20th century, World War I and preparation for U.S. entry into the war in 1917 accelerated employment. Following the war, however, unemployment began to increase and signs of an economic depression were on the horizon. Layoffs increased in 1927–1928 and the stock market crash in 1929 brought the problems to the forefront. As the Great Depression enveloped the country, closing businesses of all shapes and sizes, a handful of states attempted to confront soaring unemployment with a variety of relief programs. The most effective of these efforts were carried out in Illinois by Democratic Governor Henry Horner and in New York State by Democratic Governor Franklin D. Roosevelt. The Temporary Emergency Relief Administration (TERA) program established by Roosevelt in 1931 even became a model for Roosevelt's New Deal programs after he was elected president in 1932.

For his part, Roosevelt framed TERA as a necessary and sensible response to economic hardship:

> The serious unemployment situation which has stunned the Nation for the past year and a half has brought to our attention in a most vivid fashion the need for some sort of relief to protect those men and women who are willing to work but who through no fault of their own cannot find unemployment. This form of relief should not, of course, take the shape of a dole in any respect. The dole method of relief for unemployment is not only repugnant to all sound principles of social economics, but is contrary to every principle of American citizenship and of sound government. American labor seeks no charity, but only a chance to work for its living. (Roosevelt 1931)

Meanwhile, pressure for federal intervention to address rising homelessness, hunger, and unemployment steadily increased in 1930 and 1931. "I cannot believe that a national government will stand by while its citizens freeze and starve, without lifting a hand to help," said Democratic Pennsylvania Governor Gifford Pinchot. "I do not see how it can refuse to grant that relief which it is in honor, in duty, and in its own interest bound to supply" (Pinchot 1932). But Republican President Herbert Hoover was unmoved by these entreaties, and he maintained a policy against providing federal funds for the unemployed and for public jobs programs. The election of Democrat Franklin Roosevelt to the presidency in 1932 proved the turning point for federal job creation. FDR's Administration started various work programs including the Public Works Administration (PWA), the Tennessee Valley Authority (TVA), and the Civilian Conservation Corps (CCC). The PWA provided construction industry jobs, while the TVA's purpose was to construct dams and develop hydroelectric power, and the CCC was aimed at employing young men in the national parks and forests. While the programs provided work and gave the country a sense that the federal government was indeed doing something to reverse the downward spiral of unemployment, the programs were far from universally supported. Republican opponents charged the programs cost too much and were "make-work"—having the unemployed do no actual needed work. Business executives opposed the programs on the grounds that wages were too high and the programs were in unfair competition with private companies (Rose 2000). The economic drive that came with World War II brought the country out of the doldrums and the war economy and post-war development brought about economic prosperity through the 1950s. As one historian observed, "When the United States emerged from the war in 1945, the schools, parks, highways, airports, dams, sewer systems, and hospitals that had been created during the New Deal years gave the nation a strong foundation for explosive economic growth into the 1950s and beyond" (Hillstrom 2009).

The next major job creation programs did not appear until the 1960s, beginning under Democratic President John F. Kennedy and continuing with the Great Society programs of Democratic President Lyndon B. Johnson. These programs included the Community Work and Training Projects, the Work Incentive Program, the

Neighborhood Youth Corps and the New Careers Program. The Johnson administration, armed with a strong Democratic majority in Congress, was able to get these programs enacted despite opposition from many Republicans.

The recessions of the early 1970s again prompted calls for federal intervention to create jobs. However, Republican President Nixon opposed the creation of jobs via such means. Over time, though, continued economic pressures led to the passage of the Emergency Employment Act, which contained the Public Employment Program (PEP). PEP served to create public service jobs for the unemployed in states, counties, and cities. Although PEP was a temporary fix, it set the groundwork for the 1973 Comprehensive Employment and Training Act (CETA). Although CETA was in place for 10 years, it was often plagued with management problems and misuse of funds. Republican President Reagan eliminated CETA in 1981. The following year the Job Training and Partnership Act (JTPA) was established to work with local private companies providing job training for youth and adults, but JTPA did not involve direct federal job creation. The Republican Party tended to favor programs to assist private business expansion, asserting that such assistance would ultimately result in job growth without the direct involvement of the federal government.

Job training and re-training of laid-off workers has been the long-range emphasis of Democrats and Republicans for the past two decades. Legislation for job training was often aimed at specific types of workers, especially those engaged in manufacturing work, which steadily diminished with the rise of international trade agreements and outsourcing of factory jobs to foreign countries where workers could be paid a fraction of the wages traditionally earned by American workers.

The issue of federally sponsored job creation assumed new urgency in the wake of the Great Recession, which officially lasted from December 2007 to June 2009. After Democratic President Barack Obama was inaugurated in January 2009, he immediately joined with Democratic majorities in Congress to pass a major economic stimulus package that included massive levels of spending on public works projects. These efforts, touted by the Obama administration as having both job creation and infrastructure renewal benefits, have been strongly defended by Democrats and progressives as integral to the U.S. economic recovery. Republicans, however, have been united in decrying the stimulus as a boondoggle that wasted taxpayer dollars.

Democrats on Job Creation Programs

Many Democrats tend to favor job creation through working with the private sector and through state and local governments whenever possible. When such efforts are not enough to help the unemployed, however, Democrats have seen job creation through federal stimulus programs as a necessary option in times of high unemployment and serious economic slowdowns.

During the economic crises of 2007–2008, many Democrats blamed the administration of Republican President George W. Bush for the high rates of unemployment and failure to take measures to restore the American economy. When President Obama took office in 2009, he signed the American Recovery and Reinvestment Act into law. The first major aims of the bill were to "create new jobs and save existing ones" and to "spur economic activity and invest in long-term growth" (Naylor 2009). The bill also extended the 'Making Work Pay' tax credit for 95 percent of workers and their families. With infrastructure investment being the major focus of the bill, some $105 billion was allocated for this section, with the largest single line item in the bill being for "shovel ready" projects for highway and bridge construction.

As the programs took effect, the President and Democratic leaders reported progress. In November of 2009, Moody's Economy.com reported, "The stimulus is doing what it was supposed to do: short circuit the recession and spur recovery." At the same time, though, even some economists who praising the stimulus program cautioned that it was not large enough to lift the United States out of its deep recession (Krugman 2009).

In late 2009, the unemployment rate in the United States was still hovering just below the 10 percent level. In response to continued sluggish economic conditions, the "Jobs for Main Street Act" was proposed by the White House and hotly debated in the House of Representatives. Democratic Representative David Obey of Wisconsin described the benefits of the previous stimulus bill and challenged his colleagues to help those in need of jobs. Representative James Oberstar, a Democrat and member of the Committee on Transportation and Infrastructure, reported that, "There are 28,000 miles of highway pavement—improved, widened, expanded—underway right now. That is what we have achieved to this day, and we have more to come. There are 1,200 bridges restored, repaired, replaced, and with this addition in the Jobs for Main Street Act, we will have 56,000 miles of pavement rebuilt in the coming year. That will be 10,000 miles more than the entire Interstate Highway System just in this one bill. That is an investment in America" (Oberstar 2010).

In December of 2009, the Democratic-controlled House passed the bill by a narrow margin, with all Republicans voting against the bill. The Senate took up the bill in 2010. Senate Majority leader Harry Reid proposed a much leaner version of the original House bill. A revised version of the bill was finally passed by the Senate in March of 2010.

With unemployment continuing into the following year, President Obama addressed the nation on September 8, 2011, and proposed the "American Jobs Act." This bill focused on providing tax cuts for small businesses to increase hiring and prevent layoffs, especially for teachers, police, and firefighters, but it failed to muster the necessary support from Republicans for passage. Democrats were quick to condemn the GOP stance on the bill. "Independent analysis projected the American Jobs Act, which was fully paid for, could create as many as 2 million jobs in 2012," charged one progressive media outlet. "The Obama White House crafted a credible plan that would be helping enormously right now; and congressional

Republicans reflexively killed the Americans Jobs Act for partisan and ideological reasons" (MaddowBlog 2012).

The 2012 presidential election campaign also had jobs as a major focus. The platform of the Democratic Party included a lengthy section on "Putting Americans Back to Work." The platform highlighted the Democratic Party's self-described commitment to "to fight for measures that would strengthen the recovery and create jobs now, including keeping teachers and first responders on the job, putting construction workers back to work by investing in our roads, bridges, schools, and water supply . . . and cutting taxes for small businesses that invest and hire. . . . That's why we continue to fight for relief for the long-term unemployed, including a ban on hiring discrimination against the unemployed and a reformed and expanded universal worker training proposal to provide more training and job search assistance to all displaced workers regardless of how they lost their jobs" (Democratic Party Platform 2012).

Democrats also tend to support job-related policies such as extending unemployment benefits and raising the minimum wage. Democrats have consistently supported extending jobless benefits, as a means of continuing the safety net for the chronically unemployed. Data compiled by the Congressional Budget Office in 2014 showed that allowing unemployment benefits to expire would "cost the economy 200,000 jobs and sap 0.2% of economic growth" (Reed 2014). Raising the minimum wage is an issue many Democrats support, and they frequently cite

---

Barack Obama and Job Creation

Democrat Barack Obama was elected president of the United States in 2008—at the height of the so-called Great Recession—and re-elected in 2012. Prior to his presidency, he was a U.S. senator from Illinois, a state senator from Chicago, a civil rights attorney, and community organizer. In his first inaugural address, Obama pledged to create new jobs and "lay a foundation for growth." Due to the economic crisis that had gripped the country in 2007 and 2008, upon taking office in January of 2009, Obama quickly proposed a "New Deal"-type of stimulus package. Although the American Recovery and Reinvestment Act did spur some economic activity, high unemployment still aggravated the country. The Obama administration continued to put forth jobs programs including the Jobs for Main Street Act and the American Jobs Act. In the 2012 presidential election, the party platform included a strong emphasis on "Putting Americans Back to Work." Over the years, Obama's programs did increase jobs and unemployment declined to 5.0 percent by the close of 2015.

Sources

"Barack Obama." 2015. *Biography.com*. Accessed November 20, 2015. http://www.biography.com/people/barack-obama-12782369.

Jaffe, Greg. 2015. "Obama defends his record, rallies the base in Wisconsin." *Washington Post*, July 3.

studies that indicate that job losses from such a hike would be minimal. Their counterparts in the GOP, meanwhile, have seized on other economic studies indicating that raising the minimum wage may cost as many as half a million jobs for small businesses (Merline 2014).

Republicans on Job Creation Programs

Many Republicans favor job creation by the private sector only and are strongly opposed to public funding to create jobs. Republicans tend to advocate government support of private industry and small businesses by lowering taxes and having fewer regulations. They contend that this approach enables private sector businesses to create jobs and allow people to be employed on their own and not dependent on federal government jobs. Many Republicans subscribe to "trickle-down theory," meaning if the wealthy have lower taxes and more money to invest, they will create or expand their businesses or industry and thereby create more jobs. In the view of many Republicans, the government should get out of the way and let this process work.

During the economic crisis of 2007–2008, President Bush's major emphasis was on cutting taxes and making the earlier tax cuts permanent. Some of Bush's economic advisers did favor a stimulus package, but others held firm to tax cuts as the major way to improve the economy (Stolberg 2008).

With Obama's election to the White House in 2008, the American Recovery and Reinvestment Act became law in February 2009. Republicans criticized this stimulus package as wasteful and ineffective in addressing America's recessionary conditions. When unemployment did not quickly drop below 8 percent, as the White House predicted, but instead rose to almost 10 percent in the months following passage of the stimulus, Republican leaders pointed to the failure of the program to create as many jobs as Democrats had assured (Cooper 2009). As the employment picture improved in subsequent months and years, however, GOP critics increasingly focused on the cost of the Obama administration's economic stimulus efforts rather than its success in reducing unemployment and improving overall economic health.

When the Obama administration next proposed the Jobs for Main Street Act, Republican reaction to the "son of stimulus" bill ranged from disbelief to anger and outrage. California representative Jerry Lewis called the bill "economic insanity" and asked "why don't we just put everyone in the United States on the Federal Government payroll and call it a day?" (Lewis 2010).

Kansas representative Todd Tiahrt cautioned the bill amounted to "another $154 billion of failed economic policies that will only prolong the economic pain." He reiterated the traditional Republican economic philosophy: "Here is how you create opportunity: Stop spending, stop borrowing. You can't grow the economy from the government down. Freeze regulations, audit every one of them, and only keep the ones where the benefit exceeds the cost. Keep taxes low. When you do, people save. They invest; they spend. All of that's good for the economy." Senate Republican leader Mitch McConnell, chastised the Obama Administration for "excessive regulation, failure to pass trade deals, advocating tax increases; these are not the kinds of things that create jobs" (Tiahrt 2010). When the Obama administration in 2011 next proposed the American Jobs Act, Republicans blocked passage of the bill.

Much like the Democrats, in the 2012 presidential election, the Republican Party's platform devoted significant coverage to the issue of jobs. Consistent with traditional Republican philosophy, the platform states, "The best jobs program is economic growth. We do not offer yet another made-in-Washington package of subsidies and spending to create temporary or artificial jobs. We want much more than that. We want a roaring job market to match a roaring economy. Republicans will pursue free market policies that are the surest way to boost employment and create job growth and economic prosperity for all" (Republican Party Platform 2012).

On the issue of extending unemployment benefits, Republicans objected, citing their reluctance to support "temporary government programs." Members of the Republican Party view these extensions as doing nothing to actually help the

---

John Boehner and Job Creation

Until his retirement from the House of Representatives in October 2015, Republican Congressman John Boehner had been at the center of countless political debates over job creation and employment policies in the United States. A representative of Ohio's conservative 8th district since 1991, Boehner was consistently a driving force behind Republican initiatives to create jobs primarily by cutting government spending and supporting private sector job growth. Boehner favors lowering taxes on businesses and reducing government regulation that hampers small business development. As House Minority Leader, he led the Republican charge against President Obama's stimulus package in 2009, characterizing it as a "spending binge" that would just increase the national debt and have little long-term effect on the ability of American workers to get and keep good paying jobs. The speaker often refers to his earlier years when he ran a small business himself and hence, understands the needs of small businesses and what government can do to help or hurt the business community where the actual jobs are created. From 2011 until his retirement in October 2015, Boehner led the House of Representatives as its 53rd Speaker of the House.

Sources

Keene, David. 2015. "John Boehner's Budget Legacy." *Washington Times,* October 22. Accessed November 24, 2015. http://www.washingtontimes.com/news/2015/oct/22/david-keene-john -boehners-budget-legacy/

Sherman, Jake, et al. 2015. "John Boehner Heads for the Exits." *Politico,* September 25. Accessed November 24, 2015. http://www.politico.com/story/2015/09/speaker-john-boehner-retiring -from-congress-at-the-end-of-october-214056.

jobless move into good paying, stable jobs and at the same time adding major costs to the already sizable national debt.

Republicans have also generally opposed raising the minimum wage. In doing so, they have frequently cited March 2014 testimony given by the director of the Congressional Budget Office that predicted that raising the minimum wage from the current level of $7.25 to $10.10 per hour, as proposed by President Obama, would result in the loss of 500,000 jobs.

Vanette Schwartz

Further Reading

"American Jobs Act." 2011. *Congressional Digest* 90 (8): 235.

American Recovery and Reinvestment Act. 2015. Accessed August 2. http://www.recovery.gov/arra/About/Pages/The_Act.aspx.

"American Reinvestment and Recovery Act Jumpstarting our Economy and Investing in Our Future." 2015. Accessed August 2. https://www.whitehouse.gov/assets/documents/Recovery_Act_Overview_2-17.pdf.

Bendery, Jennifer. 2011. "Obama Jobs Plan Voted Down By Senate." *Huffington Post*, October 11. Accessed August 18, 2015. http://www.huffingtonpost.com/2011/10/11/obama-jobs-plan-senate-vote_n_1005900.html.

Cooper, Michael. 2009. "A Shot in the Arm, Not a Kick in the Pants." *New York Times*, October 7.

Cooper, Michael, and Ron Nixon. 2009. "Job Program found to Miss Many States that Need It Most." *New York Times*, October 16.

Cornyn, John. 2014. "Should the Senate Pass a Three-Month Extension of Emergency Unemployment Benefits? CON." *Congressional Digest* 93 (2): 19–21.

Democratic National Committee. 2012. "Moving America Forward: 2012 Democratic Platform." Accessed August 17, 2015. http://www.presidency.ucsb.edu/ws/index.php?pid=101962.

Garrett, Major. 2011. "McConnell Accuses White House of Extremism on Trade and Jobs." *National Journal Daily*, June 17.

Hillstrom, Kevin. 2009. *The Great Depression and the New Deal*. Detroit: Omnigraphics.

Hopkins, June. 2015. "The New York State Temporary Emergency Relief Administration: October 1, 1931." *Social Welfare History Project*. Accessed December 8, 2015. http://www.socialwelfarehistory.com/eras/great-depression/temporary-emergency-relief-administration/.

Kellam, Susan. 1994. "Worker Retraining." *CQ Researcher*, January 21.

Klebaner, Benjamin Joseph. 1952."Public Poor Relief in America, 1790–1860." PhD diss., Columbia University, New York, NY.

Krugman, Paul. 2009. "Too Little of a Good Thing." *New York Times*, November 02.

"Legislative Background in the Jobs Bill: Recent Action in Congress." 2010. *Congressional Digest* 89 (3): 79.

Lewis, Jerry. 2010. "Should the House Pass H.R. 2847, the Jobs for Main Street Act CON." *Congressional Digest* 89 (3): 81–83.

Merline, John. 2014. "Minimum Wage Hike Support Falls on CBO Jobs Warning." *Investor's Business Daily*, February 28. Accessed November 20, 2015. http://www.tipponline.com/economy/news/economy/minimum-wage-hike-support-falls-on-cbo-jobs-warning.

Naylor, Brian. 2009. "Stimulus Bill Gives 'Shovel-Ready' Projects Priority." *NPR*, February 9. Accessed July 25, 2015. http://www.npr.org/templates/story/story.php?storyId=100295436.

Oberstar, James. 2010. "Should the House Pass H.R. 2847, the Jobs for Main Street Act PRO." *Congressional Digest* 89 (3): 82–84.

Obey, David. "Should the House Pass H.R. 2847, the Jobs for Main Street Act PRO." *Congressional Digest* 89 (3): 80–82.

Pinchot, Gifford. 1932. "The Case for Federal Relief," *The Survey*, January 1.

Rachel Maddow Show. 2012. "The American Jobs Act—One Year Later." *The MaddowBlog*, September 7. Accessed January 4, 2016. http://www.msnbc.com/rachel-maddow-show/the-american-jobs-act-one-year-later.

Reed, Jack. 2014. "Should the Senate Pass a Three-Month Extension of Emergency Unemployment Benefits? PRO." *Congressional Digest* 93 (2): 14–16.

Republican National Committee. 2012. "We Believe in America: 2012 Republican Platform." August 27. Accessed August 17, 2015. http://www.presidency.ucsb.edu/ws/?pid=101961.

Roosevelt, Franklin D. 1940. "A Recommendation for a Commission to Investigate Unemployment Insurance," March 25, 1931. In *Public Papers of the Presidents of the United States: Franklin D. Roosevelt*, Vol. 9. Washington, DC: Government Printing Office.

Rose, Nancy E. 2000. *Put to Work: The WPA and Public Employment in the Great Depression*, 2nd ed. New York: Monthly Review Press.

Sautter, Udo. 1991. *Three Cheers for the Unemployed: Government and Unemployment Before the New Deal*. Cambridge: Cambridge University Press.

Stolberg, Sheryl Gay. 2008. "Two Views in the White House on an Economic Fix." *New York Times*, January 17.

Tiahrt, Todd. 2010. "Should the House Pass H.R. 2847, the Jobs for Main Street Act CON." *Congressional Digest* 89 (3): 85.

U.S. Congress. House. Committee on Education and Labor. 1985. "Direct Federal Job Creation: Key Issues," October. Accessed August 17, 2015. http://babel.hathitrust.org/cgi/pt?id=mdp.39015012872639;view=1up;seq=1.

U.S. Congress. Senate. Committee on Health, Education, Labor and Pensions. Elmendorf, Douglas W. 2014. "Testimony—Increasing the Minimum Wage: Effects on Employment and Family Income." March 12. Accessed August 18, 2015. https://www.cbo.gov/sites/default/files/113th-congress-2013-2014/reports/45138-MinimumWageTestimony.pdf.

Medicaid/Medicare

At a Glance

President Lyndon B. Johnson made history in 1965 when he amended the Social Security Act to include the Medicare and Medicaid programs. Since the adoption of these programs, the costs have increased much more dramatically than policymakers initially anticipated. As a result, both Democrats and Republicans see a need to reform these healthcare programs to alleviate their burden on federal and state budgets.

Republicans argue that the best way to mitigate these rising costs is by revising the program through the establishment of an income-adjusted contribution model for enrollees, rather than the current benefit-defined model. According to Republicans, private health insurance companies will be used to stimulate competition to drive costs down and quality of care up. In regard to Medicaid, Republicans call for reforms that would allow states increased flexibility to design and administer their own programs with fewer federal regulations.

Conversely, Democrats argue against changes in the way these programs are administered, particularly as they pertain to the use of private insurance companies. Rather than altering the entire program, Democrats advocate reforms to Medicare that would make the current program more outcome-oriented and efficient. Under Democratic reform plans for Medicaid, which are evident in the Patient Protection and Affordable Care Act of 2010, federal eligibility requirements for Medicaid will expand to cover more of the population.

Many Republicans . . .

- Favor means-testing and a higher eligibility age for Medicare
- Support increased utilization of private health insurance through a premium-support plan and a defined-contribution system
- Propose to provide states with federal block grants to increase state flexibility in operating Medicaid plans
- Favor alternatives to hospitalization for people on Medicaid with chronic health problems
- Advocate development of a separate program for Medicaid patients with long-term care needs

Many Democrats . . .

• Support reforms to the Medicare Prescription Drug Plan to reduce Medicare scams
• Favor raising the Medicare Medical Insurance premium surcharge to cover more of Part B services
• Seek increased cost-sharing measures among Medicare beneficiaries
• Favor expanding Medicaid eligibility requirements so that the program covers more people
• Support continued federal regulation of Medicaid

Overview

The year 1965 marked a year of major change for healthcare reform, and in particular, healthcare finance in the United States. On July 30, President Johnson signed the Medicare and Medicaid programs into law when Title XIX was added to the Social Security Act. Generally speaking, Medicare and Medicaid are both federally funded programs that provide assistance to specific populations with regard to financing healthcare services. Each program, however, contains systematic differences that make each unique from the other. Medicare is a system of health insurance financed through the federal government to people who: are 65 years of age or older, have certain disabilities, or suffer from permanent kidney disease (CMS 2014b). Medicaid, on the other hand, is a joint federal and state program that provides some people of limited income with health care cost assistance (CMS 2014b). Whereas Medicare is available for all individuals within the three coverage categories, not all poor people are eligible for Medicaid coverage. Additionally, Medicare is fully regulated and funded by the federal government. Conversely, the federal government provides broad guidelines for Medicaid, but allows each individual state to regulate and administer services. As a result, states set their own requirements for program eligibility and the application process, and states are also required to provide much of their own funding. Furthermore, Medicaid is a voluntary program, meaning that states are not required to participate. If, however, states choose to enact a Medicaid program, they must follow the federally established minimum guidelines to receive federal financial support. For states that participate, the federal government pays for a portion of the program based on the economic welfare of the state. "States with lower per capita incomes have a higher share of the program costs paid by the federal government than do states with higher per capita incomes" (Barr 2002, 109). In practice, all states have some form of Medicaid program in place.

The Medicare program, in general, is a joint service and insurance plan with three primary components. Part A of the Medicare program is a service plan that provides beneficiaries with hospital insurance, which "helps cover inpatient care in hospitals, including critical access to hospitals, and skilled nursing facilities (not custodial or long-term care)" (CMS 2014a). Additionally, Part B of the program provides coverage for physician and outpatient services, some physical and occupational therapy, and a portion of home health services when medically necessary. Prescription drug coverage is the newest and final component to Medicare that was incorporated as of 2006. This coverage provides all Medicare beneficiaries with access to prescription drugs at lower prices. Medicaid differs in that it is a purely insurance-based program (Barr 2002, 108). Enrollees in Medicaid programs typically have access to doctor's visits and hospital stays, some long-term services, preventive care, mental health care, prenatal and maternity care, and medically necessary medications (CMS 2014). The amount and type of coverage varies depending on the individual state's program.

Since Title XIX was passed, the Medicaid and Medicare programs have grown extensively as a result of an increase in enrollees and an increase in the cost of health care in general. During its first year, Medicare enrolled approximately 19 million people (Medicare Resource Center 2015). By 2009, 47.5 million people relied on Medicare (U.S. Census Bureau 2012). Similarly, Medicaid programs covered only around 4 million people in 1966 (Statista, Inc. 2015), and by 2009 almost 62 million people across the United States relied on Medicaid for health coverage (U.S. Census Bureau 2012). These trends were exacerbated by federal expansions of the Medicare and Medicaid programs. The first expansion of Medicare occurred in 1972, when President Nixon altered the program to provide coverage to individuals of any age with long-term disabilities or end-stage renal disease (ESRD). Medicare was further expanded in 1980 to provide beneficiaries with home health services and again in 1982 to allow for coverage of hospice services (Medicare Resource Center 2015). The most recent legislation in health care reform, the Patient Protection and Affordable Care Act (ACA) of 2010 calls for a number of major changes to Medicare to improve benefits, increase efficiency and quality of care, and promote savings (McDonough 2011, 157).

Medicaid eligibility requirements have also expanded since its inception, most notably through the Omnibus Budget Reconciliation Act of 1990, which required all Medicaid programs to provide coverage to children from low-income families (Kaiser Family Foundation 2015), and under the ACA, which expanded the eligibility of Medicaid requirements "to nearly all adults with family income at or below 138% [of the federal poverty level] ($15,856 for an individual, $26,951 for a family of three in 2014)" (Kaiser Family Foundation 2015). As a result of expanding enrollment and rising health care costs, Medicaid and Medicare expenditures have rather dramatically exceeded initial expectations, prompting discussion of reform among public policymakers at both the federal and state levels.

Democrats on Medicaid/Medicare

The Democratic Party has historically been the biggest proponent of governmental intervention in health care primarily because the party tends to follow a welfare state ideology. This means that Democrats often consider it the responsibility of the federal government to provide those in financial or social need with services and support that protects individuals' wellbeing. As a result, Democrats tend to endorse increased expansions of Medicare and Medicaid through the federal government. To illustrate this support, a 2011 report by the Pew Research Center finds that 91 percent of Democrats agree that Medicaid "has been very good/good for the country" (Pew Research Center 2011b), while 93 percent say the same about Medicare (Pew Research Center 2011a). These results indicate that Democrats generally support the continuation of these social programs. However, few Democrats believe that either program is in a good financial position. As a result, many Democrats support reform efforts to improve the financial stability of these programs. Many Democrats believe that financial reform can occur through changes within the existing framework of each program.

Generally speaking, the Democrats tend to be in favor of expanding both Medicare and Medicaid to provide more Americans with health care coverage. The ACA, which was championed almost exclusively by Democrats, expands the eligibility requirements of Medicaid to increase access for more Americans. By examining the multiple titles of the ACA, the Democratic position in regard to Medicare and Medicaid can be ascertained. Title II: Medicaid, CHIP, and the Governors; and Title III: Medical Care, Medicare, and the Cost Curve of the ACA seek to improve and advance Medicaid and Medicare respectively. Proponents of Title II, who are almost entirely Democrats, "are hopeful Medicaid will become a much more national and consistent program in the days and years ahead and will assume a larger role in shaping the U.S. health system's future" (McDonough 2011, 152). Title III highlights the democratic position to alter Medicare to promote savings and increase the quality of health care. "Many changes [in Title III] will improve the benefits and operations of the program for beneficiaries, many will improve the efficiency and quality of care provided to them, and many will generate savings" (McDonough 2011, 157). According to the Pew Report, 72 percent of Democrats believe that Medicare beneficiaries already pay enough of the costs (Pew Research Center 2011a), so they support reforms that do not shift the financial burden to the beneficiaries. Rather than shifting costs, Democrats seek to reduce the costs of the program by improving the program's effectiveness and reducing instances of misuse. They want to shift the focus of the program so that payment is determined based on health outcomes rather than simply services rendered. Democrats contend that this shift will help improve provider performance and reduce costly relapses related to previously addressed conditions. Democrats plan to use projected savings to provide uninsured Americans with health coverage.

One major area of contention between Democrats and Republicans has to do with Medicare Part C: Medicare Advantage. Medicare Advantage allows "Medicare beneficiaries to join a private health insurance plan for their covered benefits instead of participating in the traditional fee-for-service structure" (McDonough 2011, 168). Because Democrats generally support government provided health insurance over privately provided health insurance, they predominantly contest the continued reliance on private insurance through Part C. During the 2008 presidential election, Democratic candidate Obama asserted that if he could cut one federal program, he would cut Medicare Advantage (McDonough 2011, 169). Democrats argue that Medicare Advantage is regularly abused when managed care facilities assert that their patients are sicker than they really are, leading the government to regularly overpay for these plans. By reforming Medicare Advantage, Democrats contend that Medicare expenditures will decrease dramatically.

Historically, Democrats have fought for universal or government funded coverage, but these movements have proven largely unsuccessful. Therefore, while many modern Democrats promote the expansion of Medicare and Medicaid through private insurance companies, as evident in that the ACA relies on private insurance to operate, the Progressive Democrats of America, a subgroup within the Democratic Party, maintain more progressive views in regard to Medicare and Medicaid. According to Progressive Democrats, the entire healthcare system needs to be reformed into a single-payer system with the federal government as the sole payer. Progressive Democrats argue that these health programs should not rely on private insurance companies because it shifts the goals of health care away from protecting the public's health to focus on corporate profits on behalf of the insurance industry.

Democratic Praise for the Work of the Center for Medicare and Medicaid Innovation

On March 20, 2013, Max Baucus, Democratic senator from Montana, addressed the Senate Committee on Finance during a hearing to promote the continuation of the Center for Medicare and Medicaid Innovation, a program founded through the Affordable Care Act:

> Today, we are in need of new and innovative ideas for America's health care system. We know there's a better way to deliver quality health care and to lower costs. We created the Center for Medicare and Medicaid Innovation to find it.
>
> . . . The center comes with a simple mission: lower costs, and improve quality. It does so by testing new payment incentives and employing creative methods of delivering care. If the center develops a successful idea, Medicare and Medicaid work to quickly replicate it nationwide. If an idea is not successful, they go back to the drawing board and develop something different.
>
> . . . The Innovation Center is already testing many promising ideas. These include Pioneer Accountable Care Organizations, groups of doctors across the United States who work together and coordinate their care to reduce costs . . . these doctors are sharing lessons learned and best practices in an effort to provide better patient care. This is just one of the more than 30 new programs the Innovation Center has already introduced, impacting the lives of 5 million beneficiaries across all 50 states.

Health reform included specific ideas for the Innovation Center to test. But we also knew that tapping into Americans' ingenuity and entrepreneurship could lead to groundbreaking ideas on how to improve the health care delivery system.

So we told the center to ask Americans for their ideas on how to improve the quality of care without increasing costs. And as an incentive, the center would provide grants to test the most promising models.

. . . We are going to need a bold vision if we are going to get health care costs under control. So let us act boldly. Let us realize there is a way to do it better when it comes to health care costs, and as Thomas Edison said, let us find it.

Source

Baucus, Max. 2013. "Hearing Statement Regarding the Center for Medicare and Medicaid Innovation and Improving America's Health Care System." Accessed June 23, 2015. http://www.finance.senate.gov/imo/media/doc/03202013%20Baucus%20Statement%20on%20the%20Center%20for%20Medicare%20and%20Medicaid%20Innovation%20and%20Improving%20America's%20Health%20Care%20System1.pdf.

In 2009, Progressive Democrats proposed legislative bill H.R. 676: The United States National Health Care Act. Championed by Michigan representative John Conyers Jr., the bill proposed an expansion of Medicare to cover everyone within the country (U.S. Library of Congress 2015). Proponents of H.R. 676 assert that health care is a basic human right, and as such, the federal government should provide free health care to all. Other Democrats argue that the Progressive Democrats' plan for a radically different system is not possible because of current political tensions. They contend that reform must happen incrementally by building on the current system and extending private coverage options to more Americans.

Republicans on Medicaid/Medicare

Republicans have in recent decades tended to be strongly opposed to government intervention in health care, primarily because they assert that the free market is much more capable of distributing services than the federal government. As a result, they prefer allowing the market system to monitor and distribute health-care services. Consequently, Republicans tend to support the privatization of both the Medicare and Medicaid programs. They regularly advocate a reduction in the federal government's involvement in administering these programs. Historically, "In discussions about Medicare over many years, Republicans led the charge to cut the program" (McDonough 2011, 181). Republicans tend to believe that the health industry can be more efficiently regulated within the free market system than it can through government intervention and have systematically supported private intervention before government regulation. Even though they prefer privatization to government control, Republicans, like Democrats, in general recognize the social importance of both programs. According to a report by the Pew Research Center, 68 percent of Republicans agree that Medicaid "has been very good/good for the country" (Pew Research Center 2011b) and 85 percent say the same about Medicare (Pew Research Center 2011a). However, only a small percent (15 percent) believes that the programs are financially stable. While both parties recognize the need for financial improvements to both Medicare and Medicaid, Republicans differ from the Democrats in how they hope to remedy the poor financial condition of these fundamental health programs.

In response to the ACA, the Republican Party, headed by Representative Paul Ryan, proposed the *Path to Prosperity: Restoring America's Promise* in 2012. (The *Path to Prosperity* has been revised twice since 2012—once in 2013 and again in 2015—but under different subtitles.) This bill was a budget proposal that, if passed in 2012, would have substantially altered the frameworks of both Medicare and Medicaid. By examining the components of this proposed budget, the Republican position takes shape. Under this plan, Medicare would have no longer been a federally administered insurance program, but would instead have relied almost exclusively on private insurance companies. Medicare beneficiaries would have received government vouchers or subsidies to purchase private insurance benefits on their own. In 2011, approximately 40 percent of Republicans believed that the beneficiaries rather than the government should cover more of the costs of Medicare (McDonough 2011, 181), and Republicans argue that some of the financial burden would be shifted to Medicare recipients through a voucher system, reducing governmental expenditures for the program. Under the *Path to Prosperity*, the age eligibility requirement for Medicare would also have increased over the course of multiple years to better reflect current longer average lifespans. Proponents of this increase posit that this minor adjustment in age eligibility would lower government expenditures and increase overall savings.

Like the Democrats, Republicans generally support the idea of promoting Medicare savings; however, they disagree with the Democrats on what to do with the projected savings. Republicans assert that any savings should go toward deficit reductions and tax cuts to reduce the financial burden of the program on the nation as a whole (McDonough 2011, 181). Ideologically, the Republican Party supports tax cuts and reduced government expenditures to address the government deficit. This ideology is evident in their position regarding how to manage projected Medicare and Medicaid savings.

The 2015 congressional budget discussions emphasized a clear divide within the Republican Party in regard to Medicare and Medicaid. House Republicans and Senate Republicans disagreed over how to increase savings. While both Senate Republicans and House Republicans agree that there needed to be cuts to both programs, those in the Senate advocate greater costs without extensive

A Republican Senator Proposes Reforms at the Center for Medicare and Medicaid Innovation

On March 20, 2013, Republican Senator Orrin Hatch from Utah provided a statement to the Senate Committee on Finance raising concerns about the Center for Medicare and Medicaid Innovation, an agency created by the 2009 Affordable Care Act:

> Despite my long-time interest in reforming our nation's health care delivery system to reduce costs and improve quality, I was concerned with the creation of a new bureaucracy known as the Centers for Medicare and Medicaid Innovation (CMMI) and giving them $10 billion in taxpayer funds with no strings attached.
>
> We have now held two hearings in the committee where we have heard from the public and private sectors about interesting ways they are working to improve the delivery of care.
>
> I, for one, wholly support the private sector working among payers, providers, and patients to come up with solutions that best fit their communities in order to achieve more efficient and higher quality results.
>
> I have heard repeatedly from my Democratic colleagues that CMMI is tasked with letting "a thousand flowers bloom." What I really wonder is if this is simply a euphemism for barely controlled chaos.
>
> . . . With that said, I do think there is merit to trying to change the delivery of care and to focus on greater coordination of care, reducing hospital admissions, and providing better outcomes to patients. I am concerned, though, that there is confusion and a clear lack focus at CMMI . . .
>
> . . . It seems to me that CMMI would function best if it would pick a few initiatives—such as accountable care organizations (ACOs) or bundled payments—and really devote the time to those initiatives to make sure they actually work and have the intended consequences of lowering costs and increasing quality and efficiency. Coordination among initiatives that have similar goals is something the GAO has highlighted as a concern.
>
> . . . Our priority must be very clear: we need to make government as efficient as possible . . . We need the right people with expertise . . . to develop targeted approaches that can be tried quickly, studied, and assessed for measures of success.

Source

Hatch, Orrin. Hatch Statement at Finance Committee Hearing Examining the Role of the New CMS Innovation Center, 2013. Accessed June 25, 2015. http://www.finance.senate.gov /imo/media/doc/03.20.13%20Hatch%20statement%20at%20Finance%20Committee%20 hearing%20examining%20CMMI.pdf.

reform of the program. Conversely, House Republicans advocate reforms similar to those proposed in the first *Path to Prosperity* bill. Many Republicans want to implement a voucher system for Medicare, providing beneficiaries with a subsidy to purchase private insurance coverage. Representative Tom Price, Budget

Committee Chair and primary proponent of the House plan, asserts that the dramatic reform "would 'result in a government that's more efficient and effective and accountable—one that frees up the American spirit . . . to do great things and to meet great challenges'" (Taylor 2015). The House plan would also give states complete authority over their individual Medicaid programs, supported by federal lump sum funding. Senate Republicans tend to agree that states should have more flexibility in administering and designing Medicaid, but they disagree that lump sum funding should be used and federal regulation mostly eliminated.

As stated previously, Republicans and Democrats tend to clash over Medicare Part C: Medicare Advantage. Whereas Democrats want to utilize government insurance over private insurance, Republicans "prefer medical care organized and delivered by the private sector as opposed to the government; if they could do it, Republicans would prefer that all Medicare services be delivered through private plans with no fee-for-service option" (McDonough 2011, 168). The *Path to Prosperity* budget plans have all attempted to shift Medicare to a system of private insurance, but so far, they have been unsuccessful. Hence, to Republicans Medicare Advantage is a vital component of the current Medicare system because it supports their desire to utilize private insurance as a basis for Medicare. Consequently, they fight to keep it and to expand it.

Earlene A. Smith

Further Reading

Barr, Donald A. 2002. *Introduction to U.S. Health Policy: The Organization, Financing, and Delivery of Health Care in America*. San Francisco: Benjamin Cummings.

Centers for Medicare and Medicaid Services. 2014a. "Medicare Program—General Information." Home—Centers for Medicare and Medicaid Services. Last modified July 25. Accessed July 14, 2015. http://www.cms.gov/Medicare/Medicare-General-Information/MedicareGenInfo/index.html.

Centers for Medicare and Medicaid Services. 2014b. *What's Medicare? / What's Medicaid?* CMS Product No. 11306. Accessed July 23, 2015. https://www.medicare.gov/Pubs/pdf/11306.pdf.

Kaiser Family Foundation. 2015. "Medicaid Timeline." Kaiser Family Foundation—Health Policy Research, Analysis, Polling, Facts, Data and Journalism. Last modified 2015. Accessed August 4, 2015. http://kff.org/medicaid/timeline/medicaid-timeline/.

McDonough, John E. 2011. *Inside National Health Reform*. Berkeley: University of California Press.

Medicare Resource Center. 2015. "A Brief History of Medicare in America: Landmark Social Program Now Covers 47 Million Americans." Accessed March 26. http://www.medicareresources.org/basic-medicare-information/brief-history-of-medicare/.

Pew Research Center. 2011a. "Section 3: Views of Medicare." July 7. Accessed August 5, 2015. http://www.people-press.org/2011/07/07/section-3-views-of-medicare/.

Pew Research Center. 2011b. "Section 4: Views of Medicaid." July 7. Accessed September 3. http://www.people-press.org/2011/07/07/section-4-views-of-medicaid/.

Statista, Inc. 2015. "Total Medicaid Enrollment from 1966 to 2014 (in millions)." Accessed June 3. http://www.statista.com/statistics/245347/total-medicaid-enrollment-since-1966/.

Taylor, Andrew. 2015. "Senate, House GOP differ on savings approach to Medicare." *PBS News Room*, March 18. Accessed June 4, 2015. http://www.pbs.org/newshour/rundown /senate-house-gop-differ-savings-approach-medicare/.

U.S. Census Bureau. 2012. *Statistical Abstract of the United States: 2012 (131st Edition)*. Washington, DC. Accessed October 5, 2015. http://www.census.gov/compendia/statab /2012edition.html.

U.S. Library of Congress. 2015. "Bill Summary & Status: 111th Congress (2009–2010) H.R. 676 CRS Summary." Accessed August 2, 2015. http://thomas.loc.gov/cgi-bin /bdquery/z?d111:HR00676:@@@D&summ2=m&.

Minimum Wage

At a Glance

Since 2009, United States workers in most jobs have been guaranteed to make at least $7.25 per hour of work. This is known as the minimum wage. Most of the debate surrounding minimum wage centers on whether or not to raise or maintain the amount paid per hour. Support for raising the minimum wage comes primarily from Democrats. Democrats tend to believe that the current minimum wage is not enough for a person to live comfortably, keeping many people below the poverty line. They think additional money in more people's pockets will benefit all levels of the economy, as low-income people will have more money with which to buy goods. Further, Democrats find that changes to the minimum wage have not been linked to the price of consumer goods as established by the consumer price index, a set listing of the price of goods. This means that because of inflation, $7.25 does not buy as much as it did in 2009, and the minimum wage will only continue to be lowered relative to the cost of goods unless the amount is raised.

Opposition to raising the minimum wage generally comes from Republicans. Republicans believe that raising the minimum wage will cause a rise in the cost of goods and higher levels of unemployment, as employers will have to compensate for higher labor costs. They believe that many people who hold minimum wage jobs will lose their job and be unable to find another, therefore a higher minimum wage will in fact hurt the very people it is trying to help. Republicans also note that only a very small percentage of the American labor force makes minimum wage, but the increased cost of goods would harm all Americans, particularly the middle class. Finally, many Republicans argue that having a minimum wage at all is an unfair government intrusion into the private sector, and the market would be able to determine a fair wage for workers without government intervention.

Many Democrats . . .

- Assert that raising the minimum wage would help the lowest income earners live more comfortably and spend more time with their families
- Contend that a higher minimum wage would allow more low-income individuals to escape from poverty

- Argue that a higher minimum wage would increase the total amount of money in the market, making the U.S. economy stronger
- Contend that raising the minimum wage is necessary to help low-income workers keep up with rising inflation
- Claim that a minimum wage hike would not result in a meaningfully increase in unemployment

Many Republicans . . .

- Say that a minimum wage hike would increase unemployment, particularly for low wage jobs
- Claim that a minimum wage increase would spark an increase in the price of goods, harming the middle class
- Contend that minimum wage mandates are an unfair and unnecessary intrusion by the federal government into the free market

---

Overview

The Fair Labor Standards Act of 1938 first implemented a minimum wage at the national level, but several states had already attempted to establish minimum wages within their borders, beginning with Massachusetts in 1912. The Supreme Court overturned most state minimum wages on the grounds that it interfered with freedom of contract, meaning it prevented employers and employees from freely buying and selling labor (Grossman 2015). During the Great Depression, President Franklin Roosevelt began a series of sweeping economic reforms aimed at getting people back to work and helping to jumpstart the economy, known as the New Deal. Before the Fair Labor Standards Act, employees would receive very low pay, often not equivalent to the amount of work the employee had performed. This was particularly egregious for women and children, with some young people reporting earning as little as $4 a week for 60–80 hours of work (this is roughly equivalent to $70 a week in 2015 dollars) (Grossman 2015).

The Fair Labor Standards Act established a $0.25 per hour minimum rate of pay. Since then, the federal minimum wage has been raised 22 times, with the current wage set at $7.25 in 2009. While the dollar amount is the highest ever, the current minimum wage is actually on the low end when compared to the price of goods. The highest minimum wage was in 1968, at $1.60 per hour, or $8.54 in 2014 dollars (Sherk 2013).

While the federal government maintains a minimum wage, some states, and now some cities, set their own minimum wages. Twenty-two states have minimum wages above the federal level, and 15 states tie their minimum wages to the consumer price index to adjust for inflation. Several states are set to raise their minimum wage above $10 per hour in the upcoming year. In 2014, Seattle established a $15 per

An Argument for Raising the Minimum Wage

In May 2015, New York Governor Andrew Cuomo argued in support of raising the New York State minimum wage:

> More than 600 economists, including seven Nobel Prize laureates, have affirmed the growing consensus that raising wages for the lowest-paid workers doesn't hurt the economy. In fact, by increasing consumer spending and creating jobs, it helps the economy. Studies have shown that every dollar increase for a minimum wage-worker results in $2,800 in new consumer spending by household.

Source

Cuomo, Andrew. 2015. "Fast-Food Workers Deserve a Raise." *New York Times,* May 7, 2015. Accessed May 31. http://www.nytimes.com/2015/05/07/opinion/andrew-m-cuomo-fast-food -workers-deserve-a-raise.html.

hour minimum wage, and Los Angeles followed suit in 2015. San Francisco currently has a minimum wage of $12.25 per hour, which will rise to $15 per hour by 2018. The state of New York pays a minimum wage of $8.75 per hour, but under increasing pressure from low-income workers, Democratic Governor Andrew Cuomo has recently introduced a proposal to raise the minimum wage to $11.50 per hour in New York City, and $10.50 per hour in the rest of the state. Some states, such as Tennessee and Mississippi, have no minimum wage, while others, such as Georgia, have minimum wages below the federal level (NCSL 2015). In these instances, the federal minimum wage supersedes the state laws (or lack thereof).

It is important to note that not all workers receive a minimum wage. Those who work for tips, such as waiters in restaurants, have their tips included in their wages. These employees typically make $2 to $4 per hour, but with tips their average income must equal the state or federal minimum.

Since 2012, there has been a growing movement of low-wage workers demanding a higher hourly pay. The Fight for $15 movement began with a group of McDonald's employees, and now includes Walmart employees, childcare aides, airport workers, and adjunct professors, among others. The group is asking for a $15 federal minimum wage, more than double the current amount. They argue that in most parts of the country, $15 an hour is the minimum amount necessary to afford food, housing, transportation, and all other living expenses. This group, also known as the Fast Food Workers Movement, has become the most high profile social movement demanding higher wages. Another group, called Raise the Minimum Wage, is part of the National Employment Law Project, and seeks a $12 per hour federal minimum wage. While Fight for $15 is more apt to engage in walk-outs and protests, Raise the Minimum Wage tends to work on the legal end, donating to candidates and supporting bills that would raise the minimum wage.

While there are many groups, politicians, and citizens working to raise the minimum wage, there is broad disagreement about how much the minimum wage should be. As shown previously, some groups seek $15 per hour, others $12 per hour, others $10.10 per hour, and still others $9 per hour. The Congressional Budget Office (CBO) released a report in 2014 detailing the estimated effects of raising the federal minimum wage to either $9 or $10.10 per hour. The report finds that raising the minimum wage to $10.10 per hour would give a raise to 16.5 million workers, while the $9 option would give a raise to 7.6 million workers (Congressional Budget Office 2014). However, they also estimate that up to one million workers would lose their jobs as a result of the increase. The relationship between unemployment and a higher minimum wage has been a point of controversy among economists for over 100 years. Studies by UC Irvine's David Neumark and the Fed's William Wauscher have found that raising the minimum wage increases unemployment, due to the increased cost of labor to business owners (Matthews 2013). Other studies by Berkeley's David Card and Princeton's Alan Kruegar have shown increasing the minimum wage created more jobs by increasing the demand for goods and services, due to more people having more money (Matthews 2013). This remains a contested issue in the economics field, meaning that legislators must make decisions without the ability to predict what the impact of those decisions might be, but no matter which side of the issue they fall on, they are likely to find studies that support them.

Republicans on Raising the Minimum Wage

Republicans have been less supportive of raising the minimum wage, particularly of major raises or linking the minimum wage to rising inflation. However, according to Gallup, 58 percent of Republicans do support raising the minimum wage to $9 per hour, while only 43 percent support raising the minimum wage to $9 and also tying it to inflation. As the level of the minimum wage rises, Republican support tends to decrease.

A Republican Senator Speaks Out Against Raising the Minimum Wage

Republican Senator Marco Rubio of Florida has been a strong and consistent opponent of raising the minimum wage, emphasizing his belief that the federal government should not intrude into such economic matters. In his response to the 2013 State of the Union address, Rubio asserted that "more government isn't going to inspire new ideas, new businesses and new private jobs. It's going to create uncertainty. Because more government breeds complicated rules and laws that a small business can't afford to follow. Because more government raises taxes on employers who then pass the costs on to employees through fewer hours, lower pay and even layoffs. And because government programs that claims to help the middle class, often end up hurting them instead."

When President Barack Obama publicly called for Congress to pass a bill to raise the minimum wage to $9 per hour, Rubio said, "I support people making more than $9. I want people to make as much as they can. I don't think a minimum wage law works. We all support—I certainly do—having more tax payers, meaning more people who are employed. And I want people to make a lot more than $9—$9 is not enough. The problem is you can't do that by mandating it in the minimum wage laws. Minimum wage laws have never worked in terms of having the middle class attain more prosperity. What works is helping the private sector grow."

Sources

Rubio, Marco. 2013. "Republican Response to the State of the Union Address," February 12. Accessed June 3, 2015. http://abcnews.go.com/Politics/transcript-marco-rubios-state-union-response/story?id=18484413&singlePage=true.

Weiner, Rachel. 2013. "Marco Rubio: I Don't Think a Minimum Wage Law Works." February 13. Accessed June 28, 2015. http://www.washingtonpost.com/blogs/post-politics/wp/2013/02/13/marco-rubio-i-dont-think-a-minimum-wage-law-works/.

Among the 2016 Republican presidential candidates, there is broad disagreement about what the minimum wage should be, or if we should even have one at all. In an interview in May 2015, candidate Ben Carson said "I think, probably, it should be higher than it is now" (Kamisar 2015) though he did not specify how high it should be, or if he would, as president, back a plan to raise it. Later in 2015, during a Republican candidate debate, Carson reversed this position. 2012 Republican presidential nominee Mitt Romney has been, perhaps, the most notable Republican to support a minimum wage increase, encouraging Republicans to a raise because "Frankly, our party is all about more jobs and better pay" (Topaz 2014).

Other Republican politicians have been less supportive of raising the minimum wage. Former Florida Governor Jeb Bush has stated he does not believe the federal government should raise the minimum wage, suggesting instead it should be up to states to decide. Former Speaker of the House John Boehner does not support raising the minimum wage, saying in response to President Obama's plan to raise the minimum wage to $10.10 per hour, "When you raise the cost of something you get less of it. The very people the president purports to help are the ones who are going to be hurt by this" (O'Keefe 2014). In this case Boehner is referring to the increased cost of jobs leading to fewer jobs. Senate Majority Leader Mitch McConnell has said raising the minimum wage to $10.10 per hour would "destroy half a million to 1 million jobs. That's not the way to grow our economy" (Contorno 2014).

And still other Republicans find the minimum wage entirely unnecessary. In a perfect free market system, wages would be determined by balancing profits for business with the ability of workers to purchase goods. Businesses would be unable to make a profit if they are not paying workers enough to purchase the goods they are producing. Therefore, there is no need to have a government-initiated minimum wage, as the market will balance itself. Senator and 2016 presidential Candidate Marco Rubio proposes eliminating the federal minimum wage in favor of allowing the private sector to set wages. "We all support—I certainly do—having more taxpayers, meaning more people who are employed. And I want people to make a lot more than $9—$9 is not enough. The problem is you can't do that by mandating it in the minimum wage laws" (Weiner 2013). Wisconsin Governor Scott Walker said of Wisconsin's minimum wage "Well, I'm not going to repeal it, but I don't think it serves a purpose" (Kroll 2014). Finally, Senator Ted Cruz has argued that raising the minimum wage will hurt young people and minorities, preventing those workers from getting their foot in the door and gaining the necessary experience to advance to higher incomes. On President Obama's plan to raise the minimum wage, Cruz said, "The undeniable truth is if the president succeeded in raising the minimum wage, it would cost jobs from the most vulnerable" (Cruz 2014).

Republicans tend to favor small government, and find the minimum wage to be an unnecessary intrusion by the federal government into the free market. Republicans in general support higher wages for workers, but they feel the free market should establish wages rather than the federal government. Republicans suggest that setting a minimum wage traps people at that wage, and discourages companies from moving people up the ladder due to high labor costs. Raising the cost of entry-level employees also raises the costs of managers and everyone else in the organization, meaning less opportunity for advancement. Further, they find the possibility of lost jobs to be too high a cost for marginal benefits to low-income earners. They find the possibility of workers earning no money, because they lost their job as a result of a minimum wage increase, to be problematic, as those people will then be more dependent on the government to support them. Republicans find this to be an ineffective way to address poverty in America, arguing that rather than taking away jobs, the government should be encouraging job creation by lowering the cost of doing business for companies through lowering taxes, not raising their costs through requiring them to spend more on labor.

Democrats on Raising the Minimum Wage

Democrats are generally in favor of raising the minimum wage. According to the Pew Research Center, 90 percent of Democrats support increasing the minimum wage to at least $10.10 per hour (Pew Research Center 2014). Democrats tend to see increasing the minimum wage as a means to help people escape poverty, and a way to decrease the wealth gap between the richest and poorest Americans. Rather than allowing the free market to establish wages, as Republicans would prefer, Democrats support the government establishing a basic standard of living through programs such as Temporary Assistance for Needy Families (TANF), a regressive tax system, and higher wages for low-income workers. Where Republicans find increased business regulations result in costs being passed on to consumers, Democrats find regulations to be an important means for protecting workers from being exploited.

In 2013, President Barack Obama included support for raising the minimum wage in his annual State of the Union Address, saying "Tonight, let's declare that in the wealthiest nation on Earth, no one who works full time should have to live in poverty, and raise the federal minimum wage to $9 an hour" (Obama 2013). In 2014 and 2015, Obama again brought up raising the minimum wage in his annual address. In March 2013, Senator Tom Harkin introduced the Fair Minimum Wage Act of 2013, which would have raised the minimum wage to $10.10 per hour by 2015, and would subsequently have tied the minimum wage to the cost of goods. This bill died in committee (Harkin 2013). Harkin tried again, reintroducing the bill in November 2013. In April 2014, the bill was recommended to proceed to the Senate floor, but was never voted upon. In late April 2015, Senators Pat Murray and Robert C. Scott introduced the Raise the Wage Act, which would raise the federal minimum wage to $12 per hour by 2020, and then tie the wage to the cost of goods (Murray 2015). The future of this bill is uncertain, as it lacks support from Republicans who control both chambers of Congress in 2015.

Though Democrats are overall supportive of raising the minimum wage, they disagree about how much and how quickly to raise it, as well as whether or not it should be tied to the price of goods. As a Democratic presidential candidate in 2016 Hillary Clinton has expressed support for raising the minimum wage, saying she supports "fast-food and domestic workers all across the country who ask for nothing more than a living wage and a fair shot" (Scheiber 2015), but she has not stated any specifics about how much she would like to see it increased. Vermont Independent Senator and 2016 Democratic presidential candidate Bernie Sanders has called the current $7.25 per hour federal minimum wage a "starvation wage" and said, "Anyone who works 40 hours in a week in America should not be in poverty" (Hensch 2015). Sanders has further stated he supports a $15 per hour minimum wage within the "next few years" (Sanders 2015). Senator Elizabeth Warren, perhaps best known for her attempts to regulate banks after the 2008 housing meltdown, has been a very vocal supporter of raising the minimum wage. Speaking at the AFL-CIO's 2015 National Summit on Wages, Warren noted that all wages have not risen (relative to inflation) since 1980, and criticized Republican policies that have concentrated wealth in the hands of the top 1 percent of earners. She echoed Sanders' sentiments saying, "We believe no one should work full time and still live in poverty—and that means raising the minimum wage" (Warren 2015). In a presentation before the Senate Committee on Health, Education, Labor and Pensions, Warren argued the minimum wage would be $22 per hour if wages had kept up with worker productivity and the rising cost of goods (U.S. Senate 2013). While Warren stopped short of advocating for that much of a raise to the federal minimum wage, her arguments allude that a minimum wage higher than any current legislative initiatives would receive support from some Democrats.

Democrats argue that raising the minimum wage will help lift people out of poverty, and will decrease the wealth gap between the richest and poorest Americans. Some Democrats find that wages have not risen enough to keep up with the rising cost of living in the United States, and therefore the minimum wage needs to be raised significantly. Other Democrats support raising the minimum wage, but to lower amounts. With such high levels of support among Democrats, it seems likely that Democratic presidential candidates will try to make raising the minimum wage a key issue in the 2016 campaign. Whether or not they will be successful in raising the minimum wage, or whether they will be able to gain support from Republicans, remains to be seen.

Emily Schnurr

Further Reading

Congressional Budget Office. 2014. "The Effects of a Minimum-Wage Increase on Employment and Family Income." Congressional Budget Office. Accessed October 3, 2015. http://www.cbo.gov/sites/default/files/44995-MinimumWage.pdf.

Contorno, Steve. 2014. "Mitch McConnell Says Minimum Wage Hike Would 'Destroy' 500,000 to 1 Million Jobs." @politifact, October 4. Accessed May 23, 2015. http://www.politifact.com/truth-o-meter/statements/2014/oct/14/mitch-mcconnell/mitch-mcconnell-says-minimum-wage-hike-would-destr/.

Cruz, Ted. 2014. "Minimum Wage Act Kills Jobs; American Energy Renaissance Act Creates Jobs." *U.S. Senator Ted Cruz.* April 29. Accessed September 1, 2015. http://www.cruz.senate.gov/?p=press_release&id=1160.

Grossman, Jonathan. 2015. "Fair Labor Standards Act of 1938: Maximum Struggle for a Minimum Wage." U.S. Department of Labor. Accessed May 21. http://www.dol.gov/dol/aboutdol/history/flsa1938.htm.

Harkin, Tom. 2013. "S.460–113th Congress (2013–2014): Fair Minimum Wage Act of 2013." Legislation. March 5. Accessed June 3, 2015. https://www.congress.gov/bill/113th-congress/senate-bill/460.

Hensch, Mark. 2015. "Sanders Calls Minimum Wage a 'Starvation Wage.'" *The Hill*, May 2. Accessed May 24, 2015. http://thehill.com/blogs/ballot-box/dem-primaries/240871-sanders-calls-minimum-wage-a-starvation-wage.

Kamisar, Ben. 2015. "Ben Carson Backs Raising Minimum Wage." *The Hill*, May 8. Accessed May 23, 2015. http://thehill.com/blogs/ballot-box/241449-ben-carson-backs-raising-minimum-wage.

Kroll, Andy. 2014. "Gov. Scott Walker on the Minimum Wage: 'I Don't Think It Serves a Purpose.'" *Mother Jones*, October 14. Accessed May 23, 2015. http://www.motherjones.com/mojo/2014/10/scott-walker-minimum-wage-wisconsin-governor.

Matthews, Dylan. 2013. "Four Things to Know about Obama's Minimum Wage Increase." *Washington Post*, February 13. Accessed May 3, 2015. http://www.washingtonpost.com/blogs/wonkblog/wp/2013/02/13/four-things-to-know-about-obamas-minimum-wage-increase/.

Murray, Patty. 2015. "News Releases—Newsroom—MINIMUM WAGE: Murray, Scott Introduce the Raise the Wage Act—United States Senator Patty Murray." Accessed May 24, 2015. http://www.murray.senate.gov/public/index.cfm/newsreleases?ContentRecord _id=f7121681-bcd5-425b-9e73-76e33f5123bc.

NCSL. 2015. "State Minimum Wages: 2015 Minimum Wage by State." Organization. *National Conference of State Legislators*. February 24. Accessed May 4, 2015. http:// www.ncsl.org/research/labor-and-employment/state-minimum-wage-chart.aspx.

Obama, Barack. 2013. "Remarks by the President in the State of the Union Address." Speech. *State of the Union Address*. February 12. Washington, DC. Accessed March 6, 2016. https://www.whitehouse.gov/the-press-office/2013/02/12/remarks-president -state-union-address

O'Keefe, Ed. 2014. "Boehner Knocks Obama's Minimum Wage Executive Order." *Washington Post*, January 28. Accessed June 8, 2015. http://www.washingtonpost.com/blogs/post -politics/wp/2014/01/28/boehner-knocks-obamas-minimum-wage-executive-order/.

Pew Research Center. 2014. "Most See Inequality Growing, but Partisans Differ over Solutions." *Pew Research Center for the People and the Press*, January 23. Accessed May 24, 2015. http://www.people-press.org/2014/01/23/most-see-inequality-growing-but -partisans-differ-over-solutions/.

Sanders, Bernie. 2015. "Raise the Minimum Wage." *Bernie Sanders*. Accessed May 24. https://berniesanders.com/issues/raising-minimum-wage/.

Scheiber, Noam. 2015. "Wage Effort Poses Test for Clinton Campaign." *New York Times*, April 13. Accessed June 9, 2015. http://www.nytimes.com/2015/04/14/business/wage -effort-poses-test-for-clinton-campaign.html.

Sherk, James. 2013. "What Is Minimum Wage: Its History and Effects on the Economy." *The Heritage Foundation*, June 25. Accessed May 21, 2015. http://www.heritage.org/research /testimony/2013/06/what-is-minimum-wage-its-history-and-effects-on-the-economy.

Topaz, Jonathan. 2014. "Mitt Romney: Raise the Minimum Wage." *POLITICO*, May 9. Accessed May 23, 2015. http://www.politico.com/story/2014/05/mitt-romney-minimum -wage-106524.html.

U.S. Senate. 2013. *Keeping Up with a Changing Economy: Indexing the Minimum Wage*. Senate Office Building, Washington, DC: Government Publishing Office. Accessed July 8, 2015. http://www.help.senate.gov/hearings/hearing/?id=b7e4d7fc-5056-a032-52f3 -dcd089d46121.

Warren, Elizabeth. 2015. "Senator Warren's Remarks at AFL-CIO National Summit on Raising Wages." *Elizabeth Warren U.S. Senator for Massachusetts*. January 7. Accessed October 9, 2015. http://www.warren.senate.gov/?p=press_release&id=696.

Weiner, Rachel. 2013. "Marco Rubio: 'I Don't Think a Minimum Wage Law Works.'" *Washington Post*, February 13. Accessed June 28, 2015. http://www.washingtonpost .com/blogs/post-politics/wp/2013/02/13/marco-rubio-i-dont-think-a-minimum -wage-law-works/.

No-Bid Contracts

At a Glance

In general both Republicans and Democratic politicians publicly oppose the awarding of no-bid contracts. However, there are subtle differences in their policy positions on the issue.

Many Republicans . . .

- Feel that competition for government contracts increases quality and efficiency
- Say that no-bid contracts are to generally be avoided, except under certain conditions
- Believe addressing other economic issues such as spending and debt is more important for improving America's fiscal health than addressing no-bid contracts

Many Democrats . . .

- Believe the use of private organizations in the provision of public goods is to be avoided
- See use of no-bid contracts as usually unacceptable
- Contend that no-bid contracts should only be used when certain extenuating circumstances, such as pressing timetables, demand

---

Overview

The government is much larger than the individuals employed directly by government agencies. Similarly, the functions of government are vaster and more complex than the things government does directly. The garbage worker picking up household waste, the road crew filling in a pothole, and the construction worker building a new campus facility may all work for private employers. The process by which government organizations go about assigning public work to non-public entities is called contracting. In all levels of government, the procurement and management of contracts is an increasingly important and time-consuming task for public managers.

Governments contract with private and nonprofit organizations for a number of reasons. The first is cost savings. There are certain tasks for which private entities have a competitive advantage over government. For example, if a small community needs to repave a road, it is often cheaper for them to contract out the project than invest in a full-time construction crew and road repaving equipment that will have limited future utility. The second reason is reduction in administrative costs. When contracting, a public manager must only worry about the contract, and not the specifics of human resource management and labor issues such as collective bargaining. Governments also contract to lower political risk. A failed contracted project reflects poorly on the private organization doing the work, but a failed government project reflects poorly on the government as a whole. Proponents of privatization also argue that contracting promotes competition between entities seeking the contract, pushing prices down and performance up. Lastly, contracts are sometimes awarded for political reasons—including to reward political contributors for financial donations (Savas 2000).

Federal Acquisition Regulation

The Federal Acquisition Regulation (FAR) encompasses the official procurement rules for the federal government. It was created as part of the Office of Federal Procurement Policy Act of 1974. With limited exceptions, federal agencies must follow these guidelines when contracting out for services. The FAR begins with a statement of guiding principles which states:

> The vision for the Federal Acquisition System is to deliver on a timely basis the best value product or service to the customer, while maintaining the public's trust and fulfilling public policy objectives. Participants in the acquisition process should work together as a team and should be empowered to make decisions within their area of responsibility. . . . The Federal Acquisition System will:
>
> • Satisfy the customer in terms of cost, quality, and timeliness of the delivered product or service by . . . maximizing the use of commercial products and services; using contractors who have a track record of successful past performance or who demonstrate a current superior ability to perform; and Promoting competition."
> • Minimize administrative operating costs;
> • Conduct business with integrity, fairness, and openness; and
> • Fulfill public policy objectives.

The FAR also details standards of conduct in order to minimize the appearance or occurrence of corruption during the procurement process. The regulations state, in part:

- Government business shall be conducted in a manner above reproach and, except as authorized by statute or regulation, with complete impartiality and with preferential treatment for none. Transactions relating to the expenditure of public funds require the highest degree of public trust and an impeccable standard of conduct. The general rule is to avoid strictly any conflict of interest or even the appearance of a conflict of interest in Government-contractor relationships. While many Federal laws and regulations place restrictions on the actions of Government personnel, their official conduct must, in addition, be such that they would have no reluctance to make a full public disclosure of their actions.
- As a rule, no Government employee may solicit or accept, directly or indirectly, any gratuity, gift, favor, entertainment, loan, or anything of monetary value from anyone who (a) has or is seeking to obtain Government business with the employee's agency, (b) conducts activities that are regulated by the employee's agency, or (c) has interests that may be substantially affected by the performance or nonperformance of the employee's official duties. Certain limited exceptions are authorized in agency regulations.

The FAR also requires that agencies follow set guidelines for disseminating information regarding their contracting activities for the purposes of promoting transparency. Finally, the FAR outlines the parameters of a competitive procurement process.

Source

"Federal Acquisition Regulation." 2005. *General Services Administration*. Accessed August 1, 2015. https://www.acquisition.gov/sites/default/files/current/far/pdf/FAR.pdf.

Broadly, governments contract to reduce costs, fill in gaps in their service capabilities, increase performance through competition, circumvent organized labor, and boost community businesses. Contracting is a vital part of the public sector that is almost universally done by all levels of government. However, some critics argue that contracting has the potential to reduce public sector capabilities, transparency, equity, and accountability for performance. Government agencies attempt to prevent these negative consequences through a procurement process that—when done properly—states the terms of the contract, is open to all potential bidders, and is fairly awarded through a transparent and public bid process. Ideally, the end result of a procurement process is an awarded contract that is executed in a matter consistent with expectations.

However, the potential benefits of an effective procurement process are complicated by no-bid contracts. A no-bid contract is simply when a government entity awards a contract directly to a private or nonprofit organization without soliciting proposals from competing organizations. The use of no-bid contracts in government merits discussion of both operational and philosophical issues. From an operational standpoint, a no-bid contract may not bring costs down or quality up because there is no market incentive for a private or non-profit entity to minimize costs or maximize performance. When a contract is competitive, bidders must consider their competition and adjust their price and provide services accordingly if they hope to receive the contract.

However, there are situations where a no-bid contract makes sense from an operational standpoint. For example, many of the services governments contract out, such as copying services, mailings, paycheck services, are relatively inexpensive. The cost of putting these small jobs through the completing bidding process may outweigh any potential cost benefits created by a competitive procurement process. In addition, advocates of no-bid contracts point out that government agencies often have established relationships with private and nonprofit organizations with proven records of good performance. For example, if a city awards a contract for the building of a new garage to a private entity, it makes sense to work with that entity on future repairs or renovations due to their knowledge and experience with the project. In the area of national security, a bidding process is often impractical due to security concerns. In smaller rural local governments, or in highly specialized functional areas, there is often only one potential bidder for a project, making a no-bid contract the most logical and efficient approach.

Philosophically, no-bid contracts remove a layer of public accountability. Not only is government not directly providing a service, but also the providing organization did not face competition for the contract. No-bid contracts also pose equity concerns. The ability for government to include minority employment requirements in bids for contracts, or to ensure all businesses have the potential to bid on a contract, is removed when no bid is required. But, perhaps most important, no-bid contracts raise serious ethical questions. As will be discussed in the following sections, both Democrats and Republicans have accused each other of using no-bid contracts to reward political supporters. Indeed, the use of no-bid contracts creates the perception of cronyism. Basic tenets of social equity state that the burdens and benefits of government should be equitably distributed among the governed. A no-bid contract can easily be viewed as a transfer of public money to a private organization based on privileged access, rather than merit. To put in another way, the awarding of no-bid contracts gives the perceptions that elected officials use public resources to reward the wealthy and well connected at the expense of the majority of the governed.

Of course, the awarding of a no-bid contract is not always an act of corruption or cronyism. As such, the topic, in particular as it relates to the actions and positions of prominent Democrats and Republicans, demands a more nuanced discussion.

Republicans on No-Bid Contracts

Traditionally, the Republican Party is more supportive of the application of private-sector principals to the provision of public goods than their counterparts on the other side of the aisle. Ronald Reagan's 1981 *Task Force on Private Sector Initiatives*, for example, advocated the use of the private sector to solve pressing public issues and reduce the size of government in general (Reagan 1981). The Republican Party is also traditionally more supportive of initiatives like school vouchers that allow public services to be provided by private and nonprofit organizations. At the same time, Republicans in general share the Democrats' aversion to awarding no-bid contracts on the grounds they undermine the potential market-effect generated by a competitive bidding process. In recent years, the Republican Party has heavily criticized Democratic leadership for the use of no-bid contracts, and promised to increase transparency and accountability in all aspects of government, including procurement.

In 2006 President George W. Bush signed the Federal Funding Accountability and Transparency Act. The bill, which passed with bipartisan support, was designed to introduce transparency into the awarding of federal contracts to nonpublic entities. It was signed shortly before a scathing editorial in the *New York Times* relating to the awarding of no-bid contracts to the then-named Blackwater military contractor operating in Iraq (Editorial Board 2007). The *New York Times* Editorial Board accused the Bush administration of awarding contracts to Blackwater based on the connections between the corporation and former and current White House officials. In subsequent media interviews, President Bush defended the contracts, stating that his administration felt that Blackwater was uniquely qualified for the challenges of operating in an active war zone.

In response to Democratic criticism of no-bid contracting during the Bush administration, Republicans like House Minority Leader John Boehner of Ohio argued that the fiscal problems of the United States ran far deeper than the use of no-bid contracts, stating "We need to start seeing some semblance of fiscal discipline" (Feller 2009). In other words, though Republicans like Boehner generally do not support the use of no-bid contracts in federal government, they also believe the issue was being used by political opponents to cast the Bush administration in an unflattering light and distract from the larger issues of spending levels, taxation policies, and the growing national debt.

Despite the position and statements of Republican leaders like Boehner, the Republican Party became highly critical of the use of no-bid contracting when it was practiced by the administration of Democratic President Barack Obama. For example, the Republican National Committee (RNC) established two websites attacking President Obama and then–Secretary of State Hillary Clinton, respectively, for failing to reign in the use of no-bid contracting. The first website, *No Bid Failure*, first references Obama's promise to bid out all federal contracts above $25,000, and then details a list of no-bid contracts made during the president's terms in office. The second and more current website, *Breach of Contract*, is critical of 2016 presidential candidate Hillary Clinton's use of no-bid contracting during her time at the State Department. The website discusses specific instances where, according to the Republican National Committee, the awarding of no-bid contracts led to wasteful government spending.

Overall, the dominant Republican position on no-bid contracts differs only in subtle ways from the Democratic position. Prominent Republicans and the Republican National Committee all voice a general opposition to the awarding of no-bid contracts. They argue such contracts encourage cronyism, reduce accountability, and ultimately have a negative impact on the finances and performance of the federal government. However, Republicans in general are more apt than Democrats to view no-bid contracts as a distraction from more important fiscal issues. In other words, Republicans tend to be against no-bid contracts, but believe they play only a minor role in the overall fiscal health of the United States.

Republicans also have a long track record of awarding no-bid contracts despite their public opposition to their use. Interestingly, rarely if ever does a Republican (or Democrat) officially say they support the use of no-bid contracts. However, as discussed in the overview, the continued use of no-bid contracts suggests an implicit acceptance that circumstances do exist in which no-bid contracts are appropriate.

Finally, Republicans have a demonstrated willingness to attack Democrats for their use of no-bid contracts. This, as well as the Democrats' records of attacking Republicans on the same issue, shows that no-bid contracts are as much a political issue as an economic one. From an economic standpoint Republicans bemoan the lack of accountability and efficiency implicit in the awarding of no-bid contracts for government work while still using them in specific instances. However, the negative optics and political attacks surrounding the issue likely drive the continued public opposition to no-bid contracts for both major political parties.

It is also important to note that no-bid contracts are also a prominent issue in state and local politics. In general, the Republican (and Democratic) opposition to no-bid contracts seen at the federal level is also present at the state and local levels. At the local level, for example, the legacy of the progressive response to political machines in major cities, who were notorious for using no-bid contracts to award political supporters, continues to create a negative attitude toward the use of no-bid contracting in government.

Democrats on No-Bid Contracts

The Democratic Party is traditionally more skeptical than Republicans of the wisdom of contracting out core government functions to the public and nonprofit sectors. In the area of public education, for example, opposition to privatization policies such as school vouchers is the Democratic Party norm. However, Democrats' skepticism does not translate into complete opposition to the use of contracting in government. In fact, the Democratic Clinton-Gore administration actually embraced the application of market principals to government contracting. Core to the theoretical effectiveness of these principals is the competition created by bidding out government contracts. As such, it is not surprising than Democrats today are in general critical of no-bid contracts.

The official 2012 Democratic Party platform, *Moving America Forward*, includes no mention of no-bid contracts. It only includes broad statements relating to the need to ensure government is accountable to American citizens and free of corruption. However, in 2008, then presidential candidate Barack Obama explicitly stated in his *Plan for America* that he would "ensure that federal contracts over $25,000 are competitively bid" (Obama 2008, 3). That statement suggests a position that no-bid contracts for larger projects are problematic.

A closer look at more recent statements by Obama shed light into exactly why his party tends to believe that no-bid contracts for sizable federal projects are undesirable. In a 2009 unveiling of measures to reduce the use of no-bid contracts in the federal government, President Barack Obama stated that no-bid contracts are "plagued by massive cost overruns, outright fraud, and the absence of oversight and accountability." He added, "There is a fundamental public trust that we must uphold. The American people's money must be spent to advance their priorities, not to line the pockets of contractors or to maintain projects that don't work" (Feller 2009). Embedded in Obama's statements is an articulation of several Democratic positions on no-bid contracts.

First, is the position that no-bid contracts are fiscally irresponsible and linked to decreased government performance. Interestingly, this position is consistent with that of prominent Republicans, and suggests a continuing Democratic commitment to the ideas of reinventing government articulated in the 1993 Gore Report. These ideas include the use of competitive bidding as a means to reduce the size and cost of government, while in turn increasing performance via the use of market incentives. President Obama's articulated rationale for opposing no-bid contracts suggests the benefits of a reinventing government approach are lost when contracts are not put out for competitive bids.

Second, President Obama argues that no-bid contracts introduce the possibility of fraud into government spending. Simply, directing a large amount of federal spending to a private organization without a competitive bidding process subverts the goals of accountability and transparency, both of which were included in the official 2012 Democratic platform. Lastly, President Obama's statements suggest a belief that no-bid contracts subvert the public interest by benefiting a select few at the expense of the broader public good. This position is consistent with a larger Democratic belief that too much power in American society is concentrated in the hands of a small percentage of privileged Americans.

Of course, President Obama is just one Democratic voice on the issues of no-bid contracting. Former Secretary of State and 2016 presidential hopeful Hillary Clinton articulates positions that are consistent with President Obama, and the broader Democratic platform. In 2007, Clinton told a television audience, "I'm in favor of, especially after Bush and Cheney and Rove, to clean up what they're leaving behind—to end the no-bid contracts, the revolving door in government. I think it's absolutely essential that, you know, we get rid of all of the contracting out of government jobs" (Breach of Contract 2015). Clinton's statements reflect her party's general hostility to the GOP's ongoing efforts to privatize government functions and services.

Broadly speaking, the positions articulated by Barack Obama and Hillary Clinton demonstrate opposition to the awarding of no-bid contracts. The expressed rationales include the perceived abuse of federal contracting policy in the George W. Bush administration, the lack of accountability and transparency inherent in no-bid contracting, and a general belief that no-bid contracts reduce government performance by leading to cost overruns and an absence of market-incentives.

Despite the statements of Democratic leaders, however, the *Washington Post* reported that the use of no-bid contracting actually increased during Barack Obama's first term in the White House (Ivory 2013). In addition, the Obama administration received pushback for its lack of competitive bidding in the awarding of an emergency contract to address functionality issues with the *HealthCare. Gov* federal health exchange. The inconsistency between the official Democratic positions and actions on no-bid contracting reflect the reality that both parties make extensive use of no-bid contracting at the federal level of government.

In general, Democrats say that they oppose the awarding of no-bid contracts in government. However, in the day-to-day business of running government Democratic leaders still use no-bid contracts in several areas. For example, in matters of national security no-bid contracts are still used for expenses above $25,000. In emergency situations where timeliness is essential, like the changes following the troubled rollout of *HealthCare.Gov*, a no-bid contract was used. Finally, the large web of existing longstanding relationships between government agencies and contractors ensures the continued use of no-bid contracting by Democratic politicians despite party leaders' official aversion to their use.

Michael R. Ford

Further Reading

Democratic National Committee. 2012. "Moving America Forward: 2012 Democratic Platform." Accessed May 11, 2015. https://www.democrats.org/party-platform.

Editorial Board. 2007. "Blackwater's Rich Contracts." *New York Times,* October 3. Accessed June 15, 2015. http://www.nytimes.com/2007/10/03/opinion/03wed2.html?_r=0.

Feller, Ben. 2009. "Obama: Federal Contracts Need Overhaul after No-Bid Bush Era." *Associated Press,* April 4. Accessed June 15, 2015. http://www.huffingtonpost.com/2009/03/04/obama-federal-contracts-n_n_171811.html.

Ivory, Danielle. 2013. "No-bid U.S. Government Contracts Jump 9 Percent, Despite Push for Competition." *Washington Post,* March 17. Accessed April 21, 2016. https://www.washingtonpost.com/business/economy/no-bid-us-government-contracts-jump-9-percent-despite-push-for-competition/2013/03/17/9f6708fc-8da0-11e2-b63f-f53fb9f2fcb4_story.html.

"Obama's Plan for America." 2008. *Obama for America.* Accessed August 1, 2015. http://www.moveleft.org/subprime/ObamaPolicy_Fiscal.pdf.

Osborne, David, and Ted Gaebler. 1993. *Reinventing Government: How the Entrepreneurial Spirit Is Transforming the Public Sector.* New York: Plume.

Reagan, Ronald. 1981. *Executive Order 12329: President's Task Force on Private Sector Initia-tives*. Accessed August 1, 2015. http://www.presidency.ucsb.edu/ws/?pid=44377.

Republican National Committee. 2015. "Breach of Contract." Accessed August 3, 2015. https://www.gop.com/breach-of-contract/.

Republican National Committee. 2012. "We Believe in America: 2012 Republican Plat-form." Accessed May 11, 2015. https://cdn.gop.com/docs/2012GOPPlatform.pdf.

Republican National Committee. 2011. "No-Bid Failure." Accessed August 1, 2015. https://gop.com/no-bid-failure/.

Savas, E. S. 2000. *Privatization and Public Private Partnerships*. New York: Chatham House Publishers.

Pensions

At a Glance

While Democrats and Republicans tend to agree that pensions are beneficial and necessary, they disagree on how pensions should be funded and managed. Republicans often argue that responsibility for providing for one's retirement should allow for personal choice and flexibility. They tend to believe that this can best be done through privatizing pensions, especially public pensions, including Social Security (covered in a separate chapter). Republicans have encouraged the growth of defined contribution plans over traditional defined benefit models.

Democrats tend to believe that providing for one's retirement should be a shared commitment between an individual and his or her employer and the government. Retirement security is seen as being best realized with a mix of private and public pensions, including defined benefit pension plans.

Many Democrats . . .

- Believe that too much retirement risk has been moved to individuals
- Say that the move to defined contribution pensions threatens nest eggs due to the vagaries of the market
- Assert that movement away from defined benefit plans endangers retirement security for retirees

Many Republicans . . .

- Think that defined benefit pensions do not provide enough flexibility and portability to individuals
- Contend that current underfunding of pension funds would best be handled by moving toward defined contribution pension plans
- Say privatized pensions would benefit from exposure to the markets

---

Overview

By the end of 2014, according to the Towers Watson professional services firm, pensions in the United States alone amounted to $22 trillion (2015). Primarily, pensions are designed to offer financial resources to persons after they retire. Pensions are offered for employees at both private and public entities. Contributions to pensions may be made solely or by a combination of employers, employees, and the government. The two predominant types of pensions are the defined benefit plan and the defined contribution plan. The defined benefit plan is the more traditional model where a person receives guaranteed benefits based on a formula that takes into account years of service, age, and salary. Defined contribution plans, such as a 401(k), do not guarantee a certain level of benefit, but are based on contributions by the employee, his/her employer (traditionally), and the rate of return on investments in the pension fund minus administrative and management fees. Defined contribution plan funds can be invested in a variety of investments, such as stocks, government bonds, and so on.

Government pensions, as a component of social insurance, were first offered in Germany under Chancellor Otto von Bismarck in the late 19th century (Marmor, Mashaw, and Pakutka 2014). Private sector pensions in the United States began in the late 19th century in the transportation industry, primarily railroad firms, due to the dangerous working conditions faced by some workers and the capacity for rich railroad companies to provide such benefits. Expansion was aided by a change to the tax code in 1921 "that encouraged the substitution of pensions for cash compensation. Employers could deduct contributions to pension funds before taxes. The federal government would not levy taxes on pension fund investment gains. Only at the time of disbursement would payouts be taxable" (Mundel and Sundén 2004, 181). Organized labor began to develop pension plans as well, and by the late 1920s about two in five union members were acquiring retirement and/or disability benefits of one sort of another. Another major milestone in providing for the financial security of elderly Americans was the passage of Social Security Act. This landmark program, one of Democratic President Franklin D. Roosevelt's signature achievements, was signed into law in 1935.

Private sector pensions expanded after World War II. Since wartime wages were constrained by legal limitations, fringe benefits, including pensions, were more easily offered. They were further encouraged by the ability of companies to deduct pension contributions from their tax liability. After the war, "labor's drive for pension benefits was aided when the Supreme Court confirmed the National Labor Relations Board's 1948 ruling that employers had a legal obligation to negotiate the terms of pension plans. The United Steelworkers of America and the United Automobile Workers then launched successful drives for pension benefits, and other unions soon followed" (Mundel and Sundén 2004, 6).

By the start of the 1960s, many American workers were successfully experiencing the three-legged stool retirement model with the expansion of Social Security, a personal savings rate of approximately 10 percent (Federal Reserve Bank of

St. Louis 2015), and approximately 40 percent of American workers (union and non-union combined) had gained access to employment-based pensions. However, this period was also problematic because some pension programs were shoddily constructed or easily compromised. In fact, more than 1,800 pension plans failed between 1959 and 1963 (Marmor, Mashaw, and Pakutka 2014, 181).

Eventually Congress responded to these problems by passing the Employee Retirement Income Security Act (ERISA) in 1974. The ERISA provided favorable tax treatment for pensions while also requiring five-year vesting periods and broader worker participation. It also established the Pension Benefit Guaranty Corporation (PBGC), an independent agency within the U.S. government that guaranteed employee pensions up to $45,000 a year from a fund paid with premiums from private pension plans. However, a moral hazard took effect, so if there were a contentious contract issue, a corporation or union could offer more generous pension benefits in exchange for holding the line on short-term costs like higher wages. If the corporation or union were unable or unwilling to make the needed pension contributions, then the government covers the shortfall. PBGC paid out unfunded pension obligations of Bethlehem Steel, Delphi, Delta, Kaiser Aluminum, and Northwest Airlines (Marmor, Mashaw, and Pakutka 2014). In all, it has assumed pension obligations for over 1.5 million retirees from 4,700 failed plans. At the end of 2014, PBGC insured the benefits of 41 million workers and retirees in nearly 24,000 defined benefit pension plans. It also faces a shortfall of $61 billion dollars and has a 50 percent chance of becoming insolvent by 2022 according to some estimates (Marmor, Mashaw, and Pakutka 2014).

Another important piece of pension legislation was the Retirement Equity Act of 1984. That legislation, strongly supported by both Republicans and Democrats, and signed into law by President Ronald Reagan, amended ERISA to address significant concerns that working women were not receiving their fair share of benefits from private pension plans. The Retirement Equity Act of 1984 "prevented plans from penalizing parents who took time off to raise families, it allowed pension plans to make court-ordered payments to former spouses and it mandated spousal consent for workers to waive survivor benefits. In short, it began to recognize the working patterns of women . . . and provided greater retirement protection for women throughout the country" (Borzi 2013).

Underfunding issues are not limited to private pensions. According to the California Policy Center, "the total state and local government pensions in the United States at the end of 2013 had an estimated $3.6 trillion in assets. They were 74% funded, with liabilities totaling an estimated $4.86 trillion, and an unfunded liability of $1.26 trillion" (Ring 2014).

The biggest change in pensions in the last 35 years has been the growth of defined-contribution plans, namely the 401(k). The 401(k) was created during the Revenue Act of 1978. It allows employees to invest pretax income into a retirement saving account. The employer can also contribute funds to the account. The employee's account can utilize a variety of investment options, although these options may be limited by the employer in terms of their contributions. The 401(k) funds may be transferred tax-free when an employee moves to another job as long as it has a similar plan.

The transition of pensions from defined benefit models to defined contribution models has been rather extensive. According to the Center for Retirement Research at Boston College, of workers with pension plans, the number of those with only defined contribution plans decreased from 62 percent in 1983 to 17 percent in 2013, while those with only defined contribution plans jumped from 12 percent to 71 percent. The number of those with both types of plans decreased by half from 26 percent to 13 percent (2014). Changes to pension types is not restricted to private pensions, as a growing number of governments have moved from defined benefit pensions to defined contribution pensions (covered in greater detail below) (Snell 2013).

Democrats on Pensions

Democrats tend to oppose the increasing privatization of pensions. This point of view is summarized by a March 2015 report by the National Institute on Retirement Security. It notes that the shifting by greater numbers of private sector employers from defined benefit to defined contribution pension plans means that "the risk and much of the funding burden falls on individual employees, who tend to have difficulty contributing enough on their own, who typically lack investment expertise, and who may have difficulty figuring out how to spend down their nest egg in retirement." The Institute also notes that the "catastrophic financial crisis of 2008 exposed the vulnerability of the new [defined contribution]-centered retirement system. Americans saw the value of their hard-earned nest eggs plummet when the financial market crashed and destroyed trillions of dollars of household wealth" (Rhee and Boivie 2015, 2).

Democrats Renew Their Support for Workplace Pension Plans

The 2008 Democratic Party Platform provides the party's rationale for increased reliance on workplace pension plans:

> We will make it a priority to secure for hardworking families the part of the American Dream that includes a secure and healthy retirement. Individuals, employers, and government must all play a role. We will adopt measures to preserve and protect existing public and private pension plans. In the 21st Century, Americans also need better ways to save for retirement. We will automatically enroll every worker in a workplace pension plan that can be carried from job to job and we will match savings for working families who need the help. We will make sure that CEOs can't dump workers' pensions with one hand while they line their own pockets with the other.

The personal saving rate is at its lowest since the Great Depression. Currently, 75 million working Americans—roughly half the workforce—lack employer-based retirement plans. That's why we will create automatic workplace pensions. People can add to their pension, or can opt out at any time; the savings account will be easily transferred between jobs; and people can control it themselves if they become self-employed. We will ensure savings incentives are fair to all workers by matching half of the initial $1000 of savings for families that need help; and employers will have an easy opportunity to match employee savings. We believe this program will increase the saving participation rate for low- and middle-income workers from its current 15 percent to 80 percent. We support good pensions, and will adopt measures to preserve and protect existing public and private pension plans. We will require that employees who have company pensions receive annual disclosures about their pension fund's investments. This will put a secure retirement within reach for millions of working families.

Source

Democratic National Committee. 2008. Democratic Party Platform 2008. August 25. Accessed May 31, 2015. http://www.presidency.ucsb.edu/ws/index.php?pid=78283

For decades, Democratic Party platforms have stressed the importance of pensions as part of retirement. The 2012 party platform made specific reference to a right for every American to have a "secure, healthy and dignified retirement" and stated that:

We will block Republican efforts to subject Americans' guaranteed retirement income to the whims of the stock market through privatization . . . President Obama will also make it easier for Americans to save on their own for retirement and prepare for unforeseen expenses by participating in retirement accounts at work.

This stance was consistent with earlier Democratic proclamations. For example, the party's 2008 platform focused on protecting and preserving existing public and private pensions and creating automatic workplace pensions for the half of the workplace that currently lacks employer-based retirement plans. Similarly, the term "retirement security" was specifically mentioned in the 2004 platform:

We must protect the retirement security of America's workers and their families. Workers should never lose all their savings because their employer locked those savings into the company's own stock. We will bar that practice. We need to require honest information and full disclosure, and protect older workers from unfair treatment when their benefits are converted to cash balance plans. At the same time, we will strengthen and promote both defined-contribution and defined-benefit pension plans, and increase the portability of retirement savings and help all families save. (Democratic National Committee 2004)

As far back as the 1940 platform, the Democratic message has been consistent:

The Democratic Party, which established social security for the nation, is dedicated to its extension. We pledge to make the Social Security Act increasingly effective, by covering millions of persons not now protected under its terms; . . . by progressively extending and increasing the benefits of the old-age and survivors insurance system, including protection of the permanently disabled; and by the early realization of a minimum pension for all who have reached the age of retirement and are not gainfully employed. (Democratic National Committee 1940)

Republicans on Pensions

The current Republican position emphasizes moving away from traditional pensions, especially defined benefit plans, and stresses financial independence for employees with flexible and portable pension options. It can also be seen in recent efforts to partially privatize Social Security.

A number of states moved to adapt or remove defined benefit pension plans for state employees. Since the Great Recession, Republican governors have implemented mandatory hybrid pension plans in Georgia (2008), Utah (2011), Virginia (2012), and Tennessee (2013); a cash balance plan in Louisiana (2012) and Kansas (2013); and a mandatory defined contribution plan in Oklahoma (2014). Only three Democratic governors changed their state's defined benefit pensions—in Kentucky, Michigan, and Rhode Island (Bradford 2014; Kilroy 2014).

President George W. Bush, working with Republican majorities in both houses of Congress, signed the Pension Protection Act of 2006. According to the *Washington Post*, the law requires companies to fully fund defined-benefit plans over seven years, closes loopholes that allowed companies to underfund their pension plans, requires higher premiums to PBFC from companies underfunding their pension contributions, made higher contribution limits, and allows companies to automatically enroll workers in defined-contribution plans (Baker 2006).

The *Wall Street Journal* Welcomes the "End of the Defined-Benefit Pension Era"

Before final passage of the Pension Protection Act of 2006, the pro-business editors of the *Wall Street Journal* issued an editorial extolling the legislation's capacity to end the defined benefit pension:

> Most private companies long ago moved to defined-contribution plans—401(k)s, SEP IRAs and the like—as a supplement to, or replacement for, a pension system in which workers were guaranteed a company-paid retirement income for the rest of their lives. The current bill is an attempt to speed this new era of individual responsibility along, as well as clean up the deficit that Congress has made "guaranteeing" private pensions.

Source
Wall Street Journal. 2006. "The Pension Era, R.I.P." *Wall Street Journal*, August 4, A16.

The current Republican position has been consistently expressed in the party's platforms as Republican Party has grown more conservative since Reagan's election in 1980. The 2012 platform stated that "The situation of public pension systems demands immediate remedial action. The irresponsible promises of politicians at every level of government have come back to haunt today's taxpayers with enormous unfunded pension liabilities. Many cities face bankruptcy because of excessive outlays for early retirement, extravagant health plans, and overly generous pension benefits. We salute the Republican Governors and state legislators who have, in the face of abuse and threats of violence, reformed their state pension systems for the benefit of both taxpayers and retirees alike" (Republican National Committee 2012, 23).

The 2008 platform is particularly noteworthy because it contains specific mention of the party preference for defined contribution programs: "We will insist that the budget reasonably plan for the long-term costs of pension and health care programs and urge the conversion of such programs to defined contribution programs. . . . All workers should have portability in their pension plans and their health insurance, giving them greater job mobility, financial independence, and security" (Republican National Committee 2008).

Chad Kahl

Further Reading

Baker, Peter. 2006. "Bush Signs Sweeping Revision of Pension Law; Employers Forced to Bolster Traditional Retirement Plans." *Washington Post,* August 18, D1.

Borzi, Phyllis. 2013. "The Retirement Equity Act and Beyond," *U.S. Department of Labor: Promoting & Protecting Opportunity*, September 3. Accessed May 31, 2015. http://blog .dol.gov/2013/09/03/the-retirement-equity-act-and-beyond/.

Bradford, Hazel. 2014. "Pace of Pension Reform Ebbs after 49 States Change Laws: Post-Recession Focus Shifts to Making DC Plans Mandatory." *Pensions & Investments*, April 14. Accessed May 31, 2015. http://www.pionline.com/article/20140414/PRINT /304149975/pace-of-pension-reform-ebbs-after-49-states-change-laws.

Center for Retirement Research at Boston College. 2014. "Frequently Requested Data: Workers with Pension Coverage by Type of Plan, 1983, 1992, 2001, and 2013." September. Accessed May 31. http://crr.bc.edu/wp-content/uploads/1012/01/figure-15.pdf.

Democratic National Committee. 2004. "Strong at Home, Respected in the World: 2004 Democratic Platform." Accessed April 21, 2016. http://www.presidency.ucsb.edu/ws /?pid=29613.

Democratic National Committee. 1940. Democratic Platform of 1940. Accessed April 21, 2016. http://www.presidency.ucsb.edu/ws/?pid=29597.

Federal Reserve Bank of St. Louis. 2015. "Personal Saving Rate." Accessed May 31. https:// research.stlouisfed.org/fred2/series/PSAVERT.

Global Pension Assets Study 2015. 2015. New York: Towers Watson.

Hacker, Jacob S. 2002. *The Divided Welfare State: The Battle over Public and Private Social Benefits in the United States*. New York: Cambridge University Press.

Internal Revenue Service. 2015. "Definitions." Accessed May 31. http://www.irs.gov /Retirement-Plans/Plan-Participant,-Employee/Definitions.

Kilroy, Meaghan. 2014. "Oklahoma Law Creates Defined Contribution Plan for some New Public Employees." *Business Insurance*, June 2. Accessed May 31, 2015. http://www.businessinsurance.com/article/20140602/NEWS03/140609988.

Marmor, Theodore R., Jerry L. Mashaw, and John Pakutka. 2014. *Social Insurance: America's Neglected Heritage and Contested Future*. Public Affairs and Policy Administration Series. Thousand Oaks, CA: CQ Press/Sage.

Munnell, Alicia H., and Annika Sundén. 2004. *Coming Up Short: The Challenge of 401(k) Plans*. Washington, DC: Brookings Institution Press.

Pension Benefit Guaranty Corporation: Annual Report: Fiscal Year 2014. 2014. Washington, D.C.

Republican National Committee. 2012. "We Believe in America: 2012 Republican Platform." Accessed April 21, 2016. https://cdn.gop.com/docs/2012GOPPlatform.pdf.

Republican National Committee. 2008. Republican Platform of 2008. Accessed April 21, 2016. http://www.presidency.ucsb.edu/ws/?pid=78545.

Rhee, Nari, and Ilana Boivie. 2015. *The Continuing Retirement Savings Crisis*. Washington, DC: National Institute on Retirement Security.

Ring, Ed. 2014. "Estimating America's Total Unfunded State and Local Government Pension Liability." Accessed May 31, 2015. http://californiapolicycenter.org/estimating-americas-total-unfunded-state-and-local-government-pension-liability/.

Snell, Ron. 2013. "Pensions and Retirement Plan Enactments in 2012: State Legislatures." National Conference of State Legislatures, updated April. Accessed May 31, 2015. http://www.ncsl.org/research/fiscal-policy/2012-enacted-state-pension-legislation.aspx.

Woolley, John, and Gerhard Peters. 2015. "Political Platforms of Parties Receiving Electoral Votes: 1840–2012." *The American Presidency Project*. Accessed May 30. http://www.presidency.ucsb.edu/platforms.php.

Progressivity of Taxation

At a Glance

Broadly speaking, Democrats favor a more progressive tax structure than Republicans. Under progressive taxation, households with higher incomes pay higher tax rates. The income tax in the United States has been progressive for decades, but the degree has varied considerably.

For the year 2014, the highest income tax rate was 39.6 percent for married households with an income over $457,601. Under the Obama administration, the "Bush tax cut" for Americans in the highest tax bracket—a reference to temporary changes in the tax code introduced during the George W. Bush administration and congressional Republicans that significantly reduced taxes for the wealthiest Americans—was allowed to expire. The Obama administration asserted that those tax rates needed to return to their pre-Bush levels in order to reduce the deficit and help pay for necessary government services. Many Republicans, however, favor returning the top rate to the Bush-era 35 percent—or lowering it even further. The rationale for the Republican position is that lower tax rates improve economic incentives and keep income in the hands of citizens who make better spending choices than the government. Democrats counter that slashing taxes of the wealthy so dramatically would explode the deficit and force draconian cuts to social programs for poor and working-class Americans.

Many Republicans . . .

- Contend that high marginal rate tax bracket reduces worker incentives to raise their incomes, making them less productive
- Believe that high tax rates cause some to leave the workforce
- Assert that lower tax rates make business ownership more profitable and increase the ability of firms to start and expand
- Say that lower tax rates foster innovation, employment and economic growth
- Feel that high tax rates stifle savings, reducing access to commercial and home loans
- Believe that a less progressive system would allow for the development of a simpler tax code

Many Democrats . . .

- Describe progressive taxation as a fair and economically sensible approach to raising revenue for essential government services
- Believe that taxing high income households at higher rates is an equitable method for dealing with the federal debt
- Assert that progressive systems of taxation reduce economic inequality
- Dismiss the effect of higher tax rates on the work incentives of high-income households as small
- Say that the benefit of government services to low and middle income households such as Medicare and Medicaid outweighs the cost of the higher taxes for wealthier households
- Feel that eliminating loopholes that disproportionately benefit the wealthy make the tax code more transparent and equitable

---

Overview

The tax on wage income is a primary determinant of the progressivity of taxes, though the capital gains, payroll, and inheritance taxes are also important. Tax credits, loopholes, and deductions play a significant role. A tax credit is a direct reduction in the bill for certain taxpayers. For example, the Earned Income Tax Credit reduces taxes for workers with incomes below a certain level. A deduction allows for a reduction in the taxable amount of income. There are numerous deductions including the standard deduction for all filers and the mortgage interest deduction, which allow taxpayers to reduce the income they pay taxes on by the amount of mortgage interest they have paid over the year. "Loophole" is a broad term applied to many methods for avoiding taxes, often referring to accounting techniques designed to gain deductions and credits.

The present discussion almost always refers to marginal tax rates, the rate paid on the last dollar received, as opposed to an average tax rate, which is simply the fraction of the tax paid of the quantity received by the taxpayer. Alternatively, the marginal rate is the same as the average rate if there are no deductions or credits. Hence, if there are deductions and credits, the marginal rate is higher than the average rate, though raising the marginal rate would raise the average rate as well. Marginal rates are more important when discussing the change in economic incentives of a tax, while average rates are more relevant for welfare and equity considerations.

The top income tax rate has varied a great deal over U.S. history. The first peacetime income tax legislation was passed in 1894, but only when the 16th amendment to the Constitution was ratified in 1913, did the federal government have the necessary legal authority to impose a permanent income tax. When it was instituted, the highest (marginal) tax rate was less than 10 percent, but for 20 years following World War II, it was over 90 percent. Both Kennedy and Reagan instituted large cuts in the top rate at the beginning of their presidencies (IRS 2015).

Recently, the top rate reverted to 39.5 percent from 35 percent when the Bush tax cuts expired (Tax Foundation 2015c).

For 2015, there are seven income tax brackets for the U.S. The tax rate for a given bracket applies only to the income above the threshold. For example, married households pay 10 percent on taxable income (after deductions) up to $18,450 and 15 percent on taxable income up to $74,900. A household with taxable income of $20,000 would pay $1845 (10 percent of $18,450) plus $232.50 (15 percent of $1550). The other tax rates for married households are 25 percent for taxable income up to $151,200; 28 percent for taxable income up to $230,450; 33 percent for taxable income up to $411,550; 35 percent for taxable income up to $464,850, and 39.6 percent past this threshold (Tax Foundation 2015b).

Worldwide, there is a great deal of variation in income tax rates. Among developed countries, the U.S. has relatively low tax rates and a low degree of progressivity. Among, the G8 countries (excluding Russia), Japan has the highest top rate of 45 percent (Ministry of Finance of Japan 2013), and only Canada has a lower rate at 29 percent compared to 39.5 percent (Canada Revenue Agency 2015), the top income tax rate in the U.S. Even in this case, if provincial taxes for Canada and state taxes for the U.S. are taken into account, many Canadians pay a higher income tax rate than most Americans.

The capital gains tax is paid according to the change in the value of a household's assets such as stocks and bonds. Typically, wealthy citizens make a higher percentage of their income from returns on assets, so a higher capital gains tax increases the progressivity of the tax code. When the capital gains tax was instituted along with the income tax in 1913, both were taxed at the same rate (Tax Policy Center 2015b). However, the tax rate on capital gains has typically been less than the income tax rate for comparable income brackets (Feldstein 2009). Currently, the tax rate on short-term capital gains, where the asset is held less than one year, is the same as the income tax rate, but the top rate on long-term capital gains is 20 percent, lower than the top income tax rate of 39.5 percent.

Payroll taxes as implemented in the U.S. tend to reduce progressivity. Payroll taxes are paid by employers based on the incomes of workers. The most prominent of such taxes are the Social Security, Medicare, and Unemployment Insurance taxes, which are paid by workers with incomes under a cap of $106,000. While the cap is justified by the fact that workers under the cap are much more likely to use the benefits of these programs, payroll taxes are regressive (as opposed to progressive) since higher income workers do not pay them (Tax Policy Center 2015c).

Consumption taxes, such as a tax on the sale of goods and services, affect the progressivity of the tax code but are not currently levied at the federal level. Some state and local governments do have sales taxes. Since wealthy citizens save a greater fraction of their income and, hence, consume a smaller fraction, consumption taxes are inherently regressive. Though Herman Cain proposed a federal sales tax as a presidential candidate in 2007, there is little support for such a proposal at this time (Tripp and Saulny 2011).

There are significant differences among state income and consumption taxes that affect the progressivity of the code. Seven states have no income tax, but some state level income taxes are significant, the highest being California, whose rate is over 12 percent. The differences between states largely follow party lines. For example, six of the seven states with no income tax—Alaska, Florida, Nevada, South Dakota, Texas, and Wyoming—have Republican governors (Tax Foundation 2015a). An example of the range of tax policies across the states is the comparison of Washington and Oregon. Oregon has no general sales tax but a relatively high income tax of 9.9 percent, while Washington has no income tax but general sales tax of 6.5 percent, close to the highest state sales tax of 7 percent found in several states. Residents on the border would seem to have incentive to work in Washington and shop in Oregon (Tax Foundation 2015a).

Imposition of an inheritance tax is inherently progressive, since wealthier households are more likely to receive bequests. Currently, the rate for the inheritance tax, sometimes referred to as the estate tax—or death tax, in the case of Republican critics—is 40 percent on bequest income over $5.43 million. Due to the high exemption and loopholes in the code, less than 0.2 percent of taxpayers pay this tax (Marr, DeBott, and Huang 2015). This percentage takes some care to interpret since receiving inheritance does not happen every year (for most people), but paying the tax is still a rare event.

Since the 1970s, the positions of the two major political parties in the U.S. have been quite stable. Republicans tend to favor policies to lower income tax and capital gains tax rates and eliminate the estate tax that decreases progressivity. Democrats tend to favor raising income tax rates on high income households and eliminating loopholes related to the tax on capital gains and the estate tax, all of which would increase the progressivity of the tax code.

Democrats on Progressivity of Taxation

In recent years, there have been a number of Democratic proposals that would increase the progressivity of the tax structure. In the past, Democratic congressional groups have proposed higher top marginal rates. For example, the "Budget of the Congressional Progressive Caucus" for 2012 proposed a number of higher tax brackets for workers with incomes over $1 million, the highest rate being 49 percent (U.S. House of Representatives 2015). More recently, Democrats have focused on tax credits and exemptions to aid the middle class. The top ranking Democrat on the House of Representatives Budget committee Chris Van Hollen (D-Maryland) recently described a proposal (Miller and Herfinski 2015) to give a $1,000 tax rebate to those with incomes under $100,000. Because higher income workers do not benefit, this credit would increase the progressivity of the tax structure.

President Obama's most recent tax reform proposals focus on closing loopholes and providing credits to middle class families. Under the proposed reforms, the so-called "trust fund loophole," which allows some families to reduce the amount

Progressives Tout the Capacity of Tax Policies to Reduce Inequality

The People's Budget is a statement of priorities of the Congressional Progressive Caucus representing a current liberal viewpoint. Its summary statement includes:

The People's Budget levels the playing field and creates economic opportunity by increasing the pay of middle- and low-income Americans. . . . The People's Budget closes tax loopholes that companies use to ship jobs overseas. It creates fair tax rates for millionaires and provides needed relief to low- and middle-income families. It invests in debt-free college, workforce training and small businesses within our communities, helping return our economy to full employment and giving a raise to Americans who need it most.

Source

Congressional Progressive Caucus. 2015. "The People's Budget: A Raise for America." Accessed May 26. http://cpc.grijalva.house.gov/the-peoples-budget-a-raise-for-america/.

---

of the inheritance tax paid, would be eliminated. Further, the tax on long-term capital gains would be raised from 20 percent to 28 percent.

The President's proposal also includes a number of tax credits. There is an additional $500 credit for households with two wage earners, and credits of up to $300 to compensate for child care costs. In addition, some programs for credits for education are to be consolidated leading to increased credits for some families.

In sum, these proposals would increase the progressivity of the tax structure. Most of the tax credits would lower taxes on the middle class, while the higher rates and the closing of loopholes affect capital gains, which raises the effective tax rates on wealthier households. "Middle class families today bear too much of the tax burden because of unfair loopholes that are only available to the wealthy and big corporations," said the Obama White House:

[The president's plan is] to simplify our complex tax code for individuals, make it fairer by eliminating some of the biggest loopholes, and use the savings to responsibly pay for the investments we need to help middle class families get ahead and grow the economy. . . . By ensuring those at the top pay their fair share in taxes, the President's plan responsibly pays for investments we need to help middle class families get ahead, like his recent proposal to make two years of community college free for every student willing to do the work. The savings will pay for additional reforms that will help the paychecks of middle-class and working families go further to cover the cost of child care, college, and a secure retirement. (The White House 2015)

Former first lady, senator, and secretary of state Hillary Clinton also has favored tax reforms that would increase the progressivity of the tax code. A quote from her book and speech *It Takes a Village* (Clinton 1996) demonstrates her stance: "Many of you are well enough off that the tax cuts may have helped you. We're saying that for America to get back on track, we're probably going to cut that short and not give it to you. We're going to take things away from you on behalf of the common good." At various times in her political career, Clinton has proposed expansion of a number of tax credits targeted at poor and working-class Americans, such as the Earned Income Tax Credit, and credits for education and health expenditures. Furthermore, she proposed to lower the exemption for the inheritance tax so it is levied on more households. The changes in the Earned Income Tax Credit and the inheritance tax in particular, would have the effect of increasing progressivity.

The recent work of academic economist Thomas Piketty summarized in his book, *Capital for the 21st Century*, has implications for the debate of progressive taxation. In an effort to mitigate the degree of inequality, he advocates a tax on the level of wealth, as opposed to changes in wealth represented by capital gains. Important Democratic lawmakers such as Senator Elizabeth Warren of Massachusetts have spoken approvingly of such proposed changes to America's tax code (Parramore 2014).

Republicans on Progressivity of Taxation

There are a wide range of Republican proposals for changing the income tax that would reduce the progressivity of the tax code, ranging from a re-introduction of the Bush tax cuts to a flat tax. In 2012, the Republican-controlled House of Representatives passed a bill lowering the top income tax rate to 35 percent, as under the Bush tax cuts, though the bill did not pass the Democrat-controlled Senate (Weisman 2012).

A more dramatic proposal favored by some Republicans is a flat tax, with a single income bracket. Flat tax proposals usually include a deduction much larger than the present $6,200 per person. The single rate would apply to incomes above the deduction. One of the most detailed proposals is an older one (1983) by Robert Hall and Alvin Rabushka. Under their plan all wage and business income would be taxed at a rate of 19 percent, but all savings and investments (business expenditures) would be deductible. Furthermore the standard deduction for all households would depend on the size of the household, but would be much higher than it is currently. Many families could deduct over half their income under the new standard deduction, which they refer to as the family allowance.

The flat tax proposals made by GOP politicians vary in the details, both in regards to the tax rate and the elimination of other taxes and credits. Texas governor and presidential candidate Rick Perry proposed a 20 percent flat tax in a plan that would also eliminate a number of tax credits such as the Earned Income Tax Credit (Tax Policy Center 2015a). Former Speaker of the House Newt

---

The GOP Position on "Redistributive" Tax Codes

The Republican National Committee describes its priorities on tax reform with the following statement:

> Taxes, by their very nature, reduce a citizen's freedom. Their proper role in a free society should be to fund services that are essential and authorized by the Constitution, such as national security, and the care of those who cannot care for themselves. We reject the use of taxation to redistribute income, fund unnecessary or ineffective programs, or foster the crony capitalism that corrupts both politicians and corporations. Our goal is a tax system that is simple, transparent, flatter, and fair. In contrast, the current IRS code is like a patchwork quilt, stitched together over time from mismatched pieces, and is beyond the comprehension of the average citizen. A reformed code should promote simplicity and coherence, savings and innovation, increase American competitiveness, and recognize the burdens on families with children.

Source

Republican National Committee. 2015. "Restoring the American Dream: Economy and Jobs." *GOP.com*. Accessed May 27. https://gop.com/platform/restoring-the-american-dream/.

Gingrich proposed a 15 percent flat tax plan that would also eliminate some deductions.

In 2012 and 2014, House Republicans led by Paul Ryan introduced a plan with two tax brackets, as opposed to one under the flat tax and seven brackets under the present income tax code. The rates for the two brackets would be 10 percent and 25 percent, with the latter applying to corporate profits as well (Ryan 2015). Under the proposal, the alternative minimum tax, which intended to mitigate abuse of loopholes, would be eliminated as well. Both the flat tax and two rate systems would simplify the tax code, lower progressivity, and generate less government revenue.

Marco Rubio, senator from Florida and 2016 Republican candidate for President, has also proposed a two-bracket income tax system. The two rates are 15 percent for single filers making less than $75,000 or married couples making less than $150,000. Above these thresholds, the proposed income tax rate is 35 percent, the same as the current top rate and much higher than the specific proposals from other Republican candidates (Lee and Rubio 2015). Rubio's description of his proposal has some echoes of the flat tax arguments of Hall and Rabushka:

> Our reforms would help spur growth where today's tax code obstructs it. On the business side, we would cut the current 35 percent corporate tax rate to make it competitive in the global economy. The exact rate will be determined as we continue to shape the legislation, but it must be low enough to end the problem of corporate inversions and the loss of American jobs to other nations. We will also allow companies large and small to deduct their expenses and capital investments while integrating all forms of business taxation into a consolidated, single-layer tax. (Lee and Rubio 2014)

Another Republican presidential candidate for 2016, Senator Rand Paul of Kentucky, has proposed a number of tax code overhauls, most notably a flat tax scheme. He has not committed to a particular flat rate, though some in his campaign have suggested it would not be above 17 percent (Nitti 2015). As part of his plan, the inheritance tax, the alternative minimum tax, and the capital gains tax on households would all be eliminated. Business profits would be subject to the flat tax rate.

Similarly, another Republican presidential candidate, Ted Cruz from Texas, is in favor of a flat tax, lowering corporate rates, and elimination of the estate tax. "When it comes to jobs and growth and opportunity, the two most effective levers that the federal government has to facilitate small businesses creating new jobs, are tax reform and regulatory reform. I am campaigning on a flat tax that would allow every American to fill out his or her taxes on a post card that will allow us to abolish the IRS" (Drucker 2015).

George Waters

Further Reading

Canada Revenue Agency. 2015. "Canadian income tax rates for Individuals—current and previous years." Accessed May 16. http://www.cra-arc.gc.ca/tx/ndvdls/fq/txrts-eng.html.

Clinton, Hillary Rodham. 1996. *It Takes a Village*. Democratic National Committee Address, August 27. Accessed November 5, 2015. http://www.ontheissues.org/2016/Hillary _Clinton_Families_+_Children.htm#It_Takes_a_Village.

CNN Election Center. 2008. The CNN Democratic Presidential Debate in Texas—transcript, February 21. Accessed May 26, 2015. http://www.cnn.com/2008/POLITICS/02/21 /debate.transcript/.

Davis, Julie Hirschfield. 2015. "Obama Will Seek to Raise Taxes on Wealthy to Finance Cuts for Middle Class." *New York Times*, January 12. Accessed May 26, 2015. http:// www.nytimes.com/2015/01/18/us/president-obama-will-seek-to-reduce-taxes-for -middle-class.html?_r=0.

Drucker, David. 2015. "Ted Cruz Gets Specific on Abolishing the IRS." *Washington Examiner,* April 27. Accessed May 26, 2015. http://www.washingtonexaminer.com/ted-cruz -gets-specific-on-abolishing-the irs/article/2563631.

Feldstein, Martin. 2009. *The Effects of Taxation on Capital Accumulation*. Chicago: University of Chicago Press.

Gabriel, Trip, and Susan Saulny. 2011. "With Just Three Nines, Cain Refigured Math for Taxes." *New York Times*, October 12. Accessed May 26, 2015. http://www.nytimes.com /2011/10/13/us/politics/herman-cains-tax-plan-changes-gop-primary-math.html.

Hall, Robert, and Alvin Rabushka. 1983. *Low Tax, Flat Tax, Simple Tax*. New York: McGraw-Hill.

Internal Revenue Service. 2015. "A Brief History of the IRS." Accessed May 26. http://www .irs.gov/uac/Brief-History-of-IRS.

Lee, Mike, and Marco Rubio. 2014. "A Pro-Family, Pro-Growth Tax Reform." *Wall Street Journal*, September 22. Accessed May 26, 2015. http://www.wsj.com/articles/mike -lee-and-marco-rubio-a-pro-family-pro-growth-tax-reform-1411426189.

Lee, Mike, and Marco Rubio. 2015. "Economic Growth and Family Fairness Tax Plan." Accessed May 26, 2015. http://www.rubio.senate.gov/public/index.cfm/files/serve/?File_id=2d839ff1-f995-427a-86e9-267365609942.

Marr, Chuck, Brandon DeBot, and Chye-Ching Huang. 2015. "Eliminating the Estate Tax on Inherited Wealth Would Increase Deficits and Inequality." The Center for Budget and Policy Priorities. January 12. Accessed May 27, 2015, http://www.cbpp.org/research/federal-tax/eliminating-estate-tax-on-inherited-wealth-would-increase-deficits-and.

Miller, S. A., and David Herfinski. 2015. "Dems double down on liberal populism, push bolder wealth redistribution." *Washington Times*, January 12. Accessed May 27, 2015. http://www.washingtontimes.com/news/2015/jan/12/chris-van-hollen-house-democrats-push-tax-increase/.

Ministry of Finance of Japan. 2013. *Current Status of the Tax System*, July. Accessed May 16, 2015. http://www.mof.go.jp/english/tax_policy/publication/tax005/E_1117.pdf.

Nitti, Tony. 2015. "Rand Paul Announces Presidential Bid, Favors Flat Tax." *Forbes*, April 7. Accessed May 27, 2015. http://www.forbes.com/sites/anthonynitti/2015/04/07/rand-paul-announces-presidential-bid-favors-flat-tax/.

Parramore, Lynne Stuart. 2014. "Thomas Piketty and Elizabeth Warren: Trickle down Economics Is Magical Thinking." *Salon.com*, June 5. Accessed May 26, 2015. http://www.salon.com/2014/06/05/thomas_piketty_and_elizabeth_warren_trickle_down_economics_are_magical_thinking_partner/.

Paul, Rand. 2015. "Expanding Economic Opportunity." Accessed May 15. http://www.paul.senate.gov/?p=issue&id=57.

Piketty, Thomas. 2014. *Capital for the 21st Century*. Cambridge, MA: Harvard University Press.

Republican National Committee. 2012. "We Believe in America: 2012 Republican Platform." Accessed May 15, 2015. https://cdn.gop.com/docs/2012GOPPlatform.pdf.

Ryan, Paul. 2015. "The Path to Prosperity: Fiscal Year 2013 Budget Resolution." House Budget Committee, Paul Ryan chairman. Accessed May 26. http://paulryan.house.gov/uploadedfiles/pathtoprosperity2013.pdf.

Tax Policy Center. 2015a. "Governor Perry's Tax Reform Plan." Accessed May 26. http://www.taxpolicycenter.org/taxtopics/Perry-plan.cfm.

Tax Policy Center. 2015b. "Historical Capital Gains and Taxes." Accessed May 25. http://www.taxpolicycenter.org/taxfacts/displayafact.cfm?Docid=161.

Tax Policy Center. 2015c. "Historical Social Security and FICA Tax Rates for a Family of Four." Accessed November 7, 2015. http://www.taxpolicycenter.org/taxfacts/displayafact.cfm?Docid=227&Topic2id=50.

Tax Foundation. 2015a. "State Personal Income Tax Rates and Brackets 2014 Update." Accessed November 7. http://taxfoundation.org/article/state-personal-income-tax-rates-and-brackets-2014-update.

Tax Foundation. 2015b. "Tax Foundation Fiscal Fact: 2015 Tax Brackets." Accessed May 16. http://taxfoundation.orgsites/taxfoundation.org/files/docs/TaxFoundation_FF440.pdf.

Tax Foundation. 2015c. "U.S. Federal Individual Income Tax Rates History, 1862-2013." Accessed May 26. http://taxfoundation.org/article/us-federal-individual-income-tax-rates-history-1913-2013-nominal-and-inflation-adjusted-brackets.

Tripp, Gabriel, and Saulny, Susan. 2011. "With Just Three Nines, Cain Refigured Math for Taxes," *New York Times*, October 12.

U.S. House of Representatives. 2015. "The People's Budget: Budget of the Congressional Progressive Caucus, Fiscal Year 2012." Accessed May 25. http://cpc.grijalva.house.gov /files/The_CPC_FY2012_Budget.pdf.

Weisman, Jonathan. 2012. "House Approved One-Year Extension of Bush-Era Tax Cuts." *New York Times*, August 1. Accessed May 26, 2015. http://www.nytimes.com /2012/08/02/us/politics/house-votes-to-extend-bush-era-tax-cuts.html.

The White House, Office of the Press Secretary. 2015. "FACT SHEET: A Simpler, Fairer Tax Code That Responsibly Invests in Middle Class Families." January 17. Accessed May 27. https://www.whitehouse.gov/the-press-office/2015/01/17/fact-sheet-simpler -fairer-tax-code-responsibly-invests-middle-class-fami.

Road Infrastructure Investment

At a Glance

Republicans and Democrats both support infrastructure investment but differ widely on how to finance such investment, and who should control the
purse strings. Generally, Democrats tend to be in favor of infrastructure programs with overall control held by the federal government. Democrats assert
that infrastructure projects are beneficial to the system of transportation and
commerce for the country as a whole. To fairly help rural as well as urban
areas and not favor one region over another, Democrats tend to defend the
principle of equity or fairness to make needed infrastructure investment.

Generally, Republicans do not support federal government controlled
financing of roads, bridges, levees, and so on. Republicans tend to be against
'big government' and assert that federal control of infrastructure is a prime
example of federal intervention in areas that belong to state and local governments who know best how to be spend funds to benefit the greatest number
of people. Republicans also tend to favor private investment in infrastructure.

Many Democrats . . .

- Say that federally funded infrastructure provides for the country as a whole
- Believe that states and cities should work with the federal government to
  address infrastructure needs, but federal control should be maintained
- See public-private investment as a legitimate approach to addressing infrastructure needs

Many Republicans . . .

- Complain that federally funded infrastructure projects cost too much,
  waste money and are inefficient
- Assert that states and cities should exercise greater control over infrastructure
- Feel that private investment in infrastructure is best for the American
  economy
- Assert that too much federal regulation is detrimental to infrastructure
  development, adding unnecessary expense and delays in completion

---

Overview

Infrastructure investment, enacted under Democrats or Republicans, or very often in a bipartisan manner, has occurred in the United States since the early 1800s. The earliest reference to a federal role occurred in 1802–1803, when Congress passed and amended the Ohio Statehood Enabling Act. These acts specified that 5 percent of the sale of public lands be "applied to the laying out and making of public roads" (U.S. Congress 1802). In 1808 Albert Gallatin, who served in President Thomas Jefferson's cabinet, developed a plan for the federal government to build a network of roads and canals, but Gallatin's plan never came to fruition. In 1806, Jefferson signed the Cumberland Road Act, although construction did not begin until 1811. By 1822, Congress passed a bill to collect tolls on the Cumberland Road to raise revenue for repairs. President Monroe vetoed the bill on constitutional grounds. The constitutional issue continued during the 1830s as President Jackson approved large amounts of federal funds for infrastructure development and improvement in the territories of the U.S. (where the federal government had overall power), but not for states. Jackson viewed such projects as the jurisdiction of individual states only (Williamson 2015).

By the late 19th century, with America's population steadily growing due to major infusions of immigrants and its economy undergoing rapid industrialization and expansion, the demand for more and better transportation networks grew. As farmers sought to get their products to market more economically, they favored the expansion of road and rail systems, as did the United States Postal Service, which began rural free delivery (RFD) in the 1890s, necessitating a wide network of roads. The constitutional issue of spending federal funds for roads was directly addressed in the 1914 report, "Federal Aid to Good Roads." The report stated, "Federal aid to good roads will accomplish several of the objects indicated by the framers of the Constitution—establish post roads, regulate commerce, provide for the common defense and promote the general welfare" (U.S. Congress 1913).

Wars also had an effect on the development of roads and highways. From the start of World War I in 1914, the U.S. was providing material to allies in Europe. The transport of war goods was accomplished first by rail and then by trucks. The system of roads quickly began to decline with increased heavy truck traffic. Backed by the American Association of State Highway Officials, Congress passed and Democratic President Wilson signed the Federal-Aid Highway Act, providing funds for highway development. With the economic problems of the 1920s and the resulting Great Depression, Democratic President Roosevelt's Public Works Administration programs included federal funds to build roads and bridges. A succession of amended Federal-Aid Highway acts over the 1930s provided increased federal aid for the surface transportation network.

Under Republican President Eisenhower, the 1956 Federal Aid Highway and Highway Revenue Acts put billions of dollars into the interstate system and established the Highway Trust Fund as an ongoing means of providing funds for the nationwide interstate highway system. Funds for the Highway Trust Fund came from taxes on gasoline and the sale of "truck tires, trailers and heavy vehicles" (Williamson 2015).

In 1973 under Republican President Nixon, legislation was proposed to allow funds from the Highway Trust Fund to be used for urban mass transit projects. Following heavy debate over a two-month period, with legislators divided by an urban/rural split, a compromise allowed funds for urban mass transit to come from the general fund rather than the Highway Trust Fund. In 1976 the next version of the Federal-Aid Highway Act launched the 3R program, providing for highway funds to be used not only for construction of new roads, but also for the "restoration, resurfacing and rehabilitation of previously built highways" (Williamson 2015).

In 1987, the Surface Transportation and Uniform Relocation Assistance Act was passed by Congress which covered highway funding from 1988–1993. President Reagan vetoed the bill on the grounds that it was fiscally irresponsible, but Congress overrode the president's veto (Apple 1987). In 1991 additional funding for the interstate highway system was made with the passage of the Intermodal Surface Transportation and Equity Act (ISTEA). In 1998 the Transportation Equity Act for the 21st Century (TEA-21) was signed into law, providing revenue for the Highway Trust Fund until 2005. The bill included separate budget lines for highways and for mass transit. One part of TEA-21 was RABA (Revenue Aligned Budget Authority), which ensured that highway spending was directly proportional to highway revenues. In 2005 the Safe, Accountable, Flexible, Efficient, and Transportation Equity Act: A Legacy for Users (SAFETEA-LU) was passed extending funding through 2009.

In 2009, as part of President Obama's American Recovery and Reinvestment Act (ARRA), a portion of stimulus funds were designated for "shovel ready" road projects. Only 8 percent of the stimulus package funds went into infrastructure projects. In 2011, the American Jobs Act included a National Infrastructure Bank to provide loans for transportation projects. The bill was heavily opposed by Republicans. Although sections of the bill were passed, the Infrastructure Bank was defeated. In 2012, the Moving Ahead for Progress in the 21st Century bill (MAP-21) was proposed by Obama to set in place a long-term transportation plan. The bill was very controversial but eventually passed.

In the summer of 2015 Congress again was dealing with funding for a highway bill that would extend financing for the busy summer construction season. Just days before the funding was set to expire on May 31, the Senate passed a two-month extension. Republicans wanted to link the highway-funding proposal to tax reform, something that was unlikely to appeal to Democrats.

Democrats on Road Infrastructure Investment

Many Democrats tend to favor infrastructure investment funded and controlled primarily by the federal government. The 2012 Democratic Party Platform stated: "We

A Democrat Urges Passage of a Bill for New Transportation Infrastructure

In 2012 Congress signed and President Barack Obama signed into law the Moving Ahead for Progress in the 21st Century Act (MAP-21). This bill authorized over $105 billion in spending for repairing existing highways and bridges and the construction of new roadways across the country. Unlike many other spending-related proposals in Washington, MAP-21 received strong bipartisan support. The following excerpt of a 2012 speech from Senator Carl Levin (D-MI) in the days leading up to the Senate vote on the bill details some of the main reasons why both Democrats and Republicans supported it.

> We are long overdue to reauthorize our Nation's transportation programs. The last reauthorization, SAFETEA LU expired in September 2009. Since then, there have been seven short-term extensions . . . I am pleased the Senate is finally voting on a bill . . . MAP 21. This bill will improve the mobility of people and commerce while reducing traffic congestion and improving air quality. Investing in the construction and maintenance of our roads, bridges, public transit systems, trails, and rail infrastructure means people and goods move more efficiently, and that improves our international competitiveness. And investing in infrastructure will create badly needed jobs. It is one of the most obvious things we can do to help boost the economy as it struggles to emerge from the great recession. . . . Our State transportation agencies need to be able to do long-term planning, and a two-year bill helps that cause and is surely better than the short-term extensions we have been living under. . . . There are no earmarks in this bill, and nearly all discretionary grant programs allocated by the Federal Highway Administration would be eliminated. The result is that most funding is allocated to the States by formula. . . . MAP 21 makes substantial changes to transportation planning requirements at all levels . . . . and requires . . . performance measures and targets.

Source

Levin, Carl. 2012. "Should the Senate Pass S. 1813, the Moving Ahead for Progress in the 21st Century Act? PRO." *Congressional Digest* 91 (7): 210–216.

support long-term investments in our infrastructure. Roads, bridges, rail and public transit systems, airports, ports, and sewers are all critical to economic growth, as they enable businesses to grow." To fund such investments, many Democrats advocate wealthy individuals and corporations should pay a larger portion of taxes, rather than increasing the tax burden on the middle class. "We believe America prospers when everyone, . . . does their fair share and plays by the same rules" (Democratic National Committee 2012).

Democratic leaders on the Senate Budget Committee also endorse closing corporate tax loopholes to generate revenue. The committee's "Repairing Our Infrastructure" report, states: "Congress should look to close unfair loopholes that encourage multinationals to shift profits overseas to avoid paying taxes. These loopholes cost the government billions of dollars every year, and disadvantage small businesses" (U.S. Congress 2015).

Democrats tend to favor infrastructure investment as a means for the U.S. to achieve energy independence while also protecting the environment and saving money for consumers. According to the 2012 Democratic Party Platform: "We support more infrastructure investment to speed the transition to cleaner fuels. . . . Building a clean energy future means that new exploration and production needs to be approached safely and responsibly. Democrats are committed to balancing environmental protection with development, and preserving sensitive public lands from exploration, like the Arctic National Wildlife Refuge, Pacific West Coast, and Gulf of Maine. . . . We are saving consumers' money on their energy bills—both at home and at the pump." Democrats have been criticized for over-regulation of infrastructure projects, thereby imposing more barriers to development. In the 2012 platform, the Democratic Party defended its approach to regulations: "Efficient and effective regulations enforce common sense safeguards to protect the American people. . . . It's why our food is safe to eat, our water is safe to drink, and our air is safe to breathe" (Democratic National Committee 2012).

Three major infrastructure issues that have challenged both Democrats and Republicans have been the Highway Trust Fund, Public Private Partnerships and the National Infrastructure Bank. Since 1956 the Highway Trust Fund has been the major funding source for the interstate highway system. Over the years vehicles have become more fuel efficient. While automobile and truck travel tended to increase for many years, with the downturn in the economy in 2007–2008 and the increase in the cost of gasoline, travel by car declined somewhat. However, the major factor causing problems with the Highway Trust Fund has been that gas tax rates have remained the same for about twenty years, with both parties reluctant to raise the gas tax.

Given these factors, the Trust Fund dollars declined and could no longer support highway construction and repairs. With the Trust Fund about to run out of money totally, Congress passed short term financing extensions with the most recent extension expiring on July 31, 2015. Traditionally both Democrats and Republicans have been opposed to using the expansion of toll roads to fund surface transportation, considering tolls an additional tax on top of the federal and state gasoline taxes, and an added burden on the middle class and the poor. As the controversy over the shortage of funds for the Highway Trust Fund accelerated, however, the Obama administration has shown some willingness to consider this option (Halsey 2014).

Public Private Partnerships (PPP) have been a much-touted solution to the complex problem of infrastructure investment. Both parties have proposed the increased use of PPP but from very different points of view. President Obama's proposal from 2011 that continued into 2014 would have a high level of federal control. As described in the *National Journal*, "Obama and his team won't turn away investors . . . Washington would dictate the priorities for funding. . . . The unspoken message is clear. Businesses are welcome to come and play but only on the government's terms" (Johnson 2011). The National Infrastructure Bank legislation was first jointly proposed by Democrat Chris Dodd of Connecticut and Republican Chuck Hagel of Nebraska in 2007, with revised versions proposed in the House and Senate in subsequent years. The proposal would have established a fund to which states, cities, or other agencies could bring large-scale projects. The bank's board would evaluate each project and approve or reject the project for investment with the bank working with the local agency to develop a financing plan (Herbert 2008). Although the proposal was not enacted, President Obama continued to recommend infrastructure planning with the 2011 American Jobs Act, the 2014 Build America Investment Initiative, and GROW AMERICA Act.

Republicans on Road Infrastructure Investment

Many Republicans tend to favor infrastructure investment funded and controlled primarily by state and local government and private industry with much less control by the federal government. The 2012 Republican platform stated, "Interstate infrastructure has long been a federal responsibility shared with the states, and a renewed federal-state partnership and new public-private partnerships are urgently needed . . . Republicans will pursue free market policies that are the surest way to boost employment and create job growth and economic prosperity for all" (Republican National Committee 2008).

Unlike their Democratic counterparts, Republicans tend to favor lowering taxes on corporations and those who possess the capital to invest in large scale infrastructure projects. Republicans advocate a "business-like, cost-effective approach for infrastructure spending" (ibid.). Republicans also tend to advocate infrastructure development to move the U.S. forward toward energy independence. However, Republican leaders stress the role of the free market along with reining in "environmental laws that often thwart new energy exploration and production. . . . Experience has shown that, in caring for the land and water, private ownership has been our best guarantee of conscientious stewardship, while the worst instances of environmental degradation have occurred under government control" (ibid.). Republicans are especially condemning of government regulation. They see laws such as the Davis-Bacon labor law, that requires companies working on federally funded or assisted projects to pay the local prevailing wage rate, as increasing the costs of construction and repair work. Beyond direct regulation in wages, Republicans assert that related federal requirements, such as the development of regional transportation plans or environmental impact rules, impede the forward progress of infrastructure development. Another example of federal regulations noted in the Pew Trust report on Intergovernmental Challenges in Surface Transportation Funding is: "federal highway funding can carry mandates that a state submit and implement a plan to achieve minimum air quality levels, set its drinking age at 21 years old, or have sufficient laws to prevent driving while intoxicated" (Pew Charitable Trust 2014). Republican leaders stated: "overregulation is a stealth tax on everyone as the costs of compliance with the whims of federal agencies are passed along to the consumers" (Republican National Committee 2012).

Republicans have also faced major challenges with infrastructure issues posed by the Highway Trust Fund, Public Private Partnerships and the National Infrastructure Bank. With the Highway Trust Fund set to run out of money in July of 2015, Republicans strongly advocated a long-term solution. The short-term fixes have usually meant transferring funds from general tax revenues to shore up the Trust Fund. Some Republicans have proposed alternate ways of dealing with the Highway Trust Fund crisis. Former Secretary of Transportation, Ray LaHood, after leaving his position in the Obama administration, came out in favor of raising the federal gas tax. "It's just been very difficult to get conservative Republicans to think about raising the gas tax. They know that we should, but there's enough that just don't want to" (Laing 2015). Senator Mike Enzi proposed indexing the gas tax to rates of inflation as a first step in addressing the shortfall. A more radical way (devolution) was put forth by Republican Mike Lee of Utah and Tom Graves of Georgia in 2013. In contrast to recent efforts to raise the gas tax, the Transportation Empowerment Act

---

A Conservative Republican Speaks Out Against New Highway Spending

In 2012 Congress signed and President Barack Obama signed into law the Moving Ahead for Progress in the 21st Century Act (MAP-21). The measure, which authorized over $105 billion in spending for repairing existing highways and bridges and the construction of new roadways across the country, received bipartisan support. But some conservative Republicans, such as Tea Party Republican Senator Jim DeMint of South Carolina, voted against it on the grounds that it was not paid for and would thus increase the deficit:

> This bill proves that the bipartisan addiction to big spending in Washington hasn't ended. This bill requires a $13 billion dollar bailout because senators in both parties insisted on reckless spending increases far above what is available in the Highway Trust Fund. It also leaves in place wasteful and corrupt Davis-Bacon mandates [requiring the payment of prevailing wages on public works projects] that amount to taxpayer-funded kickbacks from Democrats to union bosses. There's nothing in this legislation to prevent future earmarks, and it even contains a new billion dollar slush fund for unvetted transportation projects. Congress needs to wake up and realize we're $15 trillion in debt and we can't keep doing these status quo big spending compromises. We need commonsense reforms of the highway program that would empower States with flexibility to make their own transportation decisions. If we devolved the highway program to the States, we could build and repair roads faster and less expensively.

Source

DeMint, Jim. 2012. "Should the Senate Pass S. 1813, the Moving Ahead for Progress in the 21st Century Act? CON." *Congressional Digest* 91 (7): 217.

(TEA) would lower the rate drastically over a five-year time period. The other major piece of the bill would have control over federal highways and transit programs move to individual states and shift federal funding to a block grant program.

Republicans have long been advocates of public private partnerships, as they align directly with the party's philosophy of increasing private investment and decreasing government control. "U.S. and foreign studies have found that privately financed infrastructure projects are more likely to be completed on time and on budget than traditional government projects" (Edwards 2013). John Mica, R-Florida, chair of the House Transportation and Infrastructure Committee, wants to "ensure that states have more flexibility in addressing their own infrastructure needs. . . . We will consider how we can remove barriers that prevent states from entering into public-private partnership agreements and take advantage of private-sector potential" (Johnson 2011).

The proposals for a National Infrastructure Bank (NIB) have often met with opposition from Republicans. Many Republicans assert that the NIB is yet another federal program with power and funding in Washington. Senator Orrin Hatch stated, "It is about setting up a brand new government bureaucracy . . . that will take years to get under way and will subject taxpayers, once again, to private sector risk-taking and to bail-outs" (Politi 2011). Robert Poole of the Reason Foundation commented against the NIB, "If Congress wants to assist the financing of infrastructure projects on a sustainable basis . . . it could expand a number of existing programs that already do this" (Poole 2008). In opposing Obama's proposal in 2011, Republican House Speaker John Boehner advocated instead "expanding domestic energy production, including oil drilling, and putting the proceeds toward highway infrastructure needs" (Boles 2011).

Vanette Schwartz

Further Reading

"Aging Infrastructure—Chronology." 2012. *CQ Researcher Update*, June 18.

Apple, R. W. 1987. "Senate Rejects Reagan Plea and Votes 67–33 to Override His Veto of Highway Funds." *New York Times*, April 3.

Boles, Corey. 2011. "Rival Infrastructure Plans Defeated in Senate." *Wall Street Journal*, November 3. Accessed November 20, 2015. http://www.wsj.com/articles/SB1000142 4052970203716204577016332571249456.

DeMint, Jim. 2012. "Should the Senate Pass S. 1813, the Moving Ahead for Progress in the 21st Century Act? CON." *Congressional Digest* 91 (7): 217.

Democratic National Committee. 2012. "Moving America Forward: 2012 Democratic National Platform." Accessed May 15, 2015. https://www.democrats.org/party-platform.

Edwards, Chris. 2013. "Infrastructure Investment." August. Accessed May 20, 2015. http://www.downsizinggovernment.org/infrastructure-investment.

Enzi, Mike. 2012. "Should the Senate Pass S. 1813, the Moving Ahead for Progress in the 21st Century Act? CON." *Congressional Digest* 91 (7): 207–217.

Halsey, Ashley, III. 2014. "White House Opens Door to Tolls on Interstate Highways Removing Long-standing Prohibition." *Washington Post*, April 29. https://www .washingtonpost.com/local/trafficandcommuting/white-house-opens-door-to-tolls -on-interstate-highways-removing-long-standing-prohibition/2014/04/29/5d2b9f30 -cfac-11e3-b812-0c92213941f4_story.html.

Hatch, Orrin. 2012. "Should the Senate Pass S. 1813, the Moving Ahead for Progress in the 21st Century Act? CON." *Congressional Digest* 91 (7): 219–221.

Herbert, Bob. 2008. "Investing in America," *New York Times*, January 29. Accessed May 8. 2015. http://www.nytimes.com/2008/01/29/opinion/29herbert.html?_r=0.

Johnson, Fawn. 2011. "Slow Going on Infrastructure Funding." *National Journal,* February 5, 10.

Laing, Keith. 2013. "Bill Would Eliminate Federal Transportation Funding." *The Hill*, November 15. Accessed May 25, 2015. http://thehill.com/policy/transportation/190402 -bill-would-eliminate-federal-transportation.

Laing, Keith. 2015. "Ex-DOT chief raps Congress for highway patches." *The Hill*, May 19. Accessed May 29, 2015. http://thehill.com/policy/transportation/242481-ex-dot-chief -raps-congress-for-highway-patches.

"Legislative Background on Transportation Infrastructure." 2012. *Congressional Digest* 91 (7): 204.

Marcos, Cristina. 2015. "Congress sets new deadline on highways." *The Hill*, May 23. Accessed May 25, 2015. http://thehill.com/policy/transportation/242991-congress-sets -new-deadline-on-highways.

Pew Charitable Trusts. 2014. "Intergovernmental Challenges in Surface Transportation Funding," September 23, 2014. Accessed May 19, 2015. http://www.pewtrusts.org/ en/research-and-analysis/reports/2014/09/intergovernmental-challenges-in-surface -transportation-funding.

Politi, James. 2011. "Republicans Block $60bn Infrastructure Bill." *FT.com*. November 3. Accessed November 20, 2015. http://www.ft.com/intl/cms/s/0/76b51fd2-065d-11e1 -8a16-00144feabdc0.html#axzz3s2UHdEDe.

Poole, Robert. 2009. "Should Congress Pass the National Infrastructure Bank Act? Reason Foundation." *Congressional Digest* 88 (1): 27–31.

Republican National Committee. 2012. "We Believe in America: 2012 Republican Platform." Accessed May 11, 2015. https://cdn.gop.com/docs/2012GOPPlatform.pdf.

Republican National Committee. 2008. Republican Party Platform. Accessed May 15, 2015. http://www.presidency.ucsb.edu/ws/index.php?pid=78545.

U.S. Congress. 1802. "Enabling Act for Ohio—1802," 7th Cong., 1st sess., April 30. Accessed April 21, 2016. http://www.ohiohistorycentral.org/w/Enabling_Act_of_1802 _(Transcript).

U.S. Congress, Joint Committee on Federal Aid in the Construction of Post Roads. 1913. "Federal Aid to Good Roads." April 25. Accessed May 1, 2015. http://babel.hathitrust .org/cgi/pt?id=umn.31951d03524405a;view=1up;seq=3.

U.S. Congress, Senate. Committee on the Budget. 2015. "Repairing Our Infrastructure." Accessed May 25. http://www.budget.senate.gov/democratic/public/index.cfm/repairing -our-infrastructure.

U.S. Department of Transportation. 2015. "The Grow America Act." Accessed May 29. http://www.dot.gov/sites/dot.gov/files/docs/GROW_AMERICA_Overall_Fact_Sheet .pdf.

White House Press Office. 2014. "Fact Sheet: Building a 21st Century Infrastructure: Increasing Public and Private Collaboration with the Build America Investment Initiative." July 17. Accessed May 29, 2015. https://www.whitehouse.gov/the-press-office/2014/07/17/fact-sheet-building-21st-century-infrastructure-increasing-public-and-pr.

White House Press Office. 2011. "Fact Sheet: The American Jobs Act." September 8. Accessed May 29, 2015. https://www.whitehouse.gov/the-press-office/2011/09/08/fact-sheet-american-jobs-act.

Williamson, John. 2012. "Federal Aid to Roads and Highways since the 18th Century: A Legislative History." Congressional Research Service, January 6. Accessed May 10, 2015. https://www.fas.org/sgp/crs/misc/R42140.pdf.

Scientific and Medical Research

At a Glance

In a 1945 report to Democratic President Harry S. Truman, U.S. engineer and administrator Vannevar Bush explained that industry conducts development as a matter of necessity, but industry is unable to fund basic science that expands frontiers of knowledge. Bush cautioned that while development research is needed to support industry productivity and capabilities, such development would stagnate if basic scientific research were neglected. He thus urged robust governmental support for research in science and medicine. Bush's perspective echoes in today's Democratic Party.

In 1957, in the wake of the Soviet Union's launch of the Sputnik satellite, Eisenhower administration's Secretary of Defense Charles Wilson called for major new investments in research to directly support military productivity and capabilities. But he castigated many other areas of scientific research as unimportant and wasteful of taxpayer dollars (Mieczkowski 2013). Wilson's perspective still echoes in many precincts of today's Republican Party.

Many Democrats . . .

- Believe that federal support for scientific and medical research should be strong and consistent and that the results of that research can assist lawmakers and officials in making sensible policy decisions
- Assert that precautions should be maintained to ensure that scientific and medical research is protected from political interference or pressure

Many Republicans . . .

- Believe that federal support for scientific and medical research should focus on areas of inquiry with immediate and practical applications, such as curing diseases and advancing military capabilities
- Contend that there should be enhanced oversight of government funding for research
- Wish to reduce federal funding for research in the social, behavioral, and geosciences, including research into mental health, public health, climatology, and environmental conservation

Overview

Scientific research and development includes basic, applied, and development approaches to science. Basic science builds knowledge about the natural and social world. Applied science builds knowledge about meeting a need, such as a health problem. Development science applies extant knowledge to new products and processes. Basic science engendered the Enlightenment (1651–1794) whereas development generated the Industrial Revolution (1780s–1930s).

The Enlightenment's reasoned thought led to new ideas about the natural and social world. Enlightened thinkers began developing new ideas about people being created equal, and about the rule of law that would protect individual liberties, private ownership, and free exchange of goods and ideas. Without these new ideas there would have been no New World, just old ideas transferred to another place.

The New World boasts a few late-Enlightenment era thinkers. Benjamin Franklin founded the American Philosophical Society (APS) in 1743 to "improve the common stock of knowledge" (APS 2013) in the New World. Most APS members, like Franklin, pursued science as an avocation to satisfy their curiosities. Science that satisfies general curiosity is now referred to as basic science.

After APS member Thomas Jefferson authored the Declaration of Independence, he returned home to Monticello, Virginia, to await its signing. On July 1, 1776, he commenced a science project that he continued for 50 years until his death. He recorded weather temperature twice daily to test the conventional wisdom that North American temperatures were rising as more trees were felled and more acreage cultivated (Jefferson 1787). Such studies, what we now call basic science, were so foundational to the New World that Pennsylvania deeded a building to APS. It is still there across the square from Independence Hall, where many early APS members including Franklin and Jefferson had signed the Declaration of Independence (APS 2013).

Early U.S. research occurred in the context of such avocational societies, but in the first half of the 20th century Congress established agencies with federal direct spending for R&D. These include the U.S. Department of Health and Human Services (HHS), National Science Foundation (NSF), and National Aeronautics and Space Administration (NASA). Each of these agencies were crafted in response to perceived threats, including disease epidemics, foreign governments, and economic uncertainty.

In 1912, during the presidency of Republican William Taft, Congress enacted the Public Health Service (PHS), which received funding for research into diseases such as tuberculosis and malaria. In 1930, with Republican Herbert Hoover in the White House, Congress established the National Institute (now Institutes) of Health (NIH) within the Public Health Service (PHS), which is now known as the Department of Health and Human Services. Federal funding for medical and public health research further expanded during the 1930s, carried along by the various economic stimulus and public welfare programs of Democratic President

Franklin D. Roosevelt's so-called New Deal. "In addition to providing grants to states and municipalities for new public health programs," noted one history of U.S. healthcare policy, "the Roosevelt administration orchestrated the creation of major new medical research initiatives under the auspices of federal authorities. One such initiative was a 1937 bill passed by Congress that created the National Cancer Institute (NCI)" (Hillstrom 2012, 274).

During World War II (1939–1945), Democratic President Franklin Roosevelt called on university researchers for help with expanding the nation's military capabilities. He found the resulting research collaboration to be so valuable that he wanted to maintain the government-university research relationship after the war. In 1951, Democratic President Harry S. Truman and Congress established the National Science Foundation (NSF) as a federal agency supporting university research and science education. This agency has remained an important body for advancing scientific understanding ever since.

When the Soviet Union launched Sputnik in 1957, many Americans perceived a threat to national security. Republican President Dwight Eisenhower was urged in some quarters to create a space division within the U.S. Department of Defense (DoD) capable of matching and eventually passing the Soviet space program. Instead, Eisenhower listened to scientists eager to collaborate with international peers, and in 1958 he worked with Congress to establish the National Aeronautics and Space Agency (NASA) as a federal civilian agency providing "research into the problems of flight within and outside the Earth's atmosphere, and for other purposes" ("National Aeronautics and Space Act of 1958").

For much of the second half of the 20th century, increased funding for medical and scientific research was a bipartisan goal. For example, the annual budget of the National Institutes of Health increased from $3 million in 1945 to $450 million in 1961—and to nearly $1 billion by the time the 1960s drew to a close. In 1971, meanwhile, Democrats and Republicans both supported a bill called the National Cancer Act that established a National Cancer Institute within the NIH, but with a wholly separate budget. The initial National Cancer Act, signed into law by Republican President Richard M. Nixon, provided $1.59 billion in funding just for the NCI's first three years.

In the 1980s and 1990s, however, medical and scientific research efforts that had long enjoyed uncontroversial and bipartisan support increasingly fell victim to intensifying partisanship in Washington. In the mid-1990s, for example, the HHS's Agency for Health Care Policy and Research (AHCPR), a department dedicated to medical effectiveness research for the purpose of improving the quality and cost-effectiveness of American health care—and one that had been established less than a decade earlier with the full support of Republican President George H. W. Bush—became a lightning rod for conservative lawmakers complaining about the size and influence of the federal government. Democrats staunchly defended the AHCPR (now known as the Agency for Healthcare Research and Quality, AHRQ) and through 2015 had managed to keep its doors open, but it continues to be targeted by GOP lawmakers for funding cuts or outright dissolution.

Partisan bickering also surrounds the America Creating Opportunities to Meaningfully Promote Excellence in Technology, Education, and Science (America COMPETES) Act. First signed into law by Republican President George W. Bush with bipartisan support in 2007, this legislation was touted as a tool to ensure America's continued leadership in scientific research. It boosted R&D funding for several science agencies and increased government investment in STEM (science, technology, engineering, and mathematics) education. Four years later, Democratic President Barack Obama signed a four-year reauthorization of the COMPETES Act. "It is heartening that Congress recognized that the maintenance of America's global leadership in science, technology, and innovation transcends politics and partisanship," declared the Obama White House. "Full funding of the COMPETES Act is among the most important things that Congress can do to ensure America's continued leadership in the decades ahead" (Holdren 2011). Since then, however, the future of the act has become shrouded in doubt, due in large part to persistent GOP efforts to choke off funding for the geosciences and climate research and reduce funding for the National Institute of Standards and Technology (NIST). These GOP cuts, which were included in COMPETES Act reauthorization bill passed by the GOP-controlled House in 2015, were roundly condemned both by Democrats and the scientific community. In fact, a total of 70 scientific organizations issued statements of concern about or opposition to the House bill, which Obama vowed to veto. The future of the reauthorization remains in doubt, especially as the Republican-controlled Senate did not pass a reauthorization bill of any kind in 2015.

In 2009 Democrats in Congress passed and President Barack Obama signed the American Recovery and Reinvestment Act (ARRA), which included massive new funding for a wide variety of scientific research—most notably the investigation and development of new clean energy sources. Republicans denounced the stimulus package in general, as well as the ARRA's specific "green energy" funding provisions. The Obama administration and many Democrats, however, have asserted that these investments have helped accelerate America's shift away from fossil fuels toward renewables.

Another federal agency that has an enormous budget for research and development is the Department of Defense. It has by far the largest federal direct R&D spending ($135.35 million in fiscal year 2015), more than all other federal agencies combined.

HHS has the second largest federal direct spending for R&D, about half that of the Defense Department. HHS research is divided about equally between basic and applied science. The Department of Energy receives the third largest federal direct spending for R&D. Energy research is also divided, with about 40 percent going to basic science, 30 percent to applied science, and 30 percent set aside for development. The NSF and NASA receive the fourth and fifth largest federal direct spending for R&D amounts, respectively. NSF research is primarily for basic science. NASA research is divided with about 30 percent for basic and applied science, and 70 percent for development. Other agencies with large federal R&D spending include, in order of allocation, Agriculture, Commerce, Transportation, the Interior, Homeland Security, Environmental Protection, Veterans Affairs, and Education (NSF 2012).

In addition to federal direct spending for R&D, the U.S. government supports research and development by private industry through tax credits. The tax code allows businesses to subtract R&D spending from their tax bill.

Democrats on Scientific and Medical Research

Generally speaking, the Democratic Party believes that federal investments in scientific and medical research are essential in enabling the United States to address the challenges it confronts, whether those challenges take the form of deadly and expensive diseases or threats to the natural environment. For example, Democrats have expressed grave concern with the threat of climate change, and they have advocated intensive research to better understand the severity of the threat and the benefits and drawbacks of various mitigation strategies. In his 2013 State of the Union address, for example, President Obama pledged an "all of the above" approach to energy research, including nuclear energy, clean energy (such as natural gas), and renewable energy (that does not rely on fossil fuel). Obama further proposed increased R&D funding to improve agricultural productivity and global food security.

Al Gore, Advocate for Federal Funding of Scientific Research

Throughout his many decades in the public eye—as politician, businessman, and environmental activist—Democrat Al Gore has consistently touted the benefits of federal investments in scientific research. A native of Tennessee who was the son of one of that state's most famous political figures, Gore served in the U.S. House of Representatives from 1977 through 1985, in the Senate from 1985–1993, and as vice president in the Clinton administration from 1993–2001. He continued working to stabilize the climate as chair of the Alliance for Climate Protection.

As a Representative, Gore chaired a House subcommittee on Science and Technology. Gore championed just-over-the-horizon consumer-oriented causes: toxic-waste dumping, genetic testing, global warming. In the Senate Gore returned to environmental issues. He helped probe NASA after the 1986 Challenger disaster, played an important role in funding the development of new technologies such as the Internet, and warned about the dangers of global warming.

The author of both *Earth in the Balance* and *An Inconvenient Truth*, two of the best-known book on global climate change that have ever been published, Gore was co-winner of the 2007 Nobel Peace Prize for informing the world of dangers posed by climate change. The prize committee stated that "Gore is probably the single individual who has done most to rouse the public and the governments that action had to be taken to meet the climate challenge."

Sources

"Al Gore." 2007. *The Nobel Peace Prize 2007, Intergovernmental Panel on Climate Change, Al Gore.* Accessed October 31. http://www.nobelprize.org/nobel_prizes/peace/laureates/2007 /gore-bio.html.

Gore, Al. 2006. *An Inconvenient Truth: The Planetary Emergency of Global Warming and What We Can Do About It.* New York: Rodale.

Sack, Kevin, and Robin Toner. 2000. "In Congress, Gore Selected Issues Ready for Prime Time." *New York Times,* August 13. Accessed September 25, 2015. http://partners.nytimes .com/library/politics/camp/081300wh-gore-record.html.

The Obama administration canceled NASA's moon and Mars preparations in 2009 (Malakoff 2012a). However, the 2012 Democratic platform stated its support for NASA innovation and exploration with a "stepping stone" approach to studying asteroids and observing the moons of other planets. Hopes of travel to Mars are pushed back into the 2030s (Foust 2014).

Representative Mike Honda (D-California) is a Democratic member of the GOP-controlled House Commerce, Justice, and Science (CJS) Subcommittee that makes appropriations for NSF and NASA. CJS proposed increases to NASA funding, but proposed regulations circumventing the peer review process, by identifying earth and social sciences as lesser priorities. Honda further expressed concern that the proposed regulations represented micromanagement of the NSF mission by Republicans in Congress.

The 2012 Democratic platform pledged a "world-class commitment to science and research so that the next generation of innovators and high-technology manufacturing companies thrive in America." It also called for increased investment in biomedical research and other types of scientific inquiry. Expressing concern that U.S. research was so underfunded that it could only fund a small percentage of the grant requests it received, the Democrats have repeatedly called for more generous funding for basic research agencies such as NSF, HHS, NIH, and the Department of Energy.

With funding constrained by the "small government" philosophy of the modern Republican Party, however, some Democrats have begun casting about for other means of increasing funding for federally sponsored medical and scientific research. For example, Representative Chris Van Hollen and Senator Elizabeth Warren introduced a bill to increase federal investment in medical research to be funded by pharmaceutical companies that committed wrongdoing. The funding stream seemed reasonable to Van Hollen and Warren, since pharmaceutical companies use basic NIH research to develop new drugs they sell in the marketplace for large profit (Anderson 2015).

The support expressed by Democratic lawmakers in Washington for robust investment in scientific and medical research reflects the priorities of Democratic voters as well. A 2015 Pew Research Center poll on American attitudes about science and politics found that 83 percent of respondents who identified as Democrats or "leaning" Democrats believed that government investment in basic scientific research was worthwhile, versus only 12 percent who indicated that such expenditures were not worthwhile. These levels of support were considerably higher than found among Republicans and people who lean Republican (Funk and Rainie 2015).

Republicans on Scientific and Medical Research

Republicans have complained that the characterization of Republicans as "anti-science" comes from distorted judgments about a constricted set of issues. Republicans have also emphasized that while they see themselves as watchdogs against research that is "wasteful" of taxpayer dollars, many members of their party have supported federal initiatives and research programs aimed at issues ranging from space exploration to eradicating deadly and debilitating diseases (Fisher 2013).

A GOP Champion of Space Exploration

Representative John Culberson, a lifelong Texan, has had a life-long fascination with science and space exploration. Culberson told the *Los Angeles Times* that he got his first telescope when he was 12. In high school he got excited about Europa, Jupiter's icy moon. He subscribed to the journals of *Science* and *Nature*, and the more he studied Europa, the more certain he became that NASA would discover life in the oceans of Europa.

Culberson earned a BA in History from Southern Methodist University and a JD from South Texas College of Law. He was elected to the House of Representatives in 2000 as a "fiscally conservative 'Jeffersonian Republican,'" and his since then identified himself as a member of the Tea Party. His beliefs in limited government, individual liberty, and states' rights have informed his legislative work.

Culberson is a member of the House Appropriations Committee, which funds the federal government. In 2014 he was selected by the GOP leadership to chair the Subcommittee on Commerce, Justice, and Science (CJS). The CJS Subcommittee has jurisdiction over the Department of Commerce, Department of Justice, NASA, the National Science Foundation, and other related agencies. Culberson's lifelong enthusiasm for NASA space exploration has made him one of the agency's key allies on Capitol Hill. Culberson has consistently supported high levels of science funding, with high levels of congressional oversight. Culberson has even expressed support for NASA exploration of Europa.

The Science Coalition (2015), an organization of U.S. research universities dedicated to sustaining federal investment in basic science, named Culberson their 2014 Champion of Science Award recipient. Culberson was recognized for actions reflecting his belief that "basic scientific research, conducted at universities and national labs across the country, is essential to . . . address pressing issues."

Sources

Hiltzik, Michael. 2015. "Inside the GOP's Science Policy: A Talk with Rep. John Culberson." *Los Angeles Times*, March 3. Accessed October 15, 2015. http://www.latimes.com/business /hiltzik/la-fi-mh-inside-the-gops-science-policy-20150303-column.html.

Hiltzik, Michael. 2015. "Inside GOP Science, Part 2: The Brawl over National Science Foundation Grants." *Los Angeles Times*, March 4. Accessed October 15, 2015. http://www.latimes .com/business/hiltzik/la-fi-mh-national-science-foundation-grants-20150303-column .html#page=1.

Some Republicans in leadership positions in Washington, however, have expressed skepticism about the wisdom of government-supported scientific research. Lamar Smith, chair of the U.S. House Committee on Science, Space and Technology, has denounced many NSF expenditures as a "frivolous use of taxpayer money" (Smith 2014). In an exchange of letters with NSF in 2013 and 2014, Smith challenged the agency's peer review process. He demanded copies of "every e-mail, letter, memorandum, record, note, text message, all peer reviews" (ibid.) for about 30 NSF-approved projects. He particularly questioned projects in the areas of social, behavioral and political science (Mervis 2014).

John Culberson, chair of the House Commerce, Justice, and Science Subcommittee, agreed with Smith. He expressed support for funding in space and medical research and to realize various technological advances, but objected to NSF research grants to researchers seeking the answers to "obscure or obtuse social science questions" (Culberson 2015). House Majority Whip Steve Scalise identified NSF studies he believed unnecessary, including research on human-set fires in New Zealand in the 1800s. Scalise urged Congress to invest wisely and responsibly in other biology, chemistry, math, engineering, and computer science.

The 2008 GOP platform said Republicans "share the vision of returning Americans to the moon as a step toward a mission to Mars." The party's 2012 platform lauded NASA, but did not mention travel to the moon or Mars (Malakoff 2012b). This was a disappointment to Republican House Majority Leader Kevin McCarthy, who said that "we once stood up to the challenge of the Soviet's Sputnik and made it to the moon, but today, our astronauts use Russian rockets and other nations are working to put people on Mars and beyond" (ibid.). McCarthy encouraged increased public-private partnerships and entrepreneurs in space exploration.

The Republican Party did express support for biomedical research in its 2008 and 2012 party platforms. The 2012 Republican platform supported stem cell research with "adult stem cells, umbilical cord blood, and cells reprogrammed into pluripotent stem cells" (Republican National Committee 2012). The platform opposed killing embryos for stem cells and supported banning the use of aborted fetus body parts for research. Ben Carson, retired Johns Hopkins University neurosurgeon and 2016 GOP presidential hopeful, would take a more nuanced approach. He urged room for looking at intent in decisions about fetal tissue use in medical research (Weigel 2015).

The 2012 platform called for neuroscience research for dealing with diseases and disorders such as autism spectrum disorder, Alzheimer's disease, and Parkinson's disease. In a 2015 speech to Congress, Senator Pat Toomey expressed his admiration for NIH cancer research that would soon lead to cures. He similarly supported NIH funding for Alzheimer's cures (Toomey 2014). His website pledged he would work with "colleagues on both sides of the aisle to see continued federal investment in this kind of breakthrough research" (Toomey 2015).

In recent years, however, leaders in the GOP have consistently sought to limit funding for climate science research, a stance widely attributed to conservative skepticism about whether global warming is something to be concerned about. Critics have also charged that the GOP has regularly opposed agencies and initiatives focused on improving healthcare outcomes (and saving taxpayer money) through research on best medical practices. "The federal government is now making a significant investment in health services and patient-centered outcomes research to identify waste and improve the safety, effectiveness and quality of care," wrote public policy scholar Eric Patashnik in 2015. "[But] House Republicans are trying to abolish one of the main agencies carrying out this research, the Agency for Healthcare Research and Quality (AHRQ), and cut the funding of another, the Patient-Centered Outcomes Research Institute (PCORI)," even though the same lawmakers approved a $1.1 billion increase in the NIH budget (Patashnik 2015).

Patashnik speculated that GOP opposition to "best healthcare practices" research could stem from a number of factors, including perceptions that it is tainted by its association with the Obama administration's wider healthcare reform agenda and opposition from members of the healthcare industry who are closely aligned with the GOP. Whatever the reasons, Republican lawmakers who oppose federal funding for scientific and medical research are unlikely to be reprimanded for such stances by Republican voters. A 2015 Pew Research Center poll found that Republican voters were less supportive of such expenditures than their Democratic counterparts, although roughly two out of three GOP and GOP-leaning voters still felt that such investments were worthwhile "in the long run" (Funk and Rainie 2015).

Karen Flint Stipp

Further Reading

American Philosophical Society. 2013. "About." Accessed October 12, 2015. http://www.amphilsoc.org/about/campus/philosophicalhall.

Anderson, Gerard. 2015. "Big Pharma Should Support the NIH." *Baltimore Sun*, April 17. Accessed October 1, 2015. http://www.baltimoresun.com/news/opinion/oped/bs-ed-medical-innovations-act-20150417-story.html.

Bush, Vannevar. 1945. *Science, the Endless Frontier.* Washington, DC: United States Government Printing Office. Accessed October 1, 2015. https://www.nsf.gov/od/lpa/nsf50/vbush1945.htm.

Culberson, John. 2015. "U.S Congressman John Culberson—Biography." Accessed October 16, 2015. http://culberson.house.gov/biography/.

Democratic National Committee. 2012. "Moving America Forward: 2012 Democratic National Platform." Accessed May 11, 2015. https://www.democrats.org/party-platform.

Democratic National Committee. 2015. "Science and Technology 2015." Accessed October 15. http://www.democrats.org/issues/science-and-technology.

Fisher, Mischa. 2013. "The Republican Party Isn't Really the Anti-Science Party." *The Atlantic*, November 11. Accessed October 15, 2015. http://www.theatlantic.com/politics/archive/2013/11/the-republican-party-isnt-really-the-anti-science-party/281219/.

Foust, Jeff. 2014. "NASA Facing New Space Science Cuts." *National Geographic*, May 31. Accessed October 15, 2015. http://news.nationalgeographic.com/news/2014/05/140530-space-politics-planetary-science-funding-exploration/.

Funk, Cary, and Lee Rainie. 2015. "Americans, Politics and Science Issues." Pew Research Center, July 1. Accessed January 5, 2016. http://www.pewinternet.org/2015/07/01/americans-politics-and-science-issues/.

Hillstrom, Kevin. 2012. *U.S. Health Policy and Politics: A Documentary History.* Washington, DC: CQ Press.

Jefferson, Thomas. 1787. *Notes on the State of Virginia.* Paris: John Stockdale.

Kennedy, Joseph V. 2012. "The Sources and Uses of Science Funding." *The New Atlantis* 36: 3–22.

Malakoff, David. 2012a. "Democratic Party Platform Mostly Looks Back on Science." *Science*, September 4. Accessed September 4, 2015. http://news.sciencemag.org/2012/09/democratic-party-platform-mostly-looks-back-science.

Malakoff, David. 2012b. "Republican Party Platform Has a Lot to Say about Science," *Science Magazine*, August 29. Accessed October 15, 2015. http://news.sciencemag.org/2012/08/republican-party-platform-has-lot-say-about-science.

Mervis, Jeffrey. 2014. "Battle between NSF and House Science Committee Escalates: How Did It Get This Bad?" *Science*, October 2. Accessed September 4, 2015. http://news.sciencemag.org/policy/2014/10/battle-between-nsf-and-house-science-committee-escalates-how-did-it-get-bad.

Mervis, Jeffrey. 2015. "After 2-Year Battle, House Passes COMPETE Act on Mostly Party-Line Vote." *Science Insider*, May 20. Accessed January 5, 2016. http://news.sciencemag.org/funding/2015/05/after-2-year-battle-house-passes-competes-act-mostly-party-line-vote.

Mieczkowski, Yanek. 2013. *The Race for Space and World Prestige: Eisenhower's Sputnik Moment.* Ithaca: Cornell University Press, 2013.

"National Aeronautics and Space Act of 1958." Pub. L. 85-568, 72 Stat. 426. July 29. Accessed April 21, 2016. http://history.nasa.gov/spaceact.html.

National Institutes of Health. 2012. "History of the Public Health Service." January 5. Accessed September 4, 2015. http://www.nlm.nih.gov/exhibition/phs_history/intro.html.

National Science Foundation. 2012. "Federal Funds for Research and Development: Fiscal Years 2009–11." Accessed September 4, 2015. http://www.nsf.gov/statistics/nsf12318/pdf/nsf12318.pdf.

New York Times. 2013. "The War on Cancer: From Nixon until Now." *NYTimes.com*. November 4. Accessed September 4, 2015. http://www.nytimes.com/video/us/100000002530506 /the-war-on-cancer-from-nixon-until-now.html.

Obama, Barack. 2013. "State of the Union Address." Presented to Congress, Washington, DC. January 20. Accessed September 14, 2015. https://www.whitehouse.gov/state-of -the-union-2013.

Patashnik, Eric. 2015. "Here Are the 5 Reasons Republicans Are Trying to Cut Research on Evidence-Based Medicine." *Washington Post*, Monkey Cage blog, June 22. Accessed January 5, 2016. https://www.washingtonpost.com/blogs/monkey-cage/wp/2015/06/22 /here-are-the-5-reasons-republicans-are-trying-to-cut-research-on-evidence-based -medicine/.

Republican National Committee. 2008. Republican Party Platform 2008. Accessed September 24, 2015. http://www.presidency.ucsb.edu/ws/?pid=78545.

Republican National Committee. 2012. "We Believe in America." Republican Party Platform 2012. Accessed September 4, 2015. https://www.gop.com/platform/.

Sack, Kevin, and Robin Toner. 2000. "In Congress, Gore Selected Issues Ready for Prime Time." *New York Times*, August 13. Accessed September 25, 2015. http://partners .nytimes.com/library/politics/camp/081300wh-gore-record.html.

The Science Coalition. 2015. "Mission." Accessed November 4, 2015. http://www .sciencecoalition.org/mission-and-members.

Smith, Lamar. 2014. Correspondence with NSF Director France Cordova, October 29. Accessed September 4, 2015. http://democrats.science.house.gov/sites/democrats.science .house.gov/files/documents/2014%2011%2003%20CLS%20to%20Cordova%20re%20 grant%20request%203.pdf.

Specter, Arlen. 2009. Interview by Bob Schieffer. *CBS News' Face the Nation*, May 3. Accessed September 4, 2015. http://www.cbsnews.com/htdocs/pdf/FTN_050309.pdf.

Toomey, Pat. 2014. "Pennsylvania Leads the Way in Alzheimer's Research." October 16. Accessed November 4, 2015. http://www.toomey.senate.gov/?p=op_ed&id=1429.

Toomey, Pat. 2015. "Toomey's Take: Turning the Tide in the War on Cancer." June 29. Accessed November 4, 2015. http://www.toomey.senate.gov/?p=op_ed&id=1569.

U.S. Department of Health and Human Services. 2014. "Commissioned Core of the U.S. Public Health Service: America's First Responders." September 5. Accessed August 4, 2015. http://www.usphs.gov/aboutus/history.aspx.

U.S. House of Representatives Committee on Science, Space, and Technology. 2014. "Smith: Don't Reward NSF's Frivolous Use of Taxpayer Money with More Money." May 29. Accessed May 1, 2015. https://science.house.gov/news/press-releases/smith -don-t-reward-nsf-s-frivolous-use-taxpayer-money-more-money.

Weigel, David. 2014. "Ben Carson: No Apologies for 1992 Fetal Tissue Research." *Washington Post*, August 13. Accessed November 25, 2015. http://www.washingtonpost.com/news /post-politics/wp/2015/08/13/ben-carson-no-apologies-for-1992-fetal-tissue-research/.

Small Business

At a Glance

Small business reflects the heart of American entrepreneurial spirit, and constitutes an important part of the overall U.S. economic landscape. American small business owners are driven to success, fueled by ingenuity, creativity, and the competitive marketplace of goods and ideas. "Small business" is generally defined as a company, corporation, or partnership with fewer than 500 employees. The Small Business Act states that when business receipts are less than $750,000 per annum or the company is less than three years old, it can qualify as a small business. The definition of small business varies in different countries and in different industries; the scale of small business is much bigger than the moniker "small."

According to the U.S. Department of State, "99 percent of all independent enterprises in the country employ fewer than 500 people. These small enterprises account for 52 percent of all U.S. workers. . . . Some 19.6 million Americans work for companies employing fewer than twenty workers, 18.4 million work for firms employing between twenty and ninety-nine workers, and 14.6 million work for firms with 100 to 499 workers. By contrast, 47.7 million Americans work for firms with 500 or more employees" (U.S. Department of State 2015).

Democrats and Republicans alike support the spirit of small business. Both Democrats and Republicans agree that small businesses are good for Americans and the economy, produce jobs, increase ingenuity and technological advancements, and employ a significant number of Americans. Strong partisan disagreements exist, however, concerning the ways in which the federal government interacts with, supports, and regulates small businesses. The Small Business Administration (SBA) is the primary actor in the relationship between the federal government and American entrepreneurs.

Democrats and Republicans generally agree that the entrepreneurial spirit and economic activity of small businesses are vital to America's economic health. But how does the government facilitate the establishment and growth of new small businesses? Republicans and Democrats disagree about how the federal government influences and interacts with small businesses. Democrats generally support government expenditures to promote small business, whereas Republicans generally discourage SBA loans in favor of tax breaks to help small businesses thrive.

Many Democrats . . .

- Support government assistance to small business through SBA loans, tax breaks, and other measures
- Believe sensible government regulation of small business operations is legitimate and necessary
- Believe small businesses should meet standards of care for employees mandated by government agencies and laws

Many Republicans . . .

- Believe that government regulation of small business is often burdensome and excessive
- Assert that wage and benefit packages for employees should be decided by employers

---

Overview

The Small Business Administration (SBA) was established during the Eisenhower Administration under the Small Business Act. The federal office has a number of functions, including distributing small business loans, protecting small business concerns, and encouraging the success of minority business owners. The SBA provides low interest rate loans to businesses to increase capital. Part of the loan monies is directed toward higher-risk venture projects. The SBA has other functions as well, like pairing retired entrepreneurs with young businesses—a kind of mentorship project aimed at increasing the success of business loan recipients. A smaller function built into the SBA is a quick loan program for business asset recovery in the instance of declared disaster. (Small Business Administration 2015).

There is general acknowledgment that one of the most difficult aspects of launching a new business is acquiring the necessary capital to do so. Therefore, a central component of the Small Business Act was the distribution of business loans to individuals: "The broadening of small business ownership among groups that presently own and control little productive capital is essential to provide for the well-being of this Nation by promoting their increased participation in the free enterprise system of the United States" (Small Business Act 2013, 4–5). In the administrations after Eisenhower, the SBA received widespread support from both Democrats and Republicans, enabling it to grow in scope and influence.

Over time, meanwhile, the act that brought about the creation of the SBA has evolved to include clauses and standards that emphasize the inclusion of minority groups. In other words, the federal government supports the advancement of providing SBA monies to minority small business owners. The Small Business Act and the Small Business Administration acknowledge the role of sexism and racism in the establishment and pursuit of successful business. As the amended Small Business Act of 2013 explicitly stated,

> [O]ver the past two decades there have been substantial gains in the social and economic status of women as they have sought economic equality and independence; despite such progress, women, as a group, are subjected to discrimination in entrepreneurial endeavors due to their gender; such discrimination takes many overt and subtle forms adversely impacting the ability to raise or secure capital, to acquire managerial talents, and to capture market opportunities; it is in the national interest to expeditiously remove discriminatory barriers to the creation and development of small business concerns owned and controlled by women. (Small Business Act 2013, 7)

There are also sections of the act dedicated to its specific functions for Native American and veteran business owners.

Beyond the SBA, there are numerous other laws and regulations that govern how small businesses operate in the United States. These rules and regulations are carried out by a wide assortment of agencies ranging from the federal Occupational Safety and health Administration (OSHA) to state environmental protection agencies. One of the most notable such examples is the 2009 Patient Protection and Affordable Care Act (ACA)—also known as Obamacare—which impacts business practices insofar as it is a regulatory policy outlining rules that businesses must follow (Patient Protection and Affordable Care Act 2010). ACA mandates health insurance, and that burden impacts employers. Democrats and Republicans disagree on the impact the ACA has had on small businesses, with Republicans excoriating the law as a job-killer and Democrats dismissing much of the GOP criticism as cynical partisanship. For its part, the SBA has adopted a middle ground in its assessment of the legislation's impact. "It seems unlikely that the ACA would have a large negative impact on employment," one SBA report indicated in 2013. "However, there have been numerous accounts of employers claiming to reduce employment or adjust hours to avoid the requirements and penalties in the ACA. . . . Some employers claim to have reduced employment because of the provisions of the ACA as soon as its passage in 2010, and many have blamed the ACA for the slow pace of employment growth in the years from 2010–2012. This is not plausible" (Small Business Committee Document 2013).

The Affordable Care Act is intended to protect individuals in the workforce, which Democrats tend to favor. Republicans tend to maintain that this level of interference is not necessary because the health care system will respond to the free market rather than federal interventions. Tax credits provide incentives for the adoption of health insurance programs by small businesses. For instance, "the tax credit created by the 2010 [ACA] will allow certain businesses with fewer than 25 full time employees to get a 50 percent reduction in the cost of providing health coverage. . . . Since 2010, the credit has offered up to 35 percent off health-care costs to all eligible small employers who provide coverage for their workers" (Klein 2013). Republicans discourage mandating what and how employers pay for the health care of their employees whereas Democrats tend to value employee protections and encourage this type of reform. Regardless of the bipartisan debate, the high costs of offering employees health insurance often results in uninsured employees. This is the case more than half of the time for businesses with fewer than 25 employees.

Another law, the Family Medical Leave Act (FMLA), also demonstrates the tension Democrats and Republicans feel about how the federal government interacts with and regulates small businesses. The FMLA stipulates that employers allow up to twelve weeks of leave for any number of family related reasons: birth of a child, care of family member with serious health condition, or any other "qualifying exigency" of an immediate relative (U.S. Department of Labor 2015). The financial burden of such a measure falls on employers, who lose a paid worker for the specified duration. Democrats tend to favor the FMLA because it protects workers. Republicans were largely opposed to FMLA because of party conviction that the government should not regulate the employment policies of business owners in such a heavy-handed manner.

Another interface between the federal government and small businesses lies in the realm of tax incentives and tax breaks. Tax breaks for small businesses might include things like not paying tax on the interest rates for new business-related loans. Small businesses do not generally need to pay taxes on expenses related to marketing and expanding the brand of the business (Reeves 2013). Another instance, from 2010, was an incentive of a $5,000 tax break for each new employee hired (Collins 2010). These are a few examples of incentives for small businesses to seek continued growth, increase their number of permanent jobs, and benefit from federal protections. The Obama administration boasts no fewer than 18 tax breaks for small businesses by 2016 ("Supporting Small Businesses" 2015).

Democrats on Small Business

The policy priorities of Democrats reflect an abiding interest in protecting the rights and economic fortunes of workers—including those employed by small business owners. Nonetheless, Democrats genuinely view themselves as allies of small business owners, especially when it comes to developing policies and programs to help them survive against larger competitors. As the National Democratic Party Platform stated in 2004,

> [S]mall business and entrepreneurs are the lifeblood of our economy. We will encourage small business growth with a plan to make it easier for small businesses to secure capital and loans. We support tax credits and energy investments that slash overall operating costs for small businesses and encourage them to grow and expand here in America. . . . We will help businesses cope with the skyrocketing cost of health care by . . . cutting taxes to help small businesses pay for health insurance . . . we will push for reform so that companies are not forced to choose among retirees, current workers, and their own ability to compete." (Democratic National Committee 2004)

Importantly, Democrats pay special attention to energy credits, green companies, and support growth for small business in 'clean' industries.

A Defense of the Obama Administration
Record on Small Business

In 2012 Karen Mills, administrator of the Small Business Administration (SBA) during President Obama's first term in office, gave a speech at the Democratic National Convention in which she offered a spirited defense of the Obama administration's record on small business during her time at the SBA:

> From day one, President Obama has made small businesses a top priority in his White House—giving them the tools they need to turn their dreams into small businesses, and their small businesses into world-class companies. Giving them help. And then getting out of their way.
>
> President Obama understands that small businesses are the backbone of our economy. After all, half of all Americans who work own or work for a small business. They create two-thirds of all new jobs. Small businesses are a big part of who we are.
>
> When President Obama took office, the economy was in free-fall. Credit was frozen. Small businesses weren't thinking about expansion; they were thinking about survival. The president knew that one of the most important things he could do was give small businesses a fighting chance. So, he took action.
>
> Right away, President Obama cut small business taxes—not once or twice, but 18 times. He put a record volume of guaranteed loans into the hands of America's small businesses. He eliminated pages of burdensome forms and regulations so that small business owners can focus on profits instead of paperwork. He made the federal government pay small business contractors not in 30 days, but in 15 to help entrepreneurs to make their payrolls and buy new equipment. He even gave small businesses a seat at the table in his cabinet . . .
>
> America's entrepreneurs . . . are our greatest asset. And President Obama has delivered for them. He understands that Washington doesn't create jobs; small businesses do. Government's role is to put the wind at their backs. And after the worst economic storm in generations, that's exactly what President Obama is doing—expanding access and opportunity in every corner of all 50 states. And when the American people re-elect President Obama, he will finish the work that he's started because across this country, we know when small businesses succeed, America succeeds.

Source

Daily Kos. Speech Transcript. 2012. "Transcript of Karen Mills Remarks Prepared for Delivery at the Democratic National Convention." Accessed May 1, 2015. http://www.dailykos .com/story/2012/09/06/1128222/-Transcript-of-Karen-Mills-remarks-as-prepared-for -delivery-Democratic-National-Convention.

Democrats maintain skepticism of Republican support for small business. "Democrats say that the Republicans' reputation as an ally of small business is undeserved, and that advocacy for small businesses is really a way of cloaking efforts to help big, wealthy corporate interests" (Herszenhorn and Calmes 2010). Pouring federal dollars into business interests is one strategy to jumpstart economic growth. Democrats suggest Republicans are unwilling to give these dollars to the small businesses that will continue to foster growth and ingenuity in the American economy.

Republicans on Small Business

According to the 2012 Republican Party Platform (Republican National Committee 2012), the GOP's support for small business is exemplified by its opposition to excessive governmental regulations that interfere with those enterprises. The platform expressly states support for the American entrepreneurial spirit: "America's small businesses are the backbone of the U.S. economy, employing tens of millions of workers. Small businesses create the vast majority of jobs, patents, and U.S. exporters. . . . Small businesses are the leaders in the world's advances in technology and innovation, and we pledge to strengthen that role and foster small business entrepreneurship" (Republican National Committee 2012, 2). The Republican Party acknowledges the need to tax businesses, but many GOP lawmakers say that their goal is to reform government regulatory and tax policies in ways that provide fertile soil for small business to grow and prosper.

A Republican Congressman Laments Burdensome Business Regulations

In 2012, Mike Kelly (R-PA) gave a rousing speech in Congress about the price of government regulation of small business. Although not permitted, Republican members of Congress applauded and erupted in chants of "USA!" in response to Kelly's words:

> We renovated a ballpark in my hometown. A guy named Tom Bernadowski—veteran— [spent a] couple million dollars to renovate our ballpark. The day we were gonna open up, I got a call at the dealership. He said, "Mike, would you come down?" I said, "Why? What's going on?" He said, "We're having trouble with the occupancy permit." So I went down to see it. I said, "What's the problem?" . . . "We've got a major problem. You see the mirrors in the restroom are a quarter of an inch too low."
>   "So you can't possibly open that ballpark!

So you want to know the price of regulation? You want to talk about the thousands and thousands of pages that we put on the back of the job creators? You want to talk about creating jobs in America? When you want to see a nation that doesn't want to participate but wants to dominate in the world market, then let them rise! Take the heavy boot off the throat of America's job creators and let them breathe!

The jobs we are talking about are not red jobs or blue jobs. They are red, white, and blue jobs. They are not Democrat jobs or Republican jobs or Independent jobs or Libertarian jobs. They are American jobs!

We are so out of touch with the American people. And you know what all this does? It adds layer after layer after layer of cost. And that cost is ultimately paid for by the American consumer. You want to have more revenues, then let the tide rise for all boats . . . This is not a left or right issue. This is an American issue.

Source

Kelly, Mike. 2012. U.S. House: Federal Regulations & Unemployment. July 26. Accessed on May 1, 2015. https://www.youtube.com/watch?v=F1YQDjpuY_U.

Because the platform is a broad-based ideological document, it does not include explanations for how to accomplish these tasks. Different leaders have different ideas about what tax reform, decreased regulations, and advocacy mean. Republicans tend to support movement away from government loans, shrinking the SBA, and reducing government regulations of small businesses, whereas Democrats tend to support increased government intervention and regulatory control.

Grant Walsh-Haines

Further Reading

Collins, Michael. 2010. "Republicans' Reactions Mixed to Small Business Tax Breaks." *Knoxville News Sentinel*, February 15. Accessed May 1, 2015. http://www.knoxnews.com/business/republicans-reactions-mixed-to-small-business.

Democratic National Committee. 2004. "Strong at Home, Respected in the World: 2004 Democratic National Platform." Accessed May 1, 2015. http://www.ontheissues.org/Dem_Platform_2004.htm.

Herszenhorn, David, and Jackie Calmes. 2010. "Obama Trumpets Democrats' Small-Business Bona Fides." *New York Times*, July 28. Accessed May 1, 2015. http://www.nytimes.com/2010/07/29/us/politics/29cong.html?_r=0.

Klein, Karen. 2013. "Explaining Obamacare's Baffling Tax Breaks for Small Businesses." *Bloomberg Business*, March 22. Accessed May 1, 2015. http://www.bloomberg.com/bw/articles/2013-03-22/explaining-obamacares-baffling-tax-breaks-for-small-business.

Patient Protection and Affordable Care Act. 42 U.S.C. § 18001 (2010).

Reeves, Jeff. 2013. "5 Tax Breaks for Small Business Owners." *USA Today*, March 14. Accessed May 1, 2015. http://www.usatoday.com/story/money/personalfinance/2013/03/14/taxes-entrepreneur-irs-small-business-tips/1987289.

Republican National Committee. 2012. "We Believe in America: 2012 Republican National Platform." Accessed May 11, 2015. https://cdn.gop.com/docs/2012GOPPlatform.pdf.

Small Business Act. PL 112-239. (enacted January 3, 2013). Accessed November 6, 2015. https://www.sba.gov/content/small-business-act.

Small Business Administration. 2015. Accessed May 1, 2015. http://www.sba.gov.

Small Business Committee Document 113-040. 2013. "The Effects of the Health Law's Definitions of Full-Time Employee on Small Businesses." Hearing before the Subcommittee on Health and Technology of the Committee on Small Business. United States House of Representatives. 113th Congress, 1st Session. (October 9, 2013). Accessed May 1, 2015. http://www.fdsys.gov.

"Supporting Small Businesses." 2015. The White House. Accessed September 1. https://www.whitehouse.gov/economy/business/small-business.

U.S. Department of Labor. 2015. Wage and Hour Division, Fact Sheet: "The Family and Medical Leave Act," Accessed May 1, 2015. http://www.dol.gov/whd/regs/compliance/whdfs28.pdf.

U.S. Department of State. 2015. "Small Business in the United States." Accessed May 1, 2015. http://economics.about.com/od/smallbigbusiness/a/us_business.htm.

Social Security

At a Glance

The preamble of the Social Security Acts delineates its purposes as

> An act to provide for the general welfare by establishing a system of Federal old-age benefits, and by enabling the several States to make more adequate provision for aged persons, blind persons, dependent and crippled children, maternal and child welfare, public health, and the administration of their unemployment compensation laws; to establish a Social Security Board; to raise revenue; and for other purposes. (Social Security Administration 1997, para. 1)

Each year the Board of Trustees for the Social Security Trust Fund releases a report on the long-term financial outlook of the Social Security system. Projections on the program's financial stability and future solvency are based on a number of economic and demographic factors in American society, including birth and death rates, immigration, as well as wage levels and the rates of employment. According to the Social Security Board of Trustees, program finances in 2012 reflected a surplus of $54.4 billion, with trust fund income reported to be $840.2 billion and payments at $785.8 billion (Social Security and Medicare Boards of Trustees, 2013a). However, the most recent actuarial reports predict that the growing disparity in the ratio of workers to retirees will result in long-term deficits to the Social Security Trust Fund. The program has been running a deficit in terms of payroll taxes paid into the system, with full benefits being covered by other sources such as interest from trust fund investments. Without some form of concerted action, future beneficiaries will receive only 75 percent of scheduled benefits by the year 2033 (Reno and Walker 2012). This projection, while concerning, is a marked contrast to ominous predictions that the system was fast-approaching bankruptcy, as stated by Republican President George W. Bush during his 2005 State of the Union address (*Washington Post* 2005). Nevertheless, according to a summary of the 2014 trustees report, "[n]either Medicare nor Social Security can sustain projected long-run program costs in full under currently scheduled financing, and legislative changes are necessary to avoid disruptive consequences for beneficiaries and taxpayers (Social Security and Medicare Board of Trustees 2013b, para. 2). Trustee recommendations have urged making necessary changes to the system sooner, rather than having to make major modifications abruptly due to imminent crisis.

However, the nature of the changes to be made remains an issue of contention between the major political parties. Despite stated support for Social Security among Democrats and Republicans alike, each party has proposed fundamentally different solutions for projected funding shortfalls that reflect their political values and philosophy. The primary issue of contention surrounding current debates has highlighted proposals to privatize some aspects of the Social Security system.

Many Republicans . . .

- Believe that privatizing Social Security would modernize an outdated system that does not account for demographic changes in American society
- Assert that Social Security privatization would provide younger workers with greater autonomy over their retirement decisions and yield higher benefits through market investments
- Oppose shoring up Social Security finances through tax increases
- Encourage individual savings and responsibility for retirement
- Say that raising the eligibility age for Social Security should be considered

Many Democrats . . .

- View Social Security as one of the most successful social insurance programs in American history
- Assert that privatization would place the financial security of older adults at the mercy of volatile financial markets
- Contend that there is no immediate crisis in the system's ability to pay current beneficiaries
- Say that tax increases on corporations and the wealthy, modest adjustments in benefits, and reductions in government expenditures in other areas like defense are all capable of addressing funding shortfalls in the Social Security system
- Oppose raising the eligibility age for Social Security benefits

---

Overview

Actuarial projections from the Social Security Trustees predict a future deficit of 2.72 percent in payroll taxes to the Social Security system. Excluding the interest from Treasury securities, the Trust Fund is reported to be running at a deficit in terms of payroll taxes going into the system since 2010. Consequently, one recommendation for resolving the deficit is to increase payroll taxes from its current level of 6.2 percent to 7.7 percent. A report from the Congressional Budget Office noted that in recent years incomes among the highest earners in the labor market have grown, yet the cap on taxable wages for Social Security has not increased, covering only 83 percent of all earnings in 2011. By increasing the cap to $177,500, 90 percent of all earnings would be attained, and add $470 billion to the Social Security system (Congressional Budget Office 2013). However, concerns over raising the income cap on payroll taxes have been raised regarding the potential negative impact on incentives to work. Nuschler (2012) pointed out that while Social Security recipients have historically received more in benefits than they actually paid into the system, this may not be the case for future beneficiaries due to increases in payroll taxes and the rising retirement age. Moreover, such changes may be seen as fundamentally changing the model and original intent of Social Security from a contributory system, to a system of income redistribution. Other proposals for resolving the trust fund deficit include raising the age of eligibility for receiving full benefits, lowering benefit levels, raising the cap on taxable wages, or some combination of all of the above.

Despite increased debate in recent years regarding the financial stability of the Social Security system, it may not be common knowledge that the program has faced financial shortfalls in the past. Trust fund deficits and the diminishing value of benefits due to inflation led to system modifications in both Democratic and Republican administrations in the 1970s and 1980s (Kollmann 1996). In 1977, during the Carter administration, the 95th Congress passed legislation increasing Social Security taxes. Similarly, in 1983 the 98th Congress raised payroll taxes and increased the age of retirement during the Reagan administration. These changes enabled beneficiaries to receive full payment of scheduled payments, in addition to generating a trust fund surplus that could be invested in treasury securities to offset future deficits. However, despite overcoming funding challenges in the past, surveys suggest that increasing numbers of Americans are losing faith in Social Security as a source of economic support in old age (Nuschler 2012).

Since its inception in 1935 as one of the major pieces of legislation from Democratic President Franklin D. Roosevelt's "New Deal," Social Security has evolved into one of the most popular and enduring social insurance programs in American history. The system's evolution has paralleled significant declines in the rate of poverty among older adults (Engelhardt and Gruber 2003). Republicans and Democrats alike have praised the program's effectiveness, from George W. Bush describing Social Security as "the single most successful program in government history" (PBS Newshour 2000) to Hillary Clinton extolling it as "one of the greatest inventions of American democracy" (Clinton 2006, para. 13). Its success and popular support among the general public make discussion regarding any modification to the system frequently contentious. Often called the third rail of American politics, major change to Social Security has long been seen as politically unfeasible by Republicans and Democrats alike. Indeed, over its history legislators have been more inclined to expand rather than limit eligibility and income; extending benefits to widows and dependent children, agricultural and domestic workers, and the addition of disability insurance and cost-of-living adjustments (McSteen 1985).

The Social Security system comprises two distinct trust funds: Old Age and Survivors Insurance (OASI) and Disability Insurance (DI), managed through the U.S. Department of Treasury. Despite their distinction as separate funds, OASI and DI are generally referred to jointly as the Social Security Trust Fund (Social Security Administration 2015b). In addition to payroll taxes, benefits and administrative costs of the system are financed through federal taxes on benefits among higher income beneficiaries, and interest from trust fund investments in Treasury Securities. Recipient benefits, or primary insurance amount (PIA), are not only based on earnings, but are also indexed to current national average wage levels to account for changes in the cost of living over the recipient's work history.

America's Social Security system was established as a contributory system in which beneficiaries must pay into the system for forty quarters to receive benefits, the amount of which is based on the recipient's wage history. Under the auspices of the Federal Insurance Contributions Act (FICA), employees and their employers contribute to the Social Security Trust Fund via payroll taxes. The combined payments total 12.4 percent of wages, with a cap on wages above $118,500 (Walker, Reno, and Bethell 2013; Social Security Administration 2015a). However, the original objective of America's Social Security system was not to provide universal coverage. Instead, according to Iams and Purcell (2013) in a report in the "Social Security Bulletin," the program was intended as merely one aspect of economic security for older adults, in addition to other sources such as job pensions, personal assets and savings. Nevertheless, according to recent estimates, 65 percent of total recipients receive nearly half or more of their income from Social Security, and 36 percent received 90 percent or more of their total income from the system.

The variance in pension systems around the world reflects the diverse values and political philosophies regarding social welfare in general, and old age pensions in particular. Pensions may be designed as non-contributory systems, in which guaranteed entitlements are drawn from general taxes and available to all citizens regardless of work history or financial contribution. Conversely, the contributory systems in which benefits are based on years worked and earning levels, are conceptualized as a means to mitigate poverty when a person can is no longer able to work due to advanced age. This difference mirrors the fundamental distinction between Republican and Democratic philosophies regarding Social Security. While both parties support some form of old-age pension, each party's underlying philosophy ultimately informs the purpose and structure of the pension system.

From the perspective of the Democratic Party, Social Security represents a social compact between the generations to ensure citizens a level of security and dignity in old age. According to this perspective, citizens are entitled to financial stability and a decent standard of living regardless of their socioeconomic status. As such, this view is more closely aligned with the universal basic income model, defined by Philippe Van Parijs (2003) as "an income paid by a political community to all its members on an individual basis, without means test or work requirement" (p. 8). Reflecting this outlook, a report from the Center for American Progress argued that wage stagnation among middle-class workers has contributed to the potential insolvency of the Social Security system; had middle-class wages kept pace with productivity the system would have benefited by higher payroll tax contributions relative to higher wages (Vallas et al. 2015). In addition, the Center cited the advantage to women and minorities who often receive higher benefits relative to what they pay into the system. However, this form of compensation for a history of low-wage employment is often assailed as income redistribution by economic conservatives and free market advocates, more often reflecting Republican Party beliefs. Republican philosophy is generally opposed to increased taxes and policies that promote income redistribution, or the transfer of wealth from some members of society to other members.

An important point in the Social Security debate is the immediacy, and thus the urgency, of a genuine crisis. In contrast to the congressional changes legislated during the 1970s and 1980s, in which financing problems were anticipated to occur within months, current projections predict trust fund solvency until 2033. Consequently, President Obama has challenged assertions that the Social Security system must undergo immediate and dramatic change to offset an imminent emergency. Nevertheless, Nuschler (2012) points out that recent discussion regarding Social Security differs from previous debates in the current calls among some critics—Republicans, for the most part—for fundamental transformation of the system. Transformation is justified by Republican advocates such as Paul Ryan (2012), who view the system as an outdated, Depression-era model that has limited relevancy given the economic and demographic changes to American society since the 1930s.

Republicans on Social Security

In March of 2015 congressional Republicans on the House Budget Committee released their Budget Resolution report for FY 2016. The report called attention to the "fragile" state of the Social Security system, noting that current benefits are exceeding payroll taxes. Referring to "structural deficiencies" within the system, the committee called for a bipartisan committee to address the anticipated insolvency of Social Security and provide recommendations for legislative reforms to Congress and the President (U.S. House of Representatives, House Budget Committee 2015, 21–22). Citing the need to maintain the integrity of the program the Budget Resolution indicated no intent toward major modification of Social Security. Indeed, a review of major Republican candidates and their positions on Social Security suggests it would be inaccurate to claim that the official party position advocates fundamental change or privatization of the system.

The Republican base has been identified as being comprised primarily of older, white, and working-class voters. As a group, these voters have traditionally been committed to maintaining Social Security as it is, seeing the system as an entitlement they have paid into with the expectation of financial support in their retirement. Despite this, prominent Republicans have endorsed program modifications, such as raising the retirement age and/or giving younger workers the option of investing a percentage of their payroll taxes in the financial markets.

Nonetheless, Republicans eager to make changes to Social Security have to tread carefully lest they do political damage to themselves (Roaty and Bland 2015). For example, when Republican Governor Rick Perry of Texas described Social Security as a "Ponzi scheme" (Weiner 2011, para. 6) in the 2012 presidential debates for the Republican nomination, it was viewed as a major blunder that played a significant role in Perry's loss of support among Republican voters. Similarly, 2016 Republican presidential candidate Jeb Bush strongly denied allegations that he favored cutting Social Security. Bush's 1994 candidacy for Florida state governor was impacted by automated telephone calls from the campaign of his Democratic opponent making claims to this effect, and he ultimately lost the race for governor by a narrow margin of votes (Koch 2006; McCormack 2010). While Republican Senator Marco Rubio of Florida has asserted that the Social Security system is on the verge of bankruptcy, he dismissed privatization as a viable option, writing in the *Wall Street Journal* that the option for "[p]rivatization of the accounts has come and gone" (Levy 2010, para. 13).

GOP Congressman Paul Ryan Discusses the Solvency of Social Security

In 2012 Congressman Paul Ryan (R-WI), who was House Budget Committee chairman at the time, summarized Republican concerns regarding the future solvency of the Social Security system, conveying the tone of crisis that frequently accompanies calls for modifying the current system:

> Social Security's trust funds will be exhausted by 2036. [The current] combination of policies—raid, ration, raise taxes, and deny the problem—will mean painful benefit cuts for current seniors and huge tax increases on younger working families, robbing them of the opportunity to save for their own retirements. And it will mean that those pledges of future health and retirement security that the government is currently making to younger families are nothing but empty promises. Unless government acts, Social Security will remain threatened for current seniors and will not be there for younger families. It is morally unconscionable for elected leaders to cling to an unsustainable status quo with respect to America's health and retirement security programs. Current seniors and future generations deserve better than empty promises. Current retirees deserve the benefits around which they organized their lives. Future generations deserve health and retirement security they can count on.

Source

Ryan, Paul. 2012. *The Path to Prosperity: A Blueprint for American Renewal: Fiscal Year 2013*. Accessed November 17, 2015. http://budget.house.gov/fy2013prosperity/.

In 2012 Mitt Romney emphasized his commitment to maintaining the Social Security system as a primary responsibility of the federal government, but stated his willingness to consider changes such as raising the retirement age and lowering cost-of-living adjustments for higher income recipients. However, Romney and vice-presidential candidate Paul Ryan also proposed allowing current wage earners to invest a percentage of their payroll taxes into individual accounts consisting of "a combination of stocks and bonds" (Romney 2010, 160). The candidates contended that this option would offer beneficiaries higher returns, while benefiting the overall economy through private sector investment. Significantly these proposals usually suggest directing only a portion of payroll taxes into individual accounts, rather than full privatization. A similar recommendation was offered by Republican Senator John McCain when he was a candidate for president in the 2000 Republican primaries, and later proposed by Newt Gingrich. However, Gingrich argued that the success of individual retirement accounts invested in financial markets would eventually allow workers the option to substitute personal accounts for *all* of their retirement benefits (Gingrich and DeSantis 2010).

Following his reelection in 2004, George W. Bush chose to expend political capital on reforming the Social Security system. His reform plan would have allowed younger workers the option of allocating 2 to 4 percent of payroll taxes that would normally go into the Social Security system into individual retirement accounts. However, neither Republicans nor Democrats ultimately supported the plan. In his autobiography Bush referred to his failure to modify the Social Security system as "one of the greatest disappointments of my presidency" (Bush 2010, 300).

Democrats on Social Security

Democrats have often been identified as "the creators and defenders of Social Security" (Miller 2015, para. 8). During the 2000 presidential election, Democratic candidate Al Gore spoke for most in his party when he stated, "Social Security isn't supposed to be a system of winners and losers. It's supposed to be a bedrock guarantee of a minimum decent retirement" (2015c, para. 14). Referring to the program as a social compact between the generations, Gore emphasized the party's position on maintaining the program without changes to the system that might adversely affect the most vulnerable elders. Moreover, Gore advocated expanding Social Security benefits to widows and parents who take time out of the workforce (and consequently lower average earnings calculated in their Social Security benefits upon retirement) to raise children.

Despite contentions that the Social Security system is not in any immediate crisis, Democratic candidates have also recognized potential solvency issues with the Social Security system over the long-term and have advanced various proposals to address these issues. During a 2008 primary debate with Barack Obama, then–Senator Hillary Clinton asked for a bipartisan commission similar to the committee assembled during the Reagan administration in 1983, asserting the need to bring both parties together in a working group to address projected funding deficits in the future. As noted, this recommendation was later echoed by congressional Republicans on the House Budget Committee in 2015. However, Clinton has consistently opposed any form of participation or involvement between Social Security funds and financial markets, in contrast to the recommendations of the Social Security Advisory Board (1997) during her husband's presidency. Further, she argued that any modification to COLAS, even delaying increases for a period of months, could potentially harm the most vulnerable elders. In 2008 Hillary Clinton also voiced opposition to lifting the cap on payroll taxes, suggesting that such a move could hurt some middle-class workers, and argued instead for focusing on fiscal responsibility regarding the federal deficits incurred during the presidencies of George W. Bush, before the Social Security solvency issues could be addressed. Reflecting the Democratic position, other options for sustaining Social Security have engendered debate. Calls for raising the age to receive full eligibility have been criticized on the grounds that wealthier persons are more likely to live longer and are more likely to reap the benefits of such a change. In addition, it has been argued that simply raising the age at which recipients can receive full benefits may have negligible effects on the long-term solvency of the system, given that older adults may experience physical disabilities as they age making them eligible for disability insurance. In addition, the DI Trust Fund is projected to be exhausted by 2016. Proposals by congressional Republicans to prohibit shifting funds from the OASI Trust Fund to the DI Trust Fund to make up for deficits are viewed by some Democrats as a move toward cutting Social Security benefits and cost-of-living-adjustments (Miller 2015).

Like his Republican counterparts, President Obama has raised concerns regarding the long-term stability of the Social Security system, while disputing the perception that the system is in "crisis" (Obama 2006). However, during the 2008 presidential election he distinguished his position by emphasizing his opposition to suggestions to raise the retirement age or cut benefits (National Cable Satellite Corporation 2008).

Cost-of-living adjustments to Social Security benefits are based on rates of inflation in goods and services as indicated by the consumer price index (CPI). This measure has come under criticism as an accurate measure of inflation, with some suggesting that using the chained CPI would more accurately reflect consumer spending. The chained CPI indicates how consumers modify spending due to increases in prices, and generally reflects lower levels of inflation. Consequently, employing the chained CPI would result in lower cost-of-living adjustments in Social Security benefits. President Obama has indicated a willingness to consider using the chained CPI for calculating COLAS. However, critics of such a plan warn that the chained CPI does not reflect the spending of older adults, who often cannot modify their spending on necessities such as medications and other healthcare related items.

President Obama's Prescription for Preserving Social Security

Presidential candidate Barack Obama has acknowledged the need to address the long-term financial stability of the system, while denying immediate crisis. In contrast to Republican plans, Obama has identified increasing taxes on the wealthiest Americans as a reasonable approach to address funding shortfalls in the Social Security system:

> I think that lifting the [payroll tax] cap is probably going to be the best option. Now we've got to have a process [like the one] back in 1983. We need another one. And I think I've said before everything should be on the table. My personal view is that lifting the cap is much preferable to the other options that are available. But what's critical is to recognize that there is a potential problem: young people who don't think Social Security is going to be there for them. We should be willing to do anything that will strengthen the system, to make sure that that we are being true to those who are already retired, as well as young people in the future. And we should reject things that will weaken the system, including privatization, which essentially is going to put people's retirement at the whim of the stock market.

Source

Obama, Barack H. 2007. "2007 Democratic Primary Debate at Dartmouth College." September 6. Accessed May 5, 2015. http://www.ontheissues.org/2016/Barack_Obama_Social_Security.htm.

Notwithstanding general acknowledgment of the potential financial deficits facing the system, some Democratic candidates have called for expanding Social Security benefits through increased taxes and raising the cap on wages. Consistently, Democratic candidates have reflected the primary party position opposed to directing any portion of Social Security funds toward any form of stock market participation. While the stock market generally surpasses cost-of-living adjustments in Social Security, as Obama noted, the market is made up of winners and losers. This reality presents a gamble that is viewed as contrary to the spirit and intent of Social Security. Democrats have offered plans to encourage retirement savings, while maintaining the Social Security system as it is. President Obama's Working Families Savings Account proposed a 50 percent tax credit to persons earning up to $50,000 a year who contribute to retirement plans such as an IRA. Similarly, presidential candidate Al Gore advocated a program referred to as "Social Security Plus," in which middle- and lower-income workers could direct money to retirement accounts similar to a 401(k), which would be matched by the government in tax credits. However, critics argued that this proposal amounted to simply another federal entitlement that would do little to resolve the long-term solvency issues of Social Security, and further contribute to the federal deficit.

Mark D. Olson

Further Reading

Bush, George W. *Decision Points*. 2010. New York: Crown Publishers.

Clinton, Hillary R. 2006. "Social Security: New York 2006 Senate Debate." October 22. Accessed May 5, 2015. http://www.ontheissues.org/2016/Hillary_Clinton_Social_Security.htm.

Congressional Budget Office. 2013. "Options for Reducing the Deficit: 2014 to 2023. Increase the Maximum Taxable Earnings for the Social Security Payroll Tax," November 13. Accessed July 26, 2015. https://www.cbo.gov/budget-options/2013/44811.

Engelhardt, Gary V., and Jonathan Gruber. 2003. "Social Security and the Evolution of Elderly Poverty." Paper presented at the Berkeley Symposium on Poverty, the Distribution of Income, and Public Policy, University of California, Berkeley, December 12. Accessed March 5, 2015. http://www.nber.org/papers/w10466.

Gingrich, Newt, and Joe DeSantis. 2010. *To Save America: Stopping Obama's Secular-socialist Machine*. Washington, DC: Regnery Pub.

Iams, Howard M., and Patrick J. Purcell. 2013. "The Impact of Retirement Account Distributions on Measures of Family Income." *Social Security Bulletin* 73 (2). Accessed June 5, 2015. http://www.ssa.gov/policy/docs/ssb/v73n2/v73n2p77.html.

Koch, Doro Bush. 2006. *My Father, My President: A Personal Account of the Life of George H. W. Bush*. New York: Warner Books.

Kollmann, Geoffrey. 1996. *Summary of Major Changes in the Social Security Cash Benefits Program: 1935–1996*. CRS Report 94-36 EPW. Washington, DC: Congressional Research Service.

Levy, Collin. 2015. "The Conscience of a Florida Conservative". *Wall Street Journal*. March 13, 2010. Accessed May 23. http://www.wsj.com/articles/SB10001424052748703915204575103503780254366.

McCormack, John. 2010. "Jeb Bush Rips Crist's Social Security Attack." October 5. *The Weekly Standard*. Accessed June 2, 2015. http://www.weeklystandard.com/blogs/jeb-bush-rips-crists-social-security-attack_500819.html.

McSteen, Martha A. 1985. "Fifty Years of Social Security." Social Security Bulletin 48 (): 36–44.

Miller, Mark. 2015. "Defending Social Security: Next on Obama's To-Do-List?" *Reuters*, January 8. Accessed July 25, 2015. http://www.reuters.com/article/2015/01/08/us-column-miller retirement-idUSKBN0KH1U220150108#D7kqmozSWXAKlIgZ.97.

National Cable Satellite Corporation. 2008. "Barack Obama to AARP." *Cable-Satellite Public Affairs Network (C-SPAN)*. September 6. Accessed November 10, 2015. http://www.c-span.org/video/?280932-1/barack-obama-aarp.

Nuschler, Dawn. 2012. *Social Security Reform: Current Issues and Legislation*. CRS Report No. RL33544. Washington, DC: Congressional Research Service.

Obama, Barack H. 2006. *The Audacity of Hope: Thoughts on Reclaiming the American Dream*. New York: Crown Publishers.

PBS News Hour. "George W. Bush on Social Security, May 15, 2000." Accessed March 24, 2016. http://www.pbs.org/newshour/bb/health-jan-june00-socsec_bush/.

Reno, Virginia, and Elisa Walker. 2012. "Social Security Benefits, Finances, and Policy Options: A Primer." Washington, DC: National Academy of Social Insurance. Accessed May 20, 2015. http://asi.syr.edu/wp-content/uploads/2012/06/NASI_Social_Security_Primer_PDF.pdf.

Roarty, Alex, and Scott Bland. 2015. "Republicans' Big Gamble on Social Security." *National Journal*, April 21. Accessed May 15, 2015. http://www.nationaljournal.com/2016-elections/republicans-big-gamble-on-social-security-20150421.

Romney, Mitt. 2010. *No Apology: The Case for American Greatness*. New York: St. Martin's Press.

Ryan, Paul. *The Path to Prosperity: A Blueprint for American Renewal: Fiscal Year 2013 Budget Resolution*. Washington, DC: Congressional Budget Office, 2012. Accessed May 22, 2015. http://www.ontheissues.org/2016/Paul_Ryan_Social_Security.htm.

Social Security Administration. 2015a. "Benefits Planner: Maximum Taxable Earnings (1937–2015)." *SSA.gov*. Accessed June 25. http://ssa.gov/planners/maxtax.html.

Social Security Administration. 2015b. "Frequently Asked Questions about the Social Security Trust Funds." *SSA.gov*. Accessed June 20. https://www.ssa.gov/OACT/ProgData /fundFAQ.html#a0=0.

Social Security Administration. 2015c. "Social Security Act of 1935: Preamble." *SSA.gov*. Accessed June 25. http://www.ssa.gov/history/35act.html#PREAMBLE.

Social Security Administration. 1997. "1994-96 Advisory Council Report: Findings, Recommendations and Statements." Reports and Studies. *SSA.gov*. Accessed June 26. http://www.ssa.gov/history/reports/adcouncil/report/findings.htm#option2.

Social Security and Medicare Boards of Trustees. 2013a. "Annual Report of the Board of Trustees of the Federal Old-Age and Survivors Insurance and Federal Disability Insurance Trust Funds." Washington, DC: Social Security Administration. Accessed November 9, 2015. https://www.socialsecurity.gov/OACT/TR/2013/tr2013.pdf.

Social Security and Medicare Boards of Trustees. 2013b. "Status of the Social Security and Medicare Programs: A Summary of the 2013 Annual Reports." Accessed May 25, 2015. https://www.socialsecurity.gov/oact/TRSUM/2013/tr13summary.pdf.

U.S. House of Representatives, House Budget Committee. 2015. *FY 2016 Budget Resolution: A Balanced Budget for a Stronger America*. March. Accessed July 17, 2015. http://budget .house.gov/uploadedfiles/fy16budget.pdf.

Vallas, Rebecca, Christian E. Weller, Rachel West, and Jackie Odum. 2015. "The Effect of Rising Inequality on Social Security." *The Center for American Progress*. February. Accessed July 1, 2015. https://cdn.americanprogress.org/wp-content/uploads/2015/02 /SocialSecurity-brief3.pdf.

Van de Water, Paul N. 2014. "Understanding the Social Security Trust Funds." *Center on Budget and Policy Priorities*. Washington, DC: August 17. Accessed July 10, 2015. http://www.cbpp.org/sites/default/files/atoms/files/10-5-10socsec.pdf.

Van Parijs, Philippe. 2003. "Basic Income: A Simple and Powerful Idea for the 21st Century." In *Redesigning Distribution: Basic Income and Stakeholder Grants as Alternative Cornerstones for a More Egalitarian Capitalism*, edited by Erik Olin Wright, 4–39. The Real Utopias Project, Volume V. London: Verso Books, Accessed July 30, 2015. https:// www.kcl.ac.uk/aboutkings/principal/dean/akc/archivedhandouts/general/docs07-08 /Autumn/basicincome.pdf.

Walker, Elisa A., Virginia P. Reno, and Thomas N. Bethell. "Social Security Finances: Findings of the 2013 Trustees Report." Washington, DC: National Academy of Social Insurance, 2013.

Washington Post. 2005 "Text of President Bush's 2005 State of the Union Address." *Washington Post*, February 2. Accessed November 8, 2015. http://www.washingtonpost .com/wp-srv/politics/transcripts/bushtext_020205.html.

Weiner, Rachel. 2011. "Rick Perry repeats Social Security is 'Ponzi scheme' statement." *Washington Post*, September 7. Accessed November 10, 2015. https://www.washingtonpost .com/blogs/the-fix/post/rick-perry-and-mitt-romney-come-out-swinging-in-reagan -debate/2011/09/07/gIQAhygcAK_blog.html.

Stimulus Spending

At a Glance

In 1993 Democratic President Clinton signed a major stimulus package—a set of economic measures designed to boost employment and spending—in order to jumpstart the moribund American economy. The cost of his controversial stimulus plan, passed by Democratic majorities in Congress over the objections of the GOP, was calculated at $16.3 billion (approximately $26.57 in 2016 dollars). Clinton's controversial 1993 plan, however, was dwarfed by stimulus actions taken by the Bush and Obama administrations in 2008 and 2009, respectively, when America was grappling with the worst economic downturn since the Great Depression.

In 2008, Republican President George W. Bush signed into law the first stimulus package for the American economy in 15 years. He did this in response to the Great Recession, a dramatic economic downturn that began in late 2007 with a crash in the housing market and the related collapse of several major commercial and investment banks. This intervention by a Republican president was surprising on many levels. First, the sheer size and speed of the stimulus, which was supported by a majority of congressional Democrats as well as 133 Republican representatives and 33 Republican senators, surprised many. Second, the action, undertaken at the behest of the Federal Reserve Board of Governors, violated some fundamental tenets of conservative economic theory. To many, seeing a Republican president intervene so aggressively was shocking. Stimulus supporters, however, asserted that the severity of the economic downturn was so great that governmental intervention was essential. Bush's 2008 package included $152 billion in targeted governmental funds that focused primarily on the financial services industry and on modest tax cuts for families and businesses.

Roughly a year later, with the economy still floundering, newly elected Democratic President Barack Obama and his fellow Democrats passed (with no GOP support this time) a more comprehensive additional package with an $862 billion price tag.

Both of these actions highlighted the differences in party orientation toward stimulating economic recovery (Calmes 2009). In many respects, the law passed during the Bush administration represented a violation of party ideology regarding government intervention in markets. The great potential for a systemic failure in the financial markets compelled many congressional Republicans to act. Much of the potential for widespread market failure comes from the complex and interconnected nature of modern securities markets. The concentration of assets and insurance in key institutions such as American International Group (AIG) led to political concern that if these institutions failed, so could many more firms with greater amounts of assets (Financial Crisis Inquiry Commission 2011).

The politics of stimulus spending represents an interesting example of the intersection of policy practicality and political ideology. This is especially true when it concerns billions of dollars in stimulus money designed to be quickly infused into the economy to avoid potential economic disaster. After the fact, there are always challenges with accountability and the decisions that were made to distribute stimulus funds, to say nothing of disputes about the effectiveness of said stimulus measures.

Nevertheless, with occasional economic recessions a predictable part of the American business cycle, stimulus spending is likely to remain a controversial and highly partisan political issue for the foreseeable future (Young 2013).

Many Democrats . . .

- Believe that stimulus spending is a legitimate policy tool, given the inherent volatility of the business cycle
- Favor stimulus measures targeted at both individuals and commercial firms
- Contend that Obama's 2009 stimulus package steered the U.S. economy away from economic ruin

Many Republicans . . .

- Believe that limited and targeted stimulus spending can stabilize markets until consumer spending can recover
- Assert that stimulus packages are often wasteful of taxpayer dollars
- Dismiss the idea that Obama's 2009 stimulus package helped get America back on sound financial footing

---

Overview

The process of spending to bolster financial institutions was in contrast to some of the earlier firms that, while sizable, were allowed to fail. Most notable of these failed firms was the financial company, Bear Stearns. While Republicans were not overly concerned about allowing one firm to fail, when faced with the possibility of many firms failing, congressional Republicans acted (Burrough 2008).

Democrats, on the other hand, acted more broadly to save not only financial firms but also large employers in other industries. In addition to passing a major stimulus package that paid for major new investments in roads, clean energy, and other infrastructure, the Democrats also acted to save two major domestic automakers, General Motors and Chrysler, from bankruptcy. While many congressional Republicans argued that an automobile company should not be the recipient of government funds, many Democrats countered that General Motors was a key employer and wealth creator with many more industries acting as suppliers and retailers contingent upon the corporation (Frizell 2014).

The basis for the broader interventions of the Democratic Party in the affairs of commercial firms resides in some of the fundamental economic perspectives based on the works of John Maynard Keynes. This "Keynesian" perspective argues for aggressive governmental interventions to mitigate the volatility of the business cycle. In its most basic form, Keynesian economics calls for the redistribution of money to firms and individuals to stimulate continued economic growth (Keynes 2008).

Republican orthodoxy, based on the theories and writings of Friedrich Von Hayek and Milton Friedman, originally called for minimal intervention in market corrections that are a part of the traditional business cycle. However, many contemporary Republicans believed that to weather the recession that began in late 2007, some stimulus spending was necessary. Their perspective on stimulus spending appeared to change dramatically after Bush, a member of their own party, was succeeded by a Democrat. But the GOP insisted that the shift was due more to opposition to the specific elements and large size of Obama's plan than to partisanship.

Nowadays, Republicans distinguish themselves from Democrats largely based on when, not whether, stimulus spending is appropriate. Republicans seek targeted stimulus spending that focuses on large financial firms. This acts, in their view, to stabilize the markets until tax cuts and other more fiscally conservative policy options allow for a more comprehensive recovery (Friedman 1962).

Democrats on Stimulus Spending

Democrats tend to be less reticent about using government funds to stimulate the economy. Debates within the Democratic Party usually relate to what type of stimulus package is most effective in achieving policy goals. Keynesian stimulus packages are consumer-oriented rather than business-focused. There are three general types of stimulus packages that Democrats tend to support. The first focuses on stimulating consumer spending by getting more money into the hands of consumers via tax cuts and other measures. The second type of intervention focuses on the federal government purchasing goods and services such as making infrastructure improvements, business process investments, and funding long-overdue capital projects. The third intervention relies on funding from state and local governments and their subsequent purchase of goods and services (Cogan and Taylor 2011).

In 1993, President Clinton's stimulus package was focused on restarting the economy in the short-term and consistent economic growth over the long term. It focused in large part on education and infrastructure projects. However, the scale of the plan was very small when compared to the subsequent Bush and Obama economic stimulus packages.

President Obama's 2009 stimulus package included a combination of tax cuts and federal spending on infrastructure and industry revitalization at both the national and state level. There was considerable variation in the impact that these projects had on local economies. Researchers found a relationship between the allocation of the Obama stimulus package and whether or not there was a strong union presence or a high unemployment rate in the state. In states with high employment rates and a greater union presence, there are likely to be larger numbers of people who would benefit from the types of government projects that the stimulus package funded (Howsen and Lile 2011).

In a speech at the Brookings Institution on March 13, 2009, one of President Obama's key economic advisers, Lawrence H. Summers, summarized the Democratic orientation toward the business cycle and stimulus spending. He argued that according to Keynes's general theory and the volatility of the business cycle, one can anticipate there being two or three severe recessions within each century. While the markets have the ability to self-stabilize, Summers argued that the severity of downturns do not allow the markets to police themselves effectively. This is in contrast to the perspective of a laissez-faire Republican, who would argue that even systemic economic challenges have the salutary effect of destroying ineffective firms and reallocating assets to those that are more efficient and effective (Summers 2009).

Larry Summers Defends the Obama Stimulus Plan

In March 2009 economist Larry Summers, a former Clinton administration treasury secretary and Harvard University president who served as Director of the United States National Economic Council from January 2009 until November 2010, delivered a speech at the Brookings Institution in which he explained the decision of the Obama administration and Democrats in Congress to use an economic stimulus package to lift the United States out of the so-called Great Recession that Obama had inherited when taking office in January of that year. Here are excerpts from Summers' remarks:

> How should we think about this crisis? One of the most important lessons you learn in any introductory economics course is about the self-stabilizing properties of markets. . . .
> However, it was the central insight of Keynes's General Theory that two or three times

each century, and now is one of those times, the self-equilibrating properties of markets break down as stabilizing mechanisms are overwhelmed by vicious cycles, as the right economic metaphor becomes not a thermostat but an avalanche, and that is what we are confronting today.

Consider the vicious cycles. Declining asset prices lead to margin calls and deleveraging which leads to selling, further declines in asset prices, perpetuating the cycle. Lower asset prices mean banks hold less capital. Less capital means less lending. Less lending means lower asset prices, and the cycle perpetuates. Falling home prices lead to foreclosures which lead home prices to fall even further, forcing more foreclosures, forcing losses in the mortgage sector, forcing reductions in lending, forcing housing prices further down. A weakened financial system leads to less borrowing and spending, which leads to a weakened economy, which leads to a weakened financial system. Lower incomes lead to less spending, which leads to less employment, which leads to lower incomes. And I could go on. These are not processes that are self-correcting.

Source

Summers, Lawrence H. 2009. "Responding to an Historic Economic Crisis: The Obama Program Remarks at the Brookings Institution." March 13. Accessed November 16, 2015. http://www.brookings.edu/~/media/events/2009/3/13-summers/20090313_summers.pdf.

While Republicans tend to focus on the health of the markets, Democrats tend to focus on the consequences of destabilization of the economic system for ordinary working families. Republicans and Democrats both argue for continued economic expansion. However the main distinction in their orientations toward dealing with recession rests on whether or not the negative consequences of the business cycle such as high employment or a loss of jobs should be the government's responsibility to be mitigated. Because both parties have different orientations toward these consequences, this impacts their perspectives on how economic stimulus should occur. If one assumes that the government is responsible for the negative impacts of downturns in the economy, then logically one argues for greater and faster interventions to prevent the downturns. This is because the cost of the economic downturn on government operations is so much greater when one factors in responsibility for negative impacts (Horsey 2014; Kraus 2009).

Republicans on Stimulus Spending

When Republicans are confronted with a fiscal crisis, they often focus on short-term stability. In some cases that takes the form of cutting government services in order to cut taxes to stimulate consumer action within the economy. Shortly after assuming the presidency on February 18, 1981, the administration of Republican

President Ronald Reagan issued a report detailing its plans to launch an economic recovery. Primarily the plan targeted high inflation rates that were crippling the economy. The report reads,

> We have forgotten some important lessons in America. High taxes are not the remedy for inflation. Excessively rapid monetary growth cannot lower interest rates. Well-intentioned government regulations do not contribute to economic vitality. In fact, government spending has become so extensive that it contributes to the economic problems it was designed to cure. More government intervention in the economy cannot possibly be a solution to our economic problems. (Reagan 1981)

In many respects, the statement from early in Reagan's first term as president represents the ideological foundation many Republicans hold toward stimulus. Within the Reagan presidency and subsequent Republican administrations, however, this ideological stance came in for close scrutiny. Late in Reagan's presidency, for example, he was confronted with a regional threat to financial institutions in the Midwest. The savings and loan (S&L) crisis of the 1980s cost taxpayers roughly $132 billion (General Accounting Office 1996).

Overall, the Republican Party's relationship to stimulus spending has been complex. Longer-term analysis of policies led by Republican presidents leads one to believe that responses to the recession are primarily Keynesian. While Republican Party rhetoric still stresses economic competition and austerity as the answers to economic growth, the political reality often makes this difficult (Friedman 1965; Galupo 2011). Famously, George H. W. Bush, at the 1988 Republican National Convention, uttered the phrase "Read my lips, no new taxes." This bold pledge toward austerity eventually was confronted with new economic realities. As president, Bush found that the economic growth of the mid-to-late 1980s was beginning to subside. Rather than cutting programs that he deemed important, he decided to raise more revenue (Bush 1992).

This pledge was used against President Bush in his reelection campaign in 1992 by both his primary challengers and Democratic contender Clinton in the general election. Many political analysts have argued that this was a key aspect of President Bush's defeat in his reelection campaign (Bush 1992).

Since George H. W. Bush's presidency many Republicans have focused on what form stimulus should take—as well as conditions under which such dramatic action could be excused. There has been research into understanding whether a tax cut or a one-time direct payment to taxpayers is more effective in stimulating consumer action. Research has found that the most effective direct stimulus in the economy occurs in a one-time payment rather than time lagged tax reductions (Sahm, Shapiro, and Slemrod 2012).

Others have found that in many localities tax rebates were more valuable than direct stimulus spending. This is because it allowed the funding to stay directly in these localities rather than being collected by the federal government and returned to the states (Shepherd and Shepherd 2011).

Mitt Romney Criticizes the Obama Stimulus Plan

During the 2012 presidential campaign, Republican nominee Mitt Romney repeatedly described the Obama administration's efforts to bring about an economic recovery as ineffectual and wrongheaded. Here are excerpts from a speech Romney delivered in October, just a few weeks before he lost to Obama in the November 2012 general election:

> The president invested taxpayer money—your money—in green companies, now failed, that met his fancy, and sometimes were owned by his largest campaign contributors. He spent billions of taxpayer dollars on investments like Solyndra, Tesla, Fisker, and Ener1, which only added to our mounting federal debt.
>
> Energy prices are up in part because energy production on federal lands is down. He rejected the Keystone Pipeline from Canada, and cut in half drilling permits and leases, even as gasoline prices soared to new highs.
>
> No, the problem with the Obama economy is not what he inherited; it is with the misguided policies that slowed the recovery, and caused millions of Americans to endure lengthy unemployment and poverty. That is why 15 million more of our fellow citizens are on food stamps than when President Obama was sworn into office. That is why 3 million more women are now living in poverty. That is why nearly 1 in 6 Americans today is poor. That is why the economy is stagnant.

Source

Romney, Mitt. 2012. "Remarks on the American Economy." October 26. Accessed November 15, 2015. http://mittromneycentral.com/speeches/2012-speeches/102612-remarks-on-the-american-economy/.

More recent statements of prominent Republicans regarding stimulus spending have focused on fraud, waste, and corruption, rather than attacking the ideological validity of government intervention. Presidential candidate and former Massachusetts Governor Mitt Romney specifically laid out the reasoning behind stimulus spending that many Republicans ascribe to in an October 2012 campaign speech. He argued that the size of President Obama's stimulus package was more a function of attempting to give benefits to energy companies that had been part of Obama's campaign for the presidency (Romney 2012).

Other conservative Republicans expressed similar complaints. Republican congressman (and eventual House Speaker) Paul Ryan strongly criticized the investments the federal government made in energy companies such as Solyndra and Tesla as part of the 2009 package. He charged:

> The first troubling sign [of the Obama administration's alleged inability to fix the economy] came with the stimulus. It was President Obama's first and best shot at fixing the economy, at a time when he got everything he wanted under one-party rule. It cost $831 billion—the largest one-time expenditure ever by our federal government.

It went to companies like Solyndra, with their gold-plated connections, subsidized jobs, and make-believe markets. The stimulus was a case of political patronage, corporate welfare, and cronyism at their worst. You, the working men and women of this country, were cut out of the deal. (Ryan 2012)

While the loans to Solyndra and the company's subsequent bankruptcy led many Republicans to accuse the Obama administration of inefficiently disbursing stimulus money, stimulus packages almost always focus on certain preferred industries, firms, and individuals. Defenders of the Department of Energy's clean-energy loan program funded by the Obama stimulus package also point out that the program is actually turning a profit after "weathering years of media attacks and misinformation that attempted to paint the now defunct solar energy firm Solyndra as representative of the program's failure," charged the liberal Media Matters for America. "Media outlets from the *Washington Post* to CBS News spent years profiling Solyndra, wrongly suggesting its demise was illustrative of widespread waste, fraud, failure, and political corruption among DOE loan guarantee recipients." But by November 2014, other companies funded by the program, described as an effort to "accelerate the domestic commercial deployment of innovative and advanced clean energy technologies," had been so successful that the DOE loan program was actually turning a profit (Media Matters 2014).

The federal tax code with its numerous loopholes and preferential treatment for organizations that most effectively can lobby Congress also stands to challenge the concept that effective markets will sort out the best managed and most competitive corporations. Ideologically for many Republicans, this represents less of a problem to their economic values.

Future Implications of Stimulus Spending

Economic recessions and volatility in the business cycle will always exist. Additionally, there will always be debate regarding what government's policy responses should be. While initially Republicans and Democrats hold deep philosophical differences regarding stimulus spending, it is likely that in the future, both parties will converge to more similar perspectives. Observers agree, though, that there is a strong likelihood that both parties will be willing to advocate some form of stimulus spending when the next recession occurs—at least if a member of their own party occupies the Oval Office. As economics and lawmakers alike acknowledge, the political pressure to act decisively during an economic downturn is strong. Most economists now agree that the most recent packages of stimulus spending signed by Bush and Obama served to soften the financial downturn. While fiscal conservatives in the Republican Party may argue for a return to laissez-faire economics, the reality of politics, when confronted by recessionary conditions, make this ideological position difficult to defend (Leduc and Wilson 2014; Horsey 2014; Congressional Budget Office 2012; Steinhauser 2014).

Michael R. Potter

Further Reading

Burrough, Bryan. 2008. "Bringing Down Bear Stearns." *Vanity Fair*, August. Accessed May 27, 2015. http://www.vanityfair.com/news/2008/08/bear_stearns200808-2.

Bush, George H. W. 1992. "Presidential Debate at the University of Richmond." October 15. Accessed June 3, 2015. http://www.presidency.ucsb.edu/medialist.php?presid=41.

Bush, George H. W. 1988. "Address Accepting the Presidential Nomination at the Republican National Convention in New Orleans." Accessed June 3, 2015. http://www.presidency.ucsb.edu/ws/?pid=25955.

Calmes, Jackie. 2009. "House Passes Stimulus Plan with No G.O.P. Votes." *New York Times*, January 28. Accessed April 21, 2016. http://www.nytimes.com/2009/01/29/us/politics/29obama.html?_r=0

Cogan, John F., and John B. Taylor. 2011. "Where Did the Stimulus Go? More Than $1 Trillion in Federal-Deficit Spending Did Little or Nothing to Help the Economy. Why? Because It Was Used to Pay Down Debts and Reduce Borrowing." *Commentary* 1: 23.

Congressional Budget Office. 2012. "Estimated Impact of the American Recovery and Reinvestment Act on Employment and Economic Output from October 2011 through December 2011." Washington, DC: The Congress of the United States.

Financial Crisis Inquiry Commission (FCIC). 2011. *The Financial Crisis Inquiry Report: Final Report of the National Commission on the Causes of the Financial and Economic Crisis in the United States*. Washington, DC: Government Printing Office. https://www.gpo.gov/fdsys/pkg/GPO-FCIC/pdf/GPO-FCIC.pdf.

Friedman, Milton. 1962. *Capitalism and Freedom*. Chicago, IL: University of Chicago Press.

Friedman, Milton. 1965. "The Economy: We Are All Keynesians Now." *Time*, December 31.

Frizell, Sam. 2014. "General Motors Bailout Cost Taxpayers $11.2 Billion." *Time*, April 30. Accessed April 21, 2016. http://time.com/82953/general-motors-bailout-cost-taxpayers-11-2-billion/.

Galupo, Scott. 2011. "Ronald Reagan Practiced Keynesian Economics Successfully." *U.S. News & World Report*, November 1. Accessed April 21, 2016. http://www.usnews.com/opinion/blogs/scott-galupo/2011/11/01/ronald-reagan-practiced-keynesian-economics-successfully.

General Accounting Office. 1996. "AIMD-96-123 Financial Audit: Resolution and Trust Corporations 194 and 1995 Financial Statements." Washington, DC: The Congress of the United States:14.

Horsey, David. 2014. "Economic Stimulus Was Too Small from the Start, Thanks to GOP." *Los Angeles Times*, February 20.

Howsen, Roy M., and Stephen E. Lile. 2011. "The Role of Politics and Economics in the Allocation of Federal Stimulus Spending." *Applied Economics Letters* 18 (1–3): 263–266.

Keynes, John Maynard. 2008. *General Theory of Employment, Interest and Money*. New Delhi: Atlantic Publishers and Distributors, LTD.

Kraus, Wladimir. 2009. "A Thought Experiment Comparing Austrian and Keynesian Stimulus Packages." *Libertarian Papers* 1 (26–44): 1–13.

Leduc, Sylvain, and Daniel Wilson. 2014. "Infrastructure Spending as Fiscal Stimulus: Assessing the Evidence." *Review of Economics and Institutions* 5 (1): 1–24.

Media Matters for America. 2014. "Solyndra Scandal-Mongering Hasn't Stopped the Energy Dept.'s Loan Program from Turning a Profit." *Media Matters for America*, November 13. Accessed December 10, 2015. http://mediamatters.org/blog/2014/11/13/solyndra-scandal-mongering-hasnt-stopped-the-en/201551.

Reagan, Ronald. 1981. "White House Report on the Program for Economic Recovery." Washington, DC. February 18. Accessed October 27, 2015. http://www.presidency .ucsb.edu/ws/?pid=43427.

Romney, Mitt. 2012. "Remarks on the American Economy." October 12. Accessed November 4, 2015. http://mittromneycentral.com/speeches/2012-speeches/102612-remarks -on-the-american-economy/.

Ryan, Paul. 2012. "Acceptance Speech at the Republican National Convention." August 29. Accessed November 16, 2015. https://whitehouse2012.wordpress.com/tag/full-text -of-paul-ryans-acceptance-speech-at-the-republican-national-convention/.

Sahm, Claudia R., Matthew D. Shapiro, and Joel Slemrod. 2012. "Check in the Mail or More in the Paycheck: Does the Effectiveness of Fiscal Stimulus Depend on How It Is Delivered?" *American Economic Journal* 4 (3): 216–250.

Shepherd, Ian, and Dee Ann Shepherd. 2011a. "Government Spending or Tax Cuts? The 2009 Stimulus." Accessed November 3. http://www.na-businesspress.com/JMPP /shepherd_abstract.html.

Shepherd, Ian, and Dee Ann Shepherd. 2011b. "Government Spending or Tax Cuts? The 2009 Stimulus Package for Taylor County, Texas." *Journal of Management Policy & Practice* 12 (6): 62–73.

Steinhauser, Paul. 2014. "GOP Slams Stimulus on Fifth Anniversary." *CNN.com*, February 17. Accessed March 5, 2016. http://politicalticker.blogs.cnn.com/2014/02/17/gop -slams-stimulus-on-fifth-anniversary/.

Summers, Lawrence H. 2009. "Responding to an Historic Economic Crisis: The Obama Program Remarks at the Brookings Institution." March 13. Accessed November 16, 2015. http://larrysummers.com/wp-content/uploads/2015/07/Responding-to-an-Historic -Economic-Crisis_3.13.2009.pdf.

Taylor, Jason E., and Richard K. Vedder. 2010. "Stimulus by Spending Cuts: Lessons from 1946." *Cato Policy Reports*, May/June. Washington, DC: Cato Institute.

Young, Andrew T. 2013. "Why in the World Are We All Keynesians Again? The Flimsy Case for Stimulus Spending." *Cato Policy Analysis* 721. Washington, DC: Cato Institute.

Student Loans and Debt

At a Glance

Student loan debt in the United States keeps growing (one trillion dollars and counting) with the average borrower owing over $26,000 upon graduation (Denhart 2013). The largest part of this debt is from federal student loans.

Members of the Democratic Party tend to believe the federal government has a responsibility to assist borrowers. Democrats support the government's policy of providing direct loans to students versus private sector loans, noting that the former type of loans are less expensive for students. Democrats also support policies that keep monthly payments lower, making it easier for borrowers to pay the government back, as well as savings programs for higher education.

The Republicans tend to favor loans made through the private sector. Republicans also believe that promoting competition among colleges and universities, rather than government intervention, is the best approach to keeping tuition down, and they want to make it easier for families to save for higher education.

Many Democrats . . .

- Say that student loans should come directly from the federal government
- Support federal efforts to help families save money for higher education
- Favor reducing student debt by keeping interest rates lower and increasing other forms of aid
- Contend that loans would be easier to pay off if borrowers were able to enroll in income-based repayment plans

Many Republicans . . .

- Favor having student loans handled by the private sector, with the federal government serving as insurance guarantor
- Support federal efforts to help families save money for higher education
- Feel that tuition could be reduced by encouraging increased competition between the different providers of higher education

---

Overview

The United States government's role in higher education has evolved over the years. Early on, the federal government managed and financed several institutions of higher learning including the United States Military Academy (beginning in 1802), the United States Naval Academy (1845), Gallaudet Institute for the Deaf (1864), and Howard University (1867). The evolution continued with the Morrill Act (1862). This law made states eligible to receive thousands of acres of federal land, either within or near its boundaries if the state had no federal land, to establish a college that teaches military tactics, engineering, and agriculture. Sixty-nine colleges and universities had been created under that act by 1929, with two of them privately supported. "The other sixty-seven formed the backbone of state-supported higher education in the United States" (Archibald 2002, 25).

The next major change came in 1944 with the Serviceman's Readjustment Act, also known as the GI Bill. The GI Bill provided veterans returning from World War II with many benefits, including money to cover tuition and living expenses to attend university, high school, or vocational institutions. The bill was extended to veterans of the Korean War and the Vietnam War. This benefit was popular with veterans, many of whom attended colleges or universities they would never have been able to afford without this assistance.

This evolution in higher education continued in 1957 when the Soviet Union launched Sputnik. In reaction to the launch, Congress passed the National Defense Education Act (1958). The law was a science initiative, passed on a bipartisan basis and signed by Republican President Dwight Eisenhower, to increase financial aid to students in certain science and technology professions that could provide assistance in defense, in hopes of addressing the technology gap between the Soviet Union and the United States. The assistance went to thousands of students attending colleges and universities in the 1960s.

With the Higher Education Act (1965), the federal government began offering funding to a wide portion of the American public. This law was part of Democratic President Johnson's suite of Great Society programs. The complex law was broken into eight titles, including Title IV Student Assistance. Title IV established Educational Opportunity Grants and the Guaranteed Student Loan Program, and transferred the authority for the work-study program from the Office of Economic Opportunity to the Commissioner of Education. It also amended the National Defense Education Act of 1958, and reauthorized and expanded the National Defense Student Loan Program (Archibald 2002).

The Guaranteed Student Loan Program had the federal government providing loan guarantees and interest subsidies. The private sector actually made the loans, with the federal government providing insurance in case the student eventually defaulted. In addition, the government paid the interest on a Guaranteed Student Loan that accrued while a student was in school, and the government even paid the difference between the low interest rate set on the loan and the market interest rate. With the program being expensive to administer, only students whose family income was below $15,000 qualified. The Higher Education Act has been reauthorized nine times. With each reauthorization Congress makes adjustments to the law, including adding programs and changing existing ones. In 1972, Pell Grants (then called the Opportunity Grant Program) were created. Pell Grants, which do not need to be repaid, were intended to be the foundation of an undergraduate student's financial aid package. With the 1992 reauthorization, a pilot version of the Direct Loan Program was created. The William D. Ford Federal Direct Loan Program provides low-interest loans for both students and parents to cover higher education expenses. The lender is the Department of Education. The program offers several loan products, including Stafford Loans, Perkins Loans, PLUS Loans, and Consolidation Loans. Which loan is given depends on varying factors, such as if the loan is need-based, if it is for graduate school, and whether it is a parent or a student borrowing the money. Consolidation loans allow students to consolidate Stafford Loans, PLUS Loans, and Perkins Loan into one single debt. The Direct Loan Program gave additional benefits to both students and parents, including lower interest rates.

In 2007, the College Cost Reduction and Access Act was passed by Congress. The law shifted taxpayer subsidies away from private student loan companies, increasing grants-in-aid and providing better benefits to borrowers. Pell Grants were increased from $4,310 to $5,400 by 2012. Income-based repayment (IBR) plans were also introduced. Interest rates were reduced on new subsidized Stafford Loans to undergraduate students, from 6.8 percent to 3.4 percent, although rates went back to 6.8 percent in July 2012.

The next large change to the federal government's involvement in student loans and debt came with the Student Aid and Fiscal Responsibility Act (SAFRA) in 2009. SAFRA, which was crafted and passed by Democrats as part of the Health Care and Education Reconciliation Act of 2010 despite opposition from most Republicans, increased the maximum amount available in Pell Grants to $5,500. It also ended the subsidizing of private loans by the federal government, with all federal student loan funding going for direct loans rather than through unnecessary banking "middle men." The White House estimated that the student loan reforms would save American taxpayers $68 billion in coming years.

Democrats on Student Loans and Debt

Democrats tend to support the federal government providing financing for higher education, including direct loans. Beginning on July 2, 2010, the Department of Education began making direct loans solely, stopping the government-insured loans to private lenders that had been the norm for decades. The Democrats favored this reform because private lenders charged higher interest rates and offered less favorable repayment options for borrowers than federal authorities could offer. They also saw no reason for banking institutions to reap taxpayer money from student loans, as they had done for many years.

A perennial problem for borrowers is meeting the monthly payment, especially since many of the students graduating do not have high-paying jobs yet. To address this, the Democrats have traditionally been supporters of income-based repayment (IBR) plans. The federal government currently offers three plans: the Income-Based Repayment Plan, Pay As You Earn Repayment Plan, and the Income-Contingent Repayment Plan. The payment amounts on all three plans are based on the student's discretionary income, ranging from 10 percent to 20 percent. The repayment period is longer than the standard repayment period, spanning either 20 or 25 years. Under any of the plans, the remaining loan balance is forgiven if the federal student loans are not fully repaid at the end of the repayment period. President Obama recommended the expansion of the Pay As You Earn Plan to make it is available to all borrowers.

Democrats have worked to lower the amount of loans that are needed. To achieve this, Democrats worked to increase the amount of Pell Grant scholarships and helped pass the American Opportunity Tax Credit. Pell Grants are given by the federal government to students with demonstrated financial need, who have not yet earned their first bachelor's degree. Awards do not need to be repaid. The

---

Democrats Tout Reforms to the Student Loan Program

In the 2012 Democratic National Platform, Democrats discussed their achievements regarding financing higher education. The Platform clearly shows that they believe in active involvement by the federal government in student loans and debt:

> To help keep college within reach for every student, Democrats took on banks to reform our student loan program, saving more than $60 billion by removing the banks acting as middlemen so we can better and more directly invest in students. To make college affordable for students of all backgrounds and confront the loan burden our students shoulder, we doubled our investment in Pell Grant scholarships and created the Americans Opportunity Tax Credit worth up to $10,000 over four years of college, and we're creating avenues for students to manage their federal student loans so that their payments can be only 10 percent of what they make each month. President Obama has pledged to encourage colleges to keep their costs down by reducing federal aid for those that do not, investing in colleges that keep tuition affordable and provide good value, doubling the number of work-study jobs available to students and continuing to ensure that students have access to federal loans with reasonable interest rates.

Source

Democratic National Committee. 2012. "Moving America Forward: 2012 Democratic National Platform 2012." Accessed August 26, 2015. http://assets.dstatic.org/dnc-platform/2012 -National-Platform.pdf.

maximum amount for 2014–2015 was $5,730. The American Opportunity Tax Credit is a credit worth up to $2,500 on the first $4,000 of qualifying educational expenses, which include course materials and tuition. The credit is applied on a qualifying student or parent's federal tax return.

Many Democrats also want to lower debt by working with colleges to keep tuition lower. President Obama pledged to "encourage colleges to keep their costs down by reducing federal aid for those that do not, investing in colleges that keep tuition affordable and provide good value" (Democratic National Committee 2012). As part of this, President Obama wants to create a college rating system. This system would judge colleges based on several criteria, including access (such as students receiving Pell Grants), affordability (such as net price and loan debt), and outcomes (such as graduation rates and graduate earnings). The intended result is to assist students and their families on making informed financial decisions on where to attend college.

In 2014 President Obama suggested that all Americans have the opportunity to attend community college tuition-free for two years. The plan called for the federal government to pay for 75 percent of tuition, with participating state governments having to pay the remaining amount. It was expected that a full-time community college student could save an average of $3,800 in tuition a year. "Under the proposal, students who attend at least half-time, maintain a 2.5 grade point average while in college, and make steady progress toward completing their programs would have their tuition eliminated" (Rampton and Holland 2015). Following up on President Obama's proposal, in July 2015 Democratic Senator Tammy Baldwin of Wisconsin and Democratic Representative Bobby Scott of Virginia introduced the America's College Promise Act of 2015 to their respective chambers. If passed it would provide free community college tuition to eligible students.

Massachusetts Democratic Senator Elizabeth Warren has proposed several progressive ideas for student aid reform over the past few years as well. Her first proposal was to allow students to obtain loans at the same low rate the Federal Reserve gives to banks, thus saving students money that would have gone to interest. Her second proposal was to allow borrowers to refinance their student debt at current interest rate levels. Currently students are locked into a rate at the time of graduation. This is good for borrowers if interest rates rise but bad if interest rates fall. Both proposals were blocked by Senate Republicans, due to disagreements on how to finance the proposals.

In February 2015, Senator Warren and five other Democratic senators sent a letter to the Department of Education asking for relief for students whom the senators believed had been misled by for-profit colleges (educational institutions operated by private, profit-seeking businesses). For-profit colleges tend to have more non-traditional students, which qualify to borrow more money yet the non-traditional students tend to have lower incomes, and therefore have a harder time paying back the money. Also, for-profit colleges are more likely to close down, leaving students with large amounts of debt and no degree. Citing the powers in the Higher

Education Act, the senators proposed that the Department of Education cancel some of the student loan borrowers' debts for colleges that act in ways that hurt the quality of their education or their finances or that close their doors. Warren and the other senators believe that keeping loans instead of canceling them is counterproductive. "In the long run, she's argued, regularly canceling the debts of students tricked by educational institutions would create an incentive for federal regulators to stop deceptive practices before too many students fall for them-because if they didn't, the government would take a hit to its bottom line" (Levy 2015).

Republicans on Student Loans and Debt

Republicans tend to believe the federal government's role should be limited; more of a counselor helping students and their families save for college and assisting them in making informed financial decisions. They believe competition will help keep down costs and increase innovation in higher education. Many Republicans prefer that the federal government serve as an insurance guarantor for the private sector, as they offer loans to students and their families instead of issuing direct loans. This would still provide the funds for students to attend college, but would lower the risk to the federal government if a student would default.

Republicans are generally not supportive of grants to fund higher education. The federal government makes money off the student loan interest they collect but they do not make money from grants. During the Reagan administration, "the share of federal student aid in the form of grants, which do not need to be paid back, fell to 31.8 percent, from 55.3 percent in 1979–80" (Arnone et al. 2004). Pell Grants have continued to be in danger of further cuts and freezes. In 2015, the House GOP released a budget memo that would freeze the maximum amount students receive from the federal government, currently $5,775 per year, for the next 10 years. Later, Republicans suggested that Pell Grant funding should not be guaranteed every year, but should be left for Congress to decide.

A Republican Blueprint for Reducing Student Loan Debt

In 2012, the GOP-controlled House Budget Committee laid out its vision for tackling student loans and debt in *The Path to Prosperity*, a document containing Republican policy prescriptions on a wide range of issues:

> Current federal aid structures are exacerbating a crisis in tuition inflation, plunging students and their families into unaffordable levels of debt or foreclosing the possibility of any higher education at all. This problem has been building for years and has officially reached crisis levels. In June 2010, student loan debt surpassed the national level of credit card debt for the first time in history. The graduating class of 2011 is the most indebted to date, with an average per student debt of $22,900.

These young adults are graduating with enormous loan repayments and having dif-ficulty finding jobs in our low-growth economic environment. Instead of solving the problem, schools are deflecting the mounting criticism by blaming the rising cost of health care and employee benefits, the need to compete for students by offering nicer facilities, and reductions in state subsidies and endowments as a result of the reces-sion. While these do represent contributing factors, they are merely accelerating a long-standing problem. College cost have risen at twice the rate of inflation for about thirty years, but this year fees soared 8.3 percent—more than double the inflation rate—as federal subsidies have increased at a historic pace.

But, instead of helping more students achieve their dreams, studies have shown that increased federal financial aid is simply being absorbed by tuition increases. While financial aid is intended to make college more affordable, there is growing evidence that it has had the opposite effect. Economists such as Richard Vedder point out that the decisions of colleges and universities to raise their prices would have constrained if the federal government had not stepped in so often to subsidize rising tuitions.

Source

U.S. House of Representatives, Budget Committee. 2012. "The Path to Prosperity: A Blueprint for American Renewal: Fiscal Year 2013 Budget Resolution. Accessed August 26, 2015, http://budget.house.gov/uploadedfiles/pathtoprosperity2013.pdf.

Republicans say that they understand the need for relief from the debt already incurred by borrowers. Toward this end, they worked with Democrats on sev-eral issues, including maintaining a low interest rate on Stafford Loans. Stafford Loans are guaranteed by the federal government as described by Title IV of the Higher Education Act (1965). Because they are guaranteed, they are offered at a lower interest rate than the borrower would otherwise be able to get with a private lender. There are two kinds of Stafford Loans: subsidized (the federal government pays the interest during certain authorized periods) and unsubsidized (the federal government does not pay any interest). In 2012, the interest rates on Stafford Loans were expected to jump from 3.4 percent to 6.8 percent, potentially costing borrowers thousands of dollars over the life of the loan. Democrats and Repub-licans worked together to sign a one-year extension of the lower interest rate. In 2013, the Bipartisan Student Loan Certainty Act was passed. The act links stu-dent loan rates to the federal 10-year Treasury rate, plus a set amount that varies depending on the loan.

Some Republicans also support income-based repayment plans. Income-based repayment plans are alternative plans where payment amounts are based on stu-dents' discretionary income, ranging from 10 percent to 20 percent, and often come with longer repayment periods. Representative Petri of Wisconsin has pro-posed moving to a universal income-based repayment plan. Petri's plan is different from the current income-based repayment options because it would automatically enroll every borrower to income-based repayment and there would be no loan forgiveness. The money would be taken from the borrower's paycheck and sent to the government. Several countries already have adopted this, including the United Kingdom. Borrowers could still opt to make standard payments, but would have to choose to do so.

Republicans tend to be supporters of 529 savings plans. Families use 529 plans, which are tax-advantaged investment vehicles designed to encourage saving for future higher education expenses. There are two types of 529 plans, prepaid plans and savings plans. Prepaid plans allow people to purchase tuition credits at today's rate to be used in the future by the recipient. The savings plans are administered by states and account holders can invest in the market, usually with mutual funds. The owner of the account puts money in a 529 plan and it grows, tax-free, over time. Money can be taken out, also tax-free, for approved educational expenses.

Both Republicans and Democrats have supported these plans over time, although Republicans have generally been more enthusiastic about them. President Clinton vetoed a provision in the Tax Relief Act of 1997 that would have made 529 distributions tax-free, not just tax deferred, when used for college expenses. However in 2001, President Bush signed the Economic Growth and Tax Relief Reconciliation Act and 529 distributions became tax-free. This change helped spur growth with the plans.

In early 2015, President Obama proposed rolling back the tax-free distributions in the 529 plans. This would not apply to money already invested but would apply to future contributions. The reasoning was that the plans were often used by families with a higher income, and therefore less in need of a tax break. Also, "the administration said its larger goal on college finance is to simplify the jumble of education tax credits currently in the law. The president wants to expand and make permanent the American Opportunity Tax Credit (AOTC), which provides families up to $2,500 a year for tuition, books and supplies" (Douglas-Gabriel 2015). This proved unpopular with both parties and the public, however, and the proposal was quickly tabled.

Katharine Leigh

Further Reading

Archibald, Robert B. 2002. *Redesigning the Financial Aid System: Why Colleges and Universities Should Switch Roles with the Federal Government.* Baltimore: Johns Hopkins University Press.

Arnone, Michael, Eric Hoover, Jeffery Selingo, and Welch Suggs. 2004. "Ronald Reagan Remembered." *Chronicle of Higher Education* 50 (41): A24–A25.

Democratic National Committee. 2012. "Moving America Forward: 2012 Democratic National Platform." Accessed May 11, 2015. https://www.democrats.org/party-platform.

Denhart, Chris. 2013. "How the $1.2 Trillion College Debt Crisis Is Crippling Students, Parents and the Economy." *Forbes*, July 25. Accessed May 20, 2015. http://www.forbes.com/sites/specialfeatures/2013/07/25/the-rise-and-fail-of-the-five-year-college-degree/.

Douglas-Gabriel, Danielle. 2015. "Obama Drops Proposal to Cut Tax Benefits of 529 College Savings Plans." *Washington Post*, January 27. Accessed May 20, 2015. http://www.washingtonpost.com/business/economy/obama-drops-proposal-to-cut-tax-benefits-of-529-college-savings-plans/2015/01/27/5f3f429a-a675-11e4-a2b2-776095f393b2_story.html.

Levy, Pema. 2015. "Elizabeth Warren to Obama Administration: Help Me Tackle Student Debt." *Mother Jones*, March 6. Accessed May 20, 2015. http://www.motherjones.com/politics/2015/03/warren-obama-student-debt-loans.

Rampton, Roberta, and Steve Holland. 2015. "Obama Proposes Idea of Two Free Years of Community College," *Reuters*, January 8. Accessed May 20, 2015. http://www.reuters.com/article/2015/01/09/us-obama-education-idUSKBN0KH2D120150109.

Republican National Committee. 2012. "We Believe in America: 2012 Republican Platform." Accessed May 11, 2015. https://cdn.gop.com/docs/2012GOPPlatform.pdf.

U.S. Department of Education. 2014. "Direct Loans Page for Students." Accessed on May 14, 2015. http://www.direct.ed.gov/student.html.

U.S. House of Representatives, Budget Committee. 2012. "The Path to Prosperity: A Blueprint for American Renewal: Fiscal Year 2013 Budget Resolution." Accessed August 26, 2015. http://budget.house.gov/uploadedfiles/pathtoprosperity2013.pdf.

TANF—Temporary Assistance for Needy Families

At a Glance

Aid to Families with Dependent Children (AFDC) was an entitlement program that provided financial assistance to needy dependent children in their homes or in the homes of caregivers. AFDC was replaced by the Temporary Assistance for Needy Families (TANF) program in 1996. Under TANF families and children are no longer entitled to receive assistance, and adults may only receive cash assistance for a total of 60 months during their lifetime.

Proponents of TANF believe welfare dependency should be addressed by ending the entitlement to welfare, establishing time limits for the receipt of benefits, and adopting provisions that encourage the formation of two-parent families. They also advocate a reduced federal role in the program's funding and administration, arguing in favor of increased state and local control to facilitate the tailoring of the program to meet local needs.

Opponents of TANF consider the withdrawal of the federal guarantee of welfare for needy children and families to be an abandonment of the government's moral obligation to care for its citizens. Opponents maintain that time limits succeeded only in pushing more than a million children into poverty when families lost benefits. Those opposed to TANF are also concerned that allowing states to develop their own programs will lead to markedly unequal benefits among the states.

Many Democrats . . .

- Feel that the federal government should assume primary responsibility for providing support to needy children and families
- Assert that increased investments in job support services are necessary to get families off welfare permanently
- Believe that legal immigrants are entitled to federal welfare benefits

Many Republicans . . .

* Worry that Aid to Families with Dependent Children (AFDC) created government dependency and contributes to the federal deficit
* Believe that AFDC contributed to a rise in of out-of-wedlock births and single-parent families
* Favor time limits on the receipt of services to motivate recipients to achieve self-sufficiency
* Oppose non-citizens' eligibility for social welfare benefits

---

Overview

Aid to Families with Dependent Children (AFDC) was a grant program that provided federal funds to states to provide cash welfare payments to needy families with children. States running and administering the program within federal guidelines were entitled to unlimited federal funds for "matching rate" reimbursements of benefit payments. Under AFDC, states were required to provide aid to all persons eligible under federal law whose income and resources qualified within state-established limits.

From the 1970s to the early 1990s, the divergence between Democrats' desire to raise AFDC benefit levels and Republicans' aims to cut program costs and enact strict work requirements resulted in a legislative impasse that obstructed the passage of legislation to overhaul the program. Instead, policymakers could only come to agreement on a series of incremental program reforms (Weaver 2000).

For example, President Ronald Reagan's administration wanted to restructure AFDC as a part of its *New Federalism* initiative. His administration's stated priorities were focused on balancing the budget, cutting taxes, increasing defense spending, and reducing domestic spending. As a result, the AFDC program became a major target for reduction. However, because Democrats controlled the House of Representatives, their objections to sweeping restructuring of the program meant Reagan was able to enact only modest changes in program rules and reductions in funding (O'Connor 2004).

However, by the 1990s, widespread agreement had developed among both Democrats and Republicans that the AFDC program was not working. Critics of AFDC charged it lacked sufficient state-level flexibility, discouraged work, and contributed to out-of-wedlock births and the formation of single-parent families (Sawhill 1995). In addition, expanding caseloads and rising program costs inspired strong public dissatisfaction with the program. The high level of public discontent contributed to liberal Democratic legislators' reluctance to vote against reform measures (Weaver 2000).

Within the context of this political climate, in 1992, Democratic presidential candidate Bill Clinton decided to place the issue of welfare reform back on the national political agenda. After several unsuccessful Democratic presidential bids by other Democratic candidates, Clinton planned to regain the White House for his party by positioning himself as a moderate, purposefully distancing himself from traditional liberal policies. As part of this campaign, Clinton vowed he would

---

Republicans Voice Opposition to Clinton's First Major Welfare Reform Proposal

In 1994 the Clinton administration proposed major changes to the existing welfare system through a so-called Work and Responsibility Act. Many Republicans, however, claimed that the administration's proposed reforms did not go far enough. On August 2, 1994, Tom DeLay, U.S. representative in Congress from the state of Texas, expressed concerns about the Work and Responsibility Act before the U.S. House of Representatives Committee on Education and Labor. His remarks are excerpted below. The Work and Responsibility Act did not receive sufficient support for passage, but two years later, the Clinton White House and congressional Republicans crafted a sweeping welfare reform bill called the Personal Responsibility Work Opportunity and Reconciliation Act of 1996, which was signed into law by Clinton on August 22, 1996 (DeLay voted in favor of the bill).

. . . One of the greatest problems facing our country today is illegitimacy. Several studies suggest that there may be incentives in our welfare system for young girls to have babies. Of 12 studies conducted in the past decade that looked into the relationship between welfare and rapidly rising illegitimacy rates, nine studies concluded that the availability of welfare increased the likelihood of a woman having a child out of wedlock . . .

. . . Rather than discouraging illegitimacy and encouraging two-parent families, our welfare system offers young girls the proposition of a lifetime. It says if you have a child and don't get married we will give you housing, health care, food stamps, and AFDC payments. Unfortunately, the Clinton plan does nothing to curb illegitimacy. While the Clinton plan includes an optional family cap, this measure does nothing to stop young mothers from entering the welfare rolls. It also strikes me that in my reading of the Clinton plan, the word abstinence does not even appear one time.

. . . The Clinton plan replaces the existing welfare system with a colossal and expensive government-subsidized jobs program and at a considerable expense to taxpayers. . . . It simply replaces a welfare entitlement with other entitlements. The GOP plan saves taxpayers millions of dollars, reduces the welfare rolls, puts more people to work, and instills in recipients a deepened sense of responsibility and self-worth that can be passed on to the next generation.

Source

U.S. Congress, House of Representatives, Committee on Education and Labor. 1994. *Hearing on H.R. 4605, Work and Responsibility Act of 1994: Hearing before the Committee on Education and Labor.* 103rd Cong., 2nd sess., August 2, 1994, 143–144. (Statement of Tom Delay, Representative in Congress from the State of Texas).

"end welfare as we know it" through devising and implementing a mixed ideology reform that combined liberal and conservative ideas. In his book, *A Political History of the American Welfare System: When Ideas Have Consequences*, Brendon O'Connor (2004) contends Clinton's willingness to acknowledge Republican criticism of AFDC while incorporating some Democratic views paved the way for welfare reform because his compromise diffused the liberal/conservative impasse.

Clinton's welfare reform proposal primarily called for increasing participation in education and training programs, expanding tax credits for the working poor, and limiting benefit receipt to two years, unless adults worked or performed community service. The proposal's emphasis on education, training, and tax credits represented a liberal philosophy, whereas time limits and work requirements represented conservative principles. Clinton's proposal reflected a significant departure from the Democratic Party's traditional stance on welfare since the Great Society era, and inspired significant dissension within his own political party.

Legislation embodying Clinton's plan was introduced in 1994 as the Work and Responsibility Act. Passage of the act was thwarted by his administration's initial focus on healthcare reform and later by Republican victories in the 1994 midterm elections, which transferred control of the House of Representatives to the Republican Party. Clinton's ability to enact his own welfare reform policy ended when Republicans assumed control of the House of Representatives. With Republicans now in control of setting the welfare-reform agenda, they introduced a new reform—The Personal Responsibility Act—that differed sharply from Clinton's plan. The act incorporated principles from the Republican's 1995 *Contract with America*, which promised to enact legislation to promote individual responsibility that discouraged illegitimacy and teen pregnancy, cut spending on welfare, and established tougher work requirements for welfare. The Republican plan shared the Clinton administration's emphasis on work, but sought to put recipients to work earlier. Republicans also emphasized deterrence and devolution to a greater extent than did Clinton. A key difference between the proposals was the Clinton Administration proposed spending more to reduce welfare dependency and the Republicans proposed spending less (Weaver 2000).

The nation's governors' and Republicans' political pressure helped bring the House and Senate together on a bill entitled the Personal Responsibility and Work Opportunity Reconciliation Act (PRWORA). Clinton objected to several aspects of the bill yet he faced tremendous pressure to sign the PRWORA. Clinton signed the PRWORA (P.L. 104-193) on August 22, 1996. It transformed the Aid to Families with Dependent Children (AFDC), the Job Opportunities and Basic Skills Training (JOBS) program, and the Emergency Assistance (EA) program into a new block grant called the Temporary Assistance to Needy Families (TANF) program. TANF became and continues to be the major source of cash-based welfare funding for needy families with children, as opposed to non-cash-based programs like WIC, SNAP, housing vouchers, and so on. The PRWORA block grant ended the entitlement to cash welfare benefits, capping federal funding to states and placing

---

President Clinton Comments on Welfare Reform

On July 31, 1996, Democratic President Bill Clinton made the following remarks to recognize the passage of the Personal Responsibility Work Opportunity and Reconciliation Act of 1996:

> Today, Congress will vote on legislation that gives us a chance to live up to that promise, to transform a broken system that traps too many people in a cycle of dependence to one that emphasizes work and independence, to give people on welfare a chance to draw a paycheck, not a welfare check. It gives us a better chance to give those on welfare what we want for all families in America, the opportunity to succeed at home and at work.
>
> . . . A long time ago I concluded that the current welfare system undermines the basic values of work, responsibility and family, trapping generation after generation in dependency and hurting the very people it was designed to help.
>
> Today, we have an historic opportunity to make welfare what it was meant to be: a second chance, not a way of life. And even though the bill has serious flaws that are unrelated to welfare reform, I believe we have a duty to seize the opportunity it gives us to end welfare as we know it.
>
> . . . I made my principles for real welfare reform very clear from the beginning. First and foremost, it should be about moving people from welfare to work. It should impose time limits on welfare. It should give people the child care and health care they need to move on from welfare to work without hurting children. It should crack down on child-support enforcement, it should protect our children.
>
> This legislation meets those principles. It gives us a chance we haven't had before to break the cycle of dependency that has existed for millions and millions of our fellow citizens, exiling them from the world of work. It gives structure, meaning and dignity to most of our lives.

Source

Clinton, William. 1997. "Welfare Reform Must Protect Children and Legal Immigrants." in *Welfare Reform: At Issues: An Opposing Viewpoint Series*, ed. Charles P. Cozic (San Diego, CA: Greenhaven), 40–44. (Statement of Bill Clinton, 42nd President of the United States).

---

a 60-month lifetime limit on receipt of TANF benefits, effectively turning welfare into a temporary-assistance program rather than a federal entitlement. While the block grant structure gave states more flexibility, the new structure of welfare also capped funding on levels based on 1994 expenditures, regardless of any subsequent changes in states' level of need.

Rather than issuing checks, most states provide TANF benefits via debit cards, also known as electronic benefit transfers (EBTs), which can be used to withdraw cash from automatic transfer machines (ATMs). In 2010 and 2011, a series of media stories revealed that TANF benefits were being accessed at cash machines in casinos, liquor stores, strip clubs, and even on cruise ships, an issue the media dubbed "the strip club loophole." Although several states had acted to close the so-called "strip club loophole," many members of Congress thought that problem should be addressed at the federal level.

In 2012, Congress closed the "strip club loophole" via passage of P.L. 112-96, a payroll tax bill that also reauthorized TANF through the end of the 2012. This new law required states to adopt policies that prevent recipients from spending or accessing their welfare benefits at liquor stores, casinos, gaming establishments, and adult entertainment establishments. States who failed to adopt such policies within two years risked losing 5 percent of their annual TANF block grant (Prah 2012).

However, critics of the provision charge that in some poor areas, ATMs in the prohibited establishments may be the most accessible and least costly ATM machines in the area, and that people accessing cash there might not actually be purchasing the businesses' services. In addition, states are concerned with the costs and challenges of determining and keeping updated lists of which ATMs are off-limits and which are not (Cohen 2012). Furthermore, the few states that have studied the problem found it involved less than 0.1 percent of transactions. There-fore, there is concern that states could incur substantial costs for a problem that is not prevalent (Prah 2012).

Democrats on TANF

A review of the legislative history of PRWORA reveals that, although many Demo-crats believed AFDC needed reform, there was disagreement between the liberal wing of the party and party moderates about the type of reform needed. Liberal Democrats described PRWORA as "mean spirited" and "extremist," and accused some supporters of being motivated by the desire to win reelection. Liberal Demo-crats strongly objected to the relinquishment of AFDC's entitlement status and viewed its passing as a step backward that could take decades to reinstate. To lib-eral Democrats, the devolution of the program largely to state control represented a relinquishment of the federal government's responsibility to support the nation's children, regardless of their racial or ethnic background, their geographic location, or the politics of their state. Democrats maintained transferring power to states would translate into uneven social justice in welfare distribution because poor people would be treated differently depending on the state in which they lived (U.S. Congress 1996).

During the U.S. House's floor debate for PRWORA, several liberal Democrats expressed concern about the impact welfare reform would have on victims of domestic violence, observing a significant portion of the welfare caseload is made up of victims of domestic violence, and the loss of TANF as a safety net forces many battered women either to stay with their abusers or return to them for financial support. Liberal Democrats strongly opposed the adoption of time limits, express-ing concern for the survival of those who could not find jobs or were unable to work. For liberals, it did not make sense to establish uniform time limits because although it was realistic to expect some people would successfully get off welfare quickly, other recipients who lacked skills and training would naturally need to stay enrolled in the program longer. They criticized PRWORA for failing to acknowledge not all welfare recipients would be able to find a job that paid a living wage (U.S. Congress 1996).

The more liberal wing of the party argued true welfare reform ethically should involve an increased financial investment used for education, job training and readiness supports, and job placement services. Many Democrats, however, took a more moderate stance toward welfare reform and supported time limits and stricter work provisions. Initially many Democrats joined a group of moderate Republicans to support a bipartisan proposal, known as the Castle-Tanner Proposal. But once that proposal died, most moderate Democrats agreed to support PRWORA as the only viable alternative (U.S. Congress 1996).

Although supportive of welfare reform, moderate Democrats had reservations about PRWORA because it lacked the program and financial supports necessary for states and localities actually to meet stronger work requirements. During the floor debate, moderate Democrats regularly referred to a study conducted by the Congressional Budget Office that concluded PRWORA resources fell far short of those necessary to provide meaningful job support. Some moderate Democrats maintained the block grant approach would only work if funding levels remained at a sufficient level and if federal oversight was maintained to monitor state use of funds. Many Democrats objected to turning AFDC into a block grant believing strongly in the efficacy of the federal-state partnership. They further noted that although the federal government would supply funding for state programs, the federal government would have no recourse to protect beneficiaries from the failure of states to act (U.S. Congress 1996).

Democrats acknowledged that sometimes welfare fostered dependency, but also stressed that oftentimes people could not get off welfare because they could not get a job that paid a living wage. Some Democrats believed TANF work provisions inadequate because they failed to address the root causes of the problem—the lack of adequate jobs—so the underlying conditions remained. They agreed mandatory welfare-to-work requirements could place recipients in gainful employment, but only if those programs were well-designed and given the resources necessary to succeed. They noted it was unrealistic to expect employers to hire people who did not have adequate job skills (U.S. Congress 1996).

Finally, many Democrats objected to PRWORA provisions that excluded legal and illegal immigrants from receiving AFDC and other social welfare services, seeing no justification for targeting immigrants who do not abuse the welfare system, work hard, play by the rules, pay taxes, and serve in the military. However, a few Democrats agreed with the provision to exclude immigrants, arguing the most fundamental requirement of U.S. immigration policy is that immigrants be self-reliant: in other words not dependent upon U.S. taxpayers for support. They maintained public policy should ensure funds go to needy citizens by enforcing the public-charge exclusion and public law's deportation provisions (U.S. Congress 1996).

During 2010 congressional hearings for the reauthorization of TANF, many Democrats voiced concern about low rates of participation (U. S. Congress, House of Representatives, Committee on Ways and Means 2010). Their concerns were based upon 2009 data showing fewer than two million families received TANF cash assistance, three million fewer than received AFDC in 1994 (U.S. Congress, Senate, Committee on Finance 2010). Democrats remained unconvinced declining caseloads were an indication of the program's success in making clients self-sufficient. Instead, they asserted that flat or declining caseloads should not be considered a success when rates of unemployment and poverty were high during this period (U.S. Congress, House of Representatives, Committee on Ways and Means 2010). Democrats became alarmed by TANF's rates of participation during the Great Recession because the program did not automatically expand to meet increased need, the way other safety net programs like SNAP and Medicaid had (U.S. Congress, Senate, Committee on Finance 2010).

Although the number of eligible poor families had increased substantially during the recession, participation in TANF had not increased by a similar amount and had actually declined in some states (U.S. Congress, Senate, Committee on Finance 2012). For Democrats, this indicated a substantive problem with the program as it was legislated and implemented: TANF worked well when there were plenty of jobs, but in bad economic times, when millions of people were looking for work, the program did not respond as it should.

Democrats supported funding the extant TANF contingency fund to a higher level to allow states to meet the increased demand for help. They maintained the contingency fund had supported the creation of more than 250,000 transitional jobs. Although these jobs were temporary, Democrats argued these jobs had helped recipients learn new skills and build work histories. From their point of view, the contingency fund jobs also contributed to economic development by helping small businesses hire employees on a temporary basis and sometimes on a permanent basis (U.S. Congress, Senate, Committee on Finance 2010).

Like their Republican colleagues, Democrats wanted to see the number of families on TANF decrease. However, they wanted to make sure it was not because people were falling through the cracks when assistance was needed or when people were without jobs. For Democrats, the goals of the TANF program were achieved when the number of poor families declined, not when caseloads declined due to poor families' lack of access to or eligibility for services.

Many Democrats supported closure of the "strip club loophole," but accused Republicans of overstating the problem and downplaying the genuine problems of poverty and the lack of jobs. However, a small group of Democrats voiced strong objections to the bill, believing it violated the principle of universal access by imposing additional barriers on families seeking to access essential benefits. Several representatives noted that many TANF recipients reside in rural and urban areas considered "food deserts," so they are often forced to purchase food and other necessities at casinos, clubs, and liquor stores, particularly if they lack transportation.

Finally, Democratic opponents objected to the significant costs associated with the measure. They believed it would impose additional burdens on states and financial institutions that must reconfigure thousands of ATMs. They argued the bill would not save money because it would force states to certify nearly every small business as a non-liquor store, and it would create a nationwide bureaucracy to address a problem that involved less than four one-hundredths of 1 percent (0.04 percent) of all TANF funds (U.S. Congress, House of Representatives 2012).

Republicans on TANF

During U.S. House floor debate, Republicans repeatedly raised the point that, as a candidate, President Clinton had promised welfare reform, yet had vetoed two previous bills, reneging on his promise to the American people. They argued the time had come for President Clinton to keep his commitment and reform the system entirely instead of relying on the "piecemeal" state-waiver process currently used. During debate, several Republicans made speeches describing overall attitudes to welfare reform, identifying five reform principles:

(1) welfare should not be a way of life; (2) welfare should be replaced with work; (3) power and flexibility should be shifted to the states to run welfare programs; (4) non-citizens and felons should not receive welfare; and (5) personal responsibility should be encouraged to halt the rising rates of illegitimacy in the United States. Many Republicans criticized AFDC for creating dependency and contributing to the national deficit. They argued that despite spending more than $5 trillion fighting poverty since the enactment of President Johnson's War on Poverty, the United States has yet to enjoy a reduction in the proportion of citizens living in poverty (U.S. Congress, House of Representatives 2012).

Republican arguments in favor of PRWORA emphasized the importance of individual responsibility. Republicans charged the AFDC demanded nothing from recipients in terms of responsibility, work ethic, learning, or commitment. They contended that, while legislation can design programs to help those struggling to gain financial security, government programs cannot make people succeed. According to many Republicans, changing a welfare recipient's attitude is something that can only be accomplished through the hard work of the individual, for the role of welfare is to provide an opportunity for people to lift themselves out of situations that make them dependent (U.S. Congress, House of Representatives 2012).

Republicans stressed the need for state-level flexibility, admitting the U.S. government does not have all the answers, and so what worked best in one state likely would not work as well in another. They pointed out how states have raced ahead of federal legislators in attacking poverty and developing innovative approaches so states should be given latitude to craft programs. Republicans maintained PRWORA achieved the appropriate balance of power between federal and state governments in that it gave states flexibility, yet also held them accountable in important areas such as reducing dependency and out-of-wedlock births (U.S. Congress 1996).

Republicans were uniformly in favor of enacting time limits on the receipt of welfare. For them, the establishment of time limits returned the program to its original intent, which was to be a safety net for people in crisis encouraging work and personal responsibility, and not a way of life. U.S. House member John Ensign (R-Nevada) said of the intended effects of time limits on welfare recipients, "There is no greater incentive than to know at the end of a certain period of time they are going to have to get a job, they better get their life together, they better get out there, take advantage of the job training we provide, get their life together so they can get off welfare so they can take care of their own family and have that personal responsibility" (U.S. Congress 1996).

Members of the Republican Party considered the reduction of out-of-wedlock births to be a crucial step in reducing welfare dependence. Many Republicans found it difficult to disentangle illegitimacy from welfare because they believed these two issues to be so interrelated. Many Republicans made the argument that since liberals started the War on Poverty, the number and percentage of out-of-wedlock births had skyrocketed. They charged the present welfare system contributes to soaring rates of illegitimacy and leads to family breakdown. For Republicans, PRWORA ended the ill-conceived practice of "subsidizing out-of-wedlock births" (U.S. Congress 1996) by allowing states to limit cash benefits for teen mothers and set family caps to stop the practice of increasing payments for every additional child to which a woman gives birth while on welfare. According to U.S. Representative Jan Meyers, "We are not serving the young people well when we tell them to stay in school and not have children until they are married, and then offer them money to do the opposite" (U.S. Congress 1996).

There was universal support for an increase in work requirements. Often, Republicans believe the best way to move people from dependence to independence are to get them work experience having a job in the private sector. Republicans almost unanimously supported the provisions to exclude immigrants from receiving TANF and other social welfare benefits, believing U.S. citizens to be the priority and reserving welfare benefits for citizens. They charged immigrants' receipt of social welfare benefits conflicts with U.S. law, identifying non-citizens' receipt of public assistance as grounds for deportation. According to Republicans, offering welfare benefits to non-U.S. citizens creates incentives to those who cannot support themselves to immigrate to the United States (U.S. Congress 1996).

When TANF came up for reauthorization in 2010—a year when the economy was still in early stages of recovery from the Great Recession of 2008—Republicans accused Democrats of using the reauthorization process to furtively increase welfare rolls and repeal the 1996 welfare reform that had reduced welfare dependence and poverty. In support of their claims, Republicans cited data showing welfare rolls had grown between 5 percent and 10 percent during the recession (U.S. Congress, House of Representatives, Committee on Ways and Means 2010).

Republicans objected to Democrats' proposals to increase welfare spending during the recession. They characterized such proposals as "bribes" made to states with the goal of increasing welfare rolls—which would in turn make the programs harder to control. They also saw additional funding for jobs programs as "make-work" schemes that produced only temporary improvements in employment numbers. Republicans maintained Congress should help more low-income families train for, look for, find, and keep real jobs in the real economy. They warned that returning to the pre-1996 unsuccessful system would lead to more poverty and despair, not less. Republicans were concerned that too few adult welfare recipients were engaging in activities designed to help them transition from welfare to work and prepare for life off welfare. They cited statistics that only 56 percent of work-eligible adults on welfare were failing to engage in work, education, job searches, domestic-violence counseling, substance-abuse treatment, or work-related activities. Rather than concluding such numbers were acceptable in a harsh economic climate, Republicans considered it even more important that TANF recipients engage in educational and work-readiness activities given the state of the economy (U.S. Congress, Senate, Committee on Finance 2010). According to many Republicans, reasons for the low work participation rate related to overall high unemployment, the states' fiscal resource crunch and a corresponding pull-back in programming, states' use of dubious accounting techniques to weaken the work requirement and avoid engaging adults in work and training, and a significant increase in "child-only" cases that did not include an adult benefit (U.S. Congress, House of Representatives, Committee on Ways and Means 2011, 4).

Finally, the Republican Chairman of the House Subcommittee on Human Resources of the Committee on Ways and Means, Geoff Davis of Kentucky, urged his colleagues to take steps to "plug" the "strip club loophole," noting that some states had already taken steps to prohibit such activity, and closing this "loophole" should also be done at the federal level (U.S. Congress, House of Representatives, Committee on Ways and Means 2011, 4). House of Representatives floor debate indicates that the legislative bill that closed the "strip club loophole" garnered universal Republican support. Republicans felt the measure would strengthen TANF and prevent erosion of public confidence in the program by ensuring TANF funds were used as intended. Republicans argued that closing the loophole would not be as costly or as difficult as Democratic opponents were claiming. One Republican representative noted that although the state of Washington was initially concerned about the cost of fixing the problem, one Washington casino owner reported it took approximately about 4 minutes on the phone to reprogram the casino's ATM. In response to Democratic concerns that TANF beneficiaries would be hurt by not being able to purchase groceries and other necessities at the prohibited establishments, the Republican sponsors of the bill stressed that states would be allowed to make accommodations for stores that sell groceries as well as alcohol (U.S. Congress, House of Representatives 2012).

Gardenia Harris

Further Reading

Cohen, Rick. 2012. "Congress Imposes Limitations on Accessing TANF funds." *Nonprofit Quarterly*, February 29. Accessed August 14, 2014. http://nonprofitquarterly .org/2012/02/29/congress-imposes-limitations-on-accessing-tanf-funds/.

O'Connor, Brendon. 2004. *A Political History of the American Welfare System: When Ideas Have Consequences.* Lanham, MD: Rowman & Littlefield.

Prah, Pamela M. 2012. "Congress Closes a "Strip Club Loophole" for Welfare Recipients." *Bangor Daily News*, February 29. Accessed August 14, 2015. http://bangordailynews .com/2012/02/29/news/nation/congress-closes-strip-club-loophole-for-welfare-recipients/.

Sawhill, Isabel V. 1995. "Overview," in *Welfare Reform: An Analysis of the Issues*, edited by Isabel Sawhill. Washington, DC: Urban Institute.

U.S. Congress. 1996. *Journal of the House of Representatives of the United States.* 104th Cong., 2nd Sess., July 16–22.

U.S. Congress. House of Representatives. 2012. *Welfare Integrity Now for Children and Families Act of 2011.* 112th Cong., 2nd sess. *Congressional Record*, February 1, H315–H322.

U.S. Congress. House of Representatives. Committee on Ways and Means. 2010. *The Role of TANF Program Providing Assistance to Families with Very Low Incomes: Hearing before the Subcommittee on Income Security and Family Support of the Committee on Ways and Means.* 111th Cong., 1st sess., March 11.

U.S. Congress. Senate. Committee on Finance. 2010. *Welfare Reform: A New Conversation on Women and Poverty: Hearing before the Committee on Finance.* 111th Cong., 2nd sess., September 21.

U.S. Congress. Senate. Committee on Finance. 2012. *Combating Poverty: Understanding New Challenges for Families: Hearing before the Committee on Finance.* 112th Cong., 2nd sess., June 5.

Weaver, R. Kent. 2000. *Ending Welfare as We Know It.* Washington, DC: Brookings Institution.

Tax Code Reform

At a Glance

Both the Democratic Party and the Republican Party agree that the United States tax code is too complicated and needs to be simplified. Democrats believe that individual tax rates for poor, working-class, and middle-class households should be lowered and that the "Buffett Rule" should be adopted, so millionaires would pay a higher tax rate. They also believe in lowering the corporate tax rate and providing additional tax breaks to companies willing to locate manufacturing and research and development in America. They also want to close tax loopholes that provide incentives for corporations to shift jobs overseas.

Republicans claim they want to lower individual tax rates on all citizens, regardless of income level. They also state they want to lower the corporate tax rate even further than the Democrats, via either a flat tax or the Fair Tax. Additionally, they would like the United States to join other nations in adopting a territorial tax system that would allow companies to bring back foreign cash without paying U.S. taxes on it, since those funds have already been taxed in foreign countries.

Many Democrats . . .

- Think the wealthiest Americans should shoulder a higher percentage of the overall tax burden
- Believe in lowering the corporate tax rate while also eliminating loopholes
- Believe in giving tax credits to low- and middle-income individuals
- Assert that sensible tax reform could help cut the U.S. deficit

Many Republicans . . .

- Complain that the current U.S. tax code is unnecessarily complex and confusing
- Are committed to dramatically lowering taxes paid by wealthy Americans
- Favor lowering taxes for all socioeconomic classes

- Contend that lowering the corporate tax rate will help both small business owners and large corporations
- Wish to eliminate the estate tax and taxes on interest, dividends, and capital gains
- Would like to see the Internal Revenue Service (IRS) significantly reduced or abolished outright

Overview

Americans have never been particularly fond of taxes. The American Revolutionary War was partially fought over the issue of taxes. "No taxation without representation" was a slogan often used during that period. When the war was over and Americans were creating their new government, they did not give their federal branch much power in regards to taxation. The federal government did not need a lot of funds early on; instead, it relied on tariffs on foreign goods, excise taxes (taxes paid when purchases were made on a specific good, such as alcohol), and donations from the states. The Constitution specifically limited the federal government's ability to impose direct taxes, by stating that direct taxes needed to be distributed in proportion to each state's census population. States were allowed to tax their citizens, with income taxes and other taxes.

A Landmark 1895 Supreme Court Decision on the Constitutionality of the Income Tax

The Wilson-Gorman Tariff was important because it imposed the first peacetime income tax. The income tax was legally challenged and eventually overturned by the Supreme Court, 5–4, in *Pollock v. Farmers' Loan and Trust Company* (1895). The justices found the income tax to be unconstitutional due to Article 1 Section 8. An excerpt from Chief Justice Fuller's majority opinion is below. *Pollock* would be superseded in 1913 by the 16th Amendment to the U.S. Constitution.

The mother country had taught the colonists, in the contests waged to establish that taxes could not be imposed by the sovereign except as they were granted by the representatives of the realm, that self-taxation constituted the main security against oppression. . . . The principle was that the consent of those who were expected to pay it was essential to the validity of any tax.

The States were about, for all national purposes embraced in the Constitution, to become one, united under the same sovereign authority and governed by the same laws. But as they still retained their jurisdiction over all persons and things within their territorial limits, except where surrendered to the general government or restrained by the Constitution. They were careful to see to it that taxation and representation should go together, so that the sovereignty reserved should not be impaired, and that, when Congress, and especially the House of Representatives, where it was specifically provided that all revenue bills must originate, voted a tax upon property, it should be with the consciousness, and under the responsibility, that, in so doing, the tax so voted would proportionately fall upon the immediate constituents of those who imposed it.

More than this, by the Constitution, the States not only gave to the action the concurrent power to tax persons and property directly, but they surrendered their own power to levy taxes on imports and to regulate commerce. All the 13 were seaboard States, but they varied in maritime importance, and differences existed between them in population, in wealth, in the character of property and of business interests. Moreover, they looked forward to the coming of new States from the great West into the vast empire of their anticipations. So when the wealthier States . . . gave up for the common good the great sources of revenue derived through commerce, they did so in reliance on the protection afforded by restrictions on the grant of power.

Thus, in the matter of taxation, the Constitution recognizes the two great classes of direct and indirect taxes, and lays down two rules by which their imposition must be governed, namely the rule of apportionment as to direct taxes, and the rule of uniformity as to duties, imposts and excises.

Source

Pollock v. Farmers' Loan and Trust Company, 157 U.S. 429 (1895), affirmed on rehearing, 158 U.S. 601 (1895)

The first personal income tax and the first corporate tax were the result of the federal government's efforts to pay for the American Civil War. The Revenue Act of 1861 set tax rates at 3 percent on income exceeding $600 and 5 percent on income exceeding $10,000. This law was replaced with the Revenue Act of 1862, which established the Commissioner of Internal Revenue. Several years after the Civil War, Congress allowed the direct taxation laws to expire.

During the late 19th and early 20th centuries, noted one history of taxation, "popular opposition began to mount against what were then the major sources of federal revenues: tariffs, excise taxes, and property taxes" (Slemrod and Bakiji 1996, 22). The first peacetime income tax was passed by Congress in 1894 as the Wilson-Gorman tariff. The tax was needed to make up for revenue that would be lost by tariff reductions. The rate was 2 percent on income over $4,000. Due to the high income limits, less than 10 percent of households were impacted by this legislation. The Supreme Court declared this tax unconstitutional the following year, but that would eventually be overturned with the passage of the 16th Amendment to the U.S. Constitution. Corporate taxation was not considered a violation of the Constitution, since it could be labeled as an excise tax. The corporate tax was adopted permanently in 1909.

The 16th Amendment was adopted on February 3, 1913. It states that "Congress shall have power to lay and collect taxes on incomes, from whatever source derived, without appointment among the several States, and without regard to any census or enumeration." Soon after this amendment passed, a bill was signed into law creating the first permanent personal income tax. The tax had graduated rates (the tax rate increases as the amount subject to taxation increases), ranging from 1 to 7 percent. "Many of today's most important deductions and exclusions were already there in 1913; examples include deductions for home mortgage interest and tax payments to state and local governments, and the exclusion of interest on state and local bonds" (Slemrod and Bakiji 1996, 23). Deductions for charitable contributions were added four years later. As with previous versions of the personal income tax, it did not impact many citizens.

The tax rate in the top bracket has widely fluctuated over the decades. When President Kennedy was in office the top tax rate was 91 percent. The Revenue Act of 1964 cut individual income tax rates across-the-board by about 20 percent and reduced the corporate tax rate slightly. Despite lower tax rates the law actually generated more revenue for the government in the following few years, partially due to increased compliance of taxpayers more willing pay the lower rates.

The Tax Reform Act of 1986 was a major revision to the tax code. The act simplified the income tax code, broadened the tax base, and eliminated many tax shelters. Individual income tax rates went down, with the top rate dropping from 50 percent to 28 percent. "The law also eliminated many of the loopholes that had enabled wealthy individuals and large companies to escape taxation, and it created the alternative minimum tax, which is levied on individual and corporate income that escapes taxation through remaining loopholes" (Cooper 1996, 253). Despite lowering the rate, only a few years later the top tax level was back to 39 percent.

There has not been a major revision of the tax code in almost 30 years, although there have been some changes. Tax brackets have been added back in and tax rates have fluctuated up and down since the 1980s. During the administrations of George H. W. Bush and Bill Clinton the tax rates went up, especially for wealthy taxpayers, although they came down some during the George W. Bush Administration. Currently, there are proposals to radically change the tax code that are popular with some conservatives, most notably through the introduction of a flat tax (in which Americans would pay the same percentage of their income in taxes, irrespective of their annual income) and the Fair Tax (replacing all federal incomes taxes with a national retail sales tax). According to adherents, a key feature of both of these proposals is that it would result in the diminishment or outright elimination of the Internal Revenue Service (IRS).

Democrats on Tax Code Reform

Democrats tent to support simplifying the tax code, but do not support eliminating the current tax system. The United States income tax is progressive, meaning that the tax rate increases as the taxable amount increases. Despite being progressive, some wealthy Americans pay less in taxes than those in the middle class due to loopholes. Democrats often want to close these loopholes and support tax breaks for the middle class. Democrats also tend to support deductions that can assist the poor and middle class, such as the Earned Income Tax Credit and the Child Tax Credit. In addition, they tend to support lowering the corporate tax rate, which is currently the highest of any industrialized country. Some studies indicate, however, that the "effective tax rate" paid by U.S. companies—the rate paid after deductions for pensions, health insurance, and other expenses—actually places the United States squarely in the middle of industrialized countries in terms of corporate taxation. A 2011 study by the Congressional Research Service, for example, determined that the U.S. effective rate was 27.1 percent, slightly lower than the Organization for Economic Cooperation and Development (OECD) average of 27.7 percent (Tsang 2014).

President Obama agrees with his party in regards to the tax code. He has proposed "cutting tax preferences for high-income households; eliminating special tax breaks for oil and gas companies; closing the carried interest loophole for investment fund managers; and eliminating benefits for those who buy corporate jets" (White House 2015). In 2010, President Obama signed the Tax Relief, Unemployment Insurance Reauthorization, and Job Creation Act that extended the lower tax rates passed as part of the Bush tax cut. Two years later, President Obama signed the American Taxpayer Relief Act of 2012, which made permanent the lower tax rate, but also provided for the tax rate on upper income levels to increase to what it had been prior to the Bush administration's 2001 tax cuts.

President Obama and the Democratic Party have promoted the adoption of the Buffett Rule. The Buffett Rule is named after investment billionaire Warren Buffett, who said in 2011 that he thought it was wrong that wealthy people, such as himself, could potentially pay less in federal taxes (as a portion of income) than the middle class (such as his secretary). "The Buffett Rule is the basic principle that no household making over $1 million annually should pay a smaller share of their income in taxes than middle-class families pay" (National Economic Council 2012). More specifically, the president wants no millionaire to pay less than 30 percent of their income in taxes. The rule was submitted for deliberation in the Senate as the Paying a Fair Share Act of 2012 but was stopped by a Republican filibuster. Although not passed, the Buffett Rule continues to be discussed during conversations on tax code reform.

Democrats tend to favor lowering taxes on low- and middle-income individuals, both by lowering tax rates and supporting tax credits for these groups. One such tax credit is the Earned Income Tax Credit (EITC). The EITC is a refundable tax credit for working individuals with lower or moderate income, enacted in 1975. The amount of credit a person receives is dependent on their income and their number of children. In 2013, the EITC benefit ranged from $487 for an individual without children up to $6,044 for an individual with three or more children.

Many Democrats have expressed interest in lowering the corporate tax rate, currently at 35 (2015). In their 2012 platform, Democrats said they are "committed to reforming the corporate tax code to lower tax rates for companies in the United States, with additional relief for those locating manufacturing and research and development on our shores, while closing loopholes and reducing incentives for corporations to shift jobs overseas" (Democratic National Committee 2012). Many companies based in the United States have taken as much as 60 percent of their profits, or $1.7 trillion, to other countries (Goldfarb 2013, 661). The companies do this to avoid paying taxes on this money, which the current system allows. President Obama has proposed lowering the rate to 28 percent by closing loopholes in the tax code. He would also like to give a one-time break on the tax rate to companies who bring back that money. "Obama would levy a lower tax rate—14%—on accumulated overseas cash and use the revenue raised to pay for new roads, bridges and other public infrastructure. Future foreign earnings would be taxed at 19%" (Puzzanghera 2015).

Another option that has been raised is for the United States to adopt a territorial tax system. A territorial tax system would mean that American companies would not have to pay United States taxes on all the money they earn overseas. Several countries use this system, including the United Kingdom, France, and Japan. The United States currently does not require firms to pay taxes unless the money is brought back into the United States.

Even though there have been no major revisions to the tax code recently, there have been some legislative changes that impact taxation. The Affordable Care Act of 2010 has significant implications for the tax code. The law hopes to expand health care coverage through public and private insurance coverage. One of the more controversial aspects of the law is the individual mandate that requires most Americans to obtain health insurance or pay a penalty imposed by the tax code, payable with annual tax returns. The mandate was challenged in the legal system and upheld by the Supreme Court as permissible because of Congress's taxing authority.

Republicans on Tax Code Reform

Republicans tend to believe wealthy Americans should not pay a higher tax rate just because they have more money. In fact, they favor keeping money in the hands of "job-creators" as they believe these businesses will help drive positive economic development. In the 2012 Republican Platform they proposed to extend the Bush tax cuts; reduce marginal tax rates by 20 percent across-the-board in a revenue-neutral manner; eliminate taxes on interest, dividends, and capital gains completely for lower and middle-income taxpayers; end the estate tax; and repeal the alternative minimum tax (Republican National Committee 2012).

Republicans have a potential obstacle to tax code reform in the Americans for Tax Reform (ATR), headed by Grover Norquist. The ATR created the "Taxpayer Protection Pledge," which asks officeholders and candidates to oppose any and all tax increases, whether through rate increases or the elimination of deductions and credits (unless matched dollar-for-dollar by reducing tax rates). Hundreds of Republicans and a handful of Democrats have signed the pledge. Norquist states that any politician that breaks the pledge will see campaign ads in election years that explain how they broke their promise.

The tax cuts signed by President George W. Bush are the Economic Growth and Tax Relief Reconciliation Act of 2001 and the Jobs and Growth Tax Relief Reconciliation Act of 2004. The Bush tax cuts were controversial in some quarters because they temporarily cut the tax rates for some individuals, including the wealthy. The hope was that the tax cuts would spur economic growth and eventually pay for themselves, although the evidence has been inconclusive. After a two-year extension signed in 2010, the Bush tax cuts were given a partial extension via the American Taxpayer Relief Act of 2012. With the act, the tax cuts became permanent for single people making less than $400,000 per year and couples making less than $450,000 per year, but ended for everyone else.

Several Republicans have supported the flat tax over the years. The flat tax was highlighted by Steve Forbes while he was campaigning for the Republican presidential nomination in 1996. Proponents of the flat tax argue that everyone should pay the same percentage of their income in taxes, regardless of their salary and/or accumulated wealth. Flat taxes would be easier to calculate and file, which might reduce the need for the IRS. Supporters believe that a flat tax would encourage savings and investments, as there would be no taxes on these activities. Forbes' plan included exempting low-income individuals from taxation and terminating all deductions, including the popular deductions for mortgage interest and charitable contributions (Cooper 1996, 243). Finally, the flat tax would eliminate the "double taxation" that happens under the current system. For example, business profits are taxed at the corporate level and then again as dividend income on an investor's personal income tax return.

Part of the reason a flat tax has not been adopted is because it is considered regressive, meaning that it affects some taxpayers disproportionately. Essentials that everyone needs cost the same amount of money regardless of one's wealth. For example, a gallon of gas costs the same amount for Warren Buffett as it costs his secretary, so the tax on that gallon of gas would impact the secretary more than Buffett himself. There is also disagreement over the rate that should be chosen to keep the government operational. Critics of the flat tax believe that there are potential consequences to eliminating deductions. For example, the mortgage deduction is considered to be a benefit to potential homebuyers, so eliminating it might negatively impact the housing market if less people buy homes.

Several Republicans have proposed a national sales tax to replace income taxes. Former Indiana Senator Richard Lugar proposed a 17 percent national sales tax, which would have been collected by the states. Former Arkansas Governor Mike Huckabee supported a similar version of the national sales tax, called the Fair Tax. The Fair Tax is a formal proposal that advocates replacing income tax and payroll tax with a sales tax. The tax would be a 30 percent tax on purchases of new goods and services, excluding some necessities.

There are several possible benefits to the Fair Tax. Taxpayers get to keep their entire paycheck. Since it is a sales tax, consumers can decide the amount of tax they are willing to pay (to some degree). A tax on consumption is more stable than one on wages, since most Americans purchase most of their food, shelter, clothing, and so on. Finally, the IRS could be eliminated entirely, since retailers would be responsible for collecting and remitting the taxes directly to the Treasury.

There are several potential drawbacks to the Fair Tax. Like the flat tax, the Fair Tax is regressive, since some necessities are still subject to tax. "The lower a person's income, the greater portion of that income must be spent on essential purchases, such as food and housing, and less is available for saving and investment" (Cooper 1996, 250). Also, it shifts the responsibilities of collecting the taxes to businesses, which might not be collecting taxes already. The Fair Tax provides a fee for acting as a collection agent, adding additional complications (Erb 2015). Finally, it has never been tried on a large scale, so no one knows whether it actually works.

Katharine Leigh

Further Reading

Cooper, Mary H. 1996. "Tax Reform." *CQ Researcher* 6 (11): 241–264.

Democratic National Committee. 2012. "Moving America Forward: 2012 Democratic National Platform." Accessed August 10, 2015. https://www.democrats.org/party -platform.

Erb, Kelly Phillips. 2015. "Our Current Tax v. The Flat Tax v. The Fair Tax: What's the Difference?" *Forbes*, August 7. Accessed August 7, 2015. http://www.forbes.com /sites/kellyphillipserb/2015/08/07/our-current-tax-v-the-flat-tax-v-the-fair-tax-whats -the-difference/.

Goldfarb, Sam. 2013. "On the Road to a Learner Tax Code." *CQ Weekly,* April 15, 660–663.

National Economic Council. 2012. "The Buffett Rule: A Basic Principle of Tax Fairness." Accessed August 12, 2015. https://www.whitehouse.gov/sites/default/files/Buffett_Rule _Report_Final.pdf.

Pollock v. Farmers' Loan and Trust Company, 157 U.S. 429 (1895).

Puzzanghera, Jim. 2015. "Big Differences Divide Democrats, GOP on Overhauling U.S. Tax Code." *Los Angeles Times*, April 17. Accessed December 15, 2015. http://inlandpolitics .com/blog/2015/04/18/los-angeles-times-big-differences-divide-democrats-gop-on -overhauling-u-s-tax-code/.

Republican National Committee. 2012. "We Believe in America: 2012 Republican Plat- form." Accessed August 10, 2015. https://cdn.gop.com/docs/2012GOPPlatform.pdf.

"16th Amendment to the U.S. Constitution: Federal Income Tax." 1913. *Our Documents Initiative.* Accessed November 13, 2015. http://www.ourdocuments.gov/doc.php? flash=true&doc=57.

Slemrod, Joel, and Jon Bakiji. 1996. *Taxing Ourselves: A Citizen's Guide to the Great Debate Over Tax Reform.* Cambridge and London: The MIT Press.

Tsang, Derek. 2014. "Does the U.S. Have the Highest Corporate Tax Rate in the Free World?" *PunditFact*, September 9. Accessed December 10, 2015. http://www.politifact .com/punditfact/statements/2014/sep/09/eric-bolling/does-us-have-highest-corporate -tax-rate-free-world/.

The White House. 2015. "Jobs & the Economy: Putting America Back to Work." Accessed August 12. https://www.whitehouse.gov/economy/reform/tax-reform.

Tax Cuts

At a Glance

Tax cuts have been a centerpiece of Republican domestic economic policy since the presidency of Ronald Reagan. Underpinning the political controversy regarding tax cuts are fundamental philosophical disagreements between Republicans and Democrats regarding the size and scope of government. Republicans, often suspicious of government regulation and intrusion, argue that tax cuts are an important tool in shifting resources from the public sector to the private sector where they can better encourage economic growth. Democrats, who express more confidence in government's ability—and responsibility—to encourage economic fairness, argue that tax cuts hamper society's ability to help those in need. The debate over tax cuts is a recurring theme in many national and state elections. Several high-profile legislative debates have also contributed to the prominence of tax cuts as a policy issue.

In recent years, Republicans have used budget sequestration and negotiations regarding increasing the federal government's debt to limit government's size. Stark differences in perspectives regarding tax burden and economic growth are keys to understanding the fiscal orientations and perceptions of government of both parties. The future will continue to include policy and political debates regarding tax cuts, as Democrats now argue for shifting the tax burden further away from the middle class to the wealthy. This pattern of negotiations regarding tax cuts and tax burden is unlikely to change in the near future.

Democrats and Republicans both are effective at using tax cuts as a political tool to energize different parts of the electorate. The difference in parties usually rests on whose taxes are cut and whether or not government's spending and services as a whole should be reduced. The idea of tax cuts is entrenched in elements of both parties and for that reason will continue to be a part of political rhetoric and decisions at the federal and state levels in the near future.

Many Democrats . . .

- Feel tax cuts should be targeted to benefit businesses so that they can boost employment

- Favor reducing taxes on working-class and middle-class Americans while also increasing taxes on the wealthiest Americans
- Assert that tax cuts without corresponding cuts in government spending are irresponsible and increase the deficit

Many Republicans . . .

- Believe that tax cuts are encourage economic growth
- Favor tax cuts as a measure to limit the size and scope of government
- Contend that tax cuts for the wealthiest Americans produce periods of economic expansion that ultimately benefit Americans of all income levels

---

Overview

The political issue of tax cuts and their impact on the economy, while always a part of electoral rhetoric, has become more prominent at both the federal and state levels in recent years. First, some history regarding the issue is necessary. At least since the 1980s, Republicans and Democrats have disagreed on the role of government in society. Fiscal conservatives, echoing Reagan-era politics, tend to argue that the government is too large and involved in financial markets and individuals' lives. Their reasoning is that the best manner to limit the reach of government is to "starve the beast" (Kudlow 1996) of resources. Well-resourced interest groups, such Americans for Tax Reform, lobby for limiting and reducing taxation in Washington, D.C., and all 50 states. These groups continue to argue that the government is too big, and the tax code removes too much money from the economy by funneling funds that could create economic growth to the government (Americans for Tax Reform 2015).

Democrats tend to believe that the progressive tax code is one of the most effective tools for encouraging economic mobility and ensuring that those who benefit from the economy also pay the costs of regulating it. In 2015, Maryland's Democratic Representative Chris Van Hollen argued that taxes should, in effect, be raised on the wealthiest Americans. He stated, "We have a tax code that reinforces the preference for wealth over work. It's tilted today toward those who make money off of money" (Ollstein 2015).

At the federal level, legislators raised the issue regarding two sets of congressional inaction; the first centered on requirements from the Budget Control Act of 2011 (BCA). The second debate focused on the efforts to authorize increases in the federal debt limit in 2011 and 2013. The BCA resulted from difficulties in the 111th Congress (2009–2010) in passing a budget. The resulting compromise, designed to be punitive to both Republican and Democratic interests, mandated tax increases, and spending cuts. Spending cuts were split evenly based on dollar amounts between defense and non-defense programs. For fiscal Republicans, these austerity measures could effectively achieve many of the policy ends that would typically be achieved through tax cuts, mainly limiting the size of government. This put increased pressure on Democrats to negotiate to maintain current funding levels for agencies and programs.

The second federal event standing as a proxy for tax cuts dealt with the negotiations surrounding increasing the federal debt limit. The negotiations surrounding this issue once again led to the default position that many fiscally conservative Republicans viewed as being favorable. By not increasing the federal government's ability to issue more debt, Republicans in the House of Representatives hoped to deprive the federal government of the resources needed to maintain agencies and programs. Unfortunately for their strategy, in 2011 a ratings agency downgraded the United States' public debt for the first time in history. This led to the compromise that ended the first debt-limit negotiation. Subsequently in 2013, legislators negotiated a second increase in the debt limit to avoid shutting down many federal government programs.

At the state level, this issue emerged recently in Kansas. In 2011, voters elected former U.S. Senator Sam Brownback to the office of Governor. In the following year, he signed into law one of the most aggressive packages of tax cuts an American state had proposed. Brownback, a conservative Republican, argued throughout his campaign that tax cuts were necessary to reinvigorate Kansas' economy (Siebenmark 2012). In the media release, Brownback's administration trumpeted its projections for the benefits of this new fiscal policy. It stated, "Dynamic projections show the new law will result in 22,900 new jobs, give $2 billion more in disposable income to Kansans and increase population by 35,740, all in addition to the normal growth rate of the state" (Brownback 2015).

Democrats in the legislature largely disagreed. Democratic Representative Nile Dillmore of Wichita presented research subsequent to the passing of the bill that 423,175 new jobs must be created to offset the losses that would be created by the tax cuts (Wistrom 2012). While the conclusions of Kansas' experiment in tax cuts has not led to significant economic growth and has incurred a $1 billion budgetary shortfall, voters reelected Governor Brownback in a close race in 2014 (Lowry and Tobias 2014).

The overall orientation toward government and its role in the markets underpins Republicans' and Democrats' positions regarding the tax code. At the forefront of these disagreements are differing party positions regarding the tax rates for the wealthiest Americans, corporations, and the estate tax. Republicans tend to argue that an aggressive estate tax effectively taxes money earned by individuals twice. This is because individuals subject to estate taxes frequently paid income tax when the money was initially earned (U.S. House of Representatives Republicans Conference 2015). Democrats counter that the estate tax is currently ineffective, and only two out of every 1,000 estates are subject to it. This is because of the high threshold (estates must be at least $5.43 million per person) and loopholes such as trust structures (Mahr, Debot, and Huang 2015) reduce payment of the tax.

Democrats on Tax Cuts

Throughout the 1980s and early 1990s, tax cuts were important planks in the presidencies of both Ronald Reagan and George H. W. Bush. In response, many Democrats argued, that far from stimulating growth, tax cuts hamper government's ability to provide services for the poorest people in our society. This is because Democrats oftentimes view government as a progressive force for equity in society. Therefore, taking revenue from the government in the form of tax cuts lessens government's ability to make society fairer and more just. Many Democrats are also more comfortable with using public programs to encourage economic growth. Further, many Democrats argue that the key to the progressive tax system is shifting the cost of government to the wealthy. Many Democrats view tax cuts as an effort to lessen the effective tax rates on America's most affluent citizens.

Democrats have to navigate the potential problem of a nuanced message on tax cuts. This includes squaring the idea that the middle class is overburdened by taxation, with the general belief that government can be a powerful economic force equalized through pro-consumer regulations. Therefore, Democrats in recent years have argued for targeted tax cuts for the middle class (Democratic Policy and Communications 2015). The shift in orientation toward advocating a limited form of tax relief has been subtle. This is due to the popularity among the middle class in recent years for tax cuts (White House 2012).

A Congressman Explains Democratic Opposition to Repealing the Estate Tax

Republicans have long made repeal of the estate tax a centerpiece of their tax reform efforts. Democrats, though, have been just as staunch in opposing repeal. In the following excerpt from an April 16, 2015, speech Congressman Chris Van Hollen (D-MD) detailed the main arguments employed by Democrats against the GOP's efforts in this regard:

> It was barely three weeks ago that the Republicans came to the floor with their "work harder, get less" budget. While making everyday life harder on working Americans, the Republican budget disinvests in the future of our nation by making deep cuts to education, infrastructure, and scientific research. Under their plan, Americans would face smaller paychecks and have a harder time getting ahead or buying a home; kids would have a harder time affording college; and seniors would have a harder time ensuring a secure retirement, with the end of the Medicare guarantee and immediate higher costs.
>
> . . . The estate tax is designed so that it only affects the very wealthiest households. Today, you do not have any estate tax obligation as a couple if your estate is less than $10 million. That means that only 5,500 of America's richest families will pay the estate tax this year. There are cruise ships that hold more people than that. 99.8% of households will never pay it. We do have an estate tax on the amount over $10 million, because

we do not believe that people should get ahead just by the wealth they inherited from others—Americans pride themselves on getting ahead through their own hard work.

But instead of rewarding work, Republicans are passing a massive giveaway for just 5,500 of the wealthiest households in the country. The average tax cut will be $3.3 million. Three-quarters of the cost of this bill goes to households with estates over $20 million. For households with estates worth over $50 million, the average tax cut would be $22.5 million! And right now, the wealthy have rarely been better off. The top 1% of income-earners now holds 42% of all the wealth in the United States. Last week was the 90th anniversary of *The Great Gatsby* being published, and we are heading towards levels of wealth concentration not seen since then!

Source

Van Hollen, Chris. 2015. "Congressman Van Hollen Statement of Opposition to Estate Tax Repeal." April 16. Accessed May 26, 2015. https://vanhollen.house.gov/media-center /speeches/congressman-van-hollen-statement-of-opposition-to-estate-tax-repeal.

In some states, the Democratic Party has had challenges resisting sweeping tax cuts. In North Carolina in 2010, the Republican Party successfully won control of the legislature for the first time since 1870. In 2012, the party also won the gubernatorial race (Ohlemacher 2014). Similar to Kansas, North Carolina Republicans began a program of tax cuts. In response to the new policies, a liberal group led by Reverend William Barber, the North Carolina NAACP President, argued that cuts in government services and the shift in the tax burden away from the state's wealthiest individuals was a moral issue. While garnering considerable publicity for Democrats, as of yet, these "Moral Monday" protests have had little effect on legislative fiscal policies (Lachman 2015).

Republicans on Tax Cuts

Republicans tend to believe that lowering taxes allows businesses and private individuals to aggregate capital that is then used to create private sector jobs. This argument is not new and serves as an expression of some of the deepest economic differences between the two parties. Tied to the issue of tax cuts is the idea of government efficiency. Frequently Republicans argue that by not allowing capital to stay with businesses and instead shifting it to the government, effective economic growth is stifled (Hayek 1944).

A recent controversy regarding tax cuts was the result of the economic policies of President George W. Bush. In both 2001 (Economic Growth and Tax Reconciliation Act of 2001) and 2003 (Jobs and Growth Tax Relied Reconciliation Act of 2003), President Bush signed legislation that lowered marginal tax rates for most Americans. In 2006, Bush defended his aggressive tax cuts by arguing that cuts were key to cutting the deficit. He stated, "We're on our way to cutting our deficit in half by 2009. And I'm going to give you some ideas as to how we can do that. The budget strategy has three parts. The first part is to promote economic growth by keeping taxes low. The second part is to restrain spending. And the third part is to insist that federal programs produce results" (PR Newswire 2006).

Likewise, Vice President Dick Cheney also argued that the tax cuts had been successful in creating private sector growth. In a speech in 2006, he stated, "To remain competitive, we need to keep this economy growing—and growth is more likely when Americans have more of their own money to spend, to save, and to invest. In the last five years, the Bush tax relief has left $880 billion in the hands of American workers, investors, small businesses, and families. They have used it to help produce more than four years of uninterrupted economic growth" (Cheney 2006).

With the election of Barack Obama as president in 2008 in the midst of an economic crisis, Republican positions continued to reflect a preference for lessening the tax burden on Americans. The emergence of the fiscally conservative "Tea Party" movement has also focused Republican lawmakers to a greater extent on austerity measures. The shift in rhetoric among Republicans was notable. Members of the Tea Party argued that tax cuts are a moral issue. With government debt continuing to grow, tax cuts, and decreased spending, they believe, are the appropriate actions. They state, "When given the choice between paying higher taxes and receiving fewer government services, a vast number of Americans chose receiving fewer government services" (Tea Party Patriots 2015)

George W. Bush Summarizes the Modern Republican Position on Tax Cuts

On February 8, 2006, Republican President George W. Bush laid-out the prevailing Republican position on tax cuts in succinct fashion:

> First, we're going to keep the taxes low to make sure the economy grows. My philosophy is this: When Americans are allowed to keep more of their own money to spend and save and invest, that helps the economy grow; and when the economy grows, people can find work. If entrepreneurs have more money in their pocket, they're going to use it to expand their businesses, which mean somebody is more likely to find work. If consumers have more money in their pocket, they're likely to demand additional good or services. And in a marketplace economy when somebody demands a good or a service, somebody meets that demand with product, or the service. And when that demand is met, it means somebody is more likely to find work. Cutting taxes means jobs for the American people.
>
> . . . We lowered taxes, and in doing so the message was, and the philosophy is you can spend your money better than the government can spend its money. We want

you making decisions for your families. We want you making investments. And so we cut taxes on families by lowering income tax rates and doubling the child credit. We reduced the marriage penalty. I've never understood a tax code that penalizes marriage. Seems like to me we ought to be encouraging marriage in the tax code. We put the death tax on its way to extinction. My view is, is that if you're running a small business you ought not to have to pay taxes twice, once while you're living and once after you die. If you're a farmer or a rancher, you ought to be allowed—the tax code ought to encourage you to be able to pass your property on to whomever you choose.

Source

Bush, George W. 2006. "Address on the 2007 Budget." Accessed November 13, 2015. http://www.presidentialrhetoric.com/speeches/02.08.06.html.

More recently the grassroots energy supplied by the Tea Party for conservative Republican action has focused less on tax cuts and shifted to a discussion of President Obama's Affordable Care Act. This is because, in part, many Tea Partiers view the Affordable Care Act's individual mandate as an effective tax increase.

While more centrist Republicans have attempted to link tax cuts to congressional action raising the debt limit (the total amount of money the United States is able to borrow to meet its obligations). In 2013, Republican Speaker of the House John Boehner affirmed the statements of President Bush in 2006, while adding a Tea Party perspective on tax cuts when he stated, "Fixing the tax code and lowering rates means more jobs and higher wages for the American people. Voting for this budget means supporting the Keystone pipeline and American-made energy, means more jobs and lower energy bills. Repealing Obamacare and supporting patient-centered reforms means more jobs and lower health care costs for the American people" (Boehner 2013).

While many Democrats criticized the Republican Bush-era tax cuts, President Obama was unable to undo the policy during his first two years in office. However, Obama enjoyed considerable long-term leverage because the Bush tax cuts were set to automatically expire in 2010 absent any legislation extending them. In 2010, subsequent to a midterm election during which Republicans regained control of the House, Republicans on Capitol Hill threatened a variety of legislative actions in an effort to pressure the president to extend Bush's tax cuts. They managed to secure a two-year extension of the tax cuts, but in 2012 Obama and his fellow Democrats received just enough grudging support from a minority of Republicans to pass the American Taxpayer Relief Act. This act, which Obama signed in January 2013, kept the tax cuts for middle- and working-class households but pushed the tax rate for the wealthiest Americans back up to pre-Bush levels.

Michael R. Potter

Further Reading

Americans for Tax Reform. 2015. "About." Accessed May 14, 2015. http://www.atr.org /about.

Boehner, John. 2013. "The Peoples' House Passes a Budget." Accessed May 12, 2015. http:// boehner.house.gov/the-peoples-house-passes-a-balanced-budget/.

Brownback, Samuel. 2015. "Governor Brownback Signs Pro-Growth Tax Legislation." *Media Release*. May 14, 2015. Accessed May 15. http://governor.ks.gov/media-room /media-releases/2012/05/22/governor-brownback-signs-pro-growth-tax-legislation.

Bush, George W. 2006. "Address on the 2007 Budget." February 8. Accessed November 17, 2015. http://www.presidentialrhetoric.com/speeches/02.08.06.html.

Cheney, Richard. 2006. "Remarks by the Vice President on the 2006 Agenda." February 9. Accessed November 4, 2015. http://georgewbush-whitehouse.archives.gov/news /releases/2006/02/print/20060209-9.html.

Democratic Policy and Communications Center. 2015. "Senate Democrats Reject Appro- priations Bills That Keep Devastating, Automatic Cuts." May 21. Accessed May 29. http://www.dpcc.senate.gov/?p=issue&id=416.

Hayek, Friedrich. 1944. *The Road to Serfdom*. London: George Routledge & Sons.

Kudlow, Lawrence. 1996. "Cut Taxes, Starve the Beast." *Wall Street Journal*, September 30, A18.

Lachman, Samantha. 2015. "Moral Monday Returns with Public Opinion, if Not the North Carolina Legislature on Its Side." *Huffington Post*. January 28. Accessed May 29, 2015. http://www.huffingtonpost.com/2015/01/28/moral-monday-north-carolina _n_6564352.html.

Lowry, Bryan, and Suzanne Perez Tobias. 2014. "Sam Brownback Prevails over Paul Davis for Second Term as Kansas Governor." *The Wichita Eagle*, November 4. Accessed May 15, 2015. http://www.kansas.com/news/politics-government/election/article3565951 .html.

Marr, Chuck, Brandon Debot, and Chye-Ching Huang. 2015. "Eliminating Estate Tax on Inherited Wealth Would Increase Deficits and Inequality." *Center on Budget and Pol- icy Priorities*. Updated April 13. Accessed May 12, 2015. http://www.cbpp.org/sites /default/files/atoms/files/3-24-15tax.pdf.

Ohlemacher, Stephen. 2014. "GOP Uses Historic Win to Remake North Carolina Map." *Associated Press*, October 16. Accessed on May 29, 2015. http://www.salon.com /2014/03/31/gop_uses_historic_win_to_remake_north_carolina_map/.

Ollstein, Alice. 2015. "Top Democrats in Congress to Release Unapologetically Progressive Tax Plan." *Think Progress*. January 12. Accessed May 27, 2015. http://thinkprogress.org /economy/2015/01/12/3610603/democrat-tax-plan/.

PR Newswire. 2006. "Remarks by President Bush to the Business and Industry Association of New Hampshire." February 6. Accessed November 17, 2015. http://www.prnewswire.com/ news-releases/remarks-by-president-bush-to-the-business-and-industry-association -of-new-hampshire-55249812.html.

Siebenmark, Jerry. 2012. "Kansas Small Business Owners Say Elimination of Income Tax Is a Big Help." *The Wichita Eagle*, May 24. Accessed May 14, 2015. http://www.kansas .com/news/business/article1092681.html.

Tea Party Patriots. 2015. "Tax Reform." Accessed May 12. http://www.teapartypatriots.org /ourvision/tax-reform/.

U.S. Congress. 2011. "Budget Control Act of 2011." 112th Cong., 1st Sess. January 5. Accessed November 17, 2015. http://www.gpo.gov/fdsys/pkg/BILLS-112s365enr/pdf /BILLS-112s365enr.pdf.

U.S. Congress. 2001. "Jobs and Growth Tax Relief Reconciliation Act of 2003." P.L. 108-27, 108th Cong., May 28. Accessed November 17, 2015. http://www.gpo.gov/fdsys/pkg /PLAW-108publ27/html/PLAW-108publ27.htm.

U.S. Congress. 2001. "Economic Growth and Tax Relief Reconciliation Act of 2001." P.L. 107-16, 107th Cong., June 7. Accessed November 15, 2015. http://www.gpo.gov /fdsys/pkg/PLAW-107publ16/html/PLAW-107publ16.htm.

U.S. House of Representatives Republicans Conference. 2015. "Real Estate Tax Horror Stories. Real Estate Tax Solutions." April 16. Accessed May 12, 2015. http: http://gop.gov /real-estate-tax-horror-stories-real-estate-tax-solutions/.

The White House. 2012. "Extending Middle Class Tax Cuts for 98% of Americans and 97% of Small Businesses." *Blog*. Accessed on May 29, 2015. https://www.whitehouse.gov/blog /2012/07/09/extending-middle-class-tax-cuts-98-americans-and-97-small-businesses.

The White House, Office of the Press Secretary. 2010. "Fact Sheet on the Framework Agreement on Middle Class Tax Cuts and Unemployment Insurance." December 7. Accessed May 27, 2015. https://www.whitehouse.gov/the-press-office/2010/12/07/fact -sheet-framework-agreement-middle-class-tax-cuts-and-unemployment-in.

Wistrom, Brent D. 2012. "Kansas Would Need 423,175 New Jobs to Offset Tax Cuts, Researcher Says." *The Wichita Eagle*, March 28. Accessed May 14, 2015. http://www .kansas.com/news/politics-government/article1089176.html.

Tax Shelters

At a Glance

Most people agree that corporations and individuals who evade their "fair share" of taxes should be stopped. The disagreement is over what is fair and what constitutes an abuse of the system? Members of both parties agree that there is a need to reform the tax code, particularly to simplify it and close what they believe to be tax loopholes, similar to what was done with the 1986 Tax Reform Act. That is often where the similarities end, though, for Democrats and Republicans do not always agree on what should be a legal tax shelter, what tax loopholes should be closed, or what to do with the saved revenue.

Many Republicans . . .

- Think legitimate tax shelters are too complicated and cost too much in tax preparation
- Contend tax shelters promote an unfair tax base
- Say tax shelters hinder economic growth
- Believe tax shelters should be minimized but offset with tax rate reductions

Many Democrats . . .

- Assert legitimate tax shelters are hurting the country financially
- Say tax shelters are too complicated and used disproportionately by the wealthy
- Believe tax shelters should be minimized to generate more tax revenue

---

Overview

Since the "intolerable acts" enacted by King George III during colonial times, individuals and corporations have resisted what they believed to be over-taxation. From the Boston Tea Party to the recent Tea Party rallies individuals have fought back against perceived abuses of the government's power to tax. The modern government has responded by allowing individuals and companies to decrease their taxable income base using rules that are believed to encourage other types of benefits to society. These often come in the forms of tax credits, tax subsidies, or tax shelters, although the term tax shelter is used the least as it has a negative connotation.

According to the IRS, tax shelters are "investments that yield tax benefits" when "Congress has concluded that the loss of revenue is an acceptable side effect of special tax provisions designed to encourage taxpayers to make certain types of investments" (U.S. Department of Treasury 2014, para. 1). For example, both parties generally support corporate tax credits or shelters aimed at research projects. In 2012, both President Obama and Republican presidential nominee Mitt Romney included a research credit as part of their tax plans. Some approved individual tax shelters include retirement savings, homeownership, long-term investments, and tax credits received for children (Bell 2008).

An "abusive tax shelter" is when there is believed to be "little or no benefit to society" (U.S. Department of Treasury 2014, para. 1). Where Congress draws this line makes a huge difference in what is allowed and what is considered an abuse. To ensure a fair taxation system Congress has passed laws designed to prevent abuses. Many argue, however, that the complexity of the tax code allows companies to find "tax loopholes" that are technically legal although not necessarily what Congress intended. The term "loophole" usually indicates that the person believes an individual or company is reducing their taxable income through tax shelters beyond what was intended by Congress. The term "haven" is most often used to describe overseas locations where money being sheltered to avoid paying taxes in the United States.

The last major overhaul to the Tax Code was in 1986 in a push led by Republican President Ronald Reagan with a split Congress. The Senate was controlled by Republicans and the House of Representatives by Democrats. According to Senate Finance Committee Chairman Orrin Hatch, a Republican Senator from Utah, this legislation "reformed a costly and complicated tax system into a simpler one with lower tax rates for American households and businesses, affording them greater personal prosperity" (Hatch 2015, para. 8). Nearly 30 years later, Hatch expressed his belief that similar reform is needed to address the shortcomings of an excessively "costly and complex" system.

This sentiment is echoed by members of both parties who lament the complicated tax code and many loopholes, although they tend to disagree about the specific changes that should be made. Members of both parties also point to the 1986 overhaul as proof of the success of their specific plans, but so far they have been unable to work together to create a new reform law. Two former senators who had worked together on the 1986 reform law recently discussed before the Senate Finance Committee what it took to get a reform passed then, as well as what should be done now.

Former Democratic Senator Bill Bradley of New Jersey stated in a hearing before the Senate Finance Committee that the 1986 tax reform "eliminated about $30 billion per year in loopholes, and the wealthy, even though the top rate was reduced from 50 percent to 28 percent, ended up paying a bigger percentage of the total income taxes collected" (Bradley 2015, 1). In regard to the current tax system he suggested that, "by eliminating most of the tax deductions, exclusions, and credits (now worth $911 billion), we could reduce rates, make the system fairer, and raise revenue" allowing the government to spend more on education, health, and pension security (Bradley 2015, 1). He further argued that changes to the tax code should be done as one large package, so decreasing opportunities for tax sheltering money would be offset by lower tax rates. Former Republican Senator Bob Packwood echoed this sentiment at the same hearing, describing how it took several attempts back in 1986 to balance "the attraction of the low rates versus the opposition we would get from eliminating certain deductions" (Packwood 2015, 4). He needed three groups to get onboard with the plan: Democrats who wanted loopholes eliminated, Republicans who wanted lower tax rates, and people of economic influence who would like both changes but also wanted a simpler tax code. It was a bipartisan group of seven senators, including Packwood and Bradley, who worked together to craft the bill that ultimately passed both Houses and was signed by President Reagan. According to Packwood, they created a bill that "raised the taxes significantly on corporations and rich individuals. They would pay more and middle income and the poor would pay less" (Packwood 2015, 18).

To outward appearances, the climate in recent Congresses has been much the same as it was in 1986, with the majority of Democrats wanting to close tax loopholes and the majority of Republicans focused on lower tax rates. Bradley's suggestion for how to spend the saved revenue signifies the major difference between the two parties—a difference that has intensified since the Reagan era, with dwindling enthusiasm for compromise. Democrats focus on closing loopholes particularly on corporations to increase the amount of revenue the government receives. On the other hand, Republicans focus on simplifying the tax code along with reducing rates so that most individuals and businesses will pay roughly the same amount of taxes while also spending a lot less on tax preparation and compliance, thereby keeping it revenue neutral (Ferrechio 2014).

In 2015 Democratic Senator Ron Wyden of Oregon commented that "if there's one obvious similarity between 1986 and today, it's that people are quick to say tax reform is impossible. . . . [S]o what happened three decades ago will happen again: turning the impossible into the possible" (Wyden 2015, 1). He believes "the biggest lesson from 1986 is that tax reform is possible when Democrats and Republicans set partisanship aside, come together and focus on shared principles" (Wyden 2015, 2).

An effort was made in 2013 to put partisanship aside when control of Congress was once again divided between the parties, this time with the Democrats controlling the Senate and Republicans the House. The House Ways and Means

Committee Chairman, Republican Dave Camp of Michigan, and the Senate Finance Committee Chairman Max Baucus, a Democrat from Montana, came together to create a website asking for the public's input on the tax code problem. The two committees held more than 50 joint hearings on the tax code and according to the website, "both committees heard a loud and clear message—America's tax code is broken, unpredictable and out of date" (U.S. Congress, Senate Finance Committee and House Ways and Means Committee 2014, para. 8). Republican Senator Marco Rubio of Florida reflected the sentiments of many members of both parties when he observed that "the complexity of the tax code often benefits the wealthy and well connected who can afford accountants, lawyers, and lobbyists, yet leaves many people behind" (Rubio 2015, 16). However, despite agreeing that something needs to be done and trying to work together to create a solution, the two parties prescriptions for updating the tax code—a task that inevitably requires addressing tax shelters—remained starkly different.

Republicans on Tax Shelters

Major changes to the tax code and elimination of many tax shelters in 1986 were led by President Reagan and a bipartisan group of senators led by Republican Senator Bob Packwood. There is a current push by Republicans to make changes to the tax code, including the elimination of some tax shelters. As a general rule, the Republicans require that any elimination of tax shelters be accompanied by a decrease in the current tax rate. They usually refer to the need to simplify the tax code as a top reason for reform, as well as making it more profitable for companies to bring money back to the United States.

Many tax plans proposed by Republicans intend to offset the elimination or decrease of tax shelters with a tax rate that would leave the effective percentage of tax roughly the same, but would decrease the need for complicated accounting systems and minimize the risk of abuse. These plans would keep the amount of tax paid by most individuals roughly the same amount as what they currently pay, but would aim to reduce the ability of many larger corporations from avoiding paying their fair share of taxes. Some tax shelters would remain in place, such as IRAs, that encourage people to save for their future. Republicans tend to view IRAs more favorably than Democrats in terms of allowing them to be used as tax shelters by the wealthy who already have a secure retirement future—which leaves less discussion about changes to these types of shelters.

Senator Hatch is Chairman of the Senate Finance Committee, which has held several hearings on reforming the tax code, including one on eliminating tax shelters that are perceived to be allowing companies and wealthy individuals to avoid paying their fair share of taxes. Hatch argues that "tax reforms should broaden the tax base by eliminating or reducing a number of tax expenditures, along with lowering tax rates, and removing distortions" (Hatch 2015, para. 16). He further argues that simplifying the tax code by eliminating some of the current tax shelters

---

One Republican's Call for Addressing America's "Outdated" Tax Code

Senator Orrin Hatch has served as Chairman of the Senate Finance Committee since 2014, when Republicans gained majority control of the Senate. As chairman Hatch has held several hearings on the need for tax reform, in particular lowering tax rates and reducing government regulation. He believes that the current tax code is a burden to businesses and individuals, and that it should be completely overhauled.

On February 10, 2015, Senator Hatch convened a special hearing to see "what lessons we can learn from the Tax Reform Act of 1986, the last successful overhaul of our nation's tax code." Like many in Washington, D.C., Hatch points to the 1986 reform as a model for success. He believes the vision for proposed legislation should focus on the end goals of creating opportunities for families and businesses rather than on the specific rates or changes. Hatch has highlighted seven principles that he claims are the foundation of his tax reform efforts: economic growth; fairness; simplicity; revenue neutrality; permanence; competitiveness; and promoting savings and investment.

Sources

Hatch, Orrin. 2015. "Economy & Taxes." *Orrin Hatch, United States Senator for Utah*. August 15, 2015. Accessed August 20, 2015. http://www.hatch.senate.gov/public/index.cfm /economyandtaxes.

Hatch, Orrin. 2015. "Hatch Statement at Finance Hearing on Lessons from the Tax Reform Act of 1986." *Orrin Hatch, United States Senator for Utah*. February 10. Accessed August 20, 2015. http://www.hatch.senate.gov/public/index.cfm/releases?ID=63278bbf-8acf-435f -a1da-48eccf9bb922.

---

will lead to greater clarity and make compliance easier thereby freeing up resources for businesses and families. According to Hatch, individual taxpayers and corporations currently spend six billion hours preparing taxes and over $170 billion to ensure compliance. He concludes that with reform this would be money companies could spend on innovation and job creation.

GOP Representative Paul Ryan (Wisconsin), who in 2015 left his position as Chair of the House Committee on Ways and Means to become Speaker of the House, believes our tax system "is notoriously complex, patently unfair, and highly inefficient" (Ryan 2015, para. 2). The Committee on Ways and Means promotes tax reform that it describes as being fairer and flatter than the changes recommended by President Obama and his fellow Democrats (U.S. Congress, House, Committee on Ways and Means 2015a). One of the Committee's tax reform priorities is to simplify how corporations pay taxes on international goods in an effort to encourage growth. Currently the full tax rate of 35 percent is paid on earnings only when these earnings are brought back to the United States, which discourages companies from bringing the capital back. Ryan and other Republican committee members have suggested using a system similar to many other countries' that would dramatically reduce the tax rate for foreign profits. The belief is that this would encourage companies to bring the money "home" instead of finding offshore tax shelters created to protect the money from a high tax rate (U.S. Congress, House, Committee on Ways and Means 2015b). This is one area where Republicans are likely to find cooperation with Democrats.

The GOP's inability to find common ground with the Obama administration on comprehensive tax reform has the Republicans looking to 2016, when they hope to retain control of Congress and put a Republican in the White House. To that end, congressional Republicans have been working on a comprehensive tax reform plan that they claim will significantly reduce the individual tax rate, yet increase the tax base by eliminating some of the current tax shelters to increase the tax base. As of mid-2015, however, the GOP had not issued any detailed information about what types of shelters would be adjusted, reduced, or eliminated (Snell 2015).

Democrats on Tax Shelters

Many Democrats assert the Reagan Era Tax Reform Act of 1986 fell short of solving America's tax issues by leaving in place a myriad of ways for individuals and businesses to avoid paying taxes—especially wealthy individuals and powerful multinational corporations for whom various tax shelters were available. Democrats had hoped the act would treat all income alike and eliminate tax preferences. Since it was passed, each year Congress has amended it and added thousands of pages to the code. The 1986 act did manage to limit some individual tax shelters—specifically those the organizations were not themselves actively managing but were merely created to incur big losses on paper in order to offset their earnings or investments. Many Democrats, however, believe that in the intervening three decades, the tax code has been repeatedly manipulated to favor an elite few, providing them with the means to shelter profits rather than pay taxes.

While allowing individuals to save for retirement is viewed by most Democrats as a legal tax shelter, they assert that current tax laws allow for abuse by wealthy individuals who are merely avoiding taxes because they do not need the money for retirement. Senator Wyden cited the nearly 9,000 taxpayers with IRAs worth around $5 million, which he called "mega IRAs" as proof that the current system is "out of whack" allowing some to shelter millions while others are not able to save at all (Becker 2014). Another area where Democrats believe changes have unevenly affected taxpayers is the lack of changes in capital gains tax rates, while individual income tax rates have gone up. In 1986, the top tax rate for both was 28 percent, but individual income rates now top out around 40 percent. Many wealthy individuals invest their money and are able to pay a much lower tax rate than those who work to earn their money. "Critics of lower capital gains rates say it can encourage tax sheltering" among the wealthiest Americans (Becker 2013, para. 4). Corporate tax shelters also remain a major concern of the Democratic Party.

One Democrat's Quest to Close Tax Loopholes

Democratic Senator Ron Wyden of Oregon is one of Washington's strongest advocates of tax reform, particularly closing tax loopholes for special interests. He has served at various times as both chairman and ranking member on the Senate's Finance Committee, and he is also a member of the Joint Committee on Taxation. In these assignments he has sought to work with members of the Republican Party to get a comprehensive tax reform bill that will eliminate these loopholes, keep jobs in the U.S., and promote economic growth.

In 2011, for example, he introduced the Bipartisan Tax Fairness and Simplification Act, co-sponsored by Republican Senator Dan Coats. According to Wyden's website, it "would simplify the tax system, hold down rates for individuals and families, provide tax relief to the middle class and create incentives for businesses to grow and invest in the United States." Under this plan most middle and lower income families would pay the same or less in taxes. Companies would pay less in the U.S. than they do with several U.S. trading partners, including Canada, Germany, and France. This bill did not make it out of Congress, but Wyden has not stopped pushing for reform.

In 2012, Wyden argued that "instead of investing in new jobs and innovation, U.S. businesses are investing time, energy, and resources to avoid paying taxes." As a result, he believes that it is time to eliminate tax shelters and loopholes that profit only special interests. He believes reform requires a bipartisan effort and points to the success of the 1986 tax reform as a model for both how to create bipartisan legislation as well as what needs to be done. He believes the 1986 reform "did more for the economy as a whole than special tax provisions or sweetheart deals." Wyden focuses on the corporate tax codes but he recognizes that many businesses fall under the individual tax code, which he also sees as badly in need of reform.

Sources

Wyden, Ron. 2011. "Bipartisan, Comprehensive Tax Reform Will Reform America's Competitive Edge." *Ron Wyden, United States Senator for Oregon.* Accessed August 21, 2015. https://www.wyden.senate.gov/news/blog/post/bipartisan-comprehensive-tax-reform-will-restore-americas-competitive-edge.

Wyden, Ron. 2012. "Wyden-Coats Tax Plan." *Ron Wyden, United States Senator for Oregon.* Accessed August 21, 2015. https://www.wyden.senate.gov/priorities/wyden-coats-tax-plan.

The federal government loses as much as 90 billion dollars each year to offshore corporate tax shelters (Clausing 2012). Democratic Senator Bernie Sanders of Vermont, for example, has pointed out that according to the Government Accountability Office (GAO), 83 Fortune 100 companies use offshore tax shelters. He has cited such figures in crafted legislation that would end tax sheltering by profitable corporations (Sanders 2015). One commonly utilized technique is to make a financial transaction that has losses to offset the gains—the losses are then allocated to a U.S. corporation and the gains to a taxpayer not subject to U.S. income tax. It is also common for U.S. subsidiaries of foreign companies to overpay the corporation for intangible assets to shift income abroad therefore reducing taxation in the United States.

Corporate tax reform is an area where compromise is possible between the two parties, but it is not likely to happen because Republicans want to couple it with a decrease in individual tax rates. Some Democrats, including President Obama, have publicly stated that they will not agree to a tax reform plan that lowers individual tax rates for the top income bracket, which has gone up since President Obama took office. Republicans have pointed out this would overlook small businesses, a major part of their constituency, who pay taxes as individuals. President Obama responded by signing the Small Business Jobs Act (2010), which created a number of tax cuts for small businesses. All of these "tax cuts" have come in the form of tax credits or subsidies which allow businesses to deduct expenses, although such targeted tax cuts have been criticized for further complicating the current tax code (Holan and Jacobson 2012). While most Democrats agree with the Republicans that the tax code is too complicated, the two parties seem unable to reach a compromise to simplify the tax code. The Ways and Means Committee Democrats "believes we need a simpler, fairer tax code that protects working families, encourages economic growth and domestic job creation, and is fiscally responsible" (U.S. Congress, House, Ways and Means Committee Democrats 2015, para. 1). This is why a few Democratic congressmen are joining with Republicans calling for lower overall tax rates with fewer ways to shelter income, although there are still many disagreements between the two sides about what the rates and legitimate tax shelters should be.

Looking ahead to the 2016 presidential election, Senator Bernie Sanders and former Senator and Secretary of State Hillary Clinton are the Democratic frontrunners. Clinton described what some have referred to as a "safe" tax plan in July of 2015: a "Buffett tax" on high income households, small business tax relief, new taxes on multinational corporations that benefit from offshore tax shelters, tax credits for businesses that hire or train new employees, and an end to carried interest rules that benefit investment firms (Gleckman 2015). As recently as April of 2015, Sanders has submitted bills to stop corporations from hiding income in overseas tax shelters as well as ending incentives for companies that send jobs offshore. According to Sanders, "At a time when we have a $18.2 trillion national debt and an unsustainable federal deficit; at a time when many of the largest corporations in America are paying no federal income taxes; and at a time when corporate profits are at an all-time high, it is past time for corporate America to pay their fair share in taxes so that we can create the millions of jobs this country needs" (Pianin 2015, para. 7).

Simplifying the tax code is another area where both parties tend to agree, although they also tend to disagree on how the tax code should be simplified. In 2012, the compliance costs for all Americans (individuals and corporations) filing federal taxes is estimated to have cost $37 billion, so the Democrats argue that it is only the wealthy who have the capability to find tax shelters and therefore the tax burden is more heavily borne by the lower income Americans (Tax Foundation 2014). Republicans agree individuals and companies are spending too much on tax code compliance, although they usually see it as a way to allow both to keep more of their money.

Renee Prunty and
Amanda Swartzendruber

Further Reading

Becker, Bernie. 2013. "Report: Capital gains rates could play crucial role in tax reform." *The Hill*. August 27. Accessed February 23, 2015. http//thehill.com/policy/finance/318993 -report-capital-gains-rates-could-play-key-role-in-tax-reform.

Becker, Bernie. 2014. "Wyden wants action on 'mega IRAs.'" *The Hill*. November 19. Accessed February 23, 2015. http://thehill.com/policy/finance/224811-wyden-wants -action-on-mega-iras.

Bell, Kay. 2008. "Four IRS-Approved Tax Shelters." *The Street*. March 3. Accessed July 30, 2015. http://www.thestreet.com/story/10407288/1/four-irs-approved-tax-shelters .html.

Bradley, Bill. 2015. *Testimony before the Senate Finance Committee*. 114th Cong., 1st sess., February 10. Accessed July 30, 2015. http://www.finance.senate.gov/imo/media/doc /Senator%20Bradley%20Testimony.pdf.

Clausing, Kimberly A. 2012. "A Challenging Time for International Tax Policy." *Tax Notes*, 136: 281–283.

Faller, Brian. 2015. "Ryan's Move Could Be Big Boost for Tax Reform." *Politico*. November 2. Accessed November 5, 2015. http://www.politico.com/story/2015/11/paul-ryan -tax-reform-house-speaker-215405.

Ferrechio, Susan. 2014. "Republican-Majority Congress Scales Back Tax Reform Hopes." *Washington Examiner*. December 26. Accessed July 30, 2015. http://www.washington examiner.com/republican-majority-congress-scales-back-tax-reform-hopes/article /2557753.

Gleckman, Howard. 2015. "Hillary Clinton Outlines Her Play It Safe Tax Agenda." *Forbes*. July 13. Accessed August 10, 2015. http://www.forbes.com/sites/beltway/2015/07/13 /hillary-clinton-outlines-her-play-it-safe-tax-agenda/.

Hatch, Orrin. 2015. "Hatch Statement at Finance Hearing on Lessons from the Tax Reform Act of 1986." *Orrin Hatch, United States Senator for Iowa*. February 10. Accessed August 21, 2015. http://www.hatch.senate.gov/public/index.cfm/releases?ID=63278bbf-8acf -435f-a1da-48eccf9bb922.

Holan, Angie Drobnic, and Louis Jacobson. 2012. "Barack Obama Said He's Cut Taxes for 'Middle-Class Families, Small Businesses.'" *Politifact*, September 7. Accessed November 10, 2015. http://www.politifact.com/truth-o-meter/statements/2012/sep/07/barack -obama/barack-obama-said-hes-cut-taxes-middle-class-famil/.

Packwood, Bob. 2015. *Testimony before the Senate Finance Committee*. 114th Cong., 1st sess., February 10. Accessed July 30, 2015. http://www.finance.senate.gov/imo/media /doc/Senator%20Packwood%20Testimony.pdf.

Pianin, Eric. 2015. "Corporate Tax Havens Stiff Taxpayers by $110B a Year." *The Fiscal Times*, April 15. Accessed November 5, 2015. http://www.thefiscaltimes.com/2015/04/15 /Corporate-Tax-Havens-Stiff-Taxpayers-110B-Year.

Rubio, Marco. 2015. "Economic Growth and Family Fairness Tax Reform Plan." *Marco Rubio United States Senator for Florida.* March 4. Accessed July 30, 2015. http://www.rubio.senate .gov/public/index.cfm/files/serve/?File_id=2d839ff1-f995-427a-86e9-267365609942.

Ryan, Paul. 2015. "Taxes." *U.S. Congressman Paul Ryan Serving Wisconsin's 1st Congressional District.* Accessed July 30, 2015. http://paulryan.house.gov/issues/issue/?IssueID= 12228.

Sanders, Bernie. 2015. "Offshore Tax Havens." *Bernie Sanders, United States Senator for Vermont.* April 14. Accessed July 11, 2015. http://www.sanders.senate.gov/newsroom /recent-business/offshore-tax-havens/.

Snell, Kelsey. 2015. "Paul Ryan's Presidential Campaign Play—Tax Reform." *Washington Post,* June 10. Accessed August 21, 2015. http://www.washingtonpost.com/news/powerpost /wp/2015/06/10/paul-ryans-presidential-campaign-play-tax-reform/.

Tax Foundation. 2014. "The Cost of Tax Compliance." *Tax Foundation Blog.* September 11. Accessed November 10, 2015. http://taxfoundation.org/blog/cost-tax-compliance.

U.S. Congress. House. Committee on Ways and Means. 2015a. *Getting Things Done: Fixing a Broken Tax Code.* 114th Cong., 1st sess., July 2. Accessed July 30, 2015. http:// waysandmeans.house.gov/getting-things-done-fixing-a-broken-tax-code/.

U.S. Congress. House. Committee on Ways and Means. 2015b. *LOCKOUT: Flawed U.S. Tax Structure Keeps Trillions Offshore That Could Be Invested Here.* 114th Cong., 1st sess., August 5. Accessed August 21, 2015. http://waysandmeans.house.gov/lockout-flawed -u-s-tax-structure-keeps-trillions-offshore-that-could-be-invested-here/.

U.S. Congress. House. Ways and Means Committee Democrats. 2015. *Tax Reform.* 114th Cong., 1st sess., Accessed August 1. http://democrats.waysandmeans.house.gov/issue /tax-reform.

U.S. Congress. Senate. Committee on Finance. 2015. *Getting to Yes on Tax Reform: What Lessons Can Congress Learn from the Tax Reform Act of 1986?* 114th Cong., 1st sess., February 10. Accessed November 9, 2015. http://www.finance.senate.gov/hearings /hearing/?id=2de929e6-5056-a032-5200-282bdf50915f.

U.S. Congress. Senate Finance Committee and House Ways and Means Committee. 2014. *Comprehensive Tax Reform: Building a Tax Code for the 21st Century.* 113th Cong., 2nd sess. Accessed November 9, 2015. https://taxreform.gov/.

U.S. Department of the Treasury. Internal Revenue Service. 2014. *Publication 550: Investment Income and Expenses, §2 Tax Shelters and Other Reportable Transactions.* Washington, DC. Accessed August 21, 2015. https://www.irs.gov/publications/p550/ch02 .html.

Wyden, Ron. 2015. "Wyden Statement at Finance Hearing on Lessons from Tax Reform Act of 1986." *United Sates Senate Committee on Finance.* 114th Cong., 1st sess., February 10. Accessed July 30, 2015. http://www.finance.senate.gov/imo/media/doc/021015 %20Wyden%20Statement%20at%20Finance%20Hearing%20on%20Lessons%20 from%20Tax%20Reform%20Act%20of%201986.pdf.

Unemployment

At a Glance

Economists have put forth various theories of unemployment. Neoclassical theories evolved in the 19th century as a reaction against the classical approaches represented in the works of David Ricardo and John Stuart Mill, who were concerned with accumulation of wealth. For the most part, neoclassical economists considered unemployment a matter of lower concern for policymakers and attributed the problem to imbalances in the economy. Disequilibria in the economy, for example, had much to do with markets, demand, and supply of goods.

Keynesian economics, named after John Maynard Keynes, was a direct response to neoclassical theory. Keynes and his followers were concerned primarily with restoration of full employment. Keynes argued that unemployment arose due to low effective demand for the goods and services produced in an economy. For Keynes, government could reverse unemployment through an increase in its own direct input into the economy, by cutting taxes, and controlling money markets. Economists credited Keynesian wartime deficit spending for ending the Great Depression.

Historically, both parties have long jockeyed to control perceptions of employment trends under their watch. According to Leonard Silk (1972, 185), the Nixon Administration eliminated some reports that contained unwelcome unemployment data. More recently President Obama has emphasized that the economic policies his administration crafted to combat the Great Recession were working, based in part on the number of jobs created since he took office. The Republican Party has disputed these claims, citing the work of economists with the conservative Heritage Foundation and other conservative think tanks. "According to the Bureau of Labor Statistics (BLS), in 2007 on the eve of the recession, there were 146.6 million Americans working," wrote Heritage Foundation economist Stephen Moore in July 2014. "Today, there are 145.8 million Americans in jobs. So nearly 7 years later, we are still 800,000 jobs below the previous peak. That's some jobs recovery. But the missing jobs in this economic recovery are much higher than that. A new analysis of the labor force numbers by Heritage Foundation economists places the real jobs deficit in America closer to 5.5 million, even after accounting for changes in population and demographics" (Moore 2014).

Jobs are important in other ways as well. In most societies, having a job confers a certain degree of self-worthiness and belonging. Being without a job can be a dehumanizing experience and a ticket to poverty and lowered living standards. Unemployment is linked to lower life expectancy, suicide, and disease. Without jobs, people are more likely to fall into criminal activity, substance abuse, homelessness, and overall destitution. If unemployment continues for several years, the problems are compounded. Economists refer to a state of permanent unemployment or delayed entry into the job market as "scarring" that results in a loss of critical job skills. Wage scarring may place the unemployed at the bottom level of their careers as they miss out on seniority and experience. Moreover, a wage scar can persist into middle age.

In the United States, the average unemployed worker found a job after three months of searching for a job (International Labor Organization 2014) Persistent high unemployment complicates national productivity capacities and lowers demand of goods and services, thereby creating a cycle of poverty.

In a capitalist society, labor markets are a function of economic growth and prudent management of resources. The two parties have different views on the probable causes of unemployment and how to fix it. Republicans, especially those on the far right, tend to consider programs like unemployment insurance unsuitable for helping workers gain new skills or move to places with jobs. At the opposite end, Democrats, for the most part, believe that people don't choose to be unemployed and must be offered incentives to prepare them for jobs as opportunities arise. Republicans, often persuaded by classical economists, tend to reject expansionist stimulus recovery policies that include unemployment benefits and progressive taxes. On the other hand, Democrats regard labor market recovery to be, in part, a function of expanded wages, employments benefits, and targeted subventions to key productive sectors. Although the two parties speak against deficits and reduction of the federal debt, it comes down to perspectives about which programs are most deserving of funding support.

Many Republicans . . .

- Believe unemployment can be reduced through education loans available through private money markets
- Feel government-sponsored job programs are ineffective
- Think minimum wage hikes result in higher levels of unemployment
- Feel high unemployment is best solved by reducing barriers to wealth creation and private entrepreneurship programs
- See government-subsidized housing, food stamps, and other social service programs as disincentives for working hard

- Support blocking insurance benefit extensions in all legislative bodies
- Assert that unemployment could be reduced through cutting taxes, which freezes money for investors
- Feel that unions contribute to unemployment by distorting the natural market equilibrium

Many Democrats . . .

- Believe that government job training grants and career guidance programs help people find jobs
- Say that unemployment is reduced through initiatives such as Job Corps, the Job Training and Partnership Act, and Job Start programs
- Support tax credits for firms hiring the long-term unemployed
- Contend that unemployment is attributable in part to ruthless corporate concern with "the bottom line"
- Believe that compensation programs and other social security interventions like food stamps, rent supplements, and low-income housing are worthwhile programs

Overview

An individual is said to be unemployed if she or he is "not only out of work but is available for work and, in fact, seeks work at the prevailing wage" (Lindbeck 1993, 27).

In the United States, opportunities for jobs are not uniformly accessible across racial lines. The Bureau of Labor Statistics reports, on average, the jobless rate of white Americans is half that of African Americans. For example, in Michigan in 2014, the unemployment rate of African Americans was 16.5 percent compared to 8.6 in the general population. In New Jersey, the unemployment rate was 8.2 percent for all people, but 16 percent for African Americans. In Kansas, African American unemployment was 11.8 percent compared to 5.6 among whites (Frohlich 2014).

Not surprisingly, then, African Americans are twice as likely to live in poverty, which stems from high levels of unemployment. As a result, several African American leaders doubt that policies meant to create jobs target the black community. Stemming from disparities in education quality and opportunity, African Americans have lower incomes, lower educational attainment, and live in neighborhoods with limited opportunities. Still, several sources believe even after attaining higher education degrees, African Americans have unemployment rates twice that of college-educated white Americans.

Therefore, from a sociological perspective, unemployment is linked to centuries of discrimination. Sociologists contend that the criminal justice system, which contributes to disproportionate incarceration rates among minority groups, exacerbates the problem. Recruitment, selection, and job offers obviously are skewed to make it very difficult for persons previously incarcerated to join the workforce. With limited avenues for upward mobility, groups like African Americans and veterans continue to experience unemployment and poverty.

For instance, the 2008 recession affected veterans in profound ways. An Iraq war veteran, Brook Douan, a resident of South Carolina commented, "I thought it would be easier for me to find work because people would be like, 'Oh you're a veteran, you served your country.' But now, I don't think it makes one bit of a difference" (Chen 2010). Data from the Bureau of Labor Statistics showed that in 2014, unemployment for veterans aged 18–24 was 21.6 percent, compared to 19.1 percent for their civilian counterparts (Department of Labor, Bureau of Labor Statistics 2015).

Globally, according to the International Labor Organization (ILO), the number of unemployed people is on the rise. Job creation is not expanding fast enough to keep pace with population growth. In the United States the recession of 2008–2009 exacerbated the level of unemployment. The numbers showed the economy was not creating enough jobs at a level that was sufficient for increasing national production. During the recovery, many of the new jobs were low paying, thereby continuing a structural trend that existed since the 1980s. Most economists attribute a good deal of youth unemployment to outsourcing and automation of jobs.

Unemployment constitutes a burden to the public purse since government has to spend considerable amounts of money on unemployment benefits. Unemployment also means that less money is contributed to federal coffers via taxes from both public and private investments. It also lowers demand of goods and services, thereby reducing overall domestic output (GDP).

Although state and national legislatures enact policies to reduce unemployment and move toward full employment, policy scholars consider unemployment to be intractable. In the interim, unemployment insurance policies have been implemented to help workers who lost jobs through no fault of their own "get back on their feet." Wisconsin was the first state to enact unemployment insurance laws in 1932. The programs were adopted nationwide through the Social Security Act of 1935.

Historically, the Great Depression of the late 1920s and 1930s was about economic collapse manifested in stagnation, declining productivity, and unemployment. Likewise, the Great Recession of 2008 triggered a tremendous downturn in productivity, financial investment, and employment. Subsequently, many of the provisions in the American Recovery and Reinvestment Act of 2009 that President Obama signed into law in February 2009 with the support of Democratic majorities in Congress were designed explicitly to create or save jobs. These measures were seen as essential to the overall economic recovery.

Most observers of the U.S. economy consider President Obama's advisers, such as Lawrence H. Summers, Christina Romer, and Timothy F. Geithner, as adherents to Keynesian economics. Their prescription of massive spending on public works and infrastructure, bailouts for failing corporations, and tax increases for the "super rich" were regarded as ways to rejuvenate the economy and promote job opportunities. In addition, they oversaw tax cuts to help boost consumer spending power.

The monetarist school is an offshoot of the neoclassical theory that Milton Friedman and his colleagues at the University of Chicago promoted. Friedman's influence on Republican Party thinking is unmistakable. He opposed the Keynesian thought that dominated the New Deal and Democratic Party perspectives. With respect to unemployment, Friedman contended that a natural rate of unemployment existed and that governments could increase employment above this rate, mostly through monetary measures that boosted aggregate demand. Friedman was an economic adviser to President Reagan and continues to be regarded as one of the foremost conservative economists.

Efforts to reduce unemployment continue to showcase the differences in national party approaches and philosophies. It is popular for different party spokespersons to claim that their party's policies lead to lower unemployment rates. CNN's Fact Check revealed that Republican-led states were not necessarily better performers in job creation and lowering unemployment (CNN 2012). Bureau of Labor Statistics data show insignificant differences that do not lead one to conclude that party has a causal relationship to regional unemployment. Academics such as Alan Blinder and Mark Watson, though, have conducted research that they say indicate a huge gap in economic performance between Democratic and Republican administrations (Blinder and Watson 2013).

Liberal lawmakers, voters, journalists, and academics contend that the U.S. economy grows much faster when Democrats are in the White House. Democrats argue that under their policies, the economy creates more jobs, generates higher corporate profits and higher returns on stocks (Plumer 2013).

From the philosophical arguments above, one may contend Republicans and Democrats have sharp differences in how they view and approach unemployment and job creation. These differences manifest in how different administrations approach issues of economic management in different jurisdictions.

Republicans on Unemployment

Many Republicans view unemployment security, low-income housing, food stamps, low cost education, and free medical care as factors that demotivate individuals from working hard. In other words, government programs that help the poor are considered as disincentives for hard work and job creation.

Consequently, Republican legislators frequently block unemployment insurance benefit extensions. In 2014, the number of estimated beneficiaries was around 1.7 million people. A conservative Republican group, Club for Growth, released statements that suggested that unemployment benefits breed unemployment because the benefits offer an incentive to remain unemployed. Conservative economists at the American Enterprise Institute (AEI) think unemployment benefits create an environment "where people are subsidized to become a structural unemployment problem" (Hassett 2012). A different version of this argument is that unemployment insurance did not help those without jobs learn new skills or even move to places with job opportunities.

From a macroeconomic point of view, Republicans tend to believe that unemployment would be reduced through lowering taxes. For Republicans, lower taxation rates put more money in the hands of "job creators" who, in turn, create jobs and combat unemployment. Furthermore, throughout the post–World War II period, conservative Republicans' belief in free markets as a solution to unemployment has never waned. For party adherents, full employment as an alternative to unemployment can be found in markets and not government reforms and programs like minimum wages and unemployment compensation. Republicans tend to believe that unions contribute to unemployment and job losses because they distort market equilibrium. Scholars have not found substantial evidence to support the thesis that labor unions contribute to unemployment as reflected in plant closings. In fact, the best research shows that "unionization per se has no impact on the probability of closure" (Nissen 1995, 11).

Economist and Federal Reserve Chairman Alan Greenspan

Alan Greenspan was born in 1926 in New York. He trained as an economist and worked on Wall Street. President Richard Nixon appointed him head of his Council of Economic Advisers in 1974. After Nixon's resignation, he continue din the same capacity under President Gerald Ford. In that capacity he championed anti-inflationary policies. In 1981, Greenspan served as Chairman to President Reagan's National Commission on Social Security Reform.

Following the resignation of Chairman Paul Volcker in 1987, President Reagan appointed him Chairman of the Board of Governors of the Federal Reserve. Greenspan's position as a member of the Washington elite served him well. He became the head of the Federal Reserve in 1991. As Chairman of the Federal Reserve, he helped influenced the country's economic performance. He served for 14 years in that capacity—a period that covered the presidencies of Ronald Reagan, George H. W Bush (41st president), William Clinton, and George W. Bush (43rd president). Volcker's term came to a close in 2006, when he was succeeded by Ben Bernanke.

A Libertarian Republican, Greenspan promoted policies that leveraged global capitalism and supported less regulation of derivatives. He is considered as one of the key figures in promotion of neo-liberal market economics of the past two decades. As Chairman of the Federal Reserve Board, Greenspan oversaw the longest official economic expansion in American history.

Source

"Alan Greenspan." 2015. Federal Reserve History. Accessed November 30, 2015. http://www .federalreservehistory.org/People/DetailView/6.

Republicans denounce the Patients Protection and Affordable Care Act (2010) (also called Obamacare) as a "job-killer." They view Obamacare as a tax on investments and, therefore, a disincentive for small business owners. Likewise, they believe regulations of industry may discourage job creation. Many times Republicans have spoken against regulation of the energy and environmental sectors claiming that job loss would occur.

Democrats on Unemployment

Democrats tend to believe in the creation of jobs that stay in America. Through tax policy instruments, protection of unions, and strengthening safety nets for vulnerable groups like the poor, the elderly, and disabled persons, Democrats seek to ensure that effects of unemployment are minimized. This attention may also be related to the party's desire to serve some of its core constituencies, including underserved groups.

Youth unemployment rates are highest in communities where education resources are least developed. Democrats call for more subsidized scholarships for young people in economically marginalized communities. They also support government job training grants and career guidance. Democrats sponsored initiatives such as Job Corps, the Job Training and Partnership Act, and Job Start programs.

Democrats tend to believe that in recessionary situations, job creation can be assured through government investments in infrastructure and other Keynesian strategies that stimulate growth. President Obama proposed the American Jobs Act that would provide tax credits to firms hiring the long-term unemployed.

Obama Economic Advisor Christine D. Romer

The President is often recognized as the key player in economic policy making. Presidents define the economic policy agenda and mobilize political support or opposition for other economic players including the Federal Reserve, Congress and international interests. Presidents rely on a number of advisory councils when formulating their economic policies. Among these councils is the Council of Economic Advisers (CEA), which provides economic analysis to the president. In January 2009, President Barack Obama appointed Dr. Christine D. Romer to lead the CEA. Romer earned her PhD in Economics from Massachusetts Institute of Technology (MIT). She taught at Princeton University and served as the "Class of 1957 Garff B. Wilson Professor of Economics" at the University of California, Berkeley. She is an expert in monetary and fiscal policy with a special focus on the causes of depression and macroeconomic volatility. As a New Keynesian Economist, Dr. Romer believed that to bring down unemployment, the economy had to grow first.

With that belief in mind, Romer played a key role in crafting the Obama administration's policies and programs to combat the Great Recession, the country's worst financial crisis since the Great Depression, and stimulate the economy back onto the path of recovery. In addition, she continually monitored economic data to help the Obama administration anticipate economic trends and challenges. "One of the jobs of the CEA chair is to get key data reports the night before they are going to be released to the public," she said. "My job was to let the Fed Chair and Secretary of the Treasury know if the report could cause financial market instability. It was also my job to brief the President about the numbers."

Romer resigned from the CEA in the summer of 2010, with the country firmly on the road to economic recovery. She returned to her tenured position as an economics professor at the University of California, Berkeley.

Sources

Roemer, Christina. 2011. "Unemployment or Insolvency: Strategies for a troubled Economy. Zale Lecture in Public Policy." Stanford University. May 5. Accessed November 18, 2015. http://eml.berkeley.edu//~cromer/Stanford,%20Zale%20Lecture.pdf.

Roemer, Christina. 2015. "Biography." Berkeley Economics, University of California-Berkeley. Accessed November 18, 2015. http://eml.berkeley.edu//~cromer/index.shtml.

Democrats call for minimum wage increases across the nation as part of their policy to grow the middle class. According to President Obama, examples of policies that would help the middle class and working Americans included, "raising the minimum wage, enacting fair pay, refinancing student loans, extending insurance for the unemployed" (Zezima 2014).

Democrats also tend to support unemployment compensation programs and other social security and supplementary income interventions like food stamps, rent supplements, and low income housing. Explaining why Republicans vote against extending unemployment benefits, Illinois Democrat Senator Durbin said he believed that Republicans think "unemployed people are lazy" (Sanchez 2014).

In a speech expressing support of extending unemployment benefits, Nancy Pelosi, then House Minority Leader (D-California) remarked: "The unemployment insurance extension is not only good for individuals. It has macroeconomic impact. As macroeconomic advisers have stated, it would make a difference of 600,000 jobs to our economy" (Mora 2011). According to this view, unemployment benefits not only create safety nets but also inject demand into the economy through job creation.

Still, it is important to not lose sight of some points of agreement among leaders in the two parties. Democrats and Republicans agree that unemployment is a problem, and bipartisan approaches should be utilized to fix it. Sander Levin, leading Democrat on the House Ways and Means Committee, stated while supporting the extension of unemployment benefits, "Long-term unemployment remains an enormous challenge for millions of Americans and our overall economy, which is exactly why Republicans should join with Democrats to renew this important program" (Bridge 2014).

Another area where the two parties have some agreement is in the realm of international trade. This congruence of ideas has deep historical roots. For example, in 1944, then Assistant Secretary of State, Dean Acheson, stated, "We cannot have full employment and prosperity in the United States without foreign markets" (Wasem 2013, 3). Further evidence of this bipartisan approach is evident in the 2015 Republican backing of President Obama's trade deal with 11 Pacific Rim countries at a time when policy divisions between the two parties have been remarkable.

In summary, for the most part, the two parties do not agree on how best to fix unemployment. The differences have much to do with sharp differences in their views on management of the country's domestic economy, which stems partially from different perspectives on the causes of structural unemployment.

Eric Otenyo

Further Reading

Blinder, A., and M. Watson. 2013. "Presidents and the Economy: A Forensic Investigation." Woodrow Wilson School and Department of Economics Princeton University. Accessed November 20, 2015. http://www.princeton.edu/~mwatson/papers/Presidents_Blinder _Watson_Nov2013.pdf.

Bridge, R. 2014. "Down and Out: US Unemployed without Extended Benefits Nearing 2 Million." *RT.com*. Accessed February 24, 2014. http://rt.com/usa/us-unemployment -benefits-economy-471/.

Chen, S. 2010. "After War, Young Soldiers Come Home to Fight Unemployment." CNN, July 7. Accessed October 13, 2015. http://www.cnn.com/2010/LIVING/07/07/veterans .unemployed.economy/.

CNN. 2012. "CNN Fact Check: Lower Unemployment in GOP-led States?" Accessed August 30, 2015. http://www.cnn.com.

Department of Labor, Bureau of Labor Statistics. 2015. The Unemployment Situation, 2014. Accessed October 30. http://www.bls.gov/news.release/.

Frohlich, T., A. Kent, A. E. M. Hess, D. A. Mcintyre, and A. C. Allen. 2014. "The Worst States for Black Americans." *24/7 Wall Street*. December 9. Accessed April 21, 2015. http://247wallst.com/special-report/2014/12/09/the-worst-states-for-black-americans/.

Hassett, K. A. 2012. Quoted in Shaila Dewan, "U.S. Winds Down Longer Benefits for the Unemployed." *New York Times*, May 28. Accessed April 21, 2015. http://www.nytimes .com/2012/05/29/business/economy/extended-federal-unemployment-benefits-begin -to-wind-down.html?pagewanted=all&_r=0.

Holzer, H. J., J. I. Lane, D. B. Rosenblum, and F. Andersson. 2011. *Where Are All the Good Jobs Going? What National and Local Job Quality and Dynamics Mean for U.S. Workers.* San Francisco: Russell Sage.

International Labor Organization. 2014. "Global Employment Trends 2014: The Risk of a Jobless Recovery?" Accessed October 12, 2015. http://www.ilo.org/wcmsp5/groups /public/---dgreports/---dcomm/---publ/documents/publication/wcms_233953.pdf.

Lindbeck, A. 1993. *Unemployment and Macroeconomics*. Cambridge, MA: The MIT Press.

Moore, S. 2014. "Mr. President, Where Are Our 5 Million Missing Jobs?" Heritage Foundation. July 8. Accessed July 13, 2015. http://www.heritage.org/research/commentary /2014/7/mr-president-where-are-our-5-million-missing-jobs.

Mora, E. 2011. "Pelosi: Extending Unemployment Benefits Would Create 600,000 jobs." *CNSNews.com*. December 15. Accessed October 23, 2015. http://cnsnews.com/news /article/pelosi-extending-unemployment-benefits-would-create-600000-jobs.

Nissen, B. 1995. *Fighting for Jobs: Case Studies of Labor-Community Coalitions Confronting Plant Closings*. Albany: State University of New York,.

Plumer, B. 2013. "The U.S. Economy Does Better under Democratic Presidents—Is It Just Luck?" *Washington Post*, December 2. Accessed July 27, 2015. http://www .washingtonpost.com/blogs/wonkblog/wp/2013/12/02/the-u-s-economy-does-better -under-democratic-presidents-is-it-just-luck/.

Sanchez, H. 2014. "Republicans Block Unemployment Extension, Democrats Plan to Try Again. Roll Call." *Roll Call*, February 6. Accessed October 12, 2015. http://blogs.rollcall .com/wgdb/republican-block-unemployment-extension/?dcz=.

Silk, L. 1972. *Nixonomics: How the Dismal Science of Free Enterprise Became the Black Art of Controls*. New York: Praeger.

Wasem, R. E. 2013. *Tackling Unemployment: The Legislative Dynamic of the Employment Act of 1946*. Kalamazoo, MI: W. E Upjohn Institute.

Zezima, K. 2014. "Obama Said He Wasn't Making a Campaign Speech. And He Did." *Washington Post*, October 2. Accessed October 2, 2015. http://www.washingtonpost .com/blogs/post-politics/wp/2014/10/02/obama-said-he-wasnt-making-a-campaign -speech-and-then-he-did/.

Unions

At a Glance

The growth in unions is an important feature of modern public personnel management. Typically, unions exerted pressure on management and the political system through activism geared toward workers' rights. From their inception, unions were viewed suspiciously by management, frequently in conspiracy terms. The conspiracy doctrine held that cooperation among employees was likely to infringe on commerce. There was also the view that collective action would harm the economic interests of the capitalist system. The suspicion was mutual, because unions regarded the state role in providing welfare benefits as an attempt to usurp the unions' own benefit functions and weaken the organizations.

Regardless of opposition from business interests and conservative allies in the political world, union growth in the private sector steadily increased from the late nineteenth century through the mid-1950s, only to begin a long decline in the 1960s. By 2013, the union membership rate in the United States among all workers was 11.3 percent (Bureau of Labor Statistics 2014). Nationally, 14.5 million workers belonged to unions, down from 17.7 million in 1983. Of the 14.5 million, 7.2 million employees were public sector officials, compared with 7.3 million in private sector employment. Data show that "public-sector workers had a union membership rate (35.3 percent) more than five times higher than that of private-sector workers (6.7 percent)" (Bureau of Labor Statistics 2014).

The diminishment in the size of American unions has resulted in a corresponding decline in their political clout. Still, unions remain a significant force, especially in certain state and national legislative bodies. Unions organize, develop strategies, and provide workers with opportunities to transform their numbers "into a resource of economic and political power" (Marks 1989).

Many Republicans . . .

- Believe that unions inhibit the free flow of commerce
- Charge that public unions artificially inflate the cost of state and local government operations

- Favor "open shop" and "right-to-work" policies
- Assert that workers should be protected by law so that they can opt-out of paying dues
- Oppose subjecting pensions to collective bargaining
- Favor privatization of retirement funds

Many Democrats . . .

- See unions as allies in promoting policies that grow the middle class and protect the interests of struggling and working poor
- Oppose "open shop" and "right-to-work" laws and policies
- Support the principle of equal pay for equal work

Overview

Unions exist for several political and socioeconomic reasons. The political reasons have much to do with their roles in influencing public policy while the socioeconomic reasons focus on worker benefits, which include job security, association with membership, compensation issues (i.e., wages and benefits), and improvements in the conditions of service. Department of Labor records show that public employees with memberships in unions earn more than non-members.

Samuel Gompers

Organized labor legend Samuel Gompers (1850–1924) was born in London. In 1863, his family migrated to New York City. He joined Local 15 of the United Cigar Makers in 1864. In 1875, Gompers was elected president of Local 144 of the Cigar Makers' International Union (CMIU) in New York. In 1886, Gompers and his colleagues transformed the Federation of Organized Trade and Labor Unions into the American Federation of Labor (AFL). He became the founding president of the AFL, serving from 1886 to 1924. Gompers was the longest serving president of the AFL. He is credited for promoting industrial harmony by minimizing conflicts with management. Under his leadership he secured higher wages and shorter working hours. In addition, he encouraged electing to public office "friends of labor." Gompers is credited for shaping the labor movement in America. He gave the movement its structure and strategic characteristics. At the time of his death in 1924, AFL had at least 3 million members, making it the most influential and largest labor federation in the world.

Sources

Gompers, Samuel. 1984. *Seventy Years of Life and Labor: An Autobiography.* New York: Dutton, 1925. Reprint. New York: ILR Press.

Greene, Julie. 1988. *Pure and Simple Politics: The American Federation of Labor and Political Activism, 1881–1917.* New York: Cambridge University Press.

Most employees agree that affiliation with unions protects them from arbitrary unjust managerial actions. For example, in recent years, unions participated in coalitions to challenge neoliberal free trade agreements like North Atlantic Free Trade Area (NAFTA) and the Trans-Pacific Partnership (TPP) free trade area that includes twelve Pacific Rim countries. Unions joined hands with progressive organizations like environmental groups to speak against trade and economic policies that negatively impact quality of life. Although unions opposed NAFTA, it is fair to say that both political parties support the idea of "free trade" agreements. There is a slight disagreement in how different union leaders address immigration reform. Some union leaders opposed "amnesty for illegal immigrants" and the notion that illegals take jobs away.

Yet opposition to unionism in public sector employment is a much-debated issue, especially in regard to "right-to-work states" and states that do not allow unionizing by public servants. At least 23 states have right-to-work laws. These are states that have the lowest union membership rates (below 5 percent), even within the private sector. Collective bargaining is frequently cited by conservatives as a factor in the creation of budget shortfalls that bedevil state and local governments (Methe and Perry 2003, 413). Recently, the U.S. Supreme Court added fuel to the fire by traditionally viewing unions as obstructing the free flow of commerce.

Republicans on Unions

The 2012 Republican platform encouraged all states to enact "right-to-work" laws. Such laws prohibit union contracts at private-sector firms and require employees to pay any dues or other union fees to unions. Not surprisingly, right-to-work policies have been implemented in conservative states like Arizona, Arkansas, South Carolina, North Carolina, Mississippi, and Utah that are dominated by Republican lawmakers. Right-to work laws suggest that unions must represent eligible workers, whether the member pays his or her dues or not. This means that a member who does not pay dues can still receive all benefits negotiated through collective bargaining agreement. The net effect of right-to-work laws is to reduce contributions and to deny unions cash flows. In states that do not have such restrictive laws, union members generally pay dues and fees at their workplaces.

Many Republican presidential candidates support proposals to bar mandatory members' dues for political purposes. And in states like California, which have strong union membership, Republican leaders support laws (e.g., Prop. 32) that ban the use of payroll deductions, including voluntary union subscriptions to fund political party activities.

The Republican Party also supports an end to the use of "card checks" as a way for workers to join unions. This practice stems from a 1930s Executive Order that allows, but does not require, managers to grant union recognition once employees sign cards affiliating them to unions as bona fide members. Republicans tend to reject any pressures on employers to grant recognition through "card checks" and demand that unions use secret ballot elections rather than pressuring workers to use pro-union cards. Republicans also tend to oppose the ideals of the progressive Davis-Bacon Act (1931) that required all federal construction projects pay workers at prevailing wages not below minimum union wages.

In sharp opposition to the union ideals of protecting seniority, Republicans tend to oppose tenure systems and instead promote "at-will" employment and "merit-based" performance pay reward systems. Most unions view privatization schemes as threatening their core interest of job security for their members. Republicans, for the most part, view privatization as a cost-saving managerial practice.

Wisconsin Republican Governor Scott Walker has been a particularly harsh critic of unions. Upon taking office in 2010, he repeatedly blamed public employee unions for the fiscal crisis in his state (despite the fact that the entire country was still recovering from the worst of the so-called Great Recession). Governor Walker was not alone. Other Republican governors, including Rick Scott in Florida, Rick Snyder in Michigan, Bruce Rauner in Illinois, Nikki Haley in South Carolina, and John Kasich in Ohio sought to end or limit collective bargaining in their respective states.

Walker argued that collective bargaining led to higher pensions and pay, which in turn denied states funds for schools, road repairs, and other vital expenditures. His Wisconsin Budget Repair Bill of 2010 enacted in 2011 cut compensation (including health insurance premium costs, retirement, and sick leave benefits) for most public officials, with the exception of firemen, law enforcement, and other public safety officials. The law also changed collective bargaining laws in the state of Wisconsin.

Also, at their National Leadership Conferences, conservative Republican Party caucuses argued that legislation that prohibits or limits collective bargaining is the path to secure investments. This line of thinking is supported through activities sponsored by the Koch Brothers, conservative billionaires whose interests in energy and trade make them among the wealthiest Americans. Fellow billionaire, and skin care and home cleaning supplies businessman, Dick DeVos, also supported "right-to-work" and anti-union activities. The Republican Party considers itself largely as a pro-business party and virulently anti-union (Daley 2002, 271).

Some observers believe that the modern Republican Party has shifted markedly to the right in its view of unions in recent decades. Republican presidents Richard Nixon and George H. W. Bush praised labor unions as exporters of democracy and freedom. From their speeches at various American Federation of Labor–Congress of Industrial Organizations (AFL-CIO) forums, the Republican presidents wanted to leverage labor internationalism to broaden the foreign policy agenda of spreading democracy. President Reagan, who is considered by liberal pundits as the "high priest of conservatives," was also less confrontational in his relations with unions than members of today's Tea Party. Reagan is well-known for his highly publicized 1981 dismissal of 11,345 members of the Professional Air Traffic Controllers Organization (PATCO) for violation of a back-to-work order, but before the PATCO standoff, in 1980, President Reagan, had "'reaffirmed' his party's commitment to the fundamental principle of fairness in labor relations, including the legal right of unions to organize workers and to represent them through collective bargaining" (Drum 2012).

As Kreisberg (2004) asserts, the rise of neoconservatives in the Republican Party made it more difficult for unions to engage in collective bargaining. President George W. Bush's election in 2000 ushered in an era of intensified criticisms of unions. Some observers charged that President Bush's administration set a hostile labor relations climate and he has even been described as "one of the most anti-labor presidents in U.S. history" (Kay 2011, 152).

President George W. Bush's Management Agenda privileged managerial authority and exempted several units from union coverage. Through Executive Order 13252, agencies such as the Justice Department, INTERPOL—U.S. National Bureau, the National Drug Intelligence Center, Homeland Security, and others were stripped of unionization. Consistent with data from the Pew Research Surveys, support for unions among conservative Republicans is at 23–34 percent compared with 36–44 percent among Independents, and 67–80 percent among Democrats (Easley 2013).

Democrats on Unions

The historical ties between labor unions and the Democratic Party can be traced back to President Franklin D. Roosevelt and his New Deal. Organized workers, including the Congress of Industrial Organizations (CIO), viewed President Roosevelt's job creation policies favorably and came out in droves to vote for Democrats. Most scholars agree that "unions were key players in promoting the expansion of the welfare state and the adoption of neo-Keynesian economic policies" implemented during the New Deal (Dark 1999). Political scientist Dark (1999) correctly observes that, "indeed there are few major domestic policies endorsed since the 1930s by the Democratic Party that do not in some way reveal the hand of organized labor, whether the issue be civil rights or federal funding of education, health care or war on poverty." Unions were therefore big supporters of presidents Kennedy and Johnson who steered through their preferred domestic agenda. It is noteworthy that in 1962 President Kennedy, through issuance of Executive Order 10988, ushered in the right of federal employees to collectively bargain.

Democrat President Clinton's relationship with unions was cordial but not devoid of friction. President Clinton, a former dues-paying member of the American Federation of State, County, and Municipal Employees (AFSCME), received criticism for enacting NAFTA. Clinton, in several speeches framed his political vision in terms of forging a new partnership with labor unions for enlarging and safeguarding the middle class. Robert Reich (President Clinton's Secretary of Labor from 1993–1999) was famously a strong supporter of unionization, and after his tenure, blogged about the need for unions.

Mother Jones (Mary H. Jones)

Mary Harris Jones (Mother Jones) was born in 1837. Jones was one of the most important figures in U.S. labor history. Although women have always been key members of the labor movement, they were not offered or assigned traditional leadership roles. Early unions much like the existing patriarchic society were prejudiced against women involvements in labor struggles, frequently treating women as "trying to threaten men's jobs."

Mother Jones remains a key mover and shaker of the labor movement. As a strong supporter of unions, Jones participated and organized several union activities that included strikes. She resented extreme wealth inequalities, opposed child labor and led a life of devotion to the cause of labor unions. In the 1870s to 1890s she traveled to several parts of the country to lend her support to union protests and strikes. Her activism for safety in mines is well documented. For instance in 1899 she encouraged coal miners' wives to use brooms and mops to harass strikebreakers.

Mother Jones devoted her energy fighting for the poorly paid workers in Chicago, Philadelphia and other major industrial cities. In 1903, in one of her activist marches, she sought to meet President Teddy Roosevelt but was not successful. Her march was to bring to the attention of the president the plight of mill children in the industrial north. Mother Jones died in 1930, but she has an enduring place in U.S. labor and social history. The left-leaning magazine *Mother Jones* is so named in tribute to her life of activism on behalf of working men and women.

Source

AFL-CIO. 2015. "Mother Jones, 1837–1930." Accessed November 14, 2015. http://www.aflcio
.org/About/Our-History/Key-People-in-Labor-History/Mother-Jones-1837–.

Gorn, Elliott J. 2001. *Mother Jones: The Most Dangerous Woman in America.* New York: Hill and Wang, 2001.

Since the 1960s, members of the Democratic Party continued to support the rights of workers and the freedom to form unions. Recently, debates over representation of workers have continued in Congress. For instance, Democrats supported provisions of a pending bill, the Employee Free Choice Act, which by some measures would alter collective bargaining processes. By amending the 1930s National Labor Relations Act, unions would be allowed to sidestep employees' rights to vote in private federal government-supervised organizational elections. In the proposed arrangements, "the right of unions to represent employee units if the union simply collects signed authorization cards from 50 percent-plus-one of employees in a bargaining jurisdiction" would be guaranteed (Society for Human Resource Management 2014). However, organizations like the Society for Human Resource Management (SHRM), opposed the proposed law on the ground that employees and employers would be denied the ability to shape the terms of contracts if mandatory binding interest arbitration is enacted.

Many party platforms view union activism as synonymous with those of the American middle class and working poor. As one liberal *Washington Post* columnist insisted, "Absent a substantial union movement, the American middle class will shrink. Absent a substantial union movement, the concentration of wealth will increase. Absent a substantial union movement, the corporate domination of government will grow" (Meyerson 2014).

Therefore, support of union causes is a core philosophy of the party establishment. Presidents Clinton and Obama on occasion used the middle class rhetoric to promote "pro-middle class" agendas. Obama summarized this position, "Because when hardworking Americans like Steve succeed—that's when organized labor succeeds. And when organized labor succeeds—that's when our middle class succeeds. And when our middle class succeeds—that's when the United States of America succeeds. That's what we're fighting for" (Obama 2009).

Modern Democratic Party presidential candidates often rely on union members to canvass neighborhoods for votes. Unions are considered a dependable source of campaign funds for candidates mainly associated with the Democratic Party. According to the Center for Responsive Politics (2014), unions rank among the top twenty sources of campaign funds and in many instances support primarily members of the Democratic Party. Although a few Republican candidates also benefit from union largesse, it is the exception. Unions like the American Federation of State County and Municipal Employees, the National Education Association, and the American Federation of Teachers, among other unions, frequently offer manpower to run campaigns on behalf of left-leaning Democrats.

But that doesn't mean that once in office, Democratic Party leaders endorse all labor demands. Moreover, unions do not necessarily support all Democratic Party policy prescriptions. For example, in the case of the Patient Protection and Affordable Care Act (2010), union members initially stood side-by-side with President Obama and supported the core elements of the law. However, union members' support eroded somewhat upon realization that workers might pay more for health care benefits in some of the employer-sponsored healthcare plans.

Among those outraged were United Food and Commercial Workers International Union (UFCW) members. The 1.3 million-member UFCW had twice endorsed President Obama's election. Joseph Hansen, the union's president opined the union would withdraw support for Democrats in the 2014 midterm election if it turned out that the new law (Obamacare) would cost more (Bogardus 2013). Other unions, including the United Union of Roofers, Water proofers, and Allied Workers expressed similar opposition to the policy.

Democrats often defend a broad range of labor interests, though—especially in comparison to their GOP counterparts. For example, Democrats support teacher unions in the protection of tenure systems based on the "last in-first-out" policy. Finally, unions support fair pay for all workers. The first bill President Obama signed on January 29, 2009 was the Lilly Ledbetter Fair Pay Act, which upheld the principle of equal pay for equal work. It was a symbolic victory for not only women but also the labor fraternity. Among the groups that supported the law were the American Association of University Women (AAUW), the American Civil Liberties Union (ACLU), and significantly, the American Federation of Labor–Congress of Industrial Organizations (AFL-CIO). The House voted (250–177), mainly along partisan lines, to approve the Lilly Ledbetter Fair Pay Act.

Eric Otenyo

Further Reading

Bogardus, K. 2013. "Unions Break Ranks on Obamacare." *The Hill*, May 21. Accessed May 21, 2015. http://thehill.com/business-a-lobbying/300881-labor-unions-break-ranks-on-health-law.

Center for Responsive Politics. 2014. "Heavy Hitters: Top All-Time Donors, 1989–2014." *OpenSecrets.org*. Accessed October 12, 2015. http://www.opensecrets.org/orgs/list.php?order=A.

Daley, D. M. 2002. *Strategic Human Resource Management: People and Performance Management in the Public Sector*. Upper Saddle River, NJ: Prentice Hall.

Dark, T. E. 1999. *The Unions and The Democrats: An Enduring Alliance*. Ithaca, NY: Cornell University Press.

Drum, K. 2012. "The GOP's War Against Unions Is Now Entering the Endgame." *Mother Jones*, December 12. Accessed January 23, 2015. http://www.motherjones.com.

Easley, J. 2013. "Republicans Union Busting Backfires as Support for Unions Rises 10 Points." *PoliticusUSA*, September 2. Accessed September 2, 2015. http://www.politicususa.com/2013/09/02/republicans-union-busting-backfires-support-unions-rises-10-points.html.

Kay, Tamara. 2011. *NAFTA and the Politics of Labor Transnationalism*. New York: Cambridge University Press.

Kreisberg, S. 2004. "The Future of Public Sector Unionism in the United States." *Journal of Labor Research* 25: 223–232.

Marks, G. 1989. *Unions in Politics: Britain, Germany, and the United States in the Nineteenth and Early Twentieth Centuries*. Princeton, NJ: Princeton University Press.

Methe, David T., and Perry, James L. 2003. "The Impact of Collective Bargaining on Local Government Service: A Review of Research." In *Classics of Personnel Policy*, edited by Frank J. Thompson. Belmont, CA: Wadsworth.

Meyerson, H. 2014. "If Labor Dies, What's Next?" *American Prospect*. Accessed October 23, 2015. http://prospect.org/article/if-labor-dies-whats-next.

Obama, Barack. 2009. "Remarks by the President of the United States, AFL-CIO Convention," September 15. Accessed October 30, 2015. http://www.whitehouse.gov/the_press_office/Remarks-by-the-President-at-the-AFL-CIO-convention-in-Pittsburg/.

Society for Human Resource Management (SHRM). 2014. "Employee Free Choice Act (Card Check) 2014." Accessed January 23, 2015. http://www.shrm.org/advocacy/issues/employmentandlabor/pages/employeefreechoiceact(cardcheck).aspx.

U.S. Department of Labor, Bureau of Labor Statistics. 2014. "Union Members, News Release, USDL-14-0095." Accessed January 24, 2015. www.bls.gov/cps.

Wall Street Bailout

At a Glance

Republicans reluctantly agreed to aid ailing Wall Street firms during the 2008 economic crisis by supporting "bailout" legislation to major investment banks, including hundreds of billions in taxpayer funds. After first voting to oppose financial assistance to Wall Street in September 2008, most House Republicans decided that intervention was necessary when they voted a second time in October. The risk of economic collapse from numerous firms, coupled with a large decline in the stock market, pressured Republicans to act to address a worsening financial crisis.

Democrats expressed support for the bailout throughout September and October 2008. The president-to-be, Barack Obama, worked with Republican leaders to craft a bipartisan package to assist the investment banks. Despite concerns that the legislation did little to help Main Street America, the party stressed the importance of stabilizing the economy to avoid further economic crisis.

Many Republicans . . .

- Were reluctant to support the bailout because they felt that it violated the party's free market principles
- Focus blame on the federal government for contributing to the housing market collapse

Many Democrats . . .

- Voted for the bailout, which they saw as a necessity for keeping the economy from sliding into crisis conditions
- Expressed concern that the bailout did not provide more assistance to Main Street Americans
- Claim the Republican Party's devotion to the free market was partially responsible for the economic crisis
- Demanded new banking regulations to address financial industry behavior that sparked the crisis

----

Overview

Echoing the view of many economists, President Obama maintains the 2008 economic crash created the worst economic crisis since the Great Depression (Holland 2008). It had a major impact on Main Street America by doubling the national unemployment level, and leading to a collapse in the housing market and stagnant to negative economic growth in the post-2008 era. As investment banks suffered massive housing related asset decline, the U.S. credit market froze, raising concerns that the economic crash could lead to a recession or depression if the federal government failed to respond. Congressional post-collapse efforts were aimed at unfreezing the credit market, providing Wall Street firms with financial relief, and averting a new Great Depression.

The economic bailout refers to the federal government's response to the crisis on Wall Street, which occurred due to the collapse of the housing market between 2007 and 2008. The bailout discussion emerged in Congress by September 2008, and the debate between Democrats and Republicans over whether to provide economic relief to investment firms and banks in danger of declaring bankruptcy (due to their investment losses in the real estate sector) was heated. The first vote on the bailout in late September 2008 failed to pass in the U.S. House of Representatives. The vote, which occurred on September 29, gained majority support from the Democrats, with 140 (60 percent of Democrats who cast a vote) supporting it, and 95 (40 percent) voting against. Just 65 Republicans (33 percent of Republicans who cast a vote) favored the bailout, while 133 (67 percent) voted against (Hulse and Herszenhorn 2008b).

Bipartisan Agreement on the Need for Intervention

Leaders of both political parties concluded that government aid was necessary for failing investment banks in order to prevent a more severe economic crisis. In October 2008, President George W. Bush explained that the federal bailout of the financial industry was necessary to preserve capitalism and the market system: "I'm confident by getting our markets moving, we will help unleash the key to our continued economic success: the entrepreneurial spirit of the American people."

Bush cautioned against expecting an immediate economic recovery from the 2008 crash. Speaking of the bailout funds, Bush announced: "While these efforts will be effective, they will also take time to implement . . . My administration will move as quickly as possible, but the benefits of this package will not all be felt immediately. The federal government will undertake this rescue plan at a careful and deliberate pace to ensure that your tax dollars are spent wisely."

Democratic presidential candidate Barack Obama also agreed that government action and emergency assistance was needed. In September 2008, as banks and investment firms were becoming insolvent, he stated that "we are now in a very dangerous situation where financial institutions across this country are afraid to lend money. If all that meant was the failure of a few big banks on Wall Street, that'd be one thing, but that's not what it means. What it means is that if we do not act, it will be harder for you to get a mortgage for your home or the loans you need to go to college, or a loan you need to buy a car to get to work." Obama sought to address citizens' concerns about the economy, while also acknowledging public anger over malfeasance on Wall Street. His rhetoric clearly emphasized economic instability, however, as the paramount concern: "There will be time to punish those who set this fire, but now is the moment for us to come together and put the fire out. Think about it. If your neighbor's house is burning, you're not going to spend a whole lot of time saying, well that guy was always irresponsible, he always left the stove on, he always was smoking in bed. All those things may be true, but his house could end up affecting your house. And that's the situation we're in right now." Obama's claims represented an appeal to foster a sense of togetherness on the part of the mass public. Inaction in ensuring a bailout of the banking system, Obama warned, would produce dire consequences for the rest of the country, particularly for Main Street America. The soon-to-be president's approach to the economic crisis was reinforced on a bi-partisan level in Congress, as both parties moved to provide financial relief to embattled banks and investment firms.

Sources

ABC News. 2008. "It's Wait and See After Bush Signs Rescue Plan." *ABC News*, October 4. Accessed November 16, 2015. http://abcnews.go.com/Business/story?id=5954902&page=1.

Cooper, Michael, and Jeff Zeleny. 2008. "Both Obama and McCain Make Push for Bailout." *New York Times*, September 30. Accessed November 16, 2015. http://www.nytimes.com/2008/10/01/us/politics/01campaign.html.

The debate between Democrats and Republicans centered on a number of points, specifically free market principles, concerns over whether Wall Street deserved to be bailed out, discussion of what efforts would be taken to relieve Main Street America, and concerns that government inaction would lead to disastrous economic consequences. While there was much diversity of opinion on a bailout, both political parties expressed support for granting Wall Street financial assistance. Republicans often voiced opposition to the bailout, claiming it was a violation of free market principles in which corporations and American businesses succeed due to their own hard work and smart investing, and fail when they make poor investments. Still, the collapse of the American finance sector represented a threat to the stability of the U.S. economy. This danger put pressure on many Republicans, including President George W. Bush, and Republicans in Congress, to take action in assistance of the investment sector.

Despite the controversy associated with the bailout, Congress eventually took action to assist the investment banking industry. After much deliberation, contention, and conflict, both chambers of Congress and President Bush approved a bailout measure, which authorized $700 billion to assist troubled companies in writing off poor housing investments. The legislation passed on October 3 by a vote of 263 in favor and 171 against in the House of Representatives, and on October 1 in the Senate by a vote of 74 in favor and 25 against. Support was evident among a majority of Democrats and Republicans. Nearly 71 percent of Republican Senators (34) voted for the bailout, while 29 percent voted against. The vote in the House of Representatives was closer, with 54 percent of Republicans (108) voting in favor, and 46 percent (91) voting against (Herszenhorn 2008b). Coupled with a signature from President Bush, this outcome suggests significant— albeit reluctant—support from the Republican Party. Similarly, many Democrats supported the bailout, including Democratic Senator (and later President) Barack Obama. In the Senate, 79 percent of Democrats (41) voted for the bailout, while just 21 percent (11) voted against. In total, 73 percent of House Democrats (172) voted for the bailout, while 27 percent (63) opposed it (Hulse 2008). The bailout represented a response to a crisis of the American economy, and officials in both parties felt this crisis required that they set aside partisan differences and work together to stabilize the banking and investment system.

The legislation was named the "Emergency Economic Stabilization Act of 2008," and created the "Troubled Assets Relief Program" (TARP), which enabled the U.S. Treasury Department to purchase toxic housing assets, so that they could be removed from the books of major investment firms. Purchasing these troubled assets was expected to free up liquidity for major banks, thereby allowing banks to begin loaning to each other, to various businesses, and to individuals across the country. The TARP bailout program included a number of different financial components. The hundreds of billions of dollars allocated under TARP included the following:

1. More than $200 billion in government purchases of equity shares in major banks, via the "Capital Purchase Program";
2. Nearly $68 billion in government purchases of shares from the troubled American International Group (AIG);
3. Nearly $40 billion in funds for purchasing shares from Citigroup and Bank of America, with each receiving $20 billion via the "Targeted Investment Program," with another $5 billion in loan guarantees for Citigroup;
4. Nearly $80 billion in loans and capital support for the auto industry, via the "Automotive Industry Financing Program";
5. Nearly $22 billion for the purchase of mortgage-related securities investments of questionable value and marked by significant volatility and instability (due to the housing market collapse); and
6. More than $45 billion allocated toward assisting financially-stressed homeowners to refinance their homes and avoid foreclosure (Goldman 2009).

TARP was considered controversial at the time it was created. A September 2008 CBS poll found that just 39 percent of Americans surveyed felt that the bailout would "help everyone," while more than half said it would assist "only Wall Street" (CBS News 2008). Whatever one thinks of the program, most financial experts agree that the bailout did stabilize the economy after the 2008 housing market collapse. The bailout also created a split among the American public in terms of attitudes toward subsidizing Wall Street at a time when average Americans were suffering from growing unemployment, economic stagnation, and home foreclosures. The September CBS poll also revealed that 43 percent of respondents nationally said that the government should provide financial relief to Wall Street investment firms and banks, while an equal number said it should not. These numbers suggest a fair amount of skepticism, but ultimately an even split in public opinion on whether to move forward with taxpayer assistance to Wall Street.

Democrats on the Wall Street Bailout

The Democratic Party's position on the bailout was somewhat conflicted, although a majority of its members supported it. In both the first and second House votes on the bailout in September and October, a majority of Democrats in the House voted in favor, and support grew over time, from almost two-thirds to nearly three-quarters of party members. However, a significant minority were concerned about allocating billions to Wall Street interests.

Democratic Party leaders expressed strong support for the bailout initiative. The most prominent Democrat to back the measure was Barack Obama. He expressed frustration with the House of Representatives and its initial refusal to vote for the bill, arguing that, in "a moment of national crisis," Congress's inaction had led to further public anger with Washington. Obama also expressed anger at the conditions that led to the economic collapse. He argued that Americans "should be outraged that an era of greed and irresponsibility on Wall Street and Washington had led us to this point" (CNN 2008). The president-elect also voiced support for a "financial stability fee" on investment and business transactions in the finance sector, to guarantee that taxpayers would be compensated for the money they committed to the bailout. Clearly, Obama supported aiding the banks, with some financial conditions attached.

Congressional Democratic leaders echoed Obama's support. Speaker of the House Nancy Pelosi supported the bailout, but insisted that such funds be tied to increased regulation and accountability on Wall Street, and to a stimulus program aimed at pulling the U.S. economy out of an emerging recession. "For too long, this government [referring to the Bush Administration] has followed a right-wing ideology of anything goes, no supervision, no discipline, no regulation" of Wall Street," stated Pelosi on the floor of the House (Pelosi 2008). Pelosi's comments reflected a growing public anger at Wall Street and Republican free market economics, as well as a concern that whatever created the crisis should be corrected in the months following the bailout.

Senator Harry Reid, the Democratic Senate Majority Leader, also supported the bailout. But where Representative Pelosi focused much of her anger on Republicans and the outgoing Bush presidency, Senator Reid felt quick action was needed to avoid a greater crisis. Reid warned that failure to pass a bailout could lead to economic ruin and dire consequences for Main Street America. He stated, "If we do not act responsibly today, we risk a crisis in which senior citizens across American will lose their retirement savings, small businesses won't make payroll . . . and families won't be able to obtain mortgages for their homes or cars." For Senator Reid, support for a bailout was "the only way" to "return our country to a path of economic stability, prosperity and growth" (Hulse 2008). Other party leaders such as House Whip Steny Hoyer reluctantly supported the bailout. Representative Hoyer initially insisted that any bailout be "deficit neutral" by attaching a tax increase and spending cuts to the legislation to offset the cost of the hundreds of billions granted to Wall Street firms. This measure proved politically unpopular with other members of Congress, however, leading Hoyer to reluctantly vote for a bailout without his proposed conditions. Hoyer expressed concern that "There are people who are upset we are making the deficit worse as we are trying to stabilize the economy," although this did not prevent him from prioritizing the economy over deficit concerns (Hulse 2008).

Although a majority of House and Senate Democrats voted to aid Wall Street firms during the economic collapse, many party members expressed reservations about such an action. Many refused to cast a vote for the bailout. These included representatives such as Dennis Kucinich and Peter DeFazio, and Senator Maria Cantwell, among others. Representative DeFazio expressed disdain for the bailout, complaining that hundreds of billions of dollars were being allocated to aid already wealthy interests who were responsible for creating the economic crisis while the majority of Americans received little direct forms of assistance. He opposed any bill "aimed solely at the froth of Wall Street, the speculators on Wall Street, the non-productive people on Wall Street" (DeFazio 2008). Representative Dennis Kucinich's language was even more combative, accusing Wall Street firms of coercive, criminal behavior, "If someone sticks up a bank, they get a jail sentence. Wall Street sticks up the nation, they get a $700 billion bailout. The free market doesn't mean Wall Street should be free to steal from the American taxpayer. It's a free market, not a spree market" (Kucinich 2008). One major point of protest from Kucinich was that the bailout in the House initially included no provision to help American homeowners, millions of whom had their properties foreclosed at the same time that American financial firms received billions in taxpayer subsidies. Finally, Senator Maria Cantwell protested that the bailout would set a negative historical precedent of committing public funds to bailing out private corporations that invest poorly. She worried that the bailout was akin to "giving the keys to the Treasury over to the private sector" (Sahadi 2008). Senator Cantwell's comment was in specific reference to the Treasury Department's role in buying back toxic assets from Wall Street, thereby providing new liquidity to failing investment firms.

Despite the protests from a significant, vocal minority of Democrats, most members of the party voted for the bailout. The initiative seemed distasteful or unfair to many because of the commitment of government dollars to aiding firms that are expected to succeed or fail in a free market. However, the dangers inherent in allowing the banking sector to collapse, and the broader devastation this could have brought onto the economy at large led most Democrats to believe that some form of government action was necessary.

Republicans on the Wall Street Bailout

In the initial House of Representatives vote on the bailout in late September 2008, a majority of Republicans rejected a rescue package for Wall Street, despite the fact many Democrats were voting in favor of it. Republicans rejected the bailout by a margin of two-to-one, in large part due to their long-stated commitment to free market politics, and due to their support for reducing the role of government in the private sector. Republicans routinely claim markets function most efficiently when they are subject to little or no regulation from government. In light of this position, it was difficult for many Republicans to reconcile urgent concerns about economic collapse and aid for Wall Street on the one hand, and stated preferences for a marketplace free from government interference on the other.

Republicans leaders repeatedly warned that a failure to rescue the banks would result in economic ruin. President Bush expressed "deep disappointment" after most Republicans refused to vote for a bailout in the House in late September (Hulse and Herszenhorn 2008b). Republican reluctance to sign on to a bailout meant that Democratic support became even more important. Conceding this point, President Bush, presidential candidate John McCain, House Minority Leader John Boehner, and Senate Minority Leader Mitch McConnell all met with Democratic legislators in September, seeking to work out a bipartisan bailout deal. The president understood that he needed Democratic support, because Democrats retained majority control of the House of Representatives, and approximately half of the seats in the Senate. Despite Republicans' stated commitment to reducing the government role in the private sector, the Bush administration strongly supported bailout funds for Wall Street. Acknowledging that taxpayers held reservations about TARP, Bush called the legislation "essential to the financial security of every American" (Temple-Raston 2008). Once a bipartisan agreement had been reached on the bailout, Bush thanked legislators "from both sides of the aisle" for working together to "help keep the crisis in our financial system from spreading throughout our economy" (Hulse and Herszenhorn 2008b).

Prominent Republican leaders in Congress understood the urgency of Bush's efforts and worked with the President to pass legislation. Republican presidential candidate and Senator John McCain defended the bailout as "in the best interests of the nation" (Herszenhorn 2008a). Reflecting a theme that was common among Republicans, McCain blamed the government for creating the economic crisis, presumably in reference to quasi-governmental housing agencies Freddie

Mac and Fannie Mae, and their role in supporting bundling, selling, and endorsing mortgage-backed securities—the collapse of which was responsible for causing the economic crash (Herszenhorn 2008a).

Other Republican Senate and House leaders expressed support for aiding Wall Street, although their levels of enthusiasm varied significantly. Senate Minority Leader Mitch McConnell was more favorable in describing the bailout, claiming that it as "a measure for Main Street, not Wall Street" since it would "unfreeze our credit markets and get the American economy working again" (Sahadi 2008). The comment represented a clear effort to frame the initiative in a favorable light by emphasizing the benefits to the average citizen, while downplaying the controversial nature of granting taxpayer funds to wealthy financial interests. House Minority Leader John Boehner stated that the legislation was far from ideal, referring to it as "a mud sandwich" (Hulse and Herszenhorn 2008b). But he maintained that imperfect legislation was better than no legislation, and warned that failure to act could devastate Americans' personal retirement savings. "If I didn't think we were on the brink of an economic disaster, it would be the easiest thing to say no to this. . . . We know if we do nothing this crisis is likely to worsen and put us in an economic slump the likes of which we have never seen" (Isidore 2008). The prediction of impending economic doom resonated with many members of Congress, who witnessed a 778-point decline (7 percent) in the Dow Jones industrial average following the House of Representatives' first attempt (and failure) to pass a bailout package in September (Isidore 2008).

Dissent among Republicans was strong in late September when many party members opposed bailout legislation. Even in the early October vote when most Republicans endorsed a rescue package, the measure was still controversial, with 29 percent of Republican senators and 46 percent of Republican representatives voting against. Some officials, like Senator Richard Shelby, worried that not enough time was spent on crafting an assistance package so that he could be sure that the legislation presented was "the best choice" (Sahadi 2008). Similarly, Representative Marilyn Musgrave felt that the legislation the House voted on represented "the quickest bill" rather than "the best bill" (Herszenhorn 2008). Senator Jeff Sessions worried that the bailout would empower a single person—Secretary of the Treasury Hank Paulson—to grant a massive taxpayer subsidy to Wall Street with little oversight from Congress. Representative Dana Rohrabacher described the bailout legislation as a "blank check" granted to the finance industry, and as an unfair reward for investors who behaved irresponsibly. The bill represented "socialism for the rich," in Rohrabacher's words, and "deserved to be defeated" (Rohrabacher 2008). In short, Republicans opposed the rescue package for many reasons, but all had one thing in common—they related back to a perceived sense of unfairness that the legislation did not represent the best interests of the American people. This sentiment changed somewhat post-2008. Conservative Tea Party Republicans became increasingly active in vocal opposition to the bailout, while President

Obama continued to reflect positively on the bailout's role in stabilizing the economy (Weisman, 2014).

Anthony DiMaggio

Further Reading

ABC News. 2008. "It's Wait and See after Bush Signs Rescue Plan." *ABC News*, October 4. Accessed October 2, 2015. http://abcnews.go.com/Business/story?id=5954902&page=1.

CBS News. 2008. "Poll: U.S. Concerned but Split on Bailout." *CBS News*, October 1. Accessed October 2, 2015. http://www.cbsnews.com/news/poll-us-concerned-but-split-on-bailout/.

CNN. 2008. "'Contentious' White House Meeting Ends with No Deal." *CNN.com*, September 25. Accessed October 2, 2015. http://www.cnn.com/2008/POLITICS/09/25/campaign.wrap/.

DeFazio, Peter. 2008. "Proceedings and Debates of the 110th Congress, Second Session." *Congressional Record*, October 2. Accessed October 2, 2015. http://www.gpo.gov/fdsys/pkg/CREC-2008-10-02/pdf/CREC-2008-10-02-house.pdf.

Goldman, David. 2009. "Special Report: The Rescue." *CNNmoney.com*, November 16. Accessed October 2, 2015. http://money.cnn.com/news/storysupplement/economy/bailouttracker/.

Herszenhorn, David M. 2008a. "A Curious Coalition Opposed to the Bailout." *New York Times*, October 2. Accessed October 2, 2015. http://www.nytimes.com/2008/10/03/business/03naysayers.html?_r=0.

Herszenhorn, David M. 2008b. "Bailout Plan Wins Approval; Democrats Vow Tighter Rules." *New York Times*, October 3. Accessed October 2, 2015. http://www.nytimes.com/2008/10/04/business/economy/04bailout.html?pagewanted=all\.

Holland, Steve. 2008. "Obama: U.S. in Worst Crisis Since Depression." *Reuters*, October 7. Accessed October 2, 2015. http://www.reuters.com/article/2008/10/08/usa-politics-debate-economy-idUSN0749084220081008.

Hulse, Carl. 2008. "Pressure Builds on House After Senate Backs Bailout." *New York Times*. October 1. Accessed October 2, 2015. http://www.nytimes.com/2008/10/02/business/02bailout.html?_r=.

Hulse, Carl, and David M. Herszenhorn. 2008a. "House Rejects Bailout Package, 228–205; Stocks Plunge." *New York Times*, September 29. Accessed October 2, 2015. http://www.nytimes.com/2008/09/30/business/30bailout.html?sq=&_r=0.

Hulse, Carl, and David M. Herszenhorn. 2008b. "U.S. Lawmakers Rebel Against Bailout Plan in Close Vote." *New York Times*, September 29. http://www.nytimes.com/2008/09/29/business/worldbusiness/29iht-30bailout3.16567853.html.

Isidore, Chris. 2008. "Bailout Plan Rejected—Supporters Scramble." *CNN Money*, September 29. Accessed October 2, 2015. http://money.cnn.com/2008/09/29/news/economy/bailout/.

Kucinich, Dennis. 2008. "Proceedings and Debates of the 110th Congress, Second Session." *Congressional Record*, October 2. Accessed October 2, 2015. http://www.gpo.gov/fdsys/pkg/CREC-2008-10-02/pdf/CREC-2008-10-02-house.pdf.

Pelosi, Nancy. 2008. "Transcript of Speaker Pelosi's Speech." *New York Times*, September 29. Accessed October 2, 2015. http://www.nytimes.com/2008/09/30/washington/30pelositranscript.html?pagewanted=all&_r=0.

Rohrabacher, Dana. 2008. "Speech of Hon. Dana Rohrabacher of California in the House of Representatives." *Thomas* Database, September 29. Accessed October 2, 2015. http://thomas.loc.gov/cgi-bin/thomas2.

Sahadi, Jeanne. 2008. "Senate Passes Bailout." *CNN.com*, October 2. Accessed October 2, 2015. http://money.cnn.com/2008/10/01/news/economy/senate_rescuebill2/.

Temple-Raston, Dina. 2008. "Bush Signs $700 Billion Financial Bailout." *National Public Radio*, October 3. Accessed October 2, 2015. http://www.npr.org/templates/story/story.php?storyId=95336601.

Weisman, Jonathan. 2014. "U.S. Declares Bank and Auto Bailouts Over, and Profitable." *New York Times*, December 19. Accessed November 15, 2015. http://www.nytimes.com/2014/12/20/business/us-signals-end-of-bailouts-of-automakers-and-wall-street.html?_r=0.

Glossary

Abusive tax shelter: any attempt to decrease taxable income in a way not approved by Congress, because it does not provide a significant benefit to society.

Accelerated depreciation: largest of all corporate tax expenditures. It allows companies to deduct the costs of assets faster than the values of assets actually decline. Depreciation indicates how much a physical asset's (e.g., building or equipment) value declines due to the wear and tear of use. This decline in value can be claimed as a business expense. Faster depreciation schedules allow companies to claim higher expenses to lower their short-term tax liabilities.

Affordable Care Act (also called Obamacare): federal measure requiring U.S. citizens to have access to health insurance. Developed new insurance options for Americans and includes some regulations for how businesses implement health insurance policies.

Almshouse: home for the poor.

Al Qaeda: a Sunni Muslim group formed by Osama bin Laden and other Islamic fundamentalists, and committed to engaging in terrorist attacks against governments and peoples whose actions and beliefs are deemed a threat to their fundamentalist values.

Antidumping laws: deters producers from exporting a product to the United States or other countries at prices lower than the normal value of the product (the domestic prices of the product or the cost of production) on its own domestic market.

Applied research: study used to develop knowledge about how to meet a recognized need.

At-will employment: when an employer can terminate or dismiss an employee at any time, for any cause or reason, except for an illegal one. The employer does not incur legal liability. At the same time, an employee is free to separate him or herself from work any time for any reason without incurring adverse legal actions.

Austerity: fiscal policies aimed at reducing government's expenditures.

Bailouts: government transfers public money directly to a private company to prevent the company from going out of business.

Bank runs: action when a bank is believed to have low cash reserves and depositors may begin a "run" on the bank to withdraw their deposits. These large and simultaneous withdrawals can force depository institutions into insolvency since the value of assets demanded by depositors is less than what the bank can currently supply. During the Great Depression, bank runs pushed Congress to create the Federal Deposit Insurance Corporation.

Bankruptcy: action when an individual or organization obtains legal protection from creditors after being unable to meet their financial obligations.

Basic research: an undertaking that seeks to improve understanding the natural and social world, in the belief that knowledge will prove beneficial to humankind. Basic research does not set out to develop new processes and products. It is sometimes called Pure Science, Discovery Research, and Knowledge Building.

Bear Stearns collapse: the failure of a New York-based investment bank that predated the global financial crisis of 2008–2009. The financial issues of this bank predated the more systemic subsequent issues of many other institutions, so the Federal Reserve Bank of New York allowed Bear Stearns to fail.

Block grant: funding mechanism that consolidates several smaller programs with a similar goal. States receive a fixed amount of federal money that no longer varies with the number of families needing assistance. Often designates program responsibility and discretion to states.

Budget Control Act: bipartisan legislation passed by Congress and signed by President Barack Obama in 2011, which committed the United States to more than $1 trillion in military spending cuts over the next decade.

Buffett Rule: a tax plan proposed by President Obama that would apply a minimum tax rate of 30 percent on individuals making more than a million dollars a year.

Bush-era tax cuts: package of tax cuts passed during the presidency of George W. Bush. These cuts began with the Economic Growth and Tax Reconciliation Act of 2001, continued with the Jobs and Growth Tax Relief Reconciliation Act of 2003, and ended with the Tax Relief, Unemployment Insurance Reauthorization, and Job Creation Act of 2010. This legislation lowered the highest marginal income tax rate from 39.6 percent to 35 percent.

Capital gains: the difference between the original value of an asset or investment and its value at the time of sale; "unrealized" capital gain pertains to an asset or investment that has increased in value but has not yet been sold.

Capital gains tax: a tax you pay on the increase in value of an asset (as stock or real estate) between the time it is bought and the time it is sold.

Capitalism: an economic system characterized by private or corporate ownership of capital goods, by investments that are determined by private decision, and by prices, production, and the distribution of goods that are determined mainly by competition in a free market.

Cash balance plan: a benefit plan that includes some elements that are similar to a defined contribution plan because the benefit amount is computed based on a formula using contribution and earning credits, and each participant has a hypothetical account.

Chapter 7 bankruptcy: type of bankruptcy that liquidates, or sells, a debtor's non-exempt assets to pay creditors. Priority of payment is based on the bankruptcy code.

Chapter 13 bankruptcy: type of bankruptcy sometimes referred to as a "wage earner's plan," the debtor proposes a plan to repay all or part of the debt within five years.

COBRA: federal law that may allow individuals to temporarily keep health coverage after their employment ends and requires they pay 100 percent of the premiums, including the share the employer used to pay, and an administrative fee.

Cold War: historical period of tension and conflict between competing economic forces in the world, including the United States and its allies, as supporters of capitalism, and the Soviet Union and other communist countries.

Collective bargaining: bargaining over terms and conditions of service is governed by law and involves unions, on behalf of employees and management, represented by authorized representatives.

Consumer price index: a listing of how much typical consumers pay for retail goods.

Consumption tax: a tax on the funds used for purchase of goods and service (such as a sales tax).

Contracting out: when a government agency hires a private organization to provide a good or service.

Contract with America: document presented by congressional Republicans during 1995 midterm elections providing a blueprint for the 104th congressional legislative agenda. Principles include return of program authority to states, a balanced budget, emphasis on strengthening two-parent families, reduced spending on welfare, and capping federal Aid to Families with Dependent Children (AFDC) and other means-tested programs' funds.

Contributory pension system: recipient benefits are based on the amount paid into the system by the beneficiary and his or her employer. Under the Social Security system the number of years worked and the recipient's earning level over their work history determines benefit levels.

Corporate taxes: taxes on profits that private corporations are legally required to send to state and federal government.

Cost sharing: the share of costs covered by an individual's insurance that they pay out of his or her own pocket.

Cut, Balance, and Grow Plan: 2012 presidential candidate Rick Perry's proposal to give individual taxpayers a choice between a flat tax of 20 percent or their current income tax rate.

Death tax: a widely used slang pejorative for the estate tax, misleading in that it implies a tax on death itself rather than a tax on the right to inherit wealth estate tax: a tax on the right to transfer wealth from one generation to the next.

Deduction: a reduction in the income taxed.

Deficit: the difference between budgeted government revenues and obligations.

Defined benefit pension plan: retirement plan that promises the participant a specified monthly benefit at retirement. Often, the benefit is based on factors such as the participant's salary, the participant's age, and the number of years he or she worked for the employer. The plan may state this promised benefit as an exact dollar amount, such as $100 per month at retirement or may calculate a benefit through a plan formula that considers such factors as salary and service.

Defined contribution pension plan: a retirement plan in which the employee and/or the employer contribute to the employee's individual account. The amount in the account at distribution includes the contributions and investment gains or losses, minus any investment and administrative fees with the contributions and earnings not taxed until distribution.

Deflation: occurs when the overall value of goods drops.

Democracy: a form of government in which people choose leaders by voting.

Department of Homeland Security: government bureaucracy created after the September 11, 2001, terrorist attacks designed to coordinate with other intelligence agencies in order to intercept terrorist threats.

Depression: prolonged period of increased high unemployment, diminished trade and commerce, volatility in currency values, and credit squeeze. In conditions of depression there is a downturn in general production of good and services. Depression is considered as a form of severe recession.

Development research: study to improve products and processes, for areas including but not limited to business and industry, the military, and medicine.

Devolution: the process by which a central government gives power, property, and so on, to lower levels of government, such as the elimination of the federal gas tax and transfer of funds and control from the federal government to individual states.

Direct spending: outlay of funds, such as spending federal dollars for research and development.

Discretionary spending: the portion of the annual budget over which Congress exercises control because spending on these items is optional, rather than mandatory.

Earmark: a provision in congressional legislation that allocates a specified amount of money for a specific project, program, or organization.

Earned income tax credit: a tax refund that is larger for lower income households.

Economic growth: the increase in the value of goods and services in a market over time.

Effective corporate tax rate: the rate of taxation actually paid by corporations after tax credits, allowances, exemptions, deferrals, and deductions (i.e., tax expenditures) are taken into account. Estimates suggest that the average effective corporate tax rate is between 26 percent and 30 percent as compared to the 35 percent statutory rate.

Embargo: government prohibition of exports to or imports from another country or countries.

Entitlement: all people who meet program eligibility criteria have the right to receive assistance, and federal funds flow to states in accordance to the number of people in need.

Entrepreneurial spirit: characterized by risk-taking and ingenuity in the American ethos necessary for national competition in a global economic system.

Entrepreneurship: the capacity and willingness to start a business for profit, despite risks.

Estate tax: referred to as the "death tax." This is a tax on the transfer of property after a death.

Excise taxes: taxes paid when purchases are made on specific goods, such as gasoline.

Executive order: directives issued by the president, and other legal heads of executive branches. Although executive orders have the force of law, there is no expectation for legislative approval.

Exemptions: a source or amount of income that is not taxed.

Fair Tax: a formal proposal that suggests replacing income tax with a single tax on consumption.

Family Medical Leave Act (FMLA): a federal law regulating employee medical leave. Reasons for medical leave include military leave, pregnancy, childbirth, and serious illness.

Farm Bill: an overarching piece of legislation that provides the funding for many of the programs run by the United States Department of Agriculture, including farm subsidies and food stamps.

Federal Acquisition Regulation (FAR): set of rules government agencies must follow when contracting out.

Federal Insurance Contributions Act (FICA): originally Title II of the Social Security Act of 1935 legislated payroll taxes paid by employers and employees to fund the Social Security system. Subsequent amendments assigned taxation provisions to the Internal Revenue Code under the Federal Insurance Contributions Act in 1939.

Federal tax code: a federal document, more than 75,000 pages in length, outlining federal rules of taxation for individuals and businesses.

Fight for $15: a movement of fast food and other low-income workers demanding a $15 per hour minimum wage.

Financial Stability Oversight Council: a regulatory forum created by the Dodd-Frank Wall Street Reform and Consumer Protection Act of 2010 that is charged with facilitating communication and coordination among financial regulators, collecting and evaluating financial data to monitor systemic risk, and deciding which financial institutions should be subject to added regulation by the Federal Reserve.

529 plans: education savings plans designed to help families set aside money for future college costs. They are operated by a state or by an educational institution. The money grows tax-free in the plan. Withdrawals are not taxed by the federal government as long as the money is used for qualified educational expenses.

Fixed exchange rate: when the value of currency is tied to a particular amount of a material that has an unchanging value, like gold or silver.

Flat tax: the same tax rate is applied to all taxpayers with no deductions or exemptions.

Floating exchange rate system: when the value of currency is not tied to any particular object or other currency, but rather the relative value of itself against international currencies.

Food desert: defined by the United States Department of Agriculture (USDA) as urban neighborhoods and rural towns that lack supermarkets and grocery stores that sell fresh, healthy, and affordable food. Instead, they are served by small business such as fast food restaurants, convenience stores, and liquor stores, and so on, that off few healthy, affordable food options.

Food Stamp Program: the permanent nutritional program established by the Food Stamp Act of 1964.

Fossil fuels: a hydrocarbon deposit or natural fuel formed over millions of years by the decomposition of organisms that can be used to create energy. The three main types of fossil fuels are coal, oil, and natural gas.

401(k): defined contribution plan where an employee can make contributions from his or her paycheck either before or after tax, depending on the options offered in the plan. Similar defined-contribution plans available at certain tax-exempt organizations are termed 403(b).

Fracking: process of extracting gas that uses a high-pressure mixture to release the gas.

Free enterprise: a system in which private businesses are able to compete with each other with little control by the government.

Free market: an ideology supported by conservatives, which argues that capitalism functions best when there is little to no intervention by or regulation of the private sector from government.

Free trade: absence of tariffs (tax on imports), quotas, or other governmental impediments to trade between countries.

Free trade agreement: contractual arrangement on trade between the United States and other countries. Trade agreements may be bilateral or multilateral—that is, between two countries or more than two countries.

Full employment: the natural level of employment where there is no cyclical or deficient–demand unemployment.

Geothermal energy: known as heat of the earth, it is energy from the planet's core. It is considered renewable and when harnessed, can be used for a range of heating purposes including commercial, residential, or industrial.

Glass ceiling: an unfair system or set of attitudes that prevents some people (such as women or people of a certain race) from getting the most powerful jobs.

Global Financial Crisis of 2008–2009 (also known as the Great Recession): economic crisis that threatened the collapse of many of the world major financial institutions considered by many economists to be the most significant economic downturn in the United States since the Great Depression.

Great Depression: a period of time in the United States, which occurred during the 1930s, that was marked by an economic depression, a weak economy, and a high level of poverty among Americans.

Great Recession: the largest economic downturn since the Great Depression, during which the U.S. and global economies experienced a sharp decline culminating in a global recession that began during the late 2000s. This decline began when the "bubble" of the U.S. housing market burst due to poor oversight in U.S. banking and lending practices.

Green energy: type of energy naturally replenished over a brief period of time. Examples include solar, wind, hydropower, geothermal, tidal, and biomass.

Hawkish: confrontational philosophical approach to U.S. foreign policy in which a political leader is more likely to favor military action and increased military budgets, rather than efforts to avoid military conflicts and cut military spending.

Health coverage: legal entitlement to payment or reimbursement for health care costs, generally under a contract with a health insurance company, a group health plan offered in connection with employment, or a government program.

Hydraulic fracturing: extraction process for underground resources such as oil, natural gas, geothermal, or water. Often referred to as "fracking," it is an extraction method commonly used by companies in the oil and gas industry to bring oil or natural gas to the surface by drilling deep production wells in either horizontal or vertical directional sections and creating fractures in the geologic formations containing the desired resources.

Hydropower: also known as hydroelectric energy, this is electricity formed by the gravitational movement of water. This electricity is often generated by the use of dams and large turbines at hydropower plants or stations.

Income-based repayment plans (IBRs): alternative plans to standard repayment. Payment amounts are based on students' discretionary income, ranging from 10 percent to 20 percent. Repayment periods are either 20 or 25 years. The remaining balance is forgiven at the end.

Income redistribution: the transfer of wealth from some members of society to other members through some form of government process such as taxation.

Incremental reform: public policy builds upon past programs, policies, and expenditures. Such steps focus on increases, decreases, or modifications of current policies.

Individual mandate: requirement under the Affordable Care Act requiring most individuals to have health insurance coverage or potentially to pay a penalty for noncompliance.

Inflation: a measure of the increasing cost of goods and the decreasing purchasing value of money.

Infrastructure: the foundational system of roads, highways, bridges, railroads, airports, waterways, electrical grid, and so on, serving a country, state, region, or city.

Inheritance: the wealth that is transferred from one generation to the next.

Job based health care plan (employer provided health insurance): coverage that is offered to an employee (and often his or her family) by an employer.

Keynesian economics: belief that it is the responsibility of the government to assist in stabilizing the economy of the nation that it governs through manipulation of the value of currency and public sector job creation.

Lien: the legal right to gain possession of property by a creditor and sell it if a debt is not repaid, also known as a security interest.

Lifetime limit: cap on the total lifetime benefits an individual may get from their insurance company.

Loophole: accounting techniques for increasing tax deductions and credits.

Low Income Home Energy Assistance Program (LIHEAP): federal program that lowers the cost of energy for low-income Americans.

Manifest Destiny: 19th-century American belief that the United States had the right to and ultimately would expand its territory across North America.

Marginal tax rate: the fraction of tax paid on the last dollar of income or revenue.

Medicaid: government program, administered on a state-by-state basis that provides health coverage to some subgroups of the poor.

Medicare: federal health insurance entitlement program that provides coverage to all citizens over 65 years of age, people with permanent disabilities, or people who have been diagnosed with, for example, end-stage renal disease (ESRD) or Amyotrophic Lateral Sclerosis (ALS).

Medicare Advantage (also Medicare Part C): component of Medicare that provides beneficiaries with the option to join a private health insurance plan to receive benefits instead of a traditional fee-for-service structure.

Middle-out economics: belief that economic prosperity flows outward from a thriving middle class.

Military industrial complex: description from President Dwight Eisenhower of a large political-economic system in the United States, said to include military contractors, political officials, and the military itself, that became self-sustaining after World War II, commanding a large portion of yearly federal budgets.

Minimum wage: the lowest hourly wage that a state or federal government can pay employees.

Moral hazard: tendency of those with insurance to take less care and effort to avoid risks than if they had no insurance.

Mortgage-backed securities: a financial instrument comprising numerous individual mortgages that were packaged together and sold by investment groups and government-associated agencies.

National debt: the sum of all the accumulated money from current and previous deficits in the national budget.

Natural gas: a fossil fuel formed over thousands of years as high heat and pressure convert carbon from the energy stored in layers of buried plants and animals. It is a flammable gas found naturally underground, and when combusted to generate electricity, can be used as energy. It is a nonrenewable energy source. The process of extracting natural gas is called hydraulic fracturing or fracking.

New Deal: economic policies initiated in the early days of Franklin Delano Roosevelt's administration in 1933 with the intent of mitigating the effects of the Great Depression.

New federalism: reduction of the federal government's role in providing public assistance, while returning responsibility and control for programs to states and communities.

9-9-9 Plan: 2012 presidential candidate Herman Cain's plan to replace the current income tax with a 9 percent business tax, a 9 percent personal income tax, and a 9 percent federal sales tax.

No-bid contract: when a government contract is given to a private organization without a competitive bidding process.

Non-contributory pension systems: guaranteed entitlements are drawn from general taxes and available to all citizens regardless of work history or financial contribution.

Obamacare (also known as the Affordable Care Act of 2010): the centerpiece of President Barack Obama's first presidential term, designed to comprehensively reform the system of health insurance in the United States.

Oligarchy: government by a small group of people distinguished by royalty, wealth, family ties, education, corporate, religious, or military control.

Open markets: freely competitive market operating without obstructions.

P3: combined project of a government agency with one or more private companies to build or repair a road.

Partisanship: allegiance to a political party.

Path to Prosperity (also known as the Ryan Proposal): Republican Party's 2012 budget proposal that attempted to change the Medicare program, repeal a number of components of the Affordable Care Act, and make other health care modifications.

Patient Protection and Affordable Care Act (ACA) of 2010: federal legislation that seeks to improve quality of care, expand healthcare coverage, and reduce overall healthcare costs in the United States. It is one of the most reformative healthcare bills passed since Medicare and Medicaid were created in 1965.

Pay As You Earn: an income-based repayment plan. The monthly payment is generally 10 percent of a borrower's discretionary income and has a 20-year repayment period. Any remaining balance is forgiven then if payments have been made on time.

Payroll tax: a tax paid by employers based on the wages of a worker.

Peer review: evaluation of research findings by professionals in the field, before it is accepted for publication or presentation.

Pell grants: need-based grants from the U.S. federal government awarded to students to help pay for higher education expenses. They do not need to be repaid.

Phillips curve: a graph, which illustrates the argument that employment rates and inflation rates have an inverse relationship to one another.

Political action committee (PAC): a group that is formed to give money to the political campaigns of people who are likely to make decisions that would benefit the group's interests.

Poverty line: a level of personal or family income below which one is classified as poor according to governmental standards.

Pre-existing condition: a health problem an individual had before the date that new health coverage starts.

Primary insurance amount (PIA): amount of scheduled benefits a recipient would receive upon retiring at the standard age of retirement as stipulated by the Social Security Act.

Privatization: the situation whereby a service is produced and delivered by a contractor private contractor. Privatization can also mean government selling its assets to a private vendor.

Procurement: the process by which government agencies acquire goods or services from private organizations.

Progressive Democrats of America: grassroots political action committee that promotes a progressive political agenda.

Progressive tax: the tax rate increases as the amount of income increases.

Protectionism: raising tariffs and reducing imports to protect domestic industries.

Public option: health insurance company that has been put forward by the government as an option to health insurance that is privately owned. Its role would be to drive down costs associated with private health and sit between universal care and private insurance.

Quid pro quo: something that is given to you or done for you in return for something you have given to or done for someone else.

Raise the Minimum Wage: a movement of legal professionals demanding a $12 per hour minimum wage.

Recession: when the gross domestic product declines in two successive quarters. Unemployment, falling profits, lower investment spending, reduced trade, and industrial production characterize recessionary periods.

Recovery: phase in the business cycle following a recession, characterized by increases in the gross domestic product.

Redistribution: to divide (something) among a group in a different way.

Regressive tax: a tax system in which a tax is imposed in such a manner that the tax rate decreases as the amount subject to taxation increases.

Renewable energy/renewables: energy produced by wind, solar, hydro, or another non-traditional energy source.

Renewable portfolio standards (RPS): legal mandate that requires an increase in production of energy from renewable sources such as biomass, wind, or solar. Under this requirement, electric supply companies must produce some of their energy from renewable energy sources and can then sell these to companies or consumers. RPS can encourage price competition between renewable energy types.

Revenue: money that is collected for public use by a government through taxes.

Right-to-work states: states that prohibit union collective bargaining. No worker need join or pay dues to a union as a condition of employment. A right-to-work law prohibits agreements between unions and employers on issue such as the extent of union membership dues, fees, and conditions of employment are determined.

Rule of law: notion that a nation should not be governed according to the rules set forth by individual government representatives, but rather by the law itself. Furthermore, no individual is above the law and everyone is subject to the law.

Safety net: public assistance programs for the poor, such as food stamps, unemployment benefits, and so on.

Section 1705: federal loan program that authorized loan guarantees for U.S.-based projects involving certain renewable energy systems, electric transmission, and other non-traditional energy.

Securities: financial instruments such as stocks or bonds. Stocks usually give their owners (i.e., shareholders) the right to receive portions of companies' cash flow in the form of dividends and a voice in selecting companies' management. Bonds represent debt and give their owners the right to receive interest payments and the total "face value" of the bond on the date of maturity. Financial instruments can also take the form of mortgage-backed securities that represent cash flows from home loans. Owners of securities have the right to sell securities to other investors for a profit.

Sequester: mandated cuts in government spending that were put into place by Republicans and Democrats through the Budget Control Act of 2011, which called for $1 trillion in reduced military spending from 2013 to 2021.

Shovel ready: projects for which work is able to begin immediately.

Small business: a company, corporation, or partnership with fewer than 500 employees.

Social engineering: the promotion of social goals, including enhancing the advantages derived from particular behaviors.

Social insurance programs: public programs under the auspices of the government designed to provide financial protection and assistance to vulnerable citizen populations such as the elderly or disabled.

Socialism: system of government that is defined by a combination of government and private ownership of the means of production for goods and services.

Socialized medicine: system of medical care that is financed and administered by the state.

Social Security Administration (SSA): created in 1935 as the Social Security Board to administer Social Security benefits, the Social Security Administration was established in 1946 under the direction of the Federal Security Agency and later the Department of Health, Education, and Welfare. The SSA became an independent federal agency in 1994.

Social Security Board of Trustees: six-member board made up of the secretaries of the Treasury, Labor, Health and Human Services, and the Commissioner of Social Security. The remaining two members are appointed to the board by the president. The Board of Trustees was created in 1939 and is responsible for reporting on the long-term solvency of the Social Security system.

Social Security Trust Funds: accounts holding income derived from payroll taxes and other sources to fund Old Age and Survivors Insurance (OASI) and Disability Insurance (DI) benefits. Accounts are held by the U.S. Treasury, and any surplus is invested in government guaranteed Treasury bonds.

Speculation: the practice whereby investors or investment firms manipulate the value of a stock or asset by artificially increasing demand for that item, in the process unsustainably driving up the price.

Starving the beast: saying attributed to Senator Patrick Moynihan that expresses the concept that tax cuts deprive government of the revenue necessary for them to intervene in markets and encroach on individual liberty.

Stimulus: more than $700 billion in funding allocated in 2009 by the federal government to stimulating the economy to help recover from the 2008 economic crash.

Subsidies: economic measure that ensures prices for consumers are below market rate to reduce the consumer cost or prices that keep prices for producers above market levels to reduce their costs. Examples include tax breaks, direct cash transfers, rebates, trade restrictions, or price controls.

Subsidized coverage: health coverage that's obtained through financial assistance (subsidies) from programs to help people with low and middle incomes.

Subsidized loans: loans where the U.S. Department of Education pays the interest while the student is in school at least half-time, for the first six months after leaving school, and during a period of deferment.

Substantive law: legislation that defines rights and obligations that govern society, and is differentiated from "procedural law" that determines the process for enforcing legal rights (mostly through the court system).

Supplemental Nutrition Assistance Program (SNAP): as of 2008, the new name of the food stamp program.

Supply-side economics: belief that a nation's economy should come from the natural supply and demand of goods on the open market. A healthy and diverse supply of goods and services will increase demand for those goods, thus creating a healthy economy.

Supremacy clause: Article VI, Clause 2 of the U.S. Constitution that establishes the U.S. Constitution, federal statutes, and treaties as "the supreme law of the land."

Surplus: income exceeds expenditures.

Taliban: Sunni Muslim group that has existed as an insurgent group or a part of government at various points in the last two decades in the country of Afghanistan. The Taliban gained infamy after September 11 for hosting fundamentalists affiliated with the Al Qaeda terrorist group.

Tariffs: tax imposed on imported goods and services. They are used to restrict international trade.

TARP: "Troubled Assets Relief Program," informally known as the government bailout of Wall Street financial interests.

Taxable income: the amount of income that is taxed by the government after tax credits and deductions for money put in tax shelters.

Tax base: the total amount of income that can be taxed by the government.

Tax bracket: a range of income that is taxed at the same rate.

Tax burden: total amount of taxes levied on an individual or business.

Tax credit: a payment from the government to the taxpayer.

Tax expenditure: loss to the government of taxable revenue, from the use of tax exemptions, deductions, or credits.

Tax haven: used to describe Americans who have money invested or deposited in other countries to avoid paying taxes on that money in the United States.

Tax loophole: used to negatively describe individuals or businesses who use current laws to avoid paying taxes over and above what Congress intended.

Tax rates: the graduated percentage of tax applied to an estate net value.

Tax rebates: a refund when a taxpayer files and has paid more in taxes than they owe.

Tax shelter: device that allows individuals or businesses to invest money in certain activities and thereby reduce their taxable income, but the activity must be beneficial to society as a whole.

Tax spending: exemption from taxes other groups pay, for participating in a government-sanctioned activity such as research and development.

Tax threshold: a set amount below which no estate taxes are levied; estate taxes are levied for the amount above the threshold only.

Three-legged stool: model for retirement developed by the Committee on Economic Security that relies on three elements: government pension, individual pension, and individual savings.

Trade liberalization: elimination of all trade barriers.

Traditional energy producers: providers of energy that rely nuclear, oil, or gas as their primary fuel.

Trickle-down economics, or supply-side economics: belief that economic prosperity flows downward, out of corporate investments.

Unemployment: refers to general joblessness. Persons are considered unemployed if they are actively seeking employment at prevailing wages. The unemployment rate is a metric calculated as a percentage of the unemployed to the number of persons in the labor force.

Unemployment insurance: income provided to persons who have lost jobs through no fault of their own.

Uninsured: individuals who do not receive health insurance as a job benefit and are not eligible to receive coverage through Medicare, Medicaid, or the Children's Health Insurance Program (CHIP).

Universal basic income: model of social welfare policy in which all citizens are guaranteed a standard level of income by the government.

Universal health care: ensures that all people can use the health services they need, of sufficient quality to be effective, while also ensuring that the use of these services does not expose the user to financial hardship.

U.S. Energy Information Administration (EIA): federal agency that collects, analyzes, and shares energy information with policy makers and the general public.

Vesting: minimum amount of time an employee has to work before employer contributions are permanently included in pension fund. They typically require an employee to work for a number of years before (s)he is invested in the pension fund.

War on Poverty: Kennedy-Johnson Administration's 13-point program that declared an "unconditional war on poverty" via creation of new social safety-net programs such as Head Start.

War on Terror: initiative declared by President George W. Bush after the September 11 terrorist attacks in the United States. This war has included conflicts in Afghanistan and Iraq, among other United States and allied military initiatives.

Welfare: Public assistance programs designed to help people meet their most basic needs.

William D. Ford Federal Direct Loan Program: program that provides low-interest government loans to both students and parents to help pay for higher education expenses.

Work requirement: A stipulation placed on food assistance that requires a recipient to either be actively looking for work or enrolled in a work program.

Bibliography

Amadeo, Kimberly. 2015. "Compare the 2016 Presidential Candidates on Economic Issues."
   Accessed December 15. http://useconomy.about.com/od/candidatesandtheeconomy
   /tp/candidates_and_economy.htm.

Austin, Andrew D. 2008. *The Debt Limit: History and Recent Increases*. Washington, DC:
   Congressional Research Service, April 29. Accessed December 2, 2015. http://fpc
   .state.gov/documents/organization/105193.pdf.

Barton, Stephanie. 2008. "Parties for Taxation: Republicans vs. Democrats." November 6.
   Accessed December 2, 2015. http://www.investopedia.com/articles/economics/09/us
   -parties-republican-democrat-taxes.asp.

Behravesh, Nariman. 2008. *Spin-Free Economics*. Columbus, OH: McGraw-Hill.

Bernstein, Jared. 2015. *The Reconnection Agenda: Reuniting Growth and Prosperity*. Amazon
   Digital Services, April 23. Accessed December 15, 2015. http://www.amazon.com
   /Reconnection-Agenda-Reuniting-Growth-Prosperity-ebook/dp/B00WNFRB20/ref=sr
   _1_8?ie=UTF8&qid=1450196761&sr=8-8&keywords=Democrats+and+Economic+
   Policy.

Blinder, Alan. 2015. "Keynesian Economics." *Library of Economics and Liberty, the Concise
   Encyclopedia of Economics*. Accessed December 17. http://www.econlib.org/library
   /Enc1/KeynesianEconomics.html.

Bowman, Sam. 2013. "The Keynesian Case against the Minimum Wage." Adamsmith.
   org. Accessed December 17, 2015. http://www.adamsmith.org/blog/economics/the
   -keynesian-case-against-the-minimum-wage/.

Calmes, Jackie. 2014. "Democrats Say Economic Message Was Lacking." *New York Times*,
   November 7. Accessed December 15, 2014. http://www.nytimes.com/2014/11/08/us
   /politics/democrats-losses-expose-weakness-of-economic-message.html?_r=0.

Camp-Landis, Stephen. 2006. *State Political Culture and TANF: A Case Study of Pennsylvania
   and Fifty State Analysis*. Dissertation Proposal, New York University.

Centers for Medicare and Medicaid Services. 2015. "Estimated Impact of Health Care
   Reform Proposals." Accessed December 16. https://www.cms.gov/Research-Statistics
   -Data-and-Systems/Research/ActuarialStudies/HealthCareReform.html.

Coates, David. 2000. *Models of Capitalism: Growth and Stagnation in the Modern Era*. Cambridge, UK: Polity Press.

Coates, David. 2009. *Answering Back: Liberal Responses to Conservative Argument*. New York:
   Bloomsbury Academic.

Coates, David. 2011. *Making the Progressive Case: Towards a Stronger U.S. Economy*. New
   York: Bloomsbury Academic.

Daly, Matthew. 2015. "Presidential Contenders Differ Sharply on Climate, Energy." *Denver Post*, November 27. Accessed December 15, 2015. http://www.denverpost.com
   /ci_29171646/presidential-contenders-differ-sharply-climate-energy.

DeBroux, Louis. 2014. "Democrats Hope Recycling Economic Wedge Issues Lead to 2016 Victories." *The Patriot Post*, November 26. Accessed January 2, 2015. http://patriotpost .us/commentary/31285.

"Democrat v. Republican." *Diffen.com*. Accessed November 19, 2014. http://www.diffen .com/difference/Democrat_vs_Republican.

Democratic National Committee. 2012. "Moving Forward America: 2012 Democratic Platform." Accessed November 24, 2014. http://www.democrats.org/democratic-national -platform.

"Democratic Party: On the Issues." Accessed November 26, 2014. http://www.ontheissues .org/Democratic_Party.htm.

Draper, Robert. 2013. *When the Tea Party Came to Town: Inside the U.S. House of Representatives' Most Combative, Dysfunctional, and Infuriating Term in Modern History*. New York: Simon & Schuster.

Federal Reserve Bank of Kansas City. 1998. "Income Inequality: Issues and Policy Options." A symposium sponsored by the Federal Reserve Bank of Kansas City Jackson Hole, Wyoming, August 27–29, 1998. Accessed December 15, 2015. https://www.kansascityfed .org/publications/research/escp/symposiums/escp-1998.

Financial Crisis Inquiry Commission. 2011. *The Financial Crisis Inquiry Report: Authorized Edition*. New York: Public Affairs Publishers.

Fisher, Claude S., Michael Hout, Martin Sanchez Jankowski, Samuel R. Lucas, Ann Swiddler, and Kim Voss. 1996. *Inequality by Design: Cracking the Bell Curve Myth*. Princeton, NJ: Princeton University Press.

Fleenor, Patrick. 1994. "A History and Overview of Estate Taxes in the U.S." January 1. Accessed December 11, 2015. http://taxfoundation.org/article/history-and-overview -estate-taxes-united-states.

Formisano, Robert. 2012. *The Tea Party: A Brief History*. Baltimore, MD: Johns Hopkins University Press.

Friedman, Milton. 1962. *Capitalism and Freedom*. Chicago, IL: University of Chicago Press.

Friedman, Milton. 1992. *Money Mischief: Episodes of Monetary History*. New York: Harcourt Brace.

Friedman, Milton. 2005. "Eliminate Social Security, Medicaid, Medicare." *Chicagobooth.edu*. Accessed December 16, 2015. http://www.chicagobooth.edu/news/2005-11-01_milton _friedman.aspx.

Friedman, Milton. 2012. "Milton Friedman on Minimum Wage Laws." Accessed December 16, 2015. http://www.thewelfarestatewerein.com/welfare-benefits/2012/08/milton -friedman-on-minimum-wage-laws.php.

Fuller, Dan, Richard Allston, and Michael Vaughan. 1995. "The Split Between Political Parties on Economic Issues: A Survey of Democrats, Republicans and Economists." Accessed January 5, 2015. *Eastern Economic Journal* 21 (2): 227–239.

Galbraith, John Kenneth. 1998. *The Affluent Society*. 40th Anniversary Edition. New York: Mariner Books.

"Galbraith on U.S. Economy." 1991. *Los Angeles Times*, January 23. Accessed December 15, 2015. http://articles.latimes.com/1991-01-23/local/me-434_1_free-enterprise-john -maynard-keynes-socialism.

Gomory, Alex. 2012. "Political Parties in Agreement on Student Loans." April 24. Accessed December 7, 2015. http://loans.org/student/news/political-parties-agreement-92092.

Greenspan, Alan. 2014. *The Map and the Territory 2.0: Risk, Human Nature, and the Future of Forecasting* (Revised edition). New York: Penguin Books.

Harrington, Joseph Jr. 1993. "Economic Policy, Economic Performance and Elections." *The American Economic Review* 83 (1): 27–42.

Herrnstein, Richard J., and Charles Murray. 1994. *The Bell Curve: Intelligence and Class Structure in American Life.* New York: The Free Press.

Hibbs, Douglas. 1977. "Political Parties and Macroeconomic Policy." *American Political Science Review* 71 (4): 1467–1487.

"Hillary Clinton 2016 Economic Plan." 2015. Accessed December 15. http://useconomy.about.com/od/fiscalpolicy/p/Hillary_Economy.htm.

Hood, Christopher. 1994. *Explaining Economic Policy Reversals.* New York: Open University Press.

Horn, Carolyn. 2013. "If the U.S. Economy Is Strong in 2016, Who Benefits?" CBS News, June 7. Accessed December 13, 2015. http://www.cbsnews.com/news/if-the-economys-strong-in-2016-who-benefits/.

Horowitz, Juliana Menesce. 2014. "Inequality, Poverty Divide Republicans more than Democrats." *Pew Research Center*, January 29. Accessed November 23, 2014. http://www.pewresearch.org/fact-tank/2014/01/29/inequality-poverty-divide-republicans-more-than-democrats/.

Huber, Evelyne, and John D. Stevens. 1993. "Political Parties and Public Pensions." *Acta Sociologica* 36 (4): 309–325.

"Jobs and the Economy." Accessed November 30, 2014. http://www.democrats.org/issues/economy_and_job_creation.

Jones, Jeffrey. 2015. "Economy Trumps Foreign Affairs as Key 2016 Election Issue," May 15. Accessed December 14, 2015. http://www.gallup.com/poll/183164/economy-trumps-foreign-affairs-key-2016-election-issue.aspx.

Judis, John. 2014. "The Economy Crushed the Democrats—And It Will Again in 2016 If They Don't Shape Up." *New Republic*, November 25. Accessed December 13, 2014. http://www.newrepublic.com/article/120146/2014-midterms-economy-doomed-democrats.

Keynes, John Maynard. 1936. *The General Theory of Employment, Interest and Money.* London: MacMillan.

Kotz, David M. 2015. *The Rise and Fall of Neoliberal Capitalism.* Cambridge, MA: Harvard University Press.

Krugman, Paul R. 1994. *Peddling Prosperity: Economic Sense and Nonsense in the Age of Diminished Expectations.* New York: W.W. Norton.

Krugman, Paul. 2002. "America the Polarized." *New York Times.* January 2, A21.

Krugman, Paul. 2012. *End This Depression Now!* New York: W.W. Norton & Company.

Levitt, Steven, and James M. Snyder, Jr. 1995. "Political Parties and the Distribution of Federal Outlays." *American Journal of Political Science* 39 (4): 958–980.

Long, Heather. 2015. "So What Exactly Is Donald Trump's Economic Policy?" CNN. July 28. Accessed December 13, 2015. http://money.cnn.com/2015/07/28/news/economy/donald-trump-polls-taxes-wages/index.html.

Murray, Charles. 1984. *Losing Ground.* New York: Basic Books.

Murray, Douglas. 2006. *Neoconservatism: Why We Need It.* New York: Encounter Books.

Musgrave, Richard. 1988. "U.S. Fiscal Policy, Keynes, and Keynesian Economics." *Journal of Post-Keynesian Economics* 10 (2): 171–182.

"Of Revolution, Glory and Uncertainty: A History of the U.S. Economy." 2015. Accessed December 15. http://www.randomhistory.com/us-economy-history.html.

O'Hara, John, and Michelle Malkin. 2011. *A New American Tea Party: The Counterrevolution against Bailouts, Handouts, Reckless Spending and More Taxes.* Hoboken, NJ: Wiley.

Persson, Torsten, and Guido Enrico Tabellini. 2002. *Political Economics: Explaining Economic Policy.* Boston, MA: MIT Press.

Pew Research Center. 2010. "Public Knows Basic Facts about Politics, Economics, but Struggles with Specifics," November 18. Accessed December 12, 2015. http://www.pewresearch.org/2010/11/18/public-knows-basic-facts-about-politics-economics-but-struggles-with-specifics/.

Pew Research Center. 2011. "Illegal Immigration: Gaps Within and Between Parties," December 6. Accessed November 11, 2015. http://www.people-press.org/2011/12/06/illegal-immigration-gaps-between-and-within-parties/.

Pew Research Center. 2014. "Wide Partisan Differences over the Issues that Matter in 2014," September 12. Accessed December 15, 2015. http://www.people-press.org/2014/09/12/wide-partisan-differences-over-the-issues-that-matter-in-2014/.

Phillips, Kevin. 1993. *Boiling Point: Democrats, Republicans and the Decline of Middle-Class Prosperity.* New York: Random House.

Reich, Robert B. 2015. *Saving Capitalism: For the Many, Not the Few.* New York: Knopf.

"Republican Party: On the Issues." Accessed November 23, 2014. http://www.ontheissues.org/Republican_Party.htm.

"Republican Views on the Issues." Accessed November 23, 2014. http://www.republicanviews.org/.

Rogers, Alex. 2015. "Republicans: 'Where Are the Jobs?' Democrats: 'Where Are the Wages?'" *Time,* January 5. Accessed January 6, 2015. http://time.com/3654790/congress-jobs-wages-economy/.

Scher, Bill. 2013. "The Top Five Issues Dividing Democrats." *The Week,* April 8. Accessed November 25, 2014. http://theweek.com/article/index/242383/the-top-5-issues-dividing-democrats.

Schiller, Bradley R. 2007. *The Economics of Poverty and Discrimination.* 9th ed. Upper Saddle River, NJ: Prentice Hall.

Schneider, Bill. 2014. "Political Parties Swap Roles: Can Social Issues Help Democrats?" *Reuters.* November 3. Accessed December 12, 2014. http://blogs.reuters.com/great-debate/2014/11/03/political-parties-swap-roles-can-social-issues-help-democrats/.

Skocpol, Theda, and Vanessa Williamson. 2012. *The Tea Party and the Remaking of Republican Conservatism.* Carey, NC: Oxford University Press.

Tasselmyer, Michael. 2013. *Tax Reform According to Milton Friedman.* National Taxpayers Union, July 31. Accessed December 17, 2015. http://www.ntu.org/governmentbytes/detail/Tax-Reform-According-to-Milton-Friedman.

"The Tea Party and the Economy." 2015. Accessed December 15. http://useconomy.about.com/od/Politics/p/Tea-Party-And-Economy.htm.

Thomas, Ken. 2014. "House Democrats Point to Economic Focus in 2014." *Yahoo News.* May 21. Accessed January 3, 2015. http://news.yahoo.com/house-democrats-point-economic-focus-2014-215508252--election.html;_ylt=A0LEVvCS.atUjygAG7oPxQt.;_ylu=X3oDMTBzMjNhN3Q5BHNlYwNzcgRwb3MDNDUEY29sbwNiZjEEdnRpZAM-.

"United States Elections 2016: The Economic Policies." 2015. Accessed December 15. http://internationalpoliticalforum.com/united-states-elections-2016-the-economic-policies/.

"Vice President Joe Biden's Views on the Economy." 2015. Accessed December 15. http://useconomy.about.com/od/candidatesandtheeconomy/p/Biden-Economy.htm.

"Welfare Programs: The 6 Major U.S. Welfare Programs." 2015. Accessed December 15. http://useconomy.about.com/od/fiscalpolicy/fl/Welfare-Programs.htm.

Wilke, Joy, and Frank Newport. 2014. "Democrats and Republicans Differ on Top Priorities for Government." January 28. Gallup Poll. Accessed December 28, 2014. http://www.gallup.com/poll/167084/democrats-republicans-differ-top-priorities-gov.aspx.

Winant, Howard A. 1988. *Stalemate: Political Economic Origins of Supply-Side Policy*. Westport, CT: Greenwood Press.

Winston, Clifford. 1993. "Economic Deregulation: Days of Reckoning for Microeconomists." *Journal of Economic Literature* 13: 1263–1289.

Index

About the Contributors

Osaore Aideyan holds a PhD from Claremont College in comparative politics, international studies, and public policy and is Assistant Professor of Political Science at Illinois State University.

Grace Allbaugh is Politics and Government Librarian at Illinois State University. She received her MS in information from the University of Michigan.

Joseph R. Blaney is Associate Dean of the College of Arts and Sciences and Professor of Communication at Illinois State University. He has authored/edited seven scholarly books and numerous articles related to political communication and image restoration.

Cayla Comens is a graduate student at Illinois State University working toward her master's degree in criminal justice.

Anthony DiMaggio received his PhD in political science from University of Illinois, Chicago. He is an Assistant Professor at Lehigh University.

Cassandra Dodge is a graduate student in the Department of Criminal Justice at Illinois State University.

Christopher Farrer holds a master's degree in political science from Illinois State University.

Michael R. Ford is an Assistant Professor of Public Administration at the University of Wisconsin-Oshkosh.

Gardenia Harris is Associate Professor in the School of Social Work, Illinois State University. She received her PhD in social work from the University of Illinois at Urbana-Champaign.

Jason Hochstatter holds a master's degree in political science from Illinois State University.

Chad Kahl is an interim Associate Dean and Law Librarian at Illinois State University. He has a BA and MA in political science and an MS in library and information science from the University of Illinois at Urbana-Champaign.

Katharine Leigh is the Head of Cataloging and Metadata Services at the University Libraries, Ball State University. She holds an MLIS from the University of Wisconsin-Milwaukee and an MS in political science from Illinois State University.

Daniel Liechty holds a PhD from the University of Vienna and is Professor of Social Work at Illinois State University.

Nancy S. Lind is Professor of Political Science and Public Administration at Illinois State University who has published over a dozen co-edited and co-authored books. She holds a PhD from the University of Minnesota.

Lucas Lockhart is a PhD candidate in political science at the University of Minnesota. He specializes in the politics of regulation and the comparative political economy of finance and corporate governance.

John C. Navarro is a PhD candidate in criminal justice at the University of Louisville.

Mark D. Olson is Assistant Professor in the School of Social Work at Illinois State University.

Eric Otenyo is Professor of Political Science and International Affairs at Northern Arizona University.

JiHye Park is a graduate student in the Department of Sociology, University of Iowa.

Michael R. Potter is Assistant Professor of Public Administration at the University of Wyoming. He holds a PhD from Virginia Tech.

Renee Prunty is an adjunct Assistant Professor of Political Science at Methodist College in Peoria, IL.

Cara E. Rabe-Hemp is Professor in the Department of Criminal Justice Sciences at Illinois State University.

Erik T. Rankin holds MS and MPS degrees and is Assistant to the Department Chair at Illinois State University.

Katelyn Schachtschneider is an instructional Assistant Professor in the Department of Politics and Government at Illinois State University.

Emily Schnurr is a PhD candidate in political science at Northern Arizona University.

Vanette Schwartz is Professor and Social Science librarian at Illinois State University. She holds a master's degree in library science from the University of Michigan and a master's degree in history from the University of Illinois.

Earlene A. Smith is a PhD candidate at Northern Arizona University. Her research foci are health policy and public administration.

Karen Flint Stipp is Assistant Professor in the School of Social Work at Illinois State University.

Amanda Swartzendruber is an AmeriCorps Fellow with an MS in political science. She also serves as an executive board member for the Kaga Create Foundation.

Grant Walsh-Haines is a PhD candidate at Northern Arizona University where he teaches courses in American politics and international politics.

George Waters is Professor of Economics at Illinois State University whose primary research interests are in macro/monetary economics.

Kathryn Conley Wehrmann is Associate Professor of Social Work and BSW program director in the Illinois State University School of Social Work.

Elizabeth Wheat is Assistant Professor of Public and Environmental Affairs at the University of Wisconsin-Green Bay. She holds a PhD in political science from Western Michigan University.